AF349055

WOLF
TONES

W O

T O

nancy shaver

maximilian goldfarb

sterrett smith

SOBERSCOVE PRESS | CHICAGO, IL

with appreciation to
the anonymous history of art
in the everyday

nancy shaver

maximilian goldfarb

sterrett smith

stan allen

charles curtis

pradeep dalal

stacy wakefield forte

anna friz

julia klein

ann lauterbach

catherine lord

matana roberts

david levi strauss

CONTENTS

INTRODUCTION

JULIA KLEIN

When a stringed instrument is bowed, the vibrations of certain notes can resonate at the same frequency as the vibrations of the instrument itself. The dissonant effect that results is referred to as a "wolf tone"—named for its howl—and is almost universally characterized by musicians as problematic: an unpleasant and uncontrollable deviance.

For Max Goldfarb, Nancy Shaver, and Sterrett Smith, however, the wolf tone has come to serve as a productive analogy for describing unsettling forces that may operate within a *visual* field, and a model for their ongoing artistic collaboration, Wolf Tones. Unified by a shared investment in close observation and interaction with visual and material cultures, these artists bring their differences into proximity through improvisational installations composed of found, independently created, and collectively invented objects that refuse to cohere into finite singular visions.

In this third iteration of Wolf Tones, the spatiotemporal parameters of the gallery give way to the form of the book and the site of the page. The artists have constructed a landscape of images in which they alternately foster and respond to a new set of rhythms and harmonies prompted by the convergence of their artworks with the source materials that propel their individual practices and group discourse. This is an investigation rooted in *looking* and in the artists' foundational privileging of approach over intention and mutual willingness over individual tendency.

Joining Goldfarb, Shaver, and Smith, nine new collaborators—Stan Allen, Charles Curtis, Pradeep Dalal, Anna Friz, Ann Lauterbach, Catherine Lord, Matana Roberts, David Levi Strauss, and designer Stacy Wakefield Forte—engage with Wolf Tones and the wolf tone, both literally and conceptually, from their distinct perspectives in the realms of art, architecture, art criticism, design, literature, media studies, music, and poetry. Amplifying, informing, and building upon one another, their contributions push beyond conventional modes of looking and listening to embrace dissonance—the exception, the surplus, the accident, the emergent, the unruly—and its generative possibilities.

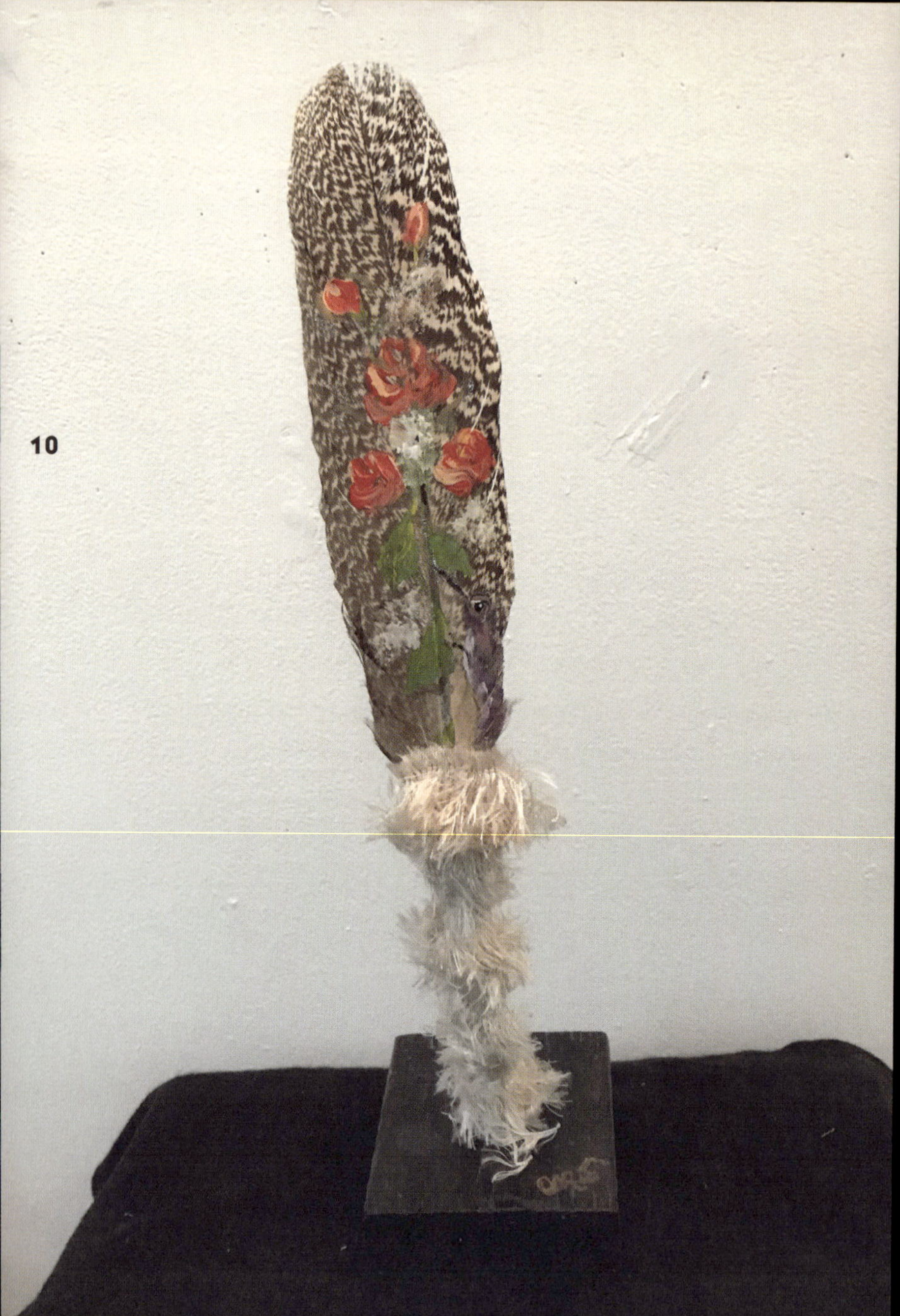
10

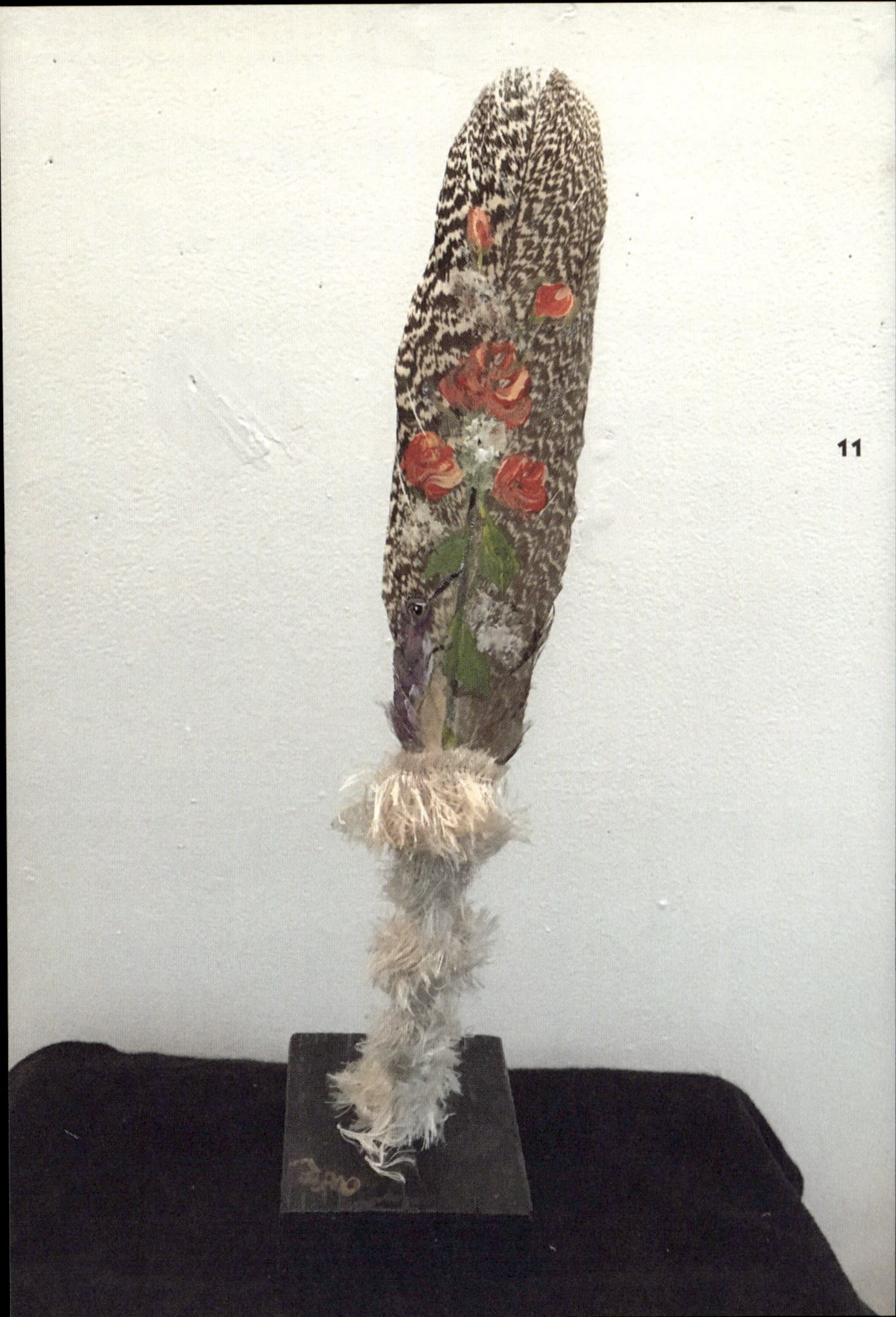

WOLFING ACTION, WOLF-CENTERED SYSTEM, WOLF STATE

13

CHARLES CURTIS

a cellist and his wolf

I can no longer reconstruct in memory my first encounter, as a youthful cellist, with the phenomenon of the wolf. It must have come early, mixed in with the countless other roughnesses, instabilities, uncertainties, and mysteries which mark this mortal instrument. A vivid sensation that I locate in those first years of cello practice is the vibrational energy returning to my hands while playing: a tactile experience, independent of sound and hearing. The instrument touches the player's body at five points: the two hands (the left through the strings, the right through the vibration of the bow), the chest on which the cello leans, and the two knees that cradle the cello. Sometimes the tuning pegs graze or join with the player's left ear, neck, or cheek; an especially exhilarating strategy was to push my earlobe hard against the tuning peg to experience the cello's sound as direct transmission, as structure-borne vibration transmitted from the solid, tensile apparatus of the cello to the bones of the jaw, cheek, and temple. Every contact point with the cellist's body is an energy juncture, and a player learns intuitively to investigate and exploit these junctures in subtle and often uncodified ways. By pulling a knee away from the cello's side, a particularly rich resonance can be allowed to resonate even more freely; by pulling the cello back against the chest, pitch and timbre can be slightly sharpened.

When playing the wolf, the energy returning from the bowed string to the hand holding the bow verges on the uncanny; the intensity of the outburst is startling. The earliest advice I recall receiving from a cello teacher on how to subdue the wolf was to squeeze the cello with my knees, and to hold down the fingers of my left hand more firmly: an attempt to dampen vibration, a kind of clenching or muzzling of the cello's vibrational mass. It was hoped that the special frequencies associated with the wolf might fall into line with the less excitable tones in its vicinity. Needless to say, the temptation to explore and enter into intimate acquaintance with such extraordinary energies was great.

touch and sound

If the wolf comes back to the cellist first as a tactile impression, it is still a sound event of considerable magnitude and fascination. But it is hard to describe as sound. Put simply, the wolf is a burst of vibrational energy that arises spontaneously when the cello is played around a particular group of frequencies. Attempting to characterize its effect or sound, I find myself reminded of driving at high speed with the rear windows open, or of being near a helicopter—both sound-pressure events more than sound images. The wolf is a sustaining sound, but one which breaks into irregular percussive strokes or pulses, like slow drum rolls; the rhythm of these pulses varies with bow direction changes, bow speed, and alterations in left hand position. Even at a relatively moderate volume, the wolf tends to fill the acoustic space in an all-around, nondirectional way, somewhat like the acoustical circumstance of standing waves; the pulsating strokes in particular seem to come from different directions than the sustaining sound that engenders them. As far as its behavior goes, we can say that the wolf moves in and out of certain frequencies on the cello depending on season, climate and weather, tuning and set-up of the cello, tension of the strings, use of mutes and special dampening devices, and probably numerous other variables that are impossible to track. Its strength relative to non-wolf frequencies likewise varies with all these factors.

The notes of the cello on which the wolf usually appears are those between the D-natural of the open D string to the F-sharp a major third above, and usually when played on the G string. But it is just as possible, under varying circumstances and across different instruments, to find wolf activity at virtually any other frequency area on the instrument. All this is to say that we are contending with a phenomenon that is variable, unpredictable, and elusive, a flickering and highly contingent presence.

eliminating wolf

All of the literature on the wolf, whether by cellists, luthiers, or physicists, starts from the position that the wolf is a problem. The wolf presents chaotic resonances and uncontrollable energies that place it in opposition to the desired smoothness of normative cello playing. One may read about strategies for containing the wolf that are far more sophisticated than squeezing the cello with one's knees. It is observed that fingering a unison or octave equivalent of the note that is wolfing tends to cancel the surplus resonances. But this is rarely practicable in the heat of musical performance, in which it is all the cellist can do to navigate the expressive and tonal demands of an urbane and involuted musical tradition. Outboard resonators and dampeners are introduced to absorb or cancel the wolfing resonances, positioned strategically around the cello. These function like the tuned mass dampers built into huge skyscrapers: massive pendulated weights which vibrate in unison with, but in phase opposition to, the (extremely low) resonant frequencies of the building itself during high winds and earthquakes.

My own experience with "wolf eliminators," or, in the more primal German, *Wolftöter*, "wolf killers," is that they tend to move the wolf to other frequency clusters, rather than eliminate it. If the wolf can be moved to a range of frequencies that lies in a no man's land between the stepped chromatic tones of the cello's desired diapason, between the named notes in our tonal system, then it is out of the way; the player can step around it, like avoiding puddles. A very resourceful cellist in an excellent German orchestra once confided to me that he drew the endpin of his cello out to a length that made the endpin itself resonate in near-unison to the wolf frequencies; by vibrating sympathetically, the endpin would presumably distribute and absorb some of the excess energy. This idea drew my attention to the extraordinary interconnectedness of all the resonating components that make up a cello.

category error

To refer to note names in connection with the wolf in fact brings up a curious impasse. Consider the commonplace statement: "The wolf in my cello is on F-sharp." This statement verges on category error. The validity of the statement could be buttressed by stating that "in the current tuning that I use, in this climate and season, today, F-sharp is one of the notes which, when I play it in a certain way, brings forth the wolf." And this tortuous formulation demonstrates how incompatible the two categories are—"note" and "wolf." You might as well say, "The letter L describes the individuality of my life on earth at this moment." The note F-sharp is an abstraction, a moveable designator, not a sound; its meaning relies on semiotic value. From a historical standpoint, one can argue that the musical note is a derivative of the seventeenth-century shift to numerical abstractions, infinitary and positional mathematical values that are independent of actual quantities or intensities. As money is to labor or physical goods, the concept of a note is to actual sounds: free of material presence and acoustical conditions, the sounds and mechanics of instruments, the human bodies and desires energizing them, anything bounded by lived time. This unboundedness provides the conditions for a manner of composition in which notes are deployed, organized, manipulated, and administered as soundless and timeless markers. None of this can be said of the wolf. The wolf cannot be "composed" in that way. All of the characteristics that are authentically its own are rooted in a moment of lived time: an instrument in the act of resonating, in a room, in a specific perspective between instrument, performer, and listener.

One could extend the category error to the relationship between wolf and cello, or to "cello" as idealized in canonical European concert music. As a transparent vessel for notes, for lyrical articulations of a most rarefied gentility, the tones and inflections of "cello" are imagined as flowing in sequences that are qualitatively contiguous, evenly spread, and applied with equal weight and emphasis, even if frequency values are acoustically disparate. The task of the cellist has evolved into one of taming the disparities and smoothing the output signal into an idealization of actual sound. Within this understanding, a "great composer" ventriloquizes the performer through the hyperrationalized commands and controls built into the notation system of the "masterpiece." The wolf clearly has no place here. Wolf cannot be ventriloquized; it must be sought and discovered according to its own immediate realities.

physical analysis

It is hard not to be curious as to the physical and acoustical sources of the wolf. But in surveying the literature we are confronted with explanations that are somewhat conjectural. Here again the wolf seems to elude a single, fixed understanding. But the prevailing explanations run approximately as follows.

The top plate of the cello, the graciously curving surface that faces outward toward the listeners when the cellist plays, is carved and thinned by its luthier in such a way that it will vibrate most intensely at a handful of related frequencies. When the cello strings are bowed at frequencies very close to these, the top plate responds so strongly that it plays back those frequencies, sending a second signal back to the string, as if it were "bowing" the string simultaneously from the other side with the power of the top plate's vibratory energy. The two signals couple, reinforcing and cancelling each other in rapid alternation. Other explanations implicate the cavity of the cello box, the resonant space inside the cello, rather than the top plate, claiming that the peak resonances of its dimensions are responsible for the returning vibration. The semi-regular rhythmic pulsations of the wolf are understood by some as acoustical beating, which would imply interference between two closely tuned frequencies; more often they are understood as the mismatched impedances of string, bridge, and top plate piling up and jostling each other. One celebrated study modeled these resonant behaviors as separate electrical circuits, the string being the primary, and the top plate, the secondary circuit. It is widely agreed

that the very finest cellos are most often those that exhibit
pronounced wolf activity.

All of the explanations point to a feedback loop. An
output signal from the bowed sound turns around, ampli-
fied by resonance within the instrument, and becomes an
input again, feeding back into and coupling with the bowed
sound. Feedback is an out-of-control state produced by the
inner mechanics of an energy system. All of the characteristics of feedback—a surplus of energy, a coupled signal
outstripping its source, the mechanical momentum of waves
boosted and erupting from within—are perfectly demon-
strated by wolf activity. Systems capable of unleashing such
power understandably provoke fear, and something like
this must prompt the reflex to mute or short-circuit such
volatility in the cello. Feedback is a power that is within the
system, that is the system itself, and over which the system
is ultimately powerless. Marcel Proust, with his uncanny
acuity at registering sensuous phenomena, identifies what
must be a kind of wolf when he writes of his experience listening to a violin: " ... at times too we think we hear a cap-
tive genie struggling deep inside the intelligent, bewitched
and tremulous box, like a devil in a holy-water basin. . . ."[1]

another category

If F-sharp belongs to the category of "notes" and "pitch
classes," and if the wolf is disqualified from membership in

this class of musical objects, then we might ask, to what category does the wolf belong? Is it a tone, a sound, a sonority, a phenomenon, an energy, an action, an effect—what kind of an object is it?

Perhaps music as we have come to know it is not about actual acoustic energy; perhaps what we experience as a cello is not really about the instrument itself. The wolf is thought of as a flaw, a malfunction, a deviant presence, a disability, a hindrance, a symptom, or a pathology, something in need of suppression. By its exclusion, it defines a streamlined system of smooth functionality and predictable results which will not tolerate its willfulness. Conversely, in turning our attention to the wolf, addressing it in its complexity and specificity, listening to it and learning to play it, we are opening toward another category, the lines of which are not explicitly drawn. Its emergence from the cello's very construction, its existential rootedness in the resonant being of the cello, would seem to suggest a way of experiencing "cello" in another depth and fullness. The force and unruly richness of the wolf mean that we must approach it with care and attentiveness, rather than domination. Its variability means that we hear it anew each time, each time in different and specific dimensions, each time as an exception: a unique aesthetic moment expressed in wave energy.

Since it is not "a" sound, a recognizable tone or sound-image to be replicated at will, and since its energy is

the result of a sequence of efforts, it seems most useful to think of it as action—wolfing action. This term is sometimes used in the acoustics literature. Seen in this way, we identify the process and not the sounding product. With each new playing, the wolf must be constructed anew. It must be built up, sought and sustained in time, without reference to something already existing. We don't know its exact properties until it has been constructed. Wolfing action highlights reciprocal energies of human initiation and feedback response, the constant cycles of asserting and responding, bowing and listening, and adjusting and reacting: an ongoing sequence of vanishingly brief life-moments devoted to initiating and sustaining the wolf.

aporia

The concept of the "wolf fifth" comes to us from the history of organ tuning. A "wolf fifth" is an out-of-tune interval that inevitably results from extending a cycle of the same in-tune interval all the way around to the tone at which one started, which then proves to deviate in tuning from the actual start point. The simplest case is the cycle of Pythagorean fifths. The same "perfect fifth" is extended in sequence from, for example, C to G to D to A and so on, until one reaches E-flat, B-flat and F, then arriving again at C. But while each sequential fifth has been the same, the C that one has cycled around to is slightly different from the beginning

C, creating a dissonance, a gap that is acoustically jarring, that beats or "howls," announcing its difference as an outburst of sonorous turbulence.[2]

One can think of this as an aberration inherent in the tuning system. The system is dutifully followed and extended, based on a "perfect," naturally in-tune unit, the justly tuned fifth; but the process escapes its own apparent rule. The "wolf fifth" is different in kind from the cello's wolf; it does not involve a feedback circuit, nor result from a spontaneous mechanical reaction. It may be more akin to inherent errors in map projections, which must be corrected for by introducing smaller errors across the entire system (and this is how the "wolf fifth" is solved in tuning systems, using the principle of "temperament"). But both wolves share the circumstance of highlighting an intrinsic anomaly that seems to defy the intended workings of the system. As well, the "wolf fifth" shows another factor which may be of considerable interest to wolfing action: the emergence of an unbridgeable gap. The dissonant note is the "same" note that we started with, but when we cycle back to it, it is different. The misalignment, a gap in the sequence, stands in the way of the projected continuity of the series—this is the "impassable path," or aporia, the self-contradiction that involuntarily reveals the reality of the system.

Something remarkably similar happens when I tune the entire cello to the perceived frequencies of the wolf. With each adjustment of string tension aimed at unison with the wolf, the wolf frequencies move slightly. It is impossible to align the tonality of the strings and the frequencies of the wolf; the differential, shifting with each attempt, appears irreducible. It cannot be smoothed over. The further I search, the more concretely this unit of distance reveals itself.

a multiplicity

Wolfing action proceeds through a network of energies and circuits. To restate the basic sequence: the bow excites a string at a given frequency; the bridge transduces this excitation to the top plate and to the box which it encloses; due to a close matching of string frequency and resonant frequencies, this energy returns as "maximal energy transfer" to the string, re-exciting it from within; and a new sound, complex and unpredictably oscillating, indexes this constellation of events and linkages. Emerging from a multiplicity of elements, this sound is likewise multiple, in all dimensions: over time, in space, and as a composite of fundamentals, partials, summation tones, and whatnot else. The sound is dissonant, by any generic application of that word, but also more literally: "sounding apart," not singular or unison, a sound that is in its very nature splayed. The wolf is additionally the sounding of the cello's own resonance together with the resonance that the cellist plays, a product of factors intrinsic to the instrument, multiplied by actions upon it.

From all of these standpoints, one might think it folly to tune the instrument to such a dense concatenation of factors. To what is one tuning? What is the reference point, the single beacon or sighting, that one steers toward? Tuning is usually understood as alignment with a standard external reference, a socially agreed-upon frequency value, like a standard unit of measure or a civil code; what might it mean to tune the cello to "itself," to an internal signal? And what of the tendency, mentioned earlier, of the wolf frequencies to slip away as one adjusts the string tension to them, presenting in effect a moving target?

wolf-centered system

Without at the time anticipating the complexities of the task, this was the challenge that I set for Éliane Radigue's solo cello composition, *Naldjorlak*, in 2004. Intuition and curiosity prompted the search for a wolf-centered tuning. Framing a new composition as a collaborative search for resonance within the instrument itself rested on the unusual circumstances of the two collaborators. Radigue, a composer of analog tape music, came to the prospect of a solo cello piece without any preconceptions of traditional cello playing or standard techniques, existing repertoire, instrument construction, or layout. In fact, it was the first

time she had composed for an acoustic instrument alone.
Her initial conception was simply that the piece should
express, or embody, the process toward union, yoga, one-
ness. The title announces this, combining the Tibetan word
for yoga, or union, *Naldjor*, with an honorific suffix, *lak*, as if
personifying and addressing the sought-after state, calling
out to it. Working from the instrument itself, and from its
most powerful internal resonance, seemed to us the proper
starting point.

What arose over the course of a nearly two-year compo-
sitional process was surprising indeed. Not only the strings
of the cello, but its tailpiece, endpin, and tailpiece wire could
be brought into a close consensus tuning, a "near-tuning,"
with the wolf. Each adjustment required retroactive adjusting
of all previous adjustments; simply tuning the instrument
became an open-ended, potentially unending, process. Not
only did the acoustical power of the wolf increase through
the tuning, the entire instrument began to resonate almost
at the limit of its physical capacity, at times even shaking
and trembling, with the allied vibrational forces transferred
across the entire body of the cello. Like a current of electricity, these energy flows connected the instrument as a unified
field, such that any bowed action produced audible sympa-
thetic resonance at almost all other points of resonance.

Naldjorlak redefined the cello for me. I found myself
involved not so much with an objectified instrument, as a

tool or implement, but with an environment. Playing meant entering into that environment and participating in the consequences: how we affect the surroundings, how they affect us, gauging the volatile behavior of the wolf in real time. The wolf as fundamental tonality makes us listen to the instrument itself, rather than *through* the instrument to a music which must be imagined, matched up to, or retrieved from elsewhere—score, tradition, habit. In fact, when a cello is tuned to *Naldjorlak*, it is impossible to play any other composition on it; the piece is inextricable from the tuning, and the tuning leads inexorably to the wolf. The wolf also suggests a paradoxical reversal of scale: the cello "contains" the wolf, yes, but, as the expression of the instrument's most vivid resonance, the wolf "contains" the entire resonance of the cello.

The differential between wolf frequencies and tuned frequencies remained, but it became very small over time. The tautological implications of tuning an instrument "to itself" brought about a new understanding of tuning. Not tuning so that the cello sounds at the "same" pitch as a given reference, but tuning to "self-sameness." But the search for self-sameness reveals a unit of difference we would not have discovered without having attempted to bridge it. We cannot bridge it, because it is inside the instrument we are tuning. The object sought is contained in the subject.

dissonance and emphasis

Wolfing action can be imagined as a native dissonance within the cello—a kind of emphasis, the rhetorical accent of the instrument itself. European music from the beginnings of tonality has relied on the accented dissonance, especially in suspensions and cadential formulas, to convey a rhetoric of stress, weight, a burden that is eased and set down in tonal resolution. Emphasis is in any case a surplus, an expressive excess beyond discourse or pure information, an added weight; and dissonance, the acoustical chafing as embodied in the tritones and sevenths of the dominant seventh and diminished chords, drives all of European tonality from at least the early Baroque.

If the dissonance does not resolve, its function changes; it is no longer in service of a rhetoric or a power exchange, but stands as a state to be resolved through direct experience, without being removed. The rhetorical notion of *catachresis* captures this change in address. Catachresis means using the wrong word intentionally. Weight and stress are embedded in the word's origin: *cata* (down) *-chresis* (use), "using downward," "misuse." One effect of catachresis is that in encountering the word where it does not belong, we see and hear the word itself, not what it stands for. Wolfing action that emerges audibly as a musical center would function in this way. Catachresis could be the sense in which category error turns productive, as a collision between meaning systems, such that the unsayable presents itself explosively, out of the realm of sense-meaning and into the realm of pure sensation.[3]

set invisibility

A dissonance that does not resolve but stands as an object of contemplation may be the manner in which a new category forms around wolfing action. This category does not legislate the terms of a meaning-system, nor the rules for interfacing with its constituent elements. Nor are its boundaries fixed. The technical notion of "diagonal constructions" and "diagonalization" found in mathematics suggests the bursting out of categories to create new and sometimes unfathomable groupings, especially when this becomes necessary due to the emergence of a self-referential factor.[4] But opening a space around wolfing action seems to have more to do with "set invisibility,"[5] the experience in which peripheral or incidental features emerge into presence that were previously excluded by the terms of the system. When the barriers lift, a new landscape comes to light, in which different or ephemeral groupings and relationships may flicker in and out of focus; meaning becomes constitutively variable.

"Set invisibility" is more an affective state than a logical formula; it gives access to states of permeability and fluidity, possibly naive, in which we hear or see or feel without the burden of conscious discrimination between meanings or categories. Dream states and the realm of poetic imagination function in this way. A poignant application of "set invisibility" is the suggestion that the most profound happiness occurs when we are not aware of being happy— the state of mind itself is not marred by an awareness or acknowledgement of being either inside or outside the boundaries of a system of happiness-indicators.

What remains is to imagine an environment in which the particular, the immediate, or the exception becomes the moment on which a system turns. In such a condition, what appeared to be marginal takes on centrality; one set of circumstances is not superimposed on another, but rather investigated as present; and reality is not generalizable from information about it. If attending to the wolf points toward these conditions, then such a state could be thought of as wolf state.

The author would like to express thanks to Dafne Vicente-Sandoval for shared work, thought, and imaginings; and to Madison Greenstone and Anthony Vine for contributions and perspectives.

ENDNOTES

1— Marcel Proust, *The Way by Swann's*, trans. Lydia Davis (London: Penguin, 2003), 349–50.

2— "The ancient Greek and Latin scales had been adjusted according to the so-called 'Pythagorean' tuning system, in which the determining interval is the perfect fifth. Such a system runs up against one fundamental physical limit: in a perfect cycle of fifths, the interval of the octave, by necessity, will be acoustically impure, because the relations of the fifth and the octave are incommensurable among themselves . . . if one extends a fifth from one discrete pitch to another and continues doing so indefinitely, one will never pass through any two pitches that sound an octave or number of octaves among themselves. Perfect fifths simply cannot be reconciled with the consonance of the octave." Daniel Heller-Roazen, *The Fifth Hammer: Pythagoras and the Disharmony of the World* (New York: Zone Books, 2011), 79–80.

3 — "Illimitable in a sense, more importantly catachresis shows the monstrous within the symbolic that points towards a heteronomy that cannot be assigned a sign." Dieter Mersch, *Epistemologies of Aesthetics* (Zürich: Diaphanes, 2015), 169.

4 — "A diagonal construction often becomes necessary, for instance, where systems encounter self-reference: if a function is taken as an argument for itself . . . the system must be expanded in some way to accommodate the self-referential case. . . . There is a singular interest attachable to diagonal and self-referential constructions which has been frequently commented upon: they may appear wherever a symbolic system is in use, whether such a system is an ordinary language, a philosophical or technical discipline, a biological system of cognition or perception, a work of art, or a system of spiritual exercises. . . . In each such system, the diagonal or self-referential case will have the appearance of singularity, a moment of confusion, an occasion for doubt, or else will seem a justification for the expansion of the system, for a mystical flight into transcendent realms." Charles Stein, *Being = Space x Action: Searches for Freedom of Mind through Mathematics, Art and Mysticism* (Berkeley, Calif: North Atlantic Books, 1988), 28–33.

5 — Charles Davy, *Words in the Mind: Exploring Some Effects of Poetry, English and French* (Cambridge: Harvard University Press, 1965).

WOLF TONES: A GAME OF WHAT IF

ANN LAUTERBACH

> *. . . Is it peace,*
> *Is it a philosopher's honeymoon, one finds*
> *On the dump? Is it to sit among mattresses of the dead,*
> *Bottles, pots, shoes and grass and murmur* aptest eve:
> *Is it to hear the blatter of grackles and say*
> *Invisible priest; is it to eject, to pull*
> *The day to pieces and cry* stanza my stone?
> *Where was it one first heard of the truth? The the.*
>
> —WALLACE STEVENS, "THE MAN ON THE DUMP"

*Then this vermilion thread becomes, strictly speaking,
unidentifiable, save as painting in action; its form
is dominated by its material, and its status as
representation by the* quasi, *in which dimension it is
precarious, neither distinct nor clear: it is perhaps
"thread-like," but it is not painted "like thread"; it is
painted like paint.*
—GEORGES DIDI-HUBERMAN, *CONFRONTING IMAGES*

1.

A school of knives heads downstream, floating on a transparent plastic platform beneath which various objects gather in quasi-clusters. Under one end of the still river is a black-and-white rug with a pattern of large pale stars, or flowers; between the rug and a set of flat, brightly colored nearly rectangular objects is a kind of sandwich, an uneasy stratified pile of nude fired clay on which we might detect the outlines of eyes; they could be discarded masks thrown down by an impatient wizard, or part of a sand sculpture made by a lonely child on the beach and abandoned to the will of the tides. We are facing tiers on a horizontal plane, the eye moving above and below as if looking at a disturbed landscape. But "landscape" is far too conventional a reference. For one, its relation to the figure is not clear. Scale—the relation of thing to thing—is turbulent and

queasy, and so the viewer has no way of knowing where or
even if she is implicated, included, connected, or simply left
out, apart; the difference between looking at and being in.
As if she might be standing in an exclusion, an elsewhere,
the place of no place. The whole vista cannot be steadied
into any formula for seeing, not only because of the sheer
disjunction of objects, but because each incident of seeing
seems to require a new consideration, a recalibration of the
total experience. Those fish-knives, for example. Each one is
hand-crafted, unique, each from each. We think of fish, and
we think of flocks of birds, leaves of grass, and we wonder
for a moment to what extent they are known to each other as
individuals. We recall the phrase *the one and the many*, and
begin to dwell for a while on the catastrophic state of our
contemporary Commons.

The general sense is of an intentional jumble, as if we
were at the very threshold between disorder and order, and
those signs of reason—numbers and letters, mathematics
and language—are not in the service of any data or information; they simply join the general visual jamboree. The
mood is exuberant, restless, as if to capture a kind of wild
plethora. But this isn't a wilderness, and nothing in or about
it points toward the accidents of nature's chance operations.
The world, and it is a world, is defiantly manufactured, artificial, constructed, but it is not a replica. The eye begins to
forsake its quest for easy identification, a thing to name: *this*

38

ANN LAUTERBACH

is this. Perhaps even the most obdurate object is on its way to a transgressive metamorphosis, desperate to escape the confines of its name, its use. The moment of subtle transition is happening just as the eye makes its way through and across the rapturous field of objects, shapes, colors; and as it does, it begins to form visual sentences, structures of sight, not in an effort to make sense but rather to draw out from the dense arena a sequence. With each movement, each angle of perception, the sequence shifts. Sequences are sometimes narratives, stories, and so the eye becomes a kind of narrator, finding for itself the story it wishes to tell.

Once upon a time, there was a fabric covered with a pattern of small flowers. After years of service as a dress, it returned to being elemental material, flat and shapeless, without either sleeves or hem. And then it found itself covering a perfectly geometrical block and standing atop a spool in a crowd of other blocks covered with other, similar patterns, in a stubborn and resilient assembly.

Once upon a time, there were barrels painted in bright flag colors. No one knew where they had come from, whether they had come by ship, air, or rail. Perhaps they had traveled up the river on a barge, filled with oil. And the oil? Where was it from and where was it now? Vanished into the scented night air.

Once upon a time, yellow happened, and happened again, elsewhere. It climbed up to the ceiling on a leaning

scaffold or tower, and then leapt onto the wall in a painting's upper-right quadrant. *Then,* but in space, not in
time, it made its way to a constellation of balls on sticks. It
reminded the eye of the dozens of tiny yellow finches that
had landed in the crabapple tree in spring, when it was
covered in a hovering cloud of palest pink. The tiny yellow
birds in the pale pink branches reminded the eye of a tapestry. Yellow seemed to punctuate the whole vista.

Once upon a time, a statue of the Buddha was beheaded
by history.

Once upon a time, a figure lay down on a rug and
was peaceful.

Once upon a time, flamboyant rupture; nerves
were exposed.

Once upon a time, the anonymity of workers became
a refusal.

2 .

And then? Then I recall how strange it was: not exactly a
dream, not exactly an exaggeration, but rather a sense that
we had lost our way and could not find a path through the
welter of things we had created and abandoned. We were
not even sure where we were going, and so being lost was
not exactly frightening, even though we began to wonder
if we would ever see a real tree or hear a real, living bird
again. After a while, we wanted to lie down, to find a respite

from the constant stimulation that made our bodies long for a clearing, a neutral; the body wished to retreat, feeling at once sated and contaminated by the visual feast.

The eye begins to think. The viewer believes that the eye conducts the world's business, informs how things happen and what choices are made to create a story among the billions of events that transpire each minute. The eye is the organ of composition, composition as explanation, as Gertrude Stein had put it. The eye composes the world and the world is fatigued, overwhelmed; the world wants the eye to stop composing and relent, let things be at rest. The world is tired of being accountable to the insatiable eye with its claims, its indiscriminate parade of possible beginnings and endings. The eye wants to stop witnessing because it is not believed.

What then is an experience? Is the narrator invited to join in this happy trio of concerted arrangement? Three persons had some fun. The narrator can tell, fun was had here. The narrator looks around and sees that this is the result of freedom of choice, of the gathering of those choices into new choices; old materials assembled into new relations, as if to suggest we might all take old materials and put them to new uses: art-making as incentive to frugal delight.

A story of means and ends.

Choice, as always, is limit; limit as declaration of care.

3.

Perhaps they were playing a game of *What If.* As if in a primordial region, before, or after, the sequence; before, or after, narrative enclosed the world's creatures in its beginnings and endings. They were playing in the ancient field of deities, perhaps in drenching rain, daisies and Queen Anne's lace bowed down by wind. "I am Ananke" said Nancy, "Nothing lasts forever." "I am Persephone," said ever-alert Gret. "I am Hermes," said Max, "Let's get to it." In the game of *What If*, the Fates are forbidden to intervene, so choices are liberated, free from final consequence, allowed to revise endlessly the topography of relation in a joyful resistance to any logic other than that of the fluid *mundo*, the anti-architectonic energies released into a choreography of motion. The eye could see these shadow figures, moving, bending, shifting. It could sense, in seeing the final pictorial display, the celebratory revisions. In the game of *What If*, there are no winners or losers, only the collaborative resonance of mutual regard.

The gods are called back to their Wiki page, to stare out from their statues.

4.

I recall, many years ago, reading a little poem by W. B. Yeats that begins with the line, "The fascination of what's difficult"; and goes on to lament bitterly the effects of such a fascination, which has "rent / Spontaneous joy and natural content / Out of my heart." Poor Yeats! But I took the opening lines to be a kind of invitation; and I began to see that a fascination with difficulty might be a kind of saving grace, a way to encounter and engage rather than avoid the facts of life's many predicaments; its turbulent, incessant facts. What is difficulty, anyway, but what causes us not to pass through to understanding or meaning instantly. *"It's too hard!"* whines the child over his homework. *"I can't do it!"* Difficulty brings us up against the limits of what we know in relation to what we need to know in order to do what comes next. I became interested in this very place of resistance, confusion, complexity. I was drawn to the less scrutable, less accessible; the undecidable or uncertain, whatever it is that contradicts the ostensible transparencies that are now on ceaseless offer. Something between a blur and an excess, a contusion and a scan; a spill. A kind of materialism, for sure, grounded in the haptic and the sensuous, a scribble on its way to something legible and lucid. So then, an interest in opacity: what cannot be seen through, like a thick knot. This would be the opposite of the digital universe in which we dwell. To choose difficulty as a value might in fact seem perverse, a recalcitrance to our notions of aesthetic perfection, which classically inscribes coherence, clarity, and simplicity on the works of art we most admire.

Well, then:

5.

Wolf Tones. A distant howl rising over an inventory of
invention: difficult beauty.

OCTOBER 2020

BEYOND THE DIALECTICAL LANDSCAPE

STAN ALLEN

There is an ecology of bad ideas, just as there is an ecology of weeds. —GREGORY BATESON

A consciousness of mud and the realms of sedimentation is necessary in order to understand the landscape as it exists. —ROBERT SMITHSON

One common thread running through the vast and diverse array of artistic and intellectual work of the last century was the struggle to come to terms with new technologies. Beginning early in the twentieth century, the rapid pace of technological change undermined previously held intellectual certainties, challenging artists to produce work as radical as the new world they saw unfolding around them. Nature was irrelevant, bound up with the romantic aesthetics of the nineteenth century: "After seeing electricity, I lost interest in Nature" (Vladimir Mayakovsky). But modernism, as a complex cultural construct, is at once dependent on technology and, at the same time, independent of its imperatives. Radical aesthetic work is rarely also technologically innovative.

The final third of the twentieth century saw an accelerated shift from hard technologies of production to soft technologies of reproduction and communication. Parallel to this was a growing awareness of a new challenge: the fraught relationship between humans and nature as it became increasingly clear that newly acquired technological prowess had the capacity to inflict environmental damage at an unprecedented scale. Many geologists assert that we are now living in a new geological era—the *Anthropocene*—characterized by the dominant and ubiquitous influence of mankind on the earth's lithosphere. Human agency, coupled with ever-more-powerful technologies, has created changes of such magnitude and duration that human history is now shifting to a geological time frame.

If the grand narrative of the twentieth century was the progress of technology, the challenge for this century will surely be to come to terms with mankind's fraught relationship to nature. A growing body of ecological theory and environmental history is doing just that, and questions of climate change and green technology are now a prominent part of mainstream media debates. Creative artists, in turn, are finding diverse ways to respond. Electricity is, after all, part of nature, as are wildfires in California, heat waves in Siberia, Greenland's melting ice sheet, and COVID-19. Ecologies, as Gregory Bateson points out, are indifferent to human notions of good and bad. To effectively address a challenge as large and as abstract as climate change, piecemeal intervention is not enough. A sea change in political will and collective consciousness is required. And one of the things that creative work in art, architecture, and landscape *can* do is shift the horizon of imagination.

The Wolf Tones collaboration accepts the often discordant and always unexpected character of nature. In their work, nature is not understood as remote, scenic beauty—something out there to be looked at—or as an exotic wilderness to be visited in passing. Instead, nature becomes part of our most intimate, everyday interior landscapes—one among many artificial natures, and one that can be constructed out of culture's castoffs. Wolf tones in music amplify and expand the frequencies of the played note. Sounds are produced that are not directly played but are a product of the resonant frequencies of the vibrating string and the body of the instrument. The oscillations between

the uneven frequencies of the natural note and the overtone
create a howling effect, often suppressed (or "tamed"), in
conventional works, by a wolf tone eliminator.[1] For Max
Goldfarb, Nancy Shaver, and Sterrett Smith, this is a model
for collaboration: a process that can thrive on controlled
discord. But their evocation of the wild is also a larger
proposition about the relationship between art and nature
today. Strategies of the informal, acceptance of decay, intentional lack of design, recycling, and recontextualization
are some of the procedures at work in their collaborative
pieces. The hand of the individual artist disappears, and the
emergent order of the assemblage asserts itself as something set in motion by the artists, yet not entirely subject to
their control.

The Wolf Tones project also mirrors another shift. For
many artists, landscape architects, and thinkers in the late
twentieth century, the most effective critique of the pas-
toral concept of nature was to insist on nature as a human
construct—that is to say, to see nature through the lens of
culture. In architecture and landscape, this took the form
of parks and landscapes that were resolutely man-made.
Proposals by Bernard Tschumi and Rem Koolhaas/OMA for
the Parc de La Villette in Paris (1983) imposed geometric
order over the landscape and emphasized the urban character and cultural history of this site on the city's periphery.
They pointed out that, while they may appear natural, the

dense plantings and meandering pathways of traditional nineteenth-century parks were entirely man-made. The critical force of their proposition was to foreground human agency—alterable, revisable—rather than accept as given the "natural" order of things. This was a powerful critique, but based on a concept of nature as primarily pictorial. By contrast, ecologists today understand nature as a vast and complex self-regulating system; geologists work with slow change and deep time. Many landscape architects today embrace ecological succession, and design for change over time. The city itself can be productively understood as an ecological system, with many variables simultaneously at work, dynamically adapting to change. If nature was once seen primarily through the lens of culture, the artists of the Wolf Tones project are among those who suggest that today we might more productively view cultural production through the lens of nature and ecology.

In his 1973 essay, "Frederick Law Olmsted and the Dialectical Landscape," Robert Smithson celebrates Olmsted as a proto–land artist who understood "the magnitude of geological change."[2] Rather than see the gentle contours of Central Park as nostalgically embedded in nineteenth-century aesthetics, Smithson expands the concept of the picturesque to encompass deep geological time. He begins the essay by exhorting the reader to "[i]magine yourself in Central Park one million years ago."[3] Through his emphasis on the long duration of geological time, Smithson anticipates a present-day philosopher such as Jane Bennett, who questions the accepted distinction between animate and inanimate matter.[4] Smithson, too, directs our attention to "mud and the realms of sedimentation."[5]

As suggestive as he is, Smithson remains a transitional figure. "My own experience," he writes, "is that the best sites for 'earth art' are sites that have been disrupted by industry, reckless urbanization or nature's own devastation." His interest is in the interplay between human activity and nature: a "concrete dialectic between nature and people."[6] This provokes his interest in degraded sites: the "monuments" of Passaic, New Jersey, for example. The terms of Smithson's dialectic are man and nature, fixity and change, order and disorder; and in works such as *Spiral Jetty* (1970), he achieved a compelling synthesis. But his dialectical consciousness retains a privileged place for the human subject, both the anonymous agents who have devastated the landscape, or the artist who interprets and refigures those sites. What would it mean to move beyond the dialectical landscape, to rethink nature not as a separate realm, not as an object or a system "out there" in a contested relationship to human agency but, as philosopher Muriel Combes has written, as "in us as much as outside of us"? Combes cites a definition of nature by Léna Balaud and Antoine Chopot as "an otherness to which we belong."[7] It's a beautiful formulation that suggests at once the essential strangeness and unknowability of nature as well as our fundamental embeddedness as human beings in the natural world. The only world, in fact.

Today, even the most remote sites on the planet are subject to man-made atmospheric disturbances. Antarctica is plagued by anthropogenic pollution, consisting of "ozone degradation, heightened CO_2 levels, increased lead concentrations, and tangible human waste." High concentrations of invisible micro-plastic particles have been found on the ocean floor and across the food chain.[8] Climate change is too big and too slow to be pictured, imagined, or confined to the space of the gallery. There is an emerging sensibility in recent work across many fields that marks a shift in our understanding of nature; rather than pictured landscape or idealized reference, it is *atmosphere*, in its expansive, always changing climatic context. Landscape is not an object, but an immersive field. It is characterized by unpredictability, prodigious diversity, and change over time.

To return to the context of music: In 2005, Éliane Radigue composed a work for cellist Charles Curtis titled *Naldjorlak* ("a diminutive of the Tibetan word referring to the motion of all life toward unity"[9]). This work does not suppress the wolf tones produced by the cello, but makes them the primary material of the piece. "The result is a kind of wild and frail, versatile and volatile world of sounds," writes Radigue. Her intention was to "follow the natural flowing of overtones and to respond to the games of the harmonics all the way up to the threshold of their disappearance beyond the limits of human hearing."[10] Human listeners, perhaps, are not the only subjects of the piece.

The Wolf Tones project belongs to this emergent sensibility. While it may seem counterintuitive to view their work through the lens of landscape, the conventional language of art criticism seems inadequate. The hand of the individual artist disappears in the process of collaboration. More than a defined artifact, these installations map out a field of potential effects, with porous boundaries. The installations, like Radigue's music, could be described as both wild and frail. The work is performative, a project that exists as much in time as in the space of the gallery. In one of his more radical insights, Smithson asserts that "Olmsted's parks exist before they are finished, which means in fact they are never finished."[11] The same could be said for the collaborative work of the Wolf Tones artists. This is literally true, in that the collaboration is ongoing; but it also suggests that the work is found as much as it is made. The work is located not in the vision of the artists; it already exists in the objects and relationships deployed in the installations and will continue to exist beyond any individual instance of their display.

ENDNOTES

1—"In a wolf tone, the air volume and the top, or the air volume and the back, want to cancel each other out. If there are two sound waves going up and down in sync the sound will be twice as loud. However, if the sound waves get slightly out of sync, the wolf note appears—the sound gets louder for a bit and then the waves cancel each other out. There is so much energy when the two notes are slightly out—so at the top of a sound wave the pitch goes up, and at the bottom it goes down." Also note: "There is some truth to the belief that good-sounding cellos and wolf tones go together. Powerful resonances are required for good-sounding cellos, but they also increase the likelihood of wolf tones." Sarah Freiberg, "How to Tame Annoying Wolf Tones," *Strings Magazine*, May 12, 2005, https://stringsmagazine.com/how-to-tame-annoying-howling-wolf-tones/.

2—Robert Smithson, "Frederick Law Olmsted and the Dialectical Landscape," *Artforum*, February 1973, 127.

3—Smithson, "Frederick Law Olmsted," 117.

4—Jane Bennett, *Vibrant Matter: a Political Ecology of Things* (Durham: Duke University Press, 2010).

5—Smithson, "Frederick Law Olmsted," 127.

6—Smithson, "Frederick Law Olmsted," 124; 123.

7—Muriel Combes, "On Nature," *LOG* 49, Summer 2020, 157.

8—Daniel T. Gieseke, "Antarctic Pollution Issues," *International Pollutions Issues*, Hunter College–CUNY, December 2014, https://intlpollution. commons.gc.cuny. edu/antarctic-pollution-issues/; Jonathan Amos, "High microplastic concentration found on ocean floor," *BBC News Science*, May 1, 2020, https://www.bbc.com/news/science-environment-52489126.

9—"Performance: Naldjorlak I, Eliane Radigue," Marfa Sounding, https://www.marfasounding.com/2016/2017/5/16/naldjorlak-i.

10—Ibid.

11—Smithson, "Frederick Law Olmsted," 119.

WE GOT TIME

MATANA ROBERTS

As a person ensconced in the world of improvisation through sound and collaboration, sometimes, in the act of reading a plan on a page (i.e., music notation), I think about the small, liminal moments of time that seem to happen, never planned and sometimes never heard again, except within that one moment, "in time." They reverberate as testaments to a spark, a glance, sometimes a call to further action. This is an excerpt from a graphic score I created called "We Got Time." It is a conceptual mixed-media score for chorus. "We Got Time" comes from the grand jury hearings following Breonna Taylor's shooting death by police. When one investigator said time constraints would prevent jurors from watching all of the collected

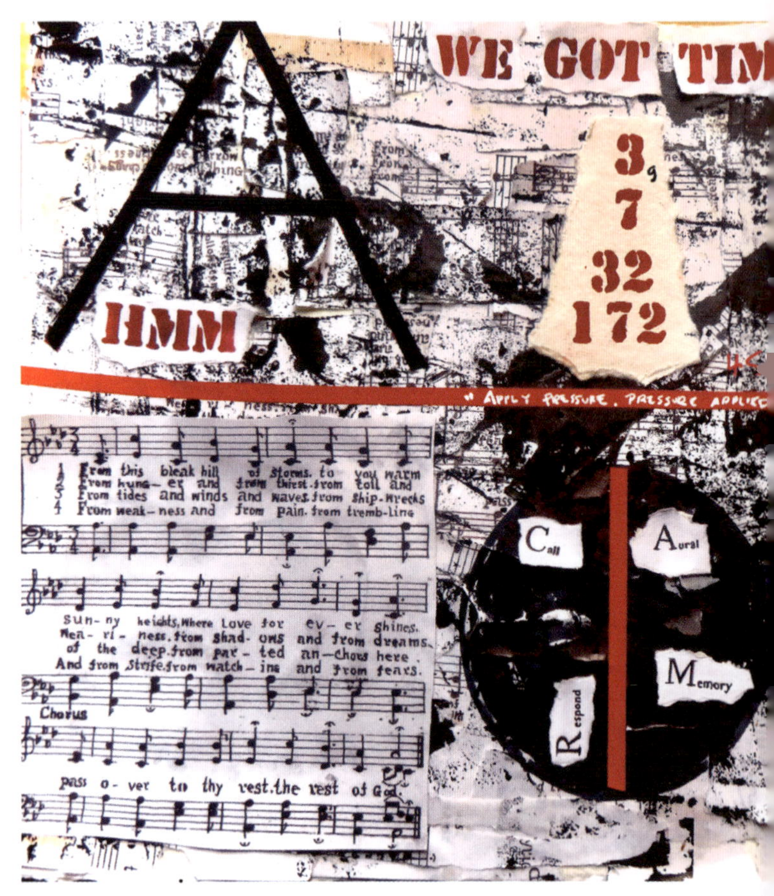
WE GOT TIM
HMM
3
7
32
172
APPLY PRESSURE. PRESSURE APPLIED
Call
Aural
Respond
Memory
From this bleak hill of storms, to you warm
From hung—er and from thirst.from toil and
From tides and winds and waves.from ship—wrecks
From weak—ness and from pain.from trem—bling
sun—ny heights,Where Love for ev—er shines.
Wea—ri—ness,from shad—ows and from dreams,
of the deep.from par—ted an—chors here
And from strife,from watch—ing and from fears.
Chorus
pass o—ver to thy rest.the rest of God.

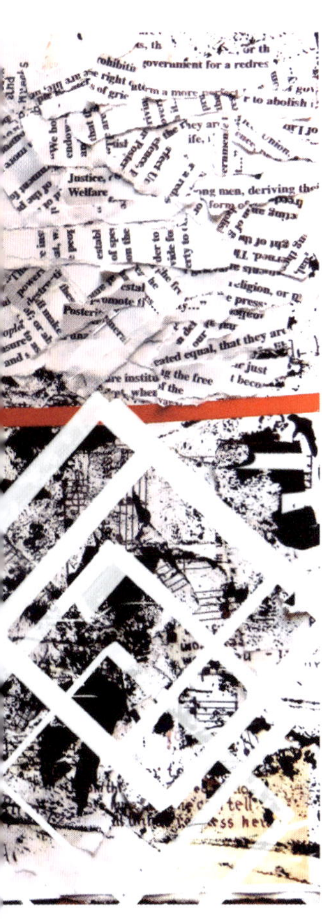

body-camera footage, a juror reacted swiftly, saying, "We got time!" The veracity of layered wolf tonage in this statement is a reminder that all we ever really have is a moment to shift direction, to place presence in ways it could never be placed again. The inferred utterance key.

Matana Roberts, "We Got Time" score excerpt, 2020. Cotton, india ink, ink jet, collage, acrylic, tape.

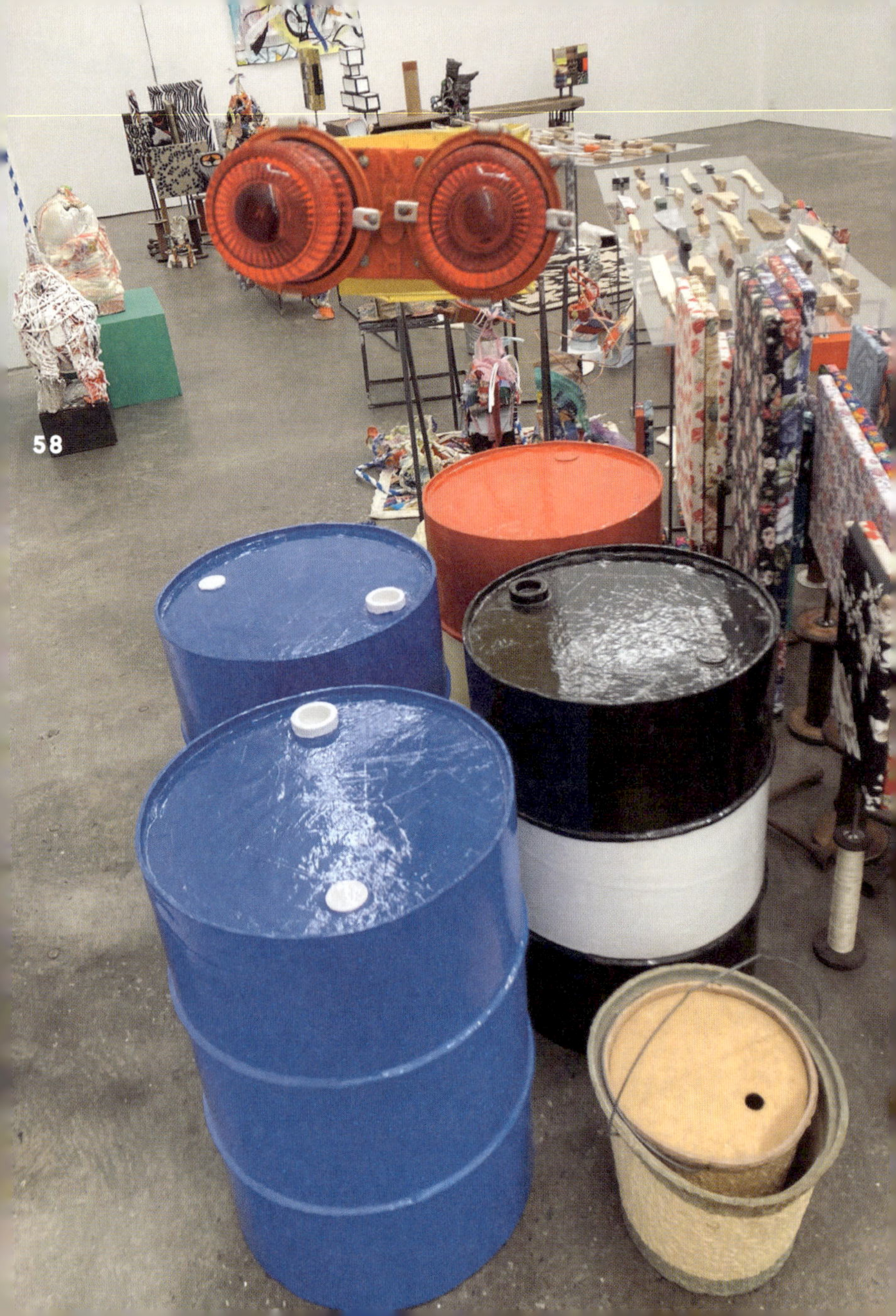

58

THE HIGHEST POINT NOT SEEN BEFOREHAND: A WOLF TONES POETICS

DAVID LEVI STRAUSS

The second exhibition of the Wolf Tones collaboration opened on Friday, March 13, 2020, at the Derek Eller Gallery on the Lower East Side in Manhattan, and closed the same night. I will always think of it as "The Last Show in New York," before the coronavirus shutdown. In retrospect, this Friday-the-13th event, near the Ides of March, marked the end of one kind of living and the beginning of another.

The night of the opening, Sterrett Smith and I drove downtown and got trapped in the heavy traffic of cars and trucks muscling and snarling to get onto the Brooklyn bridges to leave Manhattan at rush hour, and were late to the opening, after parking many blocks away, in Chinatown. When we finally arrived, we were surprised to find a not-in-significant crowd of people looking at the art. Actually, there were 32 people there, all artists and a few writers. People didn't know quite how to act around one another under these pre-pandemic but ominous circumstances, greeting each other with awkward hand gestures and sidelong looks, covering our mouths and noses with whatever was at hand (masks were a thing of the future), and keeping our (social) distance, sort of, sometimes, as we grasped at ad hoc procedures of protection and avoidance that had not yet become codified.

Eleven days earlier, on March 2, a New Rochelle lawyer had tested positive for COVID-19 after commuting to and from New York City every day. By the end of the first week in March, there were 337 cases of COVID-19 and 17 deaths, and the number of cases was doubling every few days. By March 11, there were 1,300 cases and 36 deaths. By the end of March, more than 5,500 people across the country had died.

It's now been proved that the U.S. president knew, back in March and even earlier, what the virus meant and what was to come, but elected to conceal this from the American people and then not do any of the things his epidemiologist advisors were telling him to do to check the spread of the virus, because he thought he knew better, and because he was afraid of what a viable response to the pandemic would do to his image, and especially to his chances of reelection. Today, there are more than 650,00 Americans dead, and four and a half million dead globally, with no sign of an end to it.

But this was all yet to come. On the night of March 13, 2020, there was a sense of foreboding at large, but no one knew quite what would happen next. People were expectant, vigilant, and frightened, but they still came out to look at art. Before them was a large wall piece by Nancy Shaver, a number of her wall and floor pieces made in the past two years, and a sprawling, raucous installation by something called "The Wolf Tones collective," composed of Shaver, Sterrett Smith, and Maximilian Goldfarb.

The collaborative piece was a glorious, intoxicating flow, with direction, but no conclusions. The disparate parts gradually came together to form a coherent composition, while retaining their singular properties as discrete works. The eye rested on individual pieces, then moved on to the shifting juxtapositions of forms, and roamed over migrating energy flows, like a contemporary cloud of unknowing.

The Cloud of Unknowing is a text written by an unknown author in the fourteenth century, during the deadliest pandemic in human history, called the Great Death, or *magna mortalitas*. This plague killed 200 million people, almost half of the world's population at the time, before it was done. It peaked in Europe from 1347 to 1351, starting as the bubonic plague, and eventually spread rapidly from person to person as a pneumonic plague, like COVID-19. It changed everything.

The Cloud of Unknowing is an enactment of the contemplation of God. In Don DeLillo's novel *Underworld*, one of his characters says this about *The Cloud of Unknowing*:

> We approach God through his unmadeness. We are made, created. God is unmade. How can we attempt to know such a being? We don't know him. We don't affirm him. Instead, we cherish his negation.[1]

Artists and writers make things. They are made people making things. Art and writing are forms of knowing, but they can also be forms of unknowing. In his most recent book, Michael Taussig—who was among the 32 souls present at the opening of Wolf Tones II on March 13, having walked there from Bed-Stuy—explores "the mastery of non-mastery."[2] We are mostly a materialistic people, now. We know less through experience and more through things. But this may be changing, again. Taussig's book has been called "a theoretical effort to reckon with the impulses that have fed our relentless ambition for dominance over nature," to find a new relation to mimesis.

monstrous beauty

The show at Derek Eller had an official title: *Nancy Shaver: fastness, slowness, and Monstrous Beauty*, but I will always think of it as *Nancy Shaver and the Wolf Tones, Part II*. The first appearance of the Wolf Tones had occurred from March 2 to April 14, 2019, at Soloway, an artist-run space started in 2010 by Annette Wehrhahn and other artists in a storefront in South Williamsburg, Brooklyn. The first installation of the Wolf Tones collective packed the small rooms of Soloway with a colorful riot of intersecting planes, objects, and sight-lines, as the three collaborators maxed out on the compression. There was so much going on in that small space that it felt like it had been turned inside out.

Nancy Shaver has been collaborating with other artists for some time, and including others in sometimes massive all-over installations that she orchestrates. But Wolf Tones has broken new ground in this extended exploration, and added something unique, I would argue, to the larger corpus of collaborative improvisation among artists over time.

Nancy and I were both lucky enough to be teaching in the MFA studio program at Bard College when the musician and theorist George Lewis came in for a stint, and I think we both learned a lot from George, who knows a great deal about "collaborative improvisation"—mostly in sound and music, but in terms that are applicable to other endeavors as well.

My own view is that in analyzing improvisative musical activity or behavior in structural terms, questions relating to how, when, and why are critical. On the other hand, the question of whether structure exists in an improvisation—or for that matter, in any human activity—often begs the question in a manner that risks becoming not so much exegetic as pejorative. It should be axiomatic that, both in our musical and in our human, everyday-life improvisations, we interact with our environment, navigating through time, place, and situation, both creating and discovering form.[3]

I find it intriguing that the term "improvisation," most commonly applied to music and sound, is actually based on sight. The word is formed from the negative prefix "im" + "pro" (before) + "vise," from the Latin *vide,* from the verb *videre,* to see. So, improvisation refers to something "not seen beforehand." Skeat says the word is "quite modern."[4]

Doing something "not seen beforehand" is what visual artists strive for. Doing it in collaboration is a specific approach that sounds a lot like what George Lewis describes as happening in music: "Structure, meaning, and context in musical improvisation arise from the domain-specific analysis, generation, manipulation, and transformation of sonic symbols."[5] In his essay, "Improvised Music after 1950," he methodically lays bare the contortions some European theorists have to go into to eliminate jazz improvisation

and other Afrological aesthetics from the history of "seri-
ous music." Lewis finds that "buried within this Eurological
definition of improvisation is a notion of spontaneity
that excludes history or memory," and he emphasizes
"the importance of personal narrative, of 'telling your
own story,'" in Afrological improvisation, which is tied to
"developing your own 'sound.'" He ends with this testament
from Charlie Parker: "Music is your own experience, your
thoughts, your wisdom. If you don't live it, it won't come out
of your horn."[6]

a spirit of collaboration

Ann Lauterbach, in the introduction to her 2018 interview
with Nancy Shaver published in *BOMB Magazine*, wrote of
"a spirit of collaboration innate to [Shaver's] work."[7] This
begins with Shaver's propensity to look at, accept, and work
together (collaborate) with made things, already in the
world. This activity immediately brings up a host of political
questions, beginning with *Who made it? Why did they make
it? Do they own it?* And, *If you do something with it, what
part does the original maker play in the collaboration?* And,
Is there such a thing as "the original maker"?

In her use of fabrics in her work, Shaver is attracted to
the way "they combine to make something else, which is
both of them and neither of them." Lauterbach says, "One
of the things that I've seen in your work is a love of making

something that puts unexpected things, say, some negligible, mass-produced material, right next to an extremely fine Japanese kimono fabric." So, she asks, "Is it part of your pleasure in juxtaposing things that wouldn't 'normally' be put together?" And Shaver replies, "Yes, I think this could hopefully, possibly reveal the width of beauty, and the width of beauty to all people."

But Shaver is also well known for inviting in, and collaborating directly with, other artists and non-artists in her installations. This activity has expanded over the past five years, such as in *Reconciliation* at the Aldrich Contemporary Art Museum in 2015; the show Shaver put together that same year for Soloway, called *The Look of Things*; her first "solo" show at Derek Eller, *Dress the Form*, in 2016, which included no less than 30 other artists in a massive wall-work called "Quilt"; her entry in the Venice Biennale in 2017 that included contributions from 19 other artists; and the show Helen Molesworth curated at MOCA in Los Angeles, *One Day at a Time: Manny Farber and Termite Art*, in 2018. In all of these exhibitions, Shaver has actively blurred the line between artist and curator, and, on the way, extended the definition and limned the contours of artistic "collaboration."

These massive constructions draw on a highly complex network of visual cues and symbolic meanings that can be composed by the artists and played by the viewers.[8] The

aesthetic "purity" of the readymade and the fusty con-
noisseurship of the *found object* are anathema to Shaver's
working poetics. But Duchamp's inquiry into whether one
can make works that are not "art," "to be subjected to the
interrogation of storefronts," is right at home for this shop-
keeper.[9] Shaver's combination antique shop/artwork, Henry,
in Hudson, New York, is now in its twentieth year.

In his entirely useful essay on Shaver's earlier work,
published in 2011, Jean-Philippe Antoine notes "the formal
contrasts between surface and ornament on the one hand,
and mass and depth on the other, that inform so many of
Shaver's sculptures," and points to "a major preoccupation
of Shaver's work: the relationship between visual glory (or
beauty) on the one hand, and ornamental desire on the
other."[10] And he pinpoints the singularity, and the radical
political thrust, of Shaver's oeuvre: "She allows the ornamental the portion of visual glory and of pure joy that it
deserves—that is to say, a power that it has never stopped
exercising, despite the 'modern' censorship to which it has
so often been subjected and the class contempt that, con-
sciously or not, motivates it."[11]

wolf tones II

Because of the coronavirus pandemic, the Wolf Tones II
exhibition is now and will forever be a secret exhibition, like
a performance that was seen by only a few people and then

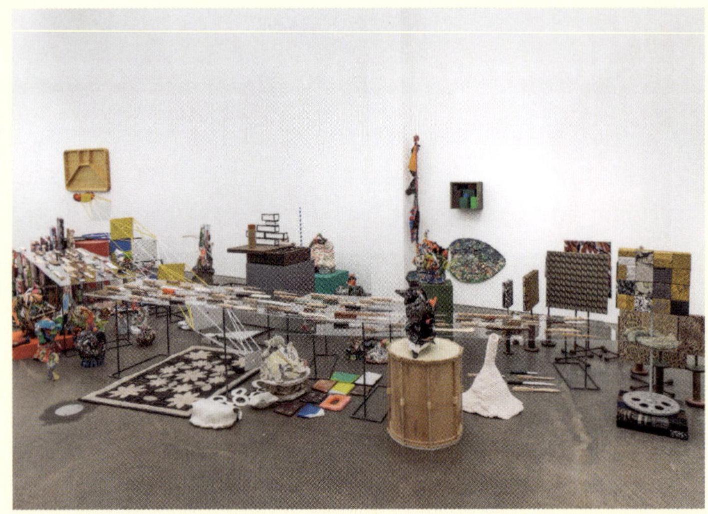

exists in extended time only in the form of photographs.[12]
Since I am one of the few people who actually saw the
exhibition, and I also saw and heard the preparations for the
show in Max Goldfarb's studio in Hudson, New York, and
in Sterrett Smith's studio, I'm compelled to try to give you a
sense of it, in an act of ephemeral ekphrasis.

The first thing one saw, entering the gallery, was
a scaled-up wood carving of a cafeteria food tray (or
TV-dinner tray) hung on the wall like a flat-screen TV, the
walls of its four compartments forming a sign of welcome,
perhaps. This preface, and the four scaled-down copies of oil
drums, two blue, one red, and one black and white, were all
made by Maximilian Goldfarb, whose work often involves a

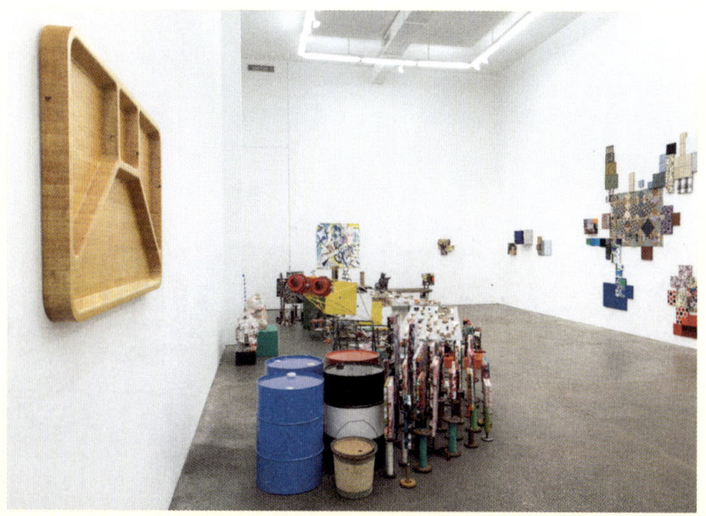

kind of pointed mimesis, where the *détournement* of manufactured and photographed objects through meticulous
handwork replicas also has a political thrust. His objects
are cultural artifacts found in source photographs of people
interacting with tools and devices, feats of epic engineering,
augmentation of abilities, telepresence, and a host of emergencies. The objects recorded in this inventory of found
imagery are then carefully made, out of scale, using incon-
gruous materials to emphasize their displacement and/or
reintegration back into the world.

In front of Goldfarb's barrels sat a bait bucket (added
by Shaver), bringing industry down to individual initia-
tive, and behind them hid one of Sterrett Smith's wrapped

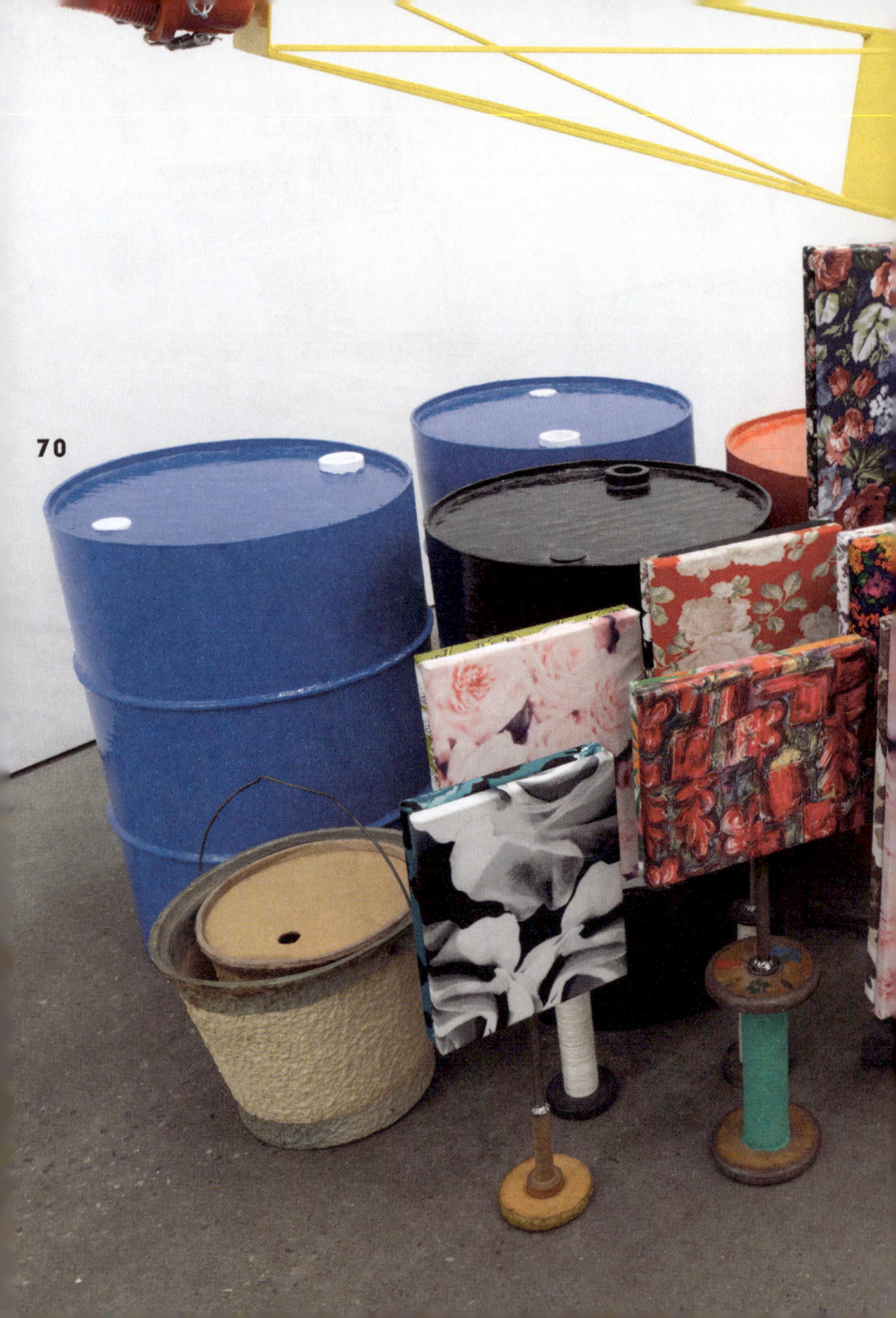

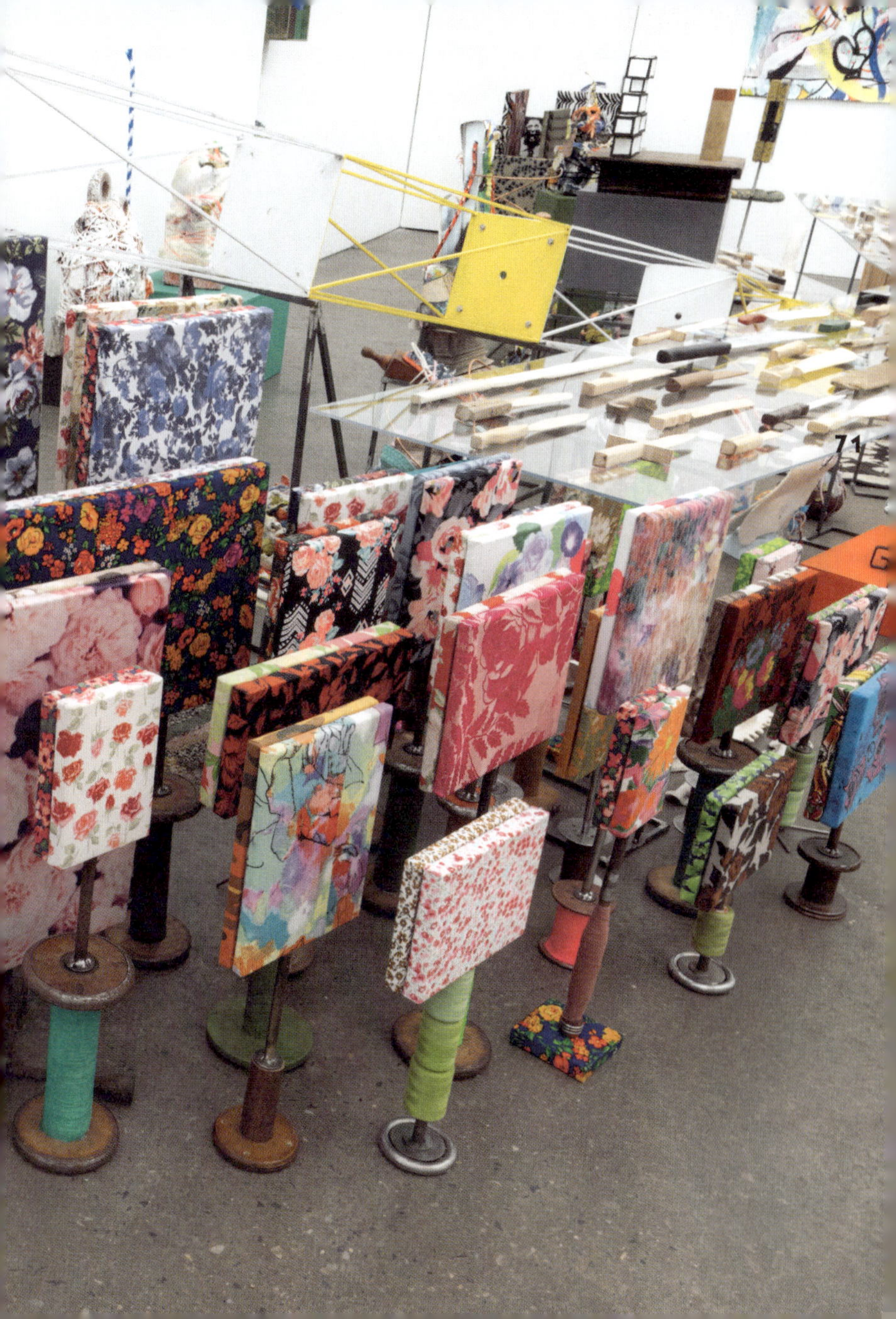
71

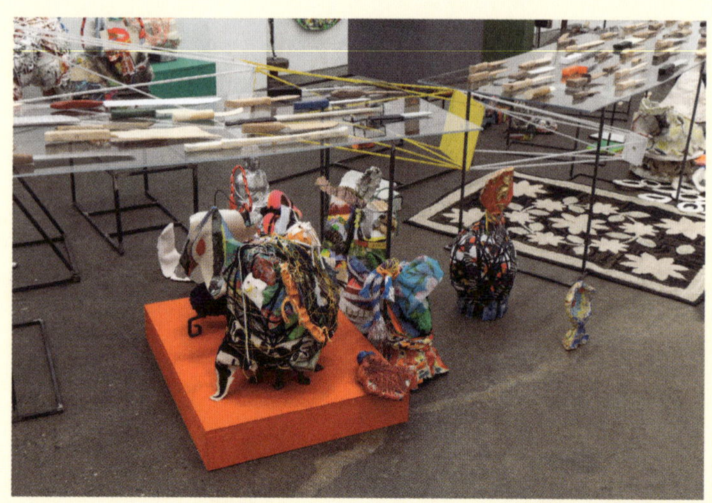

ceramic sculptures—the secret of individually conceived and expressed modeling nesting in between the faux mass-produced barrels. Smith is a painter, primarily, but she also often makes idiosyncratic sculptures that grow out of the paintings in different periods of her work. In this most recent work, she's made ceramic sculptures that are wrapped and bound in ways that make them come alive as animate bodies and beings. When Nancy Shaver first saw Smith's paintings, drawings, and sculptural investigations, and the storehouse of treasured objects in her "Utopian Parkway Garage" in the Hudson Valley in 2018, she knew that she and Smith had work to do together; and she soon introduced her to Goldfarb, and they were

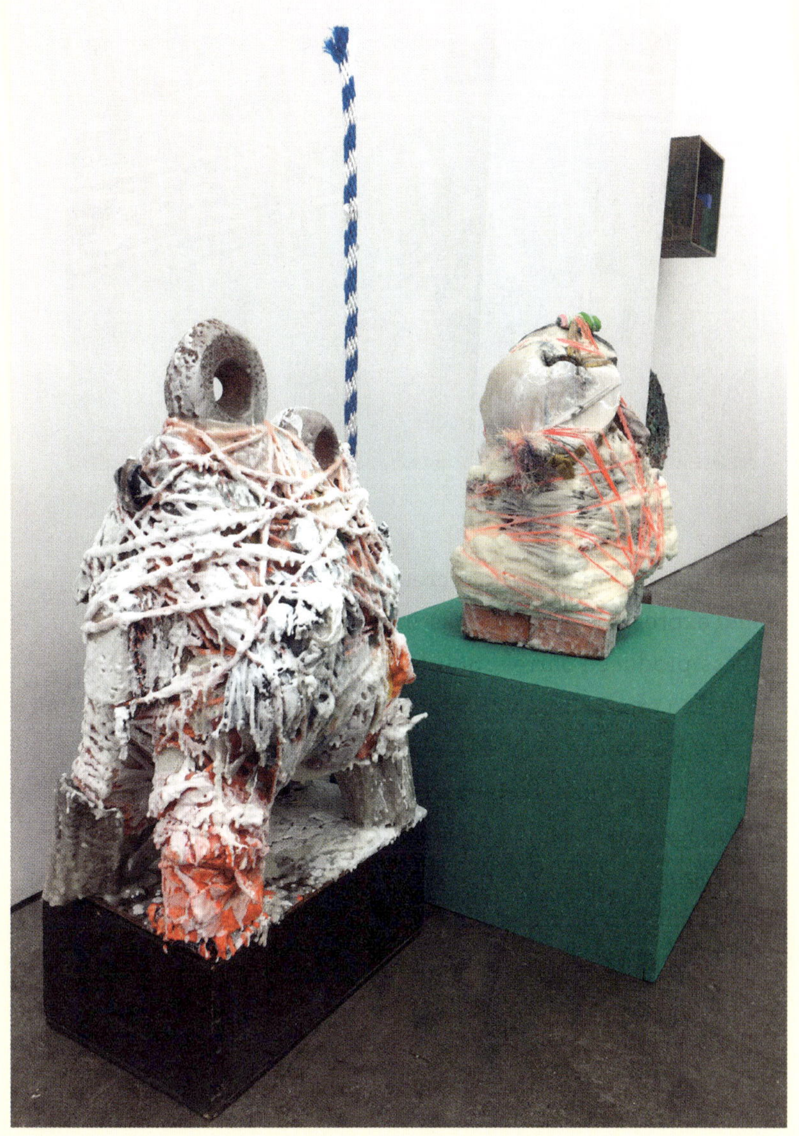

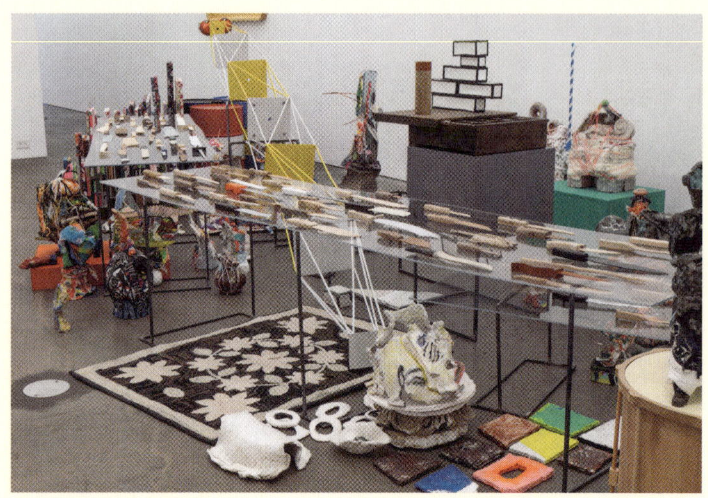

off. Smith's sculptural objects included in this installation are wildly expressive, often anthropomorphic, forms bathed in ecstatic color and wrapped, tied, or otherwise bound. These made bodies project their hand modeling, and struggle against their bonds. They are not vestiges, but emergencies: the Wolf Tones began to call them "Little Emergencies."

Nestling up against this opening salvo of the installation (introducing the collaborators) was a "garden" of Nancy Shaver's signature "sentinels," rectangles of stretched fabric mounted, like standing signs, on spools as bases. The fabrics were mostly floral designs, roses, with a few comic notes of camouflage: this garden had thorns.

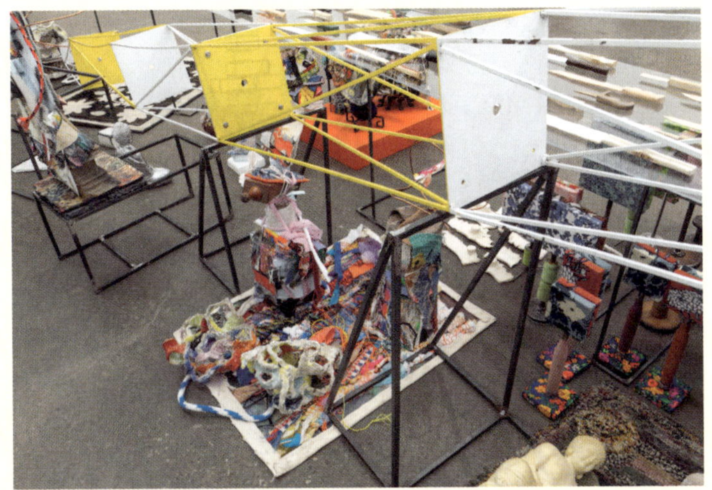

From here the arrangement opened onto split planes, above and below. Above were a phalanx of 99 knives, all different but all whittled from wood, laid out in rows on sheets of plexiglass; and a yellow-and-white replica of a radio antenna tower, placed on its side, topped by two circular, red warning lights. These elements came from Max Goldfarb. Below these see-through elements sat Sterrett Smith's white, serrated, bone-like ceramic pieces, and a grouping of "Little Emergencies," fashioned in ceramic, with brightly colored glazes, often wrapped with fabric bits and lace, works on paper, string, yarn, cord, and sometimes combined with other objects. Here, they became the expressive ground to Goldfarb's deadpan aerie.

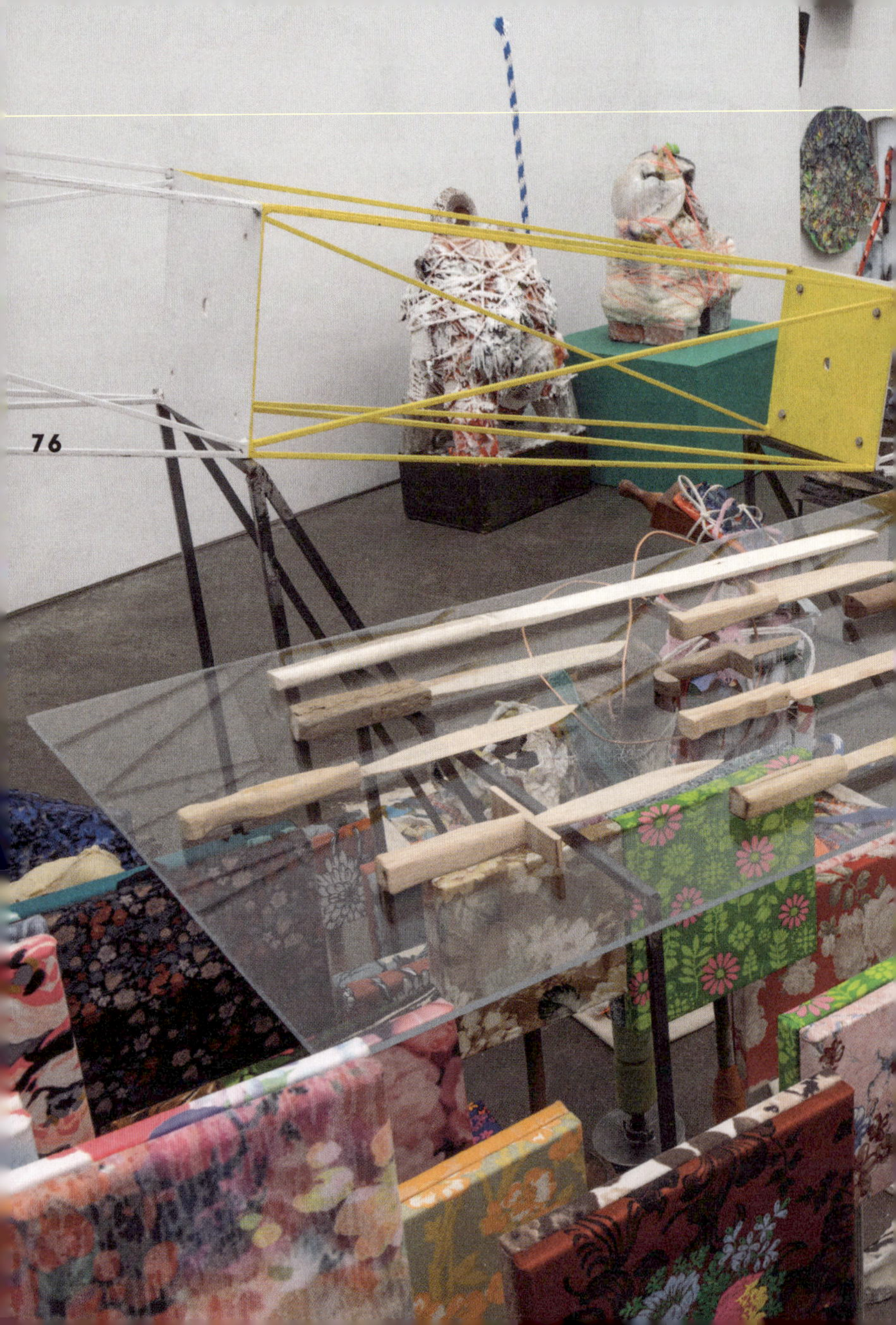

76

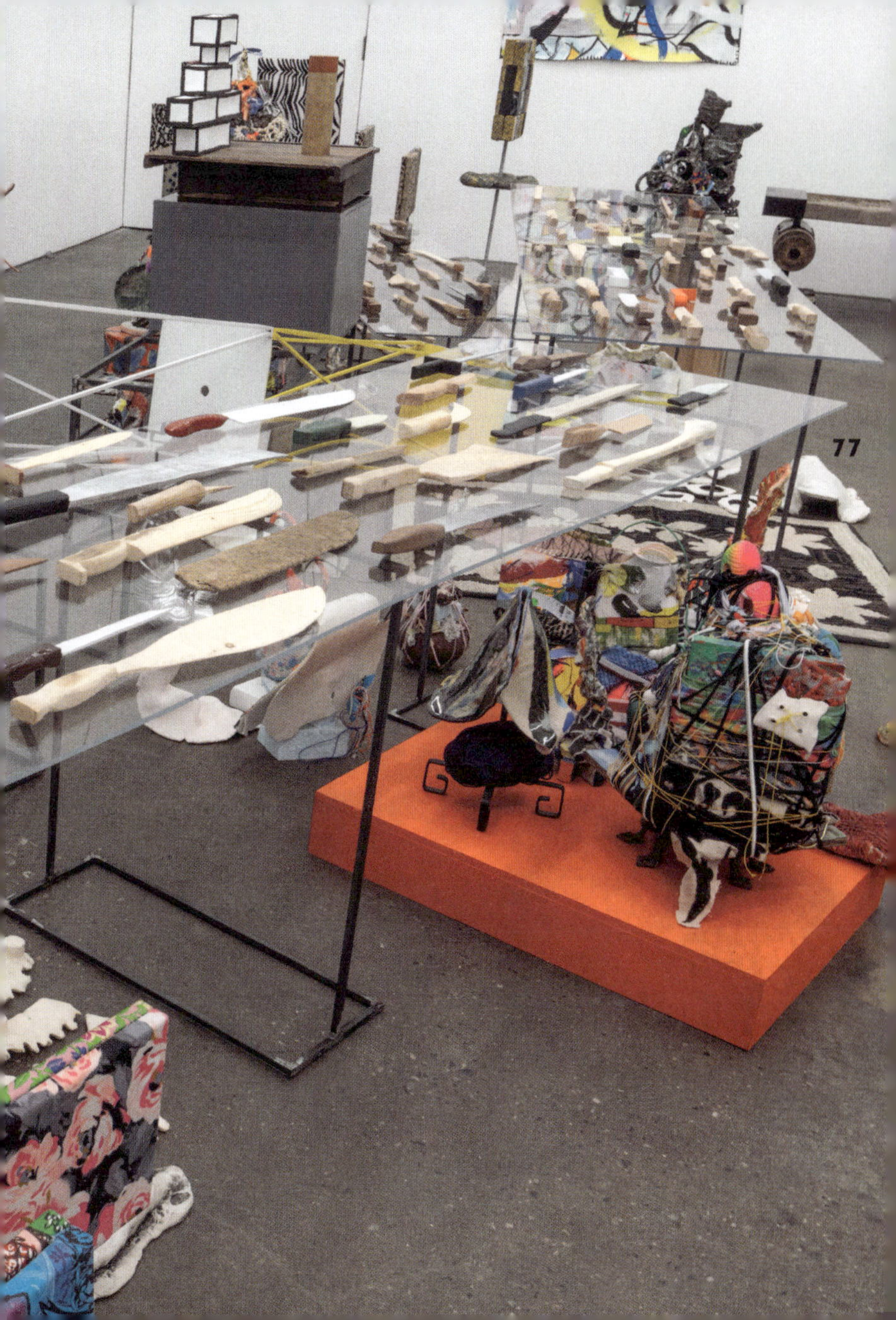
77

The knives were almost all two-edged—they were aggressively male (knife as penis, whittling as prototypical male anxiety-practice), but also protective, connective, and generous. As the knives took a turn and continued, they flew above a vernacular black-and-white rug patterned in flowers from Shaver's collection, and more ceramic pieces by Smith, including white rings, tunnels and funnels, "arteries," and a large ceramic piece that she called "Guston's Boot." It remained a question whether all of these body parts were coming together or coming apart.

As the entire archipelagic composition bent like an arm or leg, a number of larger sculptures took up positions in the crook: two large, matched, ceramic, wrapped, encaustic-coated creaturely (male and female?) sculptures and another sprouting a devil-may-care flight of copper wire, all by Sterrett Smith, and an open cash drawer topped with stacked boxes, painted white and outlined in black, and a cylinder with a red top, all from Nancy Shaver. These sculptures were all placed on wooden plinths, painted dark brown, Payne's gray, cadmium orange, and veronese and viridian green. And these were shadowed by a hanging, painted box piece by Shaver, "Elegy #1," over a spearhead-shaped boogie board from the dump, festooned with painted plastic leaves; while a piercing, celebratory vertical piece stood guard in the corner, both by Smith. On the other side was a large, wooden, musical drum by Goldfarb, to rhyme with the

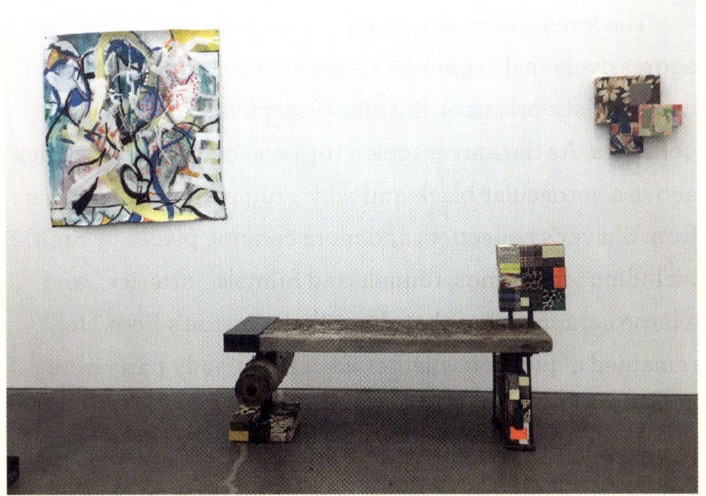

oil drums at the beginning; and a stand-alone sentinel, with crossed fish, by Shaver. A caduceus as punctuation?

The Wolf Tones part of the installation ended at the far wall with a large, abstract acrylic painting on paper by Smith, hanging over a substantial bench by Shaver, like a bitingly ironic "painting over the couch." But the show didn't end there. It continued into two walls of works by Nancy Shaver, including a large wall piece titled "Moving Left," a column of ten "blockers," another "Elegy" piece, a fabric painting, and a standing shelf piece, also elegiac, called "Mostly Blue, for E.G."

What was immediately clear to a viewer was that this entire arrangement was made to maximize one's excitement and enjoyment in looking. Every engaged moment of looking was rewarded with another revelation, and another, and another. The composition moved in three dimensions and was meant to be seen from every angle, over time. The more you looked, the more you saw.

And at the same time, the construction was a *provocation*. Like Ian Hamilton Finlay used to say, his gardens weren't only retreats, for contemplation, they were also attacks. Once you let these made things into your field of view, they act as prompts, to rethinking. Every act of generosity and grace to the senses is tinged as well with caustic reflection to the sensibilities.

It took nearly two years to make this collaborative composition, and hundreds, perhaps a thousand, distinct decisions about placement, color, and tone. And that's not to say anything about the meanings of the things juxtaposed here, and the stories they tell. Everything has a past. The world is not short of material, but it is short of meaning. What do 99 knives, painstakingly whittled, mean today, as vectors and artifacts? What do sun-bleached bones on the ground of a journey mean, or wrapped (bandaged?) beings; grouped, huddled masses, injured but not stopped? Or a garden of manufactured barbed roses as a personal gift?

As the great French-Caribbean writer and philosopher Édouard Glissant once wrote, "It is only the human imaginary that cannot be contaminated by its objects. Because

it alone diversifies them infinitely yet brings them back,
nonetheless, to a full burst of unity. The highest point of
knowledge is always a poetics."[13] That is, the highest point
of knowledge is a *making*, and in this case, a collaborative making.

The name "Wolf Tones" comes from the acoustic phenomenon whereby the material in the body of a stringed,
bowed instrument vibrates at the same frequency as the
note played, causing dissonance or noise (likened to the
ululations of a howling wolf), and sometimes requiring the
use of a "wolf tone eliminator," consisting of a metal tube
fitted over the offending string, to quell it. The collaborative
group Wolf Tones has found a way to work with and through
the unavoidable dissonance, or noise, of collaboration, as
well as the tremendous, cacophonous din being produced by
the culture at large at this time in America, to get to a clear
signal and an original tone—their own *sound*. The group
does not deny or suppress dissonance, but works through
it—kindly, conscientiously, with patience, persistence, and
an exceedingly rare amount of trust.[14]

Wolf Tones combines the works of three very different
kinds of artists: the analytic representational/conceptual
work of Max Goldfarb; the animate alchemy of Sterrett
Smith's sculptures and paintings; and the formal, gridded
rigor, cut with eccentric materials and color, of Nancy
Shaver. And these three disparate approaches are brought

together, conducted and composed, by the experienced,
searching eye and aesthetic wisdom of Nancy Shaver.

Perhaps it is significant, now, during this aggrieved time
of segregation, polarization, and isolation—when we are all
fearful and angry and tired—for forcefully distinct individuals to find a way to work together to make something
beautiful and clear.

ENDNOTES

1—Don DeLillo, *Underworld* (New York: Scribner, 1997), 295.

2—Michael Taussig, *Mastery of Non-Mastery in the Age of Meltdown* (Chicago:
University of Chicago Press, 2020).

3—George E. Lewis, "Improvised Music after 1950: Afrological and Eurological
Perspectives," *Black Music Research Journal*, vol. 16, no. 1 (Spring 1996): 117.

4—Rev. Walter W. Skeat, *An Etymological Dictionary of the English Language*
(Oxford: Oxford University Press, 1879–1882), 291.

5—Lewis, "Improvised Music," 94.

6—Lewis, "Improvised Music," 117, 119.

7—Nancy Shaver, "Liking Difficulty: Nancy Shaver Interviewed by Ann
Lauterbach," *BOMB Magazine*, August 1, 2018, https://bombmagazine.org/
articles/liking-difficulty-nancy-shaver-interviewed/.

8—I overheard Sterrett Smith talking to Max Goldfarb at one point, referring to
'the Conductor,' meaning Shaver.

9—"Can one make works that are not 'art'?" asked Duchamp, before adding to
the mix: "To be subjected to the interrogation of storefronts. / The standards of
the storefront. / The storefront proves the existence of an outside world." Marcel
Duchamp, *Duchamp du Signe*, ed. Michel Sanouillet (Paris: Flammarion, 1975),
quoted in Jean-Philippe Antoine, "Shaver's Razor: Social Values, Visual Glory,

and Ordinary Objects," trans. Anna Moschovakis, in Nancy Shaver, *The Quilt & the Truck* (Portland, OR: Publication Studio/Feature, 2011).

10—Ibid.

11—Ibid.

12—The gallery did, however, reopen with the exhibition still on view later in the pandemic, from July 7–31, 2020.

13—Édouard Glissant, *Poetics of Relation*, trans. Betsy Wing (Ann Arbor: University of Michigan Press, 1997), 140.

14—I can't help but think here also of the eighteenth-century Irish revolutionary Wolfe Tone, who was one of the very few Protestant republicans who fought for the rights of his Presbyterian and Catholic countrymen, and who inspired a later group of radical singers in Ireland who called themselves The Wolfe Tones. And the 250-year-old oak tree outside my library in the Hudson Valley is called a "wolf tree" around here, because it manages to stay wild when nearly every other tree in this area was felled in the clearing of the fields for cultivation and grazing. Wolf trees survived because they grew in the stone fence lines between the fields. They survived at the boundaries of culture.

IMAGE CREDITS

All images document Maximilian Goldfarb, Nancy Shaver, and Sterrett Smith, "Wolf Tones II," in *Nancy Shaver: fastness, slowness, and Monstrous Beauty*, 2020, Derek Eller Gallery, New York.

PAGE 58—Photo: Jeanne Liotta.

PAGES 68, 69, 70–71, 72, 74, 75, 76–77—Courtesy Derek Eller Gallery.

PAGES 73, 79—Photos: Maya Strauss.

UNEASY LISTENING: NOISE AS POTENTIAL

ANNA FRIZ

Discussions of wolf tones as a musical problem unique to violins and cellos lead to an inevitable conclusion: the wolf must be tamed. Such noises must be smoothed and all wolves soothed, or a new instrument purchased. Perhaps, though, the wolf is neither foe nor adversary, but a creature functioning as sonic evidence of relationships. The wolf tone emerges due to particular material and resonant properties of a bowed stringed instrument (for instance, a cello), and this sudden amplification of burred oscillating tones under the relationship of bow, instrument, and player is inevitably described as noise. Noise may be variably defined as surplus sounds or signals, as audible pollution, as an interruption of the regularly scheduled program, and as social or aesthetic discord. Noise is never meaningless, even if it might make for difficult listening. This same term "noise" is used in reference to both signal interference in communications networks and to spurious material sounds that exceed dominant social norms, leading to the tendency in popular discourse toward conflating those two contexts. More interesting is to reconsider noise when the wolves turn up; to rescue that bowed oscillation from its often abject status as the polar opposite of pleasant sound, song, or silence; and to consider the potential engendered by its noisy howl.

What is noise, and how to understand its social or conceptual function? The most common definition of noise in a modern Western context is that of disorderly, unpleasant, surplus sound, best eliminated if deemed intolerable; or, failing that, to be contained or controlled via insulation or masking. Without exhaustively surveying a socio-cultural history of noise, let me briefly refer to a couple of key conceptions of noise as expressed under Western modernity before returning to the question of what noise as potential might offer social life more generally and artistic collaboration in particular.

Noise as a communal experience is often associated with urban life and described as a phenomenon that plagues the bustling modern city: horse hooves on cobblestones and hawkers loudly selling their wares gave way to growing manufacturing and transport industries, commuter traffic, ubiquitous loudspeakers, and the babble of human voices issuing forth from blaring radios and televisions; all within an urban design of shrinking apartments with thin walls, tall buildings with echoing foyers, and not enough sound-absorbing green space nearby. Historian and sound studies scholar Karin Bijsterveld notes that in early modern times these complaints about noise were a class-oriented discourse—citing Schopenhauer's lament that whip-cracking in the street was a fatal interruption to his work and that the "lower classes" who seemed insensitive to such sounds were naturally also insensitive to art, philosophy, poetry, etc. Thus the category of noise proves to be a loaded ideological construct, a product of its cultural and historical matrix. Bijsterveld's study of early modern noise abatement campaigns in North America and Europe reflected relationships of power between economic classes and technological culture. "Loud sounds, if positively evaluated, have been attributed with characteristics such as power, strength, progress, prosperity, energy, dynamics, masculinity, and control."[1] These same sounds, if unwanted or associated with lower classes, are considered an unpleasant disruption, i.e., noise. Consumer technologies are brought to bear on such instances of social discord and friction, and contribute to social inequality in our contemporary moment such that those with means may invest in evermore soundproofed private vehicles or noise-cancellation head-phones, allowing a commuter to move through the city in a self-contained bubble accompanied by their own sound-scape, undisturbed by jackhammers or verbal interactions with other people in the street or on a subway.

Noise as a problem of signal interference is a common refrain around the operations of communications when engaging with technology and distance, particularly with the rise of complex networked systems. The transmission model of communication was put forward by Claude Shannon and Warren Weaver in 1949, and the assumptions beneath this constitutive theory of early communications studies and information theory continue to circulate in popular culture in dispersed but powerful ways. In Weaver's introduction to Claude Shannon's *The Mathematical Theory of Communication*,[2] he describes the communication process as originating with information generated at the source (by the sender), which is emitted through a transmitter as a signal that then reaches the receiver. Noise is introduced in the equation with the signal during transmission. Entropy is factored into the system as a measure of information, and a certain amount of redundancy is allowed to combat noise accompanying the signal, thus ensuring better reception. Successful communication is gauged by the accuracy of the transmission of symbols, the ability of the receiver to

decode the semantic meaning of the symbols transmitted by
the sender, and the effectiveness of the message on the sub-
sequent actions or behaviors of the receiver. Weaver emphasizes that without the technological accuracy of noise-free
transmission, the semantic and affective aspects cannot be
expected to function, making the technical transmission of
a message paramount.

Noise is thus distortion, error, and surplus signal that
results in more uncertainty. Weaver characterizes this
surplus as "spurious and undesirable" noise which must
be removed. N. Katherine Hayles, in revisiting the Macy
Conferences on Cybernetics where Shannon discussed his
theories, notes that Shannon was adamant that his information theory "concerned only the efficient transmission
of messages through communication channels, not what
those messages mean."[3] She goes on to suggest that, taken
in the context of engineering, this may have been a sensible
course to follow, but taken out of context (i.e., applied to the
structure and function of communication generally), "the
definition allowed information to be conceptualized as if it
were an entity that can flow unchanged between different
material substrates."[4] Decontextualization and reification
of information in this way also suggests that information is
static (unchanging), and that change would be the (undesirable) result of noise in the signal.[5] Thus the problem of
(mis)communications is defined by the procedural problem

of signal to noise ratios, while the ideological and material contexts of communication, such as infrastructures, social practices, and physical bodies fade from view.

Communications scholar Ian Angus suggests that noise may function as resistance by increasing the noise of the signal beyond control, effectively creating a rupture in the containment and ordering of things to enable change.[6] His preferred social remedy is a renewed focus on the local in order to recover embodied oral culture. Angus posits that noise may be employed as potential—an opening—as well as a means of command and control. Contemporary media culture under hypercapitalism may generate masses of commercial noise as distraction and thus social control, but noise may also be an unoccupied FM radio frequency waiting for a radio pirate to come along and occupy it. Noise may temporarily reclaim mediated commercial space—be it the boomboxes of the 1980s, pounding hip-hop and Cuban jazz into the North American streets to drown out the Muzak and the humdrum of everyday life in the city, or be it raucous marching and sonic resistance by protesters without a city permit. Angus champions the noise of local democratic life taking place in public—which he defines as unordered sound and difference, such as a rumble of conversation punctuated by kids running squealing around picnic tables at a community dinner in the park—as a reclamation of cultural codes.

To return to musical examples, artists and composers have long sought to upend the canonized aesthetic of Western musical and performance traditions, and since the early twentieth century, noise can also be understood as an expressive, deliberate, and often political counter-narrative to dominant aesthetics, formal restrictions, and social hierarchies of class, race, and gender. For instance, if noise is historically described as the antithesis of music—accused of being loud, unstructured, unpredictable, tonally non-conformist, etc.—in the twentieth century, the boundaries between noise and music dissolved through radical new practices, from jazz improvisation and bebop, to composing experimental radio and sound works from everyday sounds such as traffic and industry, to the advent of various forms of electronic and industrial music, to all manner of sample-based music practices that introduce an ever-expanding sonic vocabulary such as scratch DJing, to deep dub cuts, to ultra-fast beats made by manipulating presets on cheap repurposed electronic devices. Such practices also challenge the imperative for control described in sender-receiver models of communications, as communal sound-making and repurposing of technologies and techniques propose multiple trajectories and complex relations that privilege the shared project of presence, improvisation, and variation.[7] In the end, notes Angus, the idea of noise is as indeterminate as its function: "Who decides what is spurious? Even more important, what is the function of noise? Not only Shannon and Weaver, but mainstream communication theory as a whole has no answer to this question. Indeed, it never even formulates the question clearly."[8] In reassigning the label of noise to mainstream media, Angus engages in a struggle over the meaning of cultural codes: if the norm is the message and surplus is noise, then Angus suggests a reversal, such that the norm might instead be local, embodied relationships, upon which consumer society under capitalism acts as interference.

But the struggle to define noise also has subtle potential to address power relations in addition to flipping the scripts of normative behavior and listening. Audible noise itself, in its purported chaos and changefulness, with its broad spectrum of sounds, with its lack of stable form, might also be understood as being made of myriad tiny relational differences.[9] To return to the wolf tone howling on the cello string: the noise of the wolf tone is not merely a sound to be judged for its aesthetics; the wolf tone is an index of relationship between the sonic frequency produced by the vibrating string, the resonant frequency of the body of the instrument, and the bodily effort to play on the part of the musician. The wolf tone is an avowal of material relations, of bodies in space. The wolf tone is a declarative eruption: these bodies exist, they have specificity. The defining characteristics of the wolf tone are both these embodied relationships that produce it and their resulting audible dissonance. If the misapplied goal of information theory is the accurate reception of the message from the sender and the effective change in conduct on the part of the receiver, or if the study of human communications has often over-privileged the desire for union or consensus,[10] the wolf tone proposes that dissonance and discord are also valu-able, meaning-filled communication tropes. Reframing the "problem" of the wolf tone contributes to understanding the reality of dissonance in communication and relationships, where distance and noise may be generative, and discord may serve as embodied, audible evidence of the work of collaboration.

ENDNOTES

1 — Karin Bijsterveld, "The Diabolical Symphony of the Mechanical Age: Technology and Symbolism of Sound in European and North American Noise Abatement Campaigns, 1900–40," in *The Auditory Culture Reader*, eds. Les Back and Michael Bull (Oxford: Berg, 2003), 182.

2 — Claude Shannon and Warren Weaver, *The Mathematical Theory of Communication* (Urbana: University of Illinois Press, 1949), 4-5.

3 — N. Katherine Hayles, *How We Became Posthuman: Virtual Bodies in Cybernetics, Literature, and Informatics* (Chicago: University of Chicago Press, 1999), 54.

4 — Ibid.

5 — Ibid., 63.

6 — Ian H. Angus, *Primal Scenes of Communication: Communication, Consumerism, and Social Movements* (Albany: State University of New York Press, 2000).

7 — For instance, see Alexander G. Weheliye, *Phonographies: Grooves in Sonic Afro-Modernity* (Durham: Duke University Press, 2005); and George E. Lewis, "Improvised Music after 1950: Afrological and Eurological Perspectives," *Black Music Research Journal,* vol. 16, no. 1 (Spring 1996): 91–122.

8 — Angus, *Primal Scenes of Communication*, 128.

9 — Georgina Born, "On Nonhuman Sound—Sound As Relation," in *Sound Objects*, eds. Rey Chow and James A. Steintrager (Durham: Duke University Press, 2019), 185–207.

10 — John Durham Peters, *The Marvelous Clouds: Toward a Philosophy of Elemental Media* (Chicago: University of Chicago Press, 2015).

DISCORDANT NOTES

CATHERINE LORD

The school of knives strikes the eye first, something like a hundred knives, I think (should I have written down the number?), but precision is not essential, rather the fact of many, many, way too many, knives to bother to count. Each knife is its own snowflake, allegedly unique, hand-whittled, all more or less life-size. They are placed on three metal and plexiglass stands, each one longer rather than wider. The knives slice in one direction, schooling above and beside groups of bulky, bound, weighty, ceramic roughnesses and battalions of thrift store fabric warriors, serene in their class rebellion. Discordant notes. The mess sits under a construction that looks like a reconstituted yellow derrick, a ghost of a cell phone tower. Buddhas are present, in corners and voids, but they provide as much, or as little, ethical guidance as the occasional chicken. The transfer station has vanquished the grid. Just like regular school, when school is actually about learning, this is both a collaboration and a confrontation. Three artists are involved, so the evolving results never collapse into good taste or ego. The rules of the game forbid such moves, and the game is played individually, like solitaire, and together, like poker. Who made what is not the point. Nothing is claimed, nothing is signed. This is an experienced adjacency of materials, a mature friendship, maybe even a thrupple, a small pod of artists vehemently agreeing to disagree wildly, without rocking the proverbial boat. Balance is a delicate business. These are strong-willed artists. It's easy to see how quickly the whole house of battered cards could tumble. The three artists entangled (Max Goldfarb, Nancy Shaver, and Sterrett Smith) have conducted all manner of quiet conversations. They have refined their eyes for discordance and for collaboration. In their different ways, they engage, they persuade, they tweak, they argue. They forget who thought to do what, and when. Intimacy is neither a simple thing, nor a static triumph. The sentences in which I write lack the muscle to describe this, or even to stand and watch, but this is in fact the thrill.

CATHERINE LORD

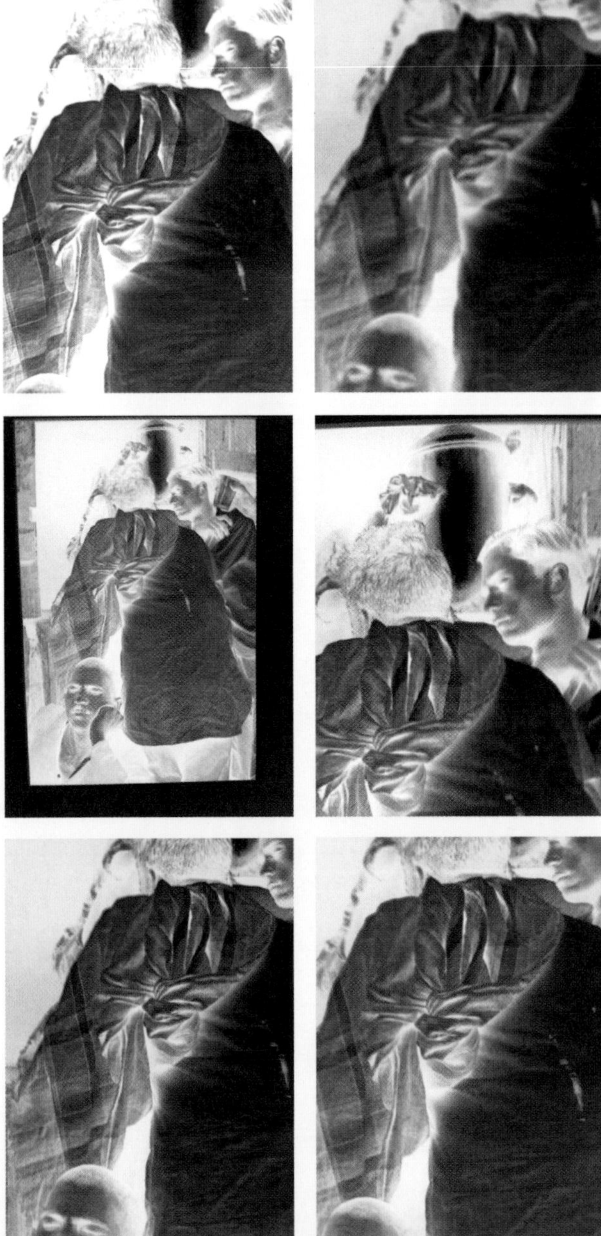

HAND AND LOOM

PRADEEP DALAL

1 / the gamcha, benares

Impulsively and rapidly, I rephotographed photographs made by William Gedney in Benares, India, in the early 1970s. I found myself drawn to the articles of clothing on the various people in Gedney's photographs—the folds of a dhoti, the casual wrapping of a gamcha, a folded piece of fabric held in the hand.[1]

I was familiar with most of Gedney's photographs, especially his India work, and was delighted to see the exhibition, *Gedney in India,* at the Chhatrapati Shivaji Maharaj Vastu Sangrahalaya in Mumbai in 2017. I made several hundred images on my phone. Probing each of his photographs, I isolated details of clothing worn by the subjects of Gedney's desirous eye. I sometimes made a dozen or more images from a single photograph.

In his diary, Gedney lists the subjects of his pictures in Benares: the setting of the ghats on the riverfront, religious

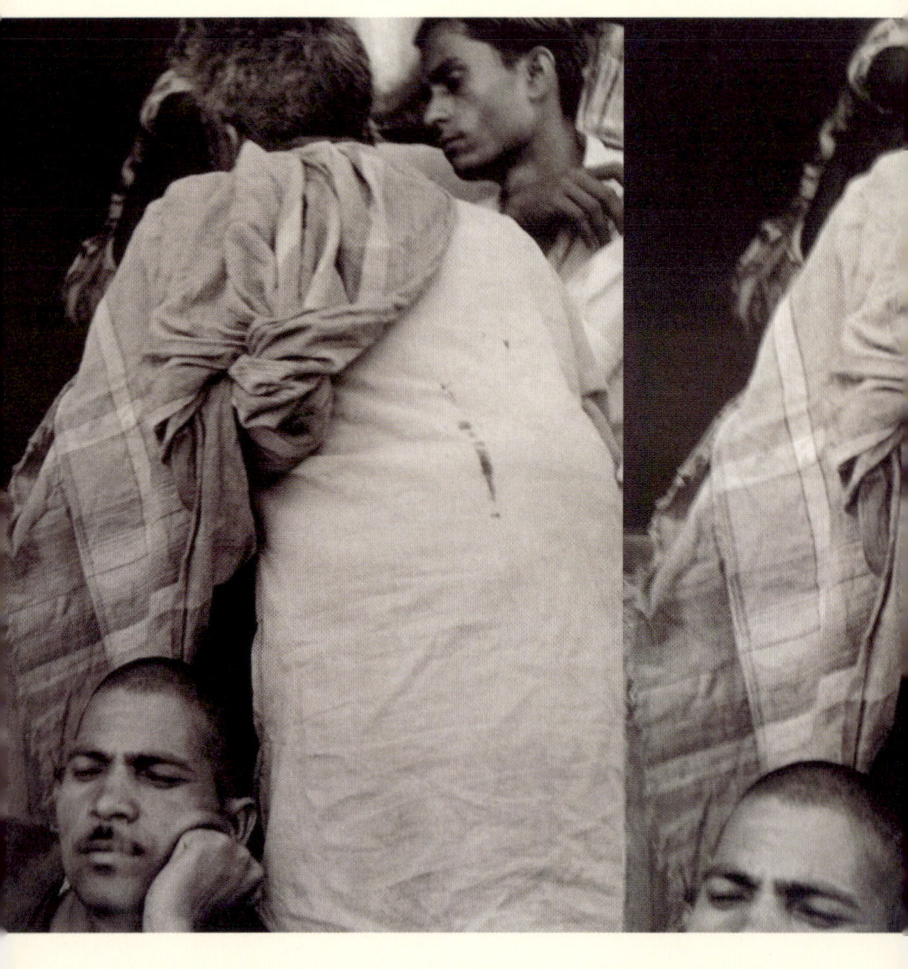

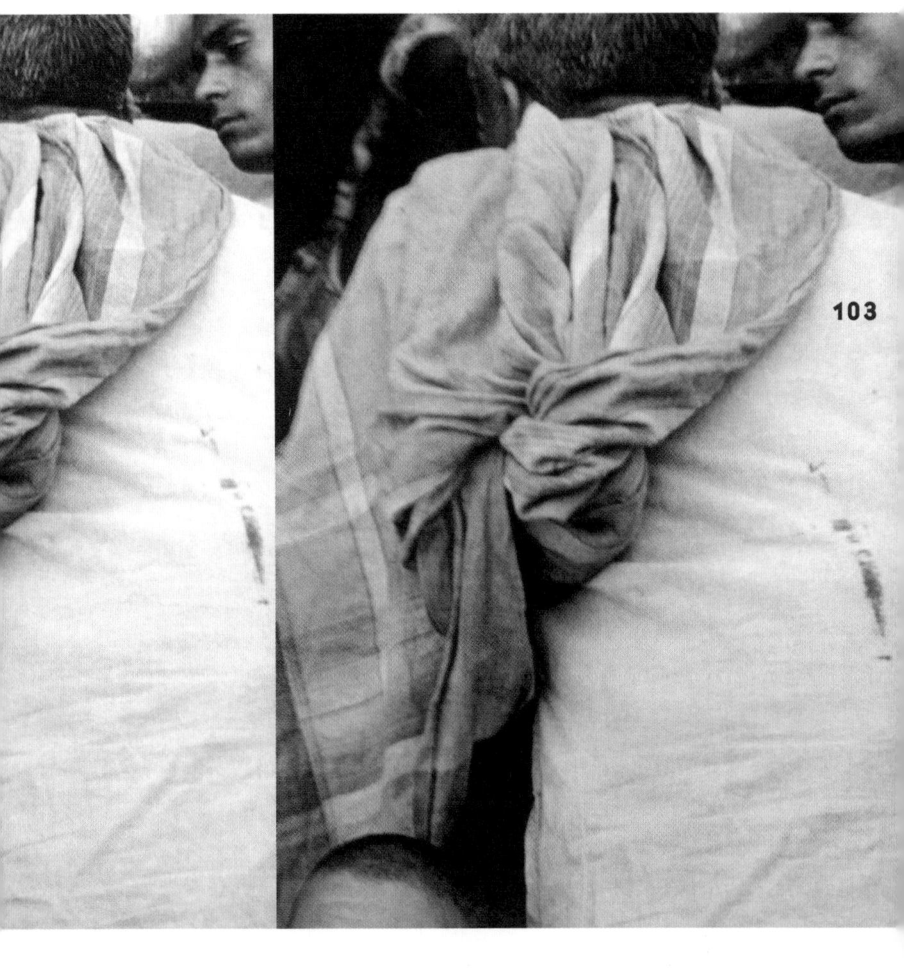

103

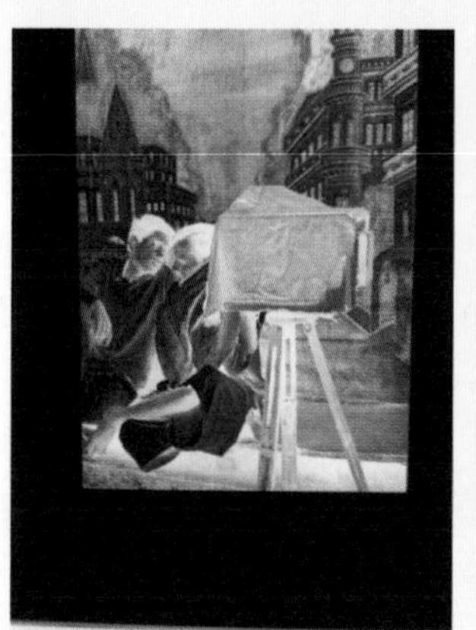
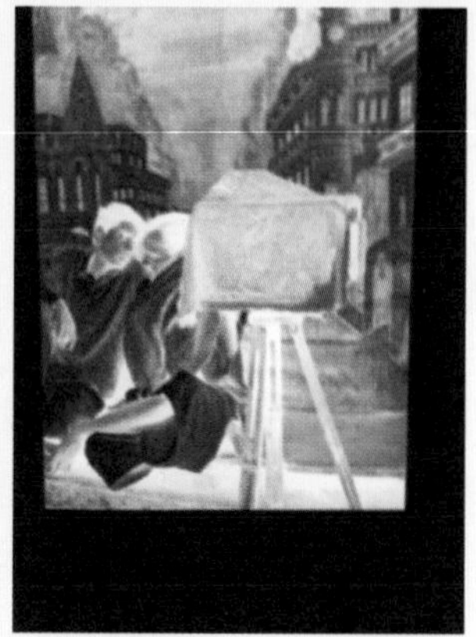
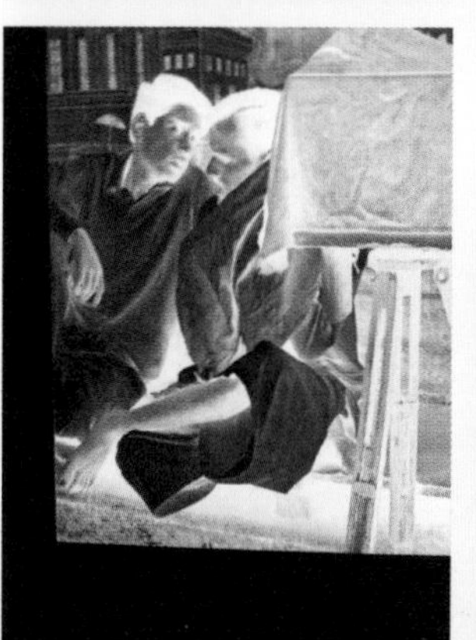
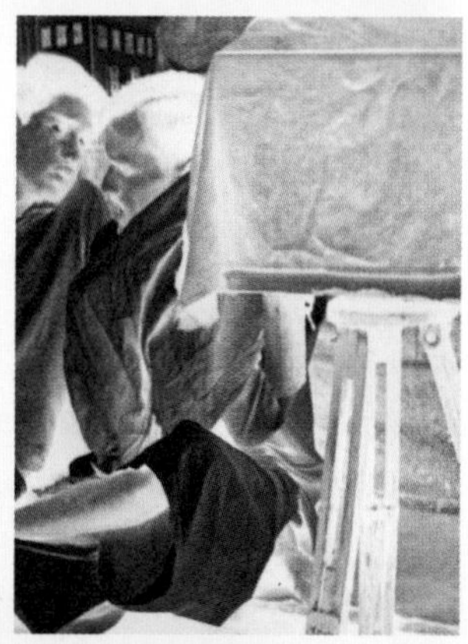
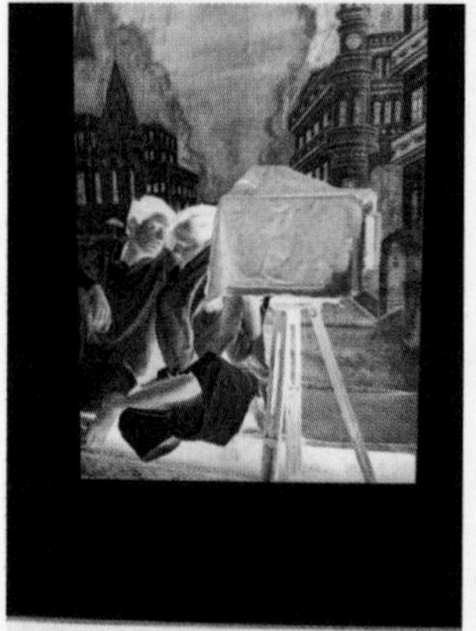
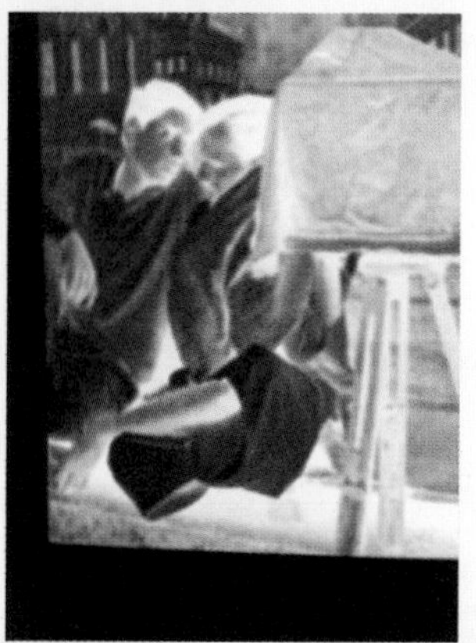

celebrations, temples, portraits, and, he adds, "clothes—dressing draping of dhoti . . ."[2] He emphasizes "not wanting to photograph the body as abstract form but as the embodiment of the physical: grace of movement, sexual attraction, desire, intimacy, the privacy of one's own body . . . to give some feeling of the body as three dimensional, textural[,] the feeling of skin its softness . . ."[3]

The cotton gamcha is a multipurpose cloth, indispensable in a hot and humid climate. In Gedney's photographs, you see this simple, unstitched rectangle of cloth draped and used in elegant and inventive ways: a rickshaw puller clasps it to stop his hand from slipping due to sweat; some wear it wrapped around the neck, shoulders, or around the waist as a sash, or over the head. Some even fully mask their face with it to keep out dust. It also serves as a cushion while sleeping on the ground, is sometimes rolled and placed on the head to cushion heavy loads, and even knotted into bundles to carry objects and belongings.

WG, India, 1970 #1. A swift arc can be drawn from the blissed-out person on the lower left, with smoke coming out of his nostrils, to the tableau of three figures at the tea shop—one person's face in profile with his hand against his shoulder connects with the outstretched hand of a figure outside the frame holding a glass. The central figure—his back to us, a loosely draped gamcha over his left shoulder trailing over the entire stretch of his left hand, the knotted

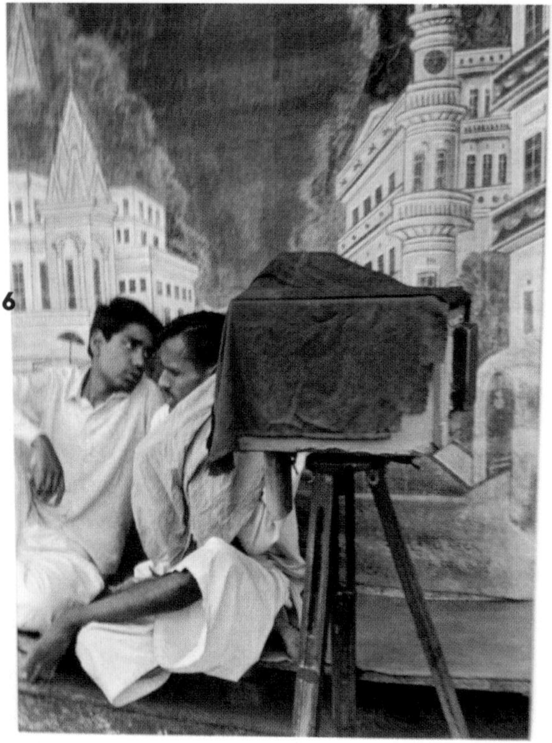

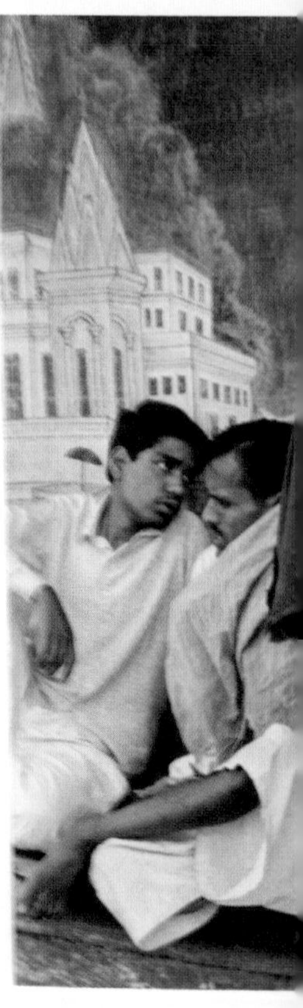

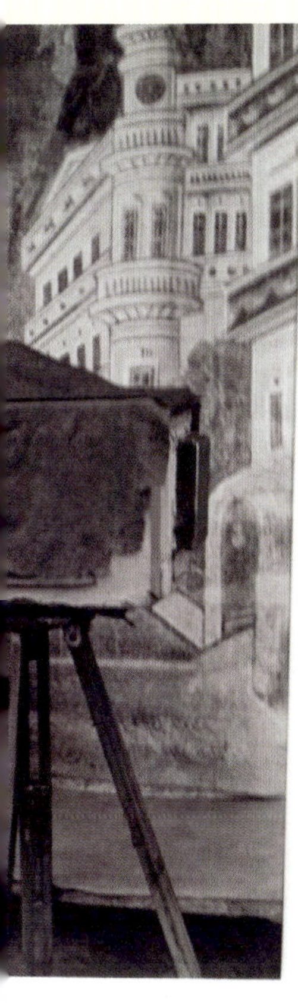

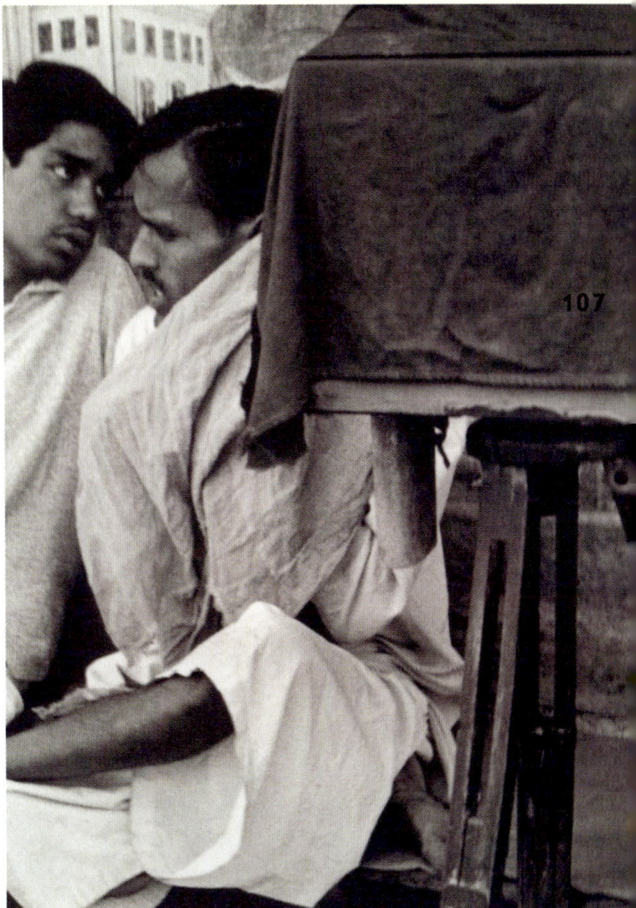

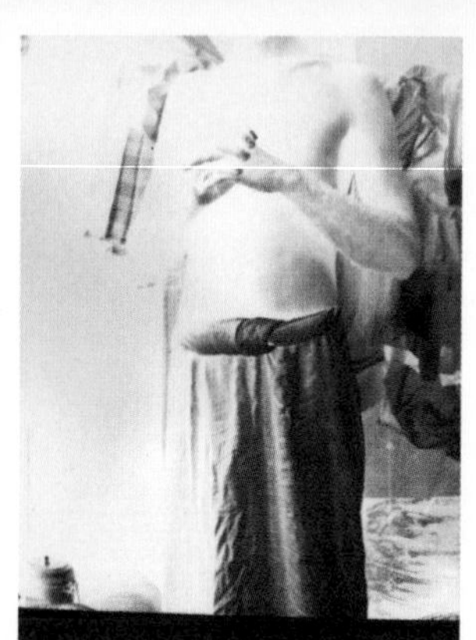
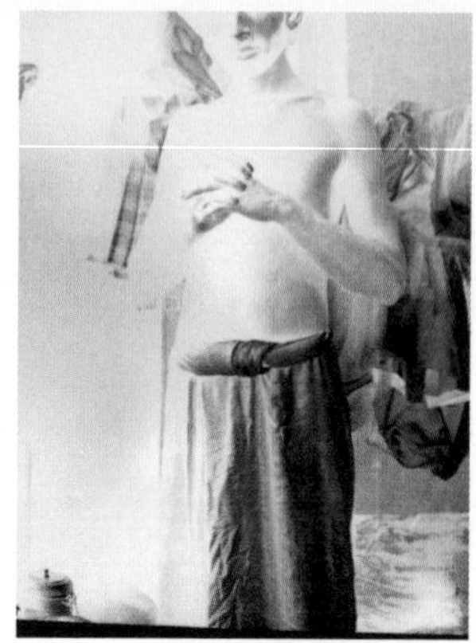
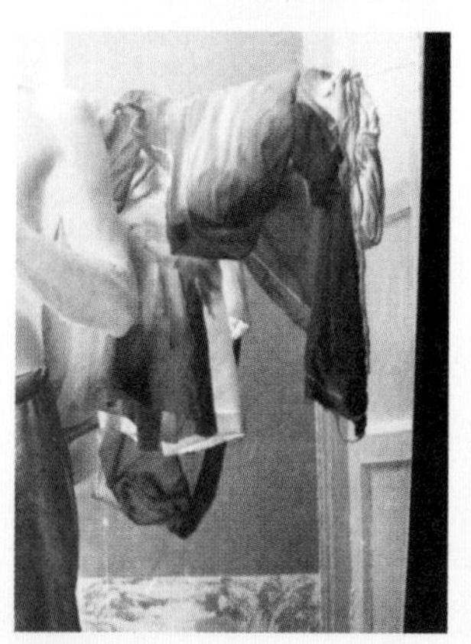
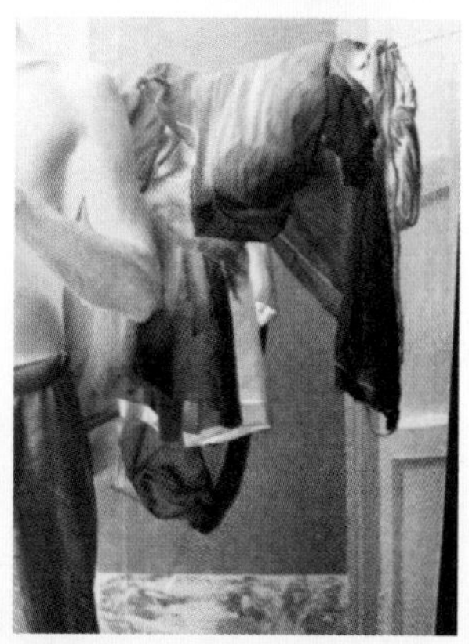
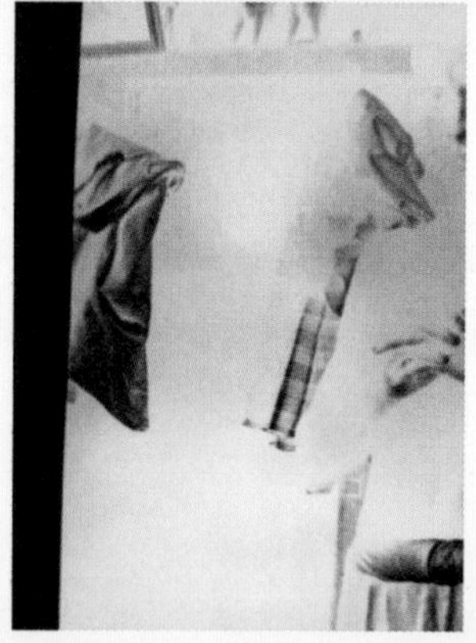
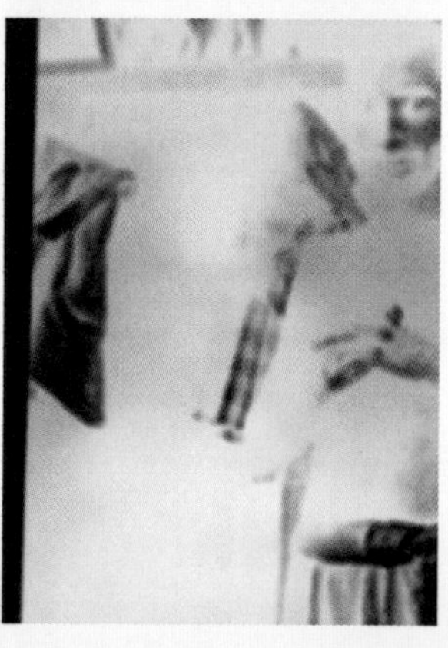

portion on the back—is particularly striking. How is the whorled, furrowed, bunched portion made? Does it hold something, some currency notes and coins perhaps? Or is it just a knot to give some form of ballast to the loose shawl-like fabric? There is a nonchalance to the draping of the fabric; it does not come in the way of the movement of the hands, of the upper body—it is so light that it does not register. There is no stylized drape with the cloth. It just fits ever so loosely on the white kurta, the faded striped pattern on the ends distinct from the plain, white, soiled garment below, with a slight gash mark on the lower back. There is exceptional beauty in the casual clothing of these working men—seemingly inattentive and unconscious, an unforced styling perhaps, yet powerfully attractive.

WG, India, 1970 #2: The architectural backdrop—a city scene with a central perspective and a large camera on a bulky wooden tripod—is immediately compelling in Gedney's photograph. The painted cloth backdrop has a vaguely Hindu temple structure facing a more imposing colonial building with a clock. The camera is covered by two pieces of cloth, with a carefully folded line where one rests on the other. The two men are huddled close and conversing, though not looking at each other. The way one of them holds his gamcha tenderly to the side of his face, his hands underneath the cloth making a sort of support, is endearing. He is sitting cross-legged with one leg resting comfortably

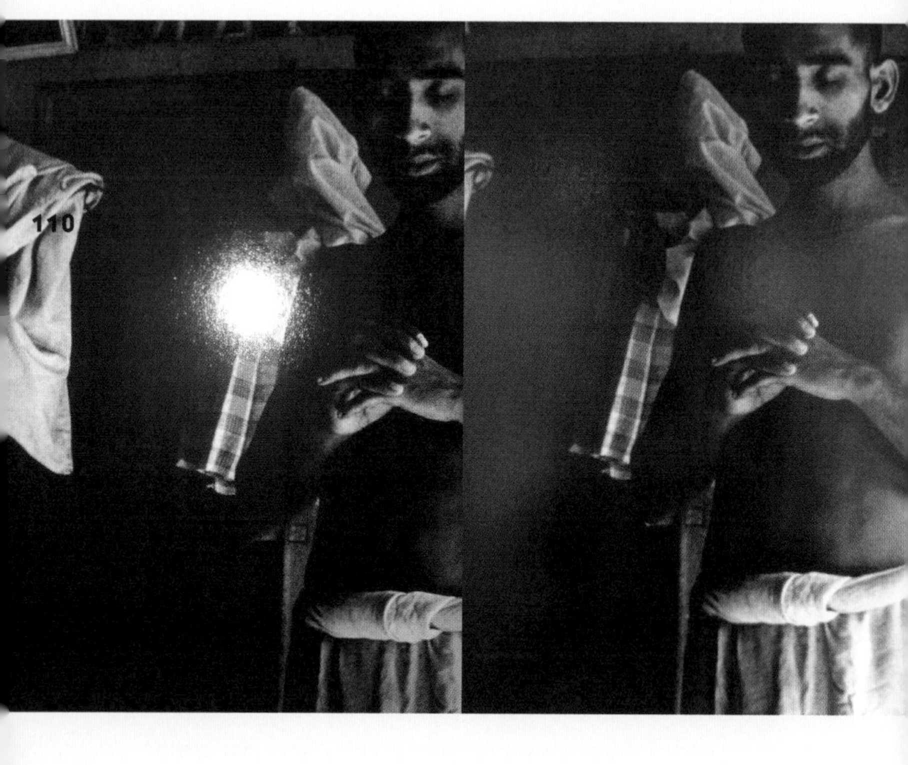

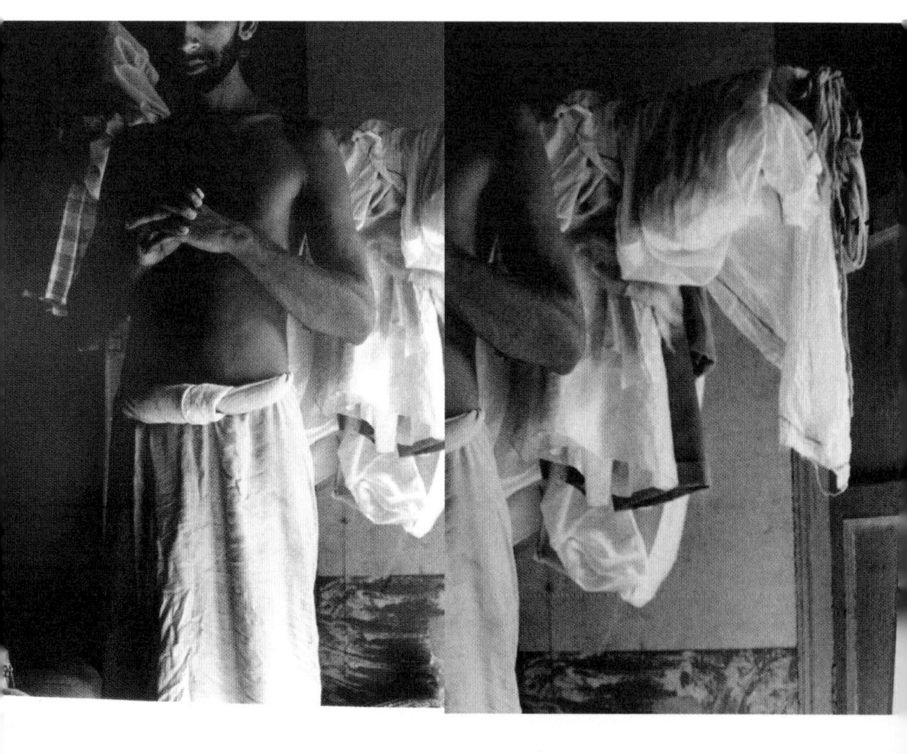

on the opposite knee. The very wide leg of his lengha allows ease of air flow. Cloth carries the image of the imposing buildings of the city, cloth cloaks the camera that makes the image, cloth shields the body from the unbearable intensity of heat and humidity.

WG, India, 1970 #3: A slender, young, bearded man, wearing a simple wraparound lungi—hands folded against his chest, fingers loosely steepled, eyes closed in prayer. My eyes snag on the rolled-over portion of fabric that rests like a bolster at his slender waist. It seems unusually bulky. Behind him on a clothesline are many casually, untidily draped cloths—perhaps billowy, soft, white lungis. The fore-shortening in the photograph suggests that this backdrop cushions the bare torso and the elbows. The image suggests a hot room and the need for soft, thin cotton against the body. There is a folded trouser and a checked fabric on the line too. In one of the dark images, the cloths stand out in relief against the shadowed background; the circle of bright white is the flash.

Describing another type of cloth, also from Benares, the extraordinary handloom revivalist Pupul Jayakar writes that the cotton jamdani is woven as a response to "the challenge of the terrific summer heat of the Gangetic plains. The fierce scorching sun demands a cloth that is bereft of colour and yet has its tones and nuances. A cloth that is light on the body, that moves to the gentlest breeze. . . ."[4]

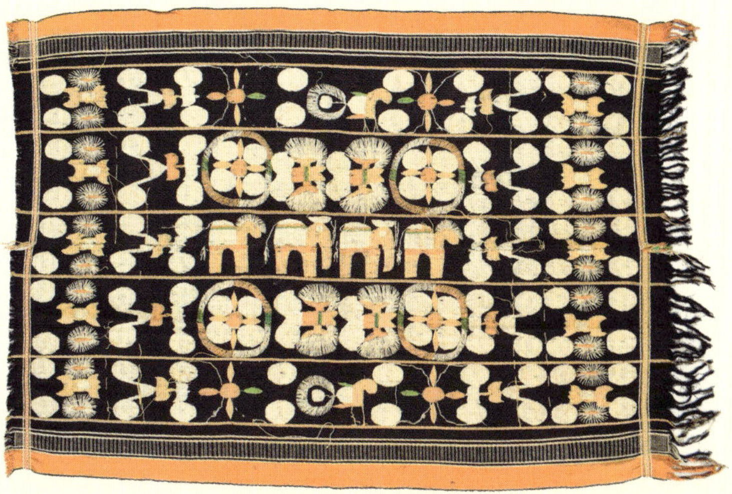

2 / the elephant cloth, nagaland

When I moved to New York in 2003, I became friendly with
Luis, who sold marvelous textiles and votive figurines from
the Philippines at various flea markets in New York. He had
a superb eye, especially for textiles, and shared articles with
me on different weaving traditions, especially the fantasti-
cally dizzying optical Binakul weaves from the Ilcos region.
Over many years, I got a few of these from him, along with
an indigo "x"-pattern cloth from Mindoro Island. Luis also
introduced me to a friend who had a few old Indian textiles that she wanted to sell. I met her in the lobby of the
Salvation Army hostel, where she showed me some small

mirrored and embroidered pieces from Gujarat and the Kutch, and a few from the Northeast region in India. While I always gravitate toward fine-grained geometric patterns, one of the pieces she showed me was a striking blue cloth with tufted yellow-and-green animal and bird figures. I did not know then that it was an elephant cloth woven by the Angami tribe in Nagaland.

EC #1: A copy of the catalog from a 1956 MoMA show, *Textiles and Ornaments from India,* has been sitting on my shelf for dozens of years. Reading it during lockdown via a full high-resolution scan on the MoMA website, alongside installation views of that landmark exhibition, was surprisingly immersive. I was delighted to find several examples of tribal Naga weaving among the finest brocades, ikats, silks, and other storied textiles.

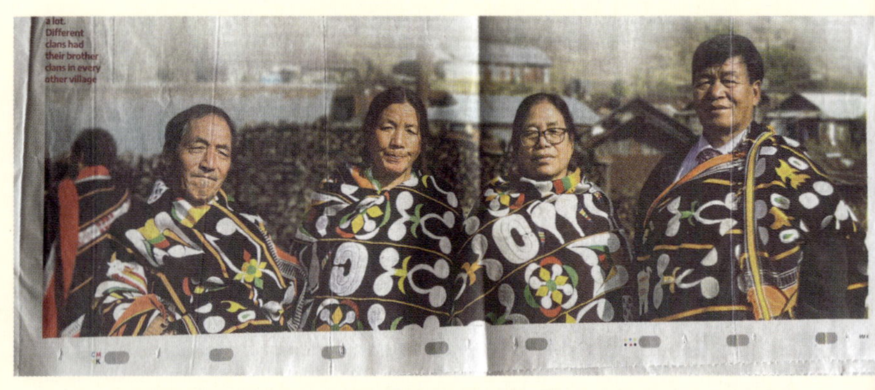

In the catalog essay, John Irwin explains that:

> "[T]he loom here used is the single-heddle tension-
> loom of simple type, usually associated with
> Indonesia. The weaver sits on the ground, regulat-
> ing the tension of the warps with the aid of a belt
> anchored around the small of the back. On the side
> opposite, the warps are fixed to a beam, which is
> attached to a wall or simply to two small stakes
> driven into the ground. Patterns are made partly by
> using differently colored warp and weft yarns, and
> partly by insertion of separate pieces of colored
> thread at intervals in the weaving—a technique
> which could be described as the simplest kind of
> brocading or loom-embroidery."[5]

It is only by seeing images of older Naga textiles from the 1940s in the collections of the Victoria & Albert Museum (V&A) in London and the National Museum in New Delhi that you get a sense of the superb shadings of color and precision of drawing in the extraordinary variations in patterns. The geometry of liquid bars of vertical and horizontal lines, studded with crosses, squares, diamonds, and rhombuses reveal a pleasure in, and mastery of, order and system. Yet it is disheartening that I cannot find images of the elephant cloth and other Naga textiles on the websites of any of the Indian museums. Hence, we have to make a formal request and then pay the V&A to use the image of an elephant cloth donated by W.G. Archer. He acquired it in India while serving as a deputy commissioner in the Naga Hills for the British administration before Indian independence in 1947.

EC #2: In this fine elephant cloth, I marvel at the clusters of petal-like forms, the variegated shadings of color and texture, the spidery tessellated lines, and the felt-like egg forms, encircled and open, that allow for shapes in the nestled negative spaces. Subtle shadings in the colors—yellow, peach, ochre, orange, and specks of green. Line, shape, and color come together in a remarkable manner.

EC #3: However, in a recent newspaper photograph, the contemporary versions of the elephant cloth seem overly bright and vivid. I hear that instead of cotton, today they use acrylic. And the plant and natural dyes have been replaced by chemical dyes, and perhaps have been for many decades.

T'ai Smith, in her article, "Limits of the Tactile and the Optical: Bauhaus Fabric in the Frame of Photography," relates ideas of tactility very directly to photography. She looks at the impact of Moholy-Nagy's ideas of tactility on those of his student Otti Berger and frames their perceptual methods with the ideas of art historian Alois Riegl. Smith says Berger's "touch panels" remind the viewer that touch is used with vision and vice versa. "One must grasp the structure not only with one's brain, but also feel it out with the subconscious."[6] On Berger's theory, Smith explains that "her tactile capability applied not only to the physical, but also the psychical sense of touch."[7]

In Riegl's account of the shifting modes of perception and production from the ancient Egyptian period to the Greek Classical to the late Roman, he outlines a clear progression from the haptic to the optical. But the path toward the optical *Kunstwollen* (the will to form through which art becomes not an imitation of reality but an expression of a desired reality) is marked by a battle that leaves the winner with the repressed memory of its other. While the optical perception takes the privileged position in his account, Riegl recognizes the degree to which these terms always collide. Thus, he lays out an opposition between two sensory modes only to show how they are interdependent aspects of perception.

3 / the saora cloth, orissa

I saw a thick, ivory-colored cloth with a wide brown border in a small government museum in Bhubaneswar, Orissa, a few years ago. I photographed it extensively. I photographed many different textiles in their collection, including the celebrated bomkai, maniabandha, and vichitrapuri sarees, the latter with chessboard squares in ikat weaves that my mother wears. Somehow, this plain textile pulled me in—the rich ivory-brown color combination felt just right,

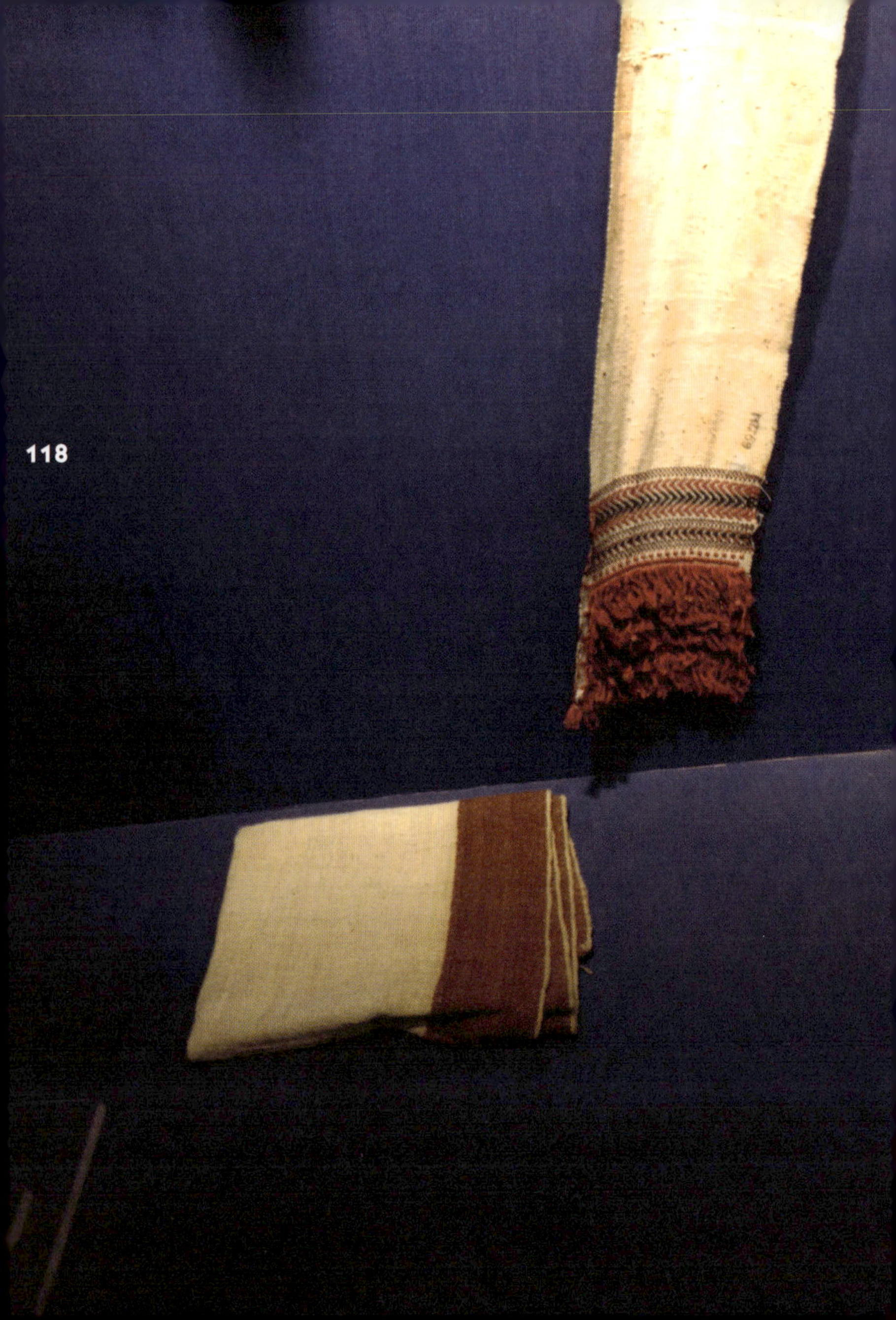
118

the proportion of the band of loamy chocolate brown was substantial, and the soft, felt-like texture registered even through the display glass.

"[The] Hill Saoras had large substantial villages," writes anthropologist Verrier Elwin. "[T]heir men put on a long brightly-coloured loin-cloth and their women wore a handwoven brown-bordered skirt and did not usually wear anything else . . ."[8] And the museum label description notes that the "Lanjia Saora [are] so called by their neighbors for their distinct style of male dress in which the long and narrow strip of male loin is worn in such a fashion that both the red embroidered ends hang down in front and back like a tail. The traditional dress of a Saora woman is a coarse waist cloth with grey/red borders about three feet in length and about two feet in breadth which hardly reaches the knees. In chilly weather she covers the upper part of her body with another piece of cloth tied at the back with a knot."[9]

4 / the tie-dyed patola, gujarat

About 10 years ago, I was in Ahmedabad with my mother. She had brought along a bunch of her old sarees to sell, including the saree she was married in. It was an exceptional, all-white saree with a pulsating grid of squares in gold thread—beautiful and spectacularly modern, even after 60-plus years. Pleading with her to keep it, I awkwardly

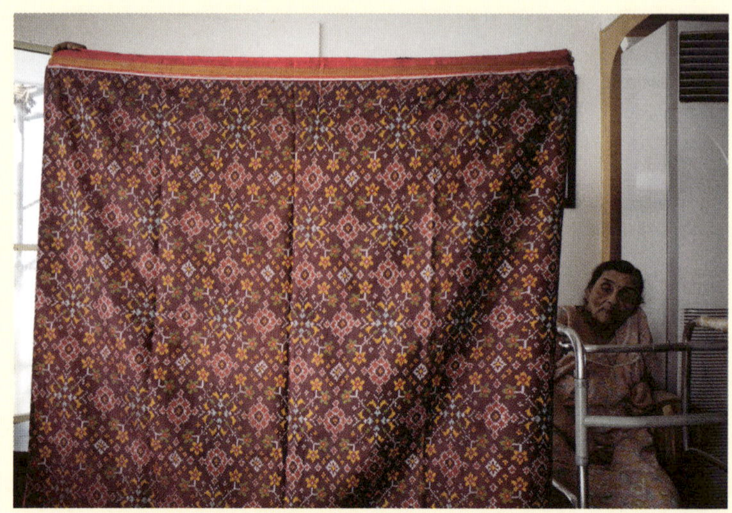

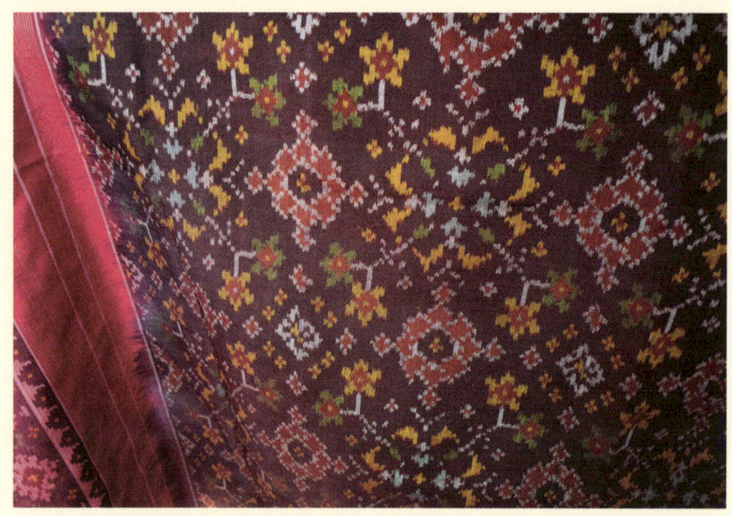

offered to give her the amount that the vendor would pay. She refused. The saree remains vivid in my memory, and I have been unable to find even an image of one like it. The buyer would have burnt the saree in order to melt the jari, or gold thread. My mother described a line of women waiting in front of a small fire that would be set on the sidewalk in the old city. The old and torn sarees would be burned, and the melted gold thread would be recovered in the form of a small lump. Some women would then take that to the jeweler to make bangles or a necklace.

PS #1–2: Some years after she was married, my mother bought a patola saree for herself. In many parts of Gujarat, it is tradition to be married in one. The richness of the geometrical patterning—the gridded, pointillist dot-matrix-like shapes, both floral and vegetal, are extraordinary, as are the other traditional designs: the five-flower design (panch ful bhat), leaf design (pan bhat), jewel-square design (rattan chok bhat), basket design (chhabadi bhat), open-spaced design (gala vali bhat), and many more. The patola design originates in a pattern drawn on graph paper. Further, the master weaver Kanaiyalal M. Salvi explains that the loom used for patola sarees is the most traditional loom in the handloom industry, and that craftsmen make all the different elements of the loom themselves.[10] He lists some of the Gujarati names of the parts: ver, lumki, tor, teleja, katar, pachanda, adania lakdi, khara, makdi, gol lakdi.

I am struck by the modest room in which Salvi's loom is housed, and the rough-hewn handmade loom itself. From the humble graph-paper drawing that sets the design of the patola textile, to the immense labor of dyeing multiple colors in each thread, the tie-dye method and the complexity and dexterity of the process are almost unfathomable. As is the huge effort: Salvi says it takes them two years to make a single nine-yard saree. The absolute command over an endlessly rich vocabulary of dense pattern and color combinations is a fast-disappearing reminder of the supreme sensibility and skill that produce these textile wonders.

The finest Indian textile was the renowned Dacca muslin described by the Mughals as "baft hawa," or woven air. Agha Shahid Ali, in his poem, "Dacca Gauzes," says of the weaving:

> *a dead art now, dead over*
> *a hundred years. "No one*
> *now knows," my grandmother says,*
>
> *"what it was to wear*
> *or touch that cloth." She wore*
> *it once, an heirloom sari from*
>
> *her mother's dowry, proved*
> *genuine when it was pulled, all*
> *six yards, through a ring.*

In understated clipped phrases, the poem braids an intimate family story with harsh colonial tactics. The impact of unbridled commerce on weaving traditions built over generations is told with a deceptively light touch.

> *In history we learned: the hands*
> *of weavers were amputated,*
> *the looms of Bengal silenced,*
>
> *and the cotton shipped raw*
> *by the British to England.*
> *History of little use to her,*
>
> *my grandmother just says*
> *how the muslins of today*
> *seem so coarse and that only*
>
> *in autumn, should one wake up*
> *at dawn to pray, can one*
> *feel that same texture again.*[11]

5/ drapery

G #1–5: I came across a small thumbnail image of the dramatic drapery study by Anne-Louis Girodet for *Scène* de *Déluge* (1806) in a design magazine's art-show listings.[12] It was only when I saw a larger, high-resolution image of the

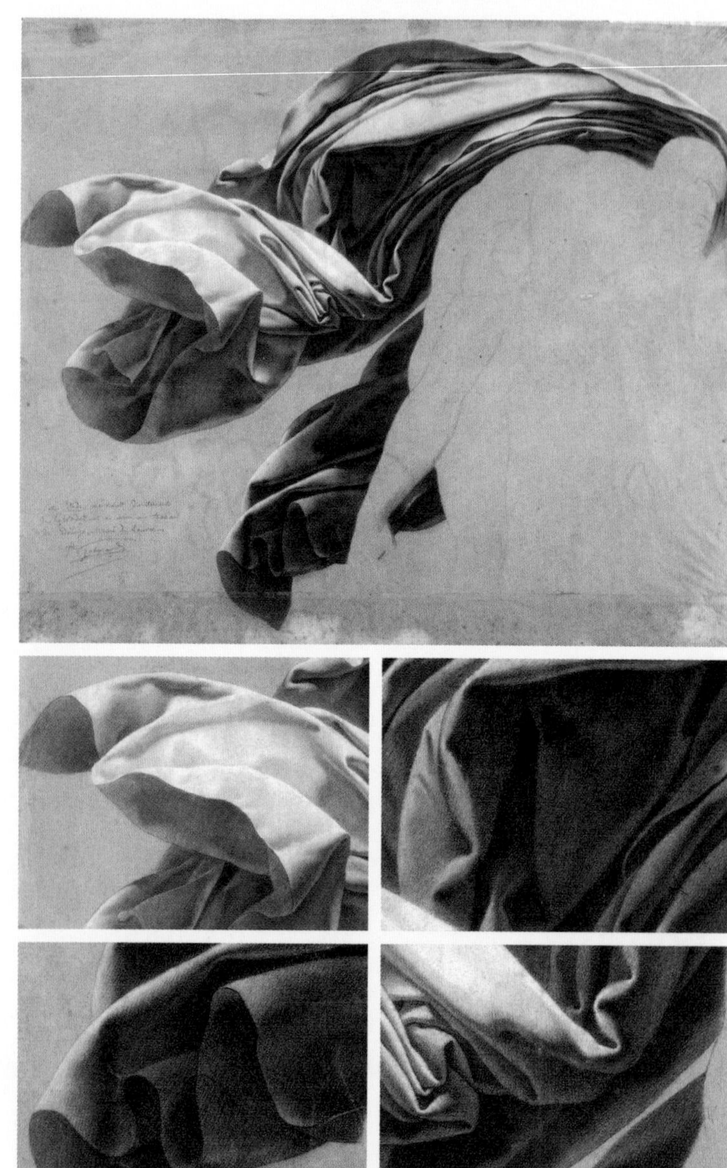

drawing that I could sense the weight and power of the fabric—the folds and creases flowing, molten, windborne.[13] The merest outline of the hand of the figure wearing the cloak hints at a body beneath. However, the drapery is alive, moving and creature-like. The drawing is powerful, the sweeping arc of the cloth conveying the human gesture and regal political muscle underneath it all. The figure is galloping on a horse, cinematic, like a Roman emperor, the cape flowing in the wind.

The drapery is unlike any fabric I know. The folds, whorls, creases, and pinched bits are all greatly exaggerated, as though Girodet is already imagining it in marble: three-dimensional, dense, solid. Like Michelangelo's sculptures, or his drapery studies for both sculpture and painting. Still, Girodet's study is for a painting, not a sculpture. Marble and cloth, marble and chalk and graphite, graphite and wool or cotton. I am struck by the displacements which transpose the vitality and energy to a piece of cloth in the most striking, bold, and unexpected ways.

Several years ago, I made a set of photographs based on purely tactile manipulation of pieces of cloth on a scanner. No composing, just a set of movements with bits of fabric and small objects—folding, bunching, brushing, shifting, squeezing, spreading, sliding, swiping, pinching, molding, swirling, twisting, fanning—on a tabloid-sized rectangle of scanner glass. A lilac bandhani saree fragment with tiny

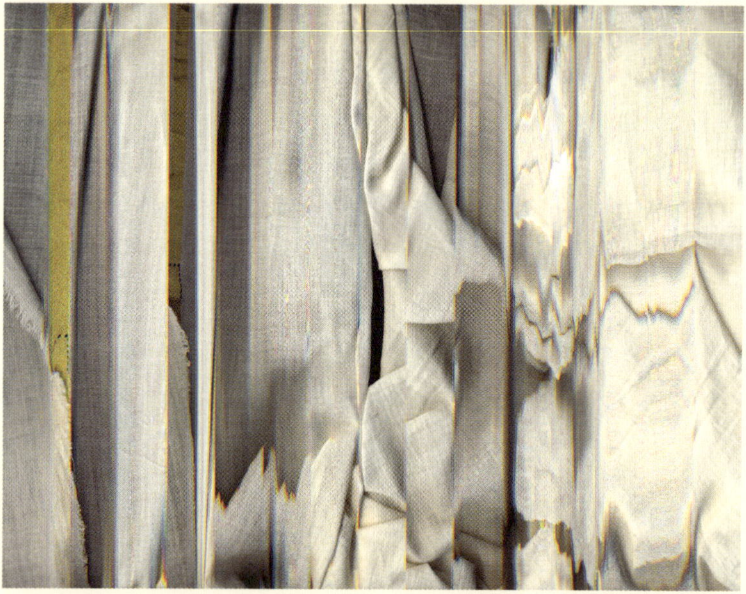

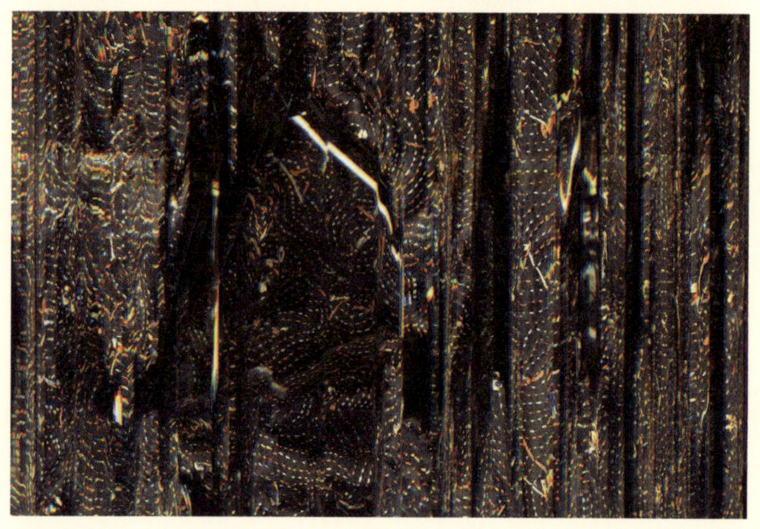

ochre-and-white diamond guls from my mother; a dark
brown kantha cloth with swirling embroidery in threads
of orange, green, yellow and white; a silk mundu in lus-
trous ivory cotton with a gold jari border—I had needed
to buy and wear this lungi when I photographed a temple
in Thrissur. In each of the images, paper, glass, plexi, and
copper objects read as one with the fabric, albeit uneasily. A
line, a fold, a pattern, an embossing. Each reveals an inexpli-
cable interruption in the material. The inability of the eye to
decode this in the images is thrilling.

ENDNOTES

1— "Gamucha is produced as a primary handloom product by traditional weavers.
A gamucha (also gamchcha, gamcha) is a traditional thin, coarse, cotton cloth
found in various parts of South and Southeast Asia; it is used to dry the body
after bathing or wiping sweat. It is often worn on one side of the shoulder."
Wikipedia, s.v. "gamucha," last accessed August 3, 2021, https://en.wikipedia.org/
wiki/Gamucha.

2— William Gedney, "Writings: Brooklyn and India, 1969–71," in William Gedney
Photographs and Writings, Digital Collection #RL.10032, Archive of Documentary
Arts, Duke University Libraries, Durham, North Carolina, https://repository.duke.
edu/dc/gedney.

3— William Gedney, "Notes on Photographing Nudes, 1968," in William Gedney
Photographs and Writings, Digital Collection #RL.10032, Archive of Documentary
Arts, Duke University Libraries, Durham, North Carolina, https://repository.duke.
edu/dc/gedney.

4— Pupul Jayakar, "Cotton Jamdanis of Tanda and Banaras," *Lalit Kala*, no. 6
October 1959): 37–44.

5 — John Irwin, "Indian Textiles in Historical Perspective," *Textiles and Ornaments of India, A Selection of Designs* (New York: The Museum of Modern Art, 1956), 31.

6 — T'ai Smith, "Limits of the Tactile and the Optical: Bauhaus Fabric in the Frame of Photography," *Grey Room*, no. 25 (2006): 20.

7 — Ibid.

8 — Verrier Elwin, *The Tribal World of Verrier Elwin: An Autobiography* (New York: Oxford University Press, 1964).

9 — Wall text, Textile Gallery, Odisha State Museum, Bhubaneswar, Orissa, India, http://odishamuseum.nic.in.

10 — "Patan Patola: In conversation with Kanaiyalal M. Salvi," video, 31:48, Jan. 4, 2018, produced by Sahapedia, https://www.youtube.com/watch?v=PYWWP39Aqv8.

11 — Agha Shahid Ali, "The Dacca Gauzes," *The Half-Inch Himalayas* (Middletown, CT: Wesleyan University Press, 1987), 42.

12 — "Exposition DRAPÉ," Musée Des Beaux-Arts de Lyon (website), https://www.mba-lyon.fr/en/node/41.

13 — "Drapery Study, Anne-Louis Girodet-Trioson," *Fine Art America* (website), https://fineartamerica.com/ featured/drapery-study-anne-louis-girodet-trioson.html.

IMAGE CREDITS

PAGES 100, 102–103—Pradeep Dalal, digital images of photograph on exhibition in *Gedney in India*, Chhatrapati Shivaji Maharaj Vastu Sangrahalaya, Jehangir Nicholson Art Foundation (JNAF), 2017. Original photograph: William Gedney, "India, 1970," William Gedney photographs, David M. Rubenstein Rare Book & Manuscript Library, Duke University, https://repository. duke.edu/dc/gedney/gedst003007009. Courtesy David M. Rubenstein Rare Book & Manuscript Library, Duke University.

PAGES 104, 106-107—Pradeep Dalal, digital images of photograph on exhibition in *Gedney in India*, Chhatrapati Shivaji Maharaj Vastu Sangrahalaya, Jehangir Nicholson Art Foundation (JNAF), 2017. Original photograph: William Gedney, "India, 1970," William Gedney photographs, David M. Rubenstein Rare Book & Manuscript Library, Duke University, https://repository.duke.edu/dc/gedney/gedst003008005. Courtesy David M. Rubenstein Rare Book & Manuscript Library, Duke University.

PAGES 108, 110-111—Pradeep Dalal, digital images of photograph on exhibition in *Gedney in India*, Chhatrapati Shivaji Maharaj Vastu Sangrahalaya, Jehangir Nicholson Art Foundation (JNAF), 2017. Original photograph: William Gedney, "Benares, India, 1969-1971," William Gedney photographs, David M. Rubenstein Rare Book & Manuscript Library, Duke University, https://repository.duke.edu/dc/gedney/gedst005001005. Courtesy David M. Rubenstein Rare Book & Manuscript Library, Duke University.

PAGE 113—Embroidered cotton cloth shawl, Manipur, ca. 1940. © Victoria and Albert Museum, London.

PAGE 114—"Esteemed members of the Chakesang tribe pose in Hapidasa Shawls, 2021," *The Hindu Magazine*, Sunday, March 7, 2021. Photo: Daniel Krocha.

PAGE 118—Lanjia Saora Women's Waist Cloth and Men's Loin Cloth, Textile Gallery, Odisha State Museum, Bhubaneswar, Orissa, India. Photo: Pradeep Dalal.

PAGE 120 (top and bottom detail)—Patola Saree belonging to Mrs Kunjlata R. Dalal. Photo: Pradeep Dalal.

PAGE 124 (top and bottom details)—Anne-Louis Girodet de Roussy Trioson ou Girodet-Trioson, *Etude de draperie pour "Scène de déluge,"* 1806. Collection du Musée d'arts de Nantes, inv.1523. © Musée d'arts de Nantes. Photo: Cécile Clos. Courtesy Musée d'arts de Nantes.

PAGE 126 (top)—Pradeep Dalal, *Matter* (LKA/Ramkinker), 2013. Digital C Print, 19 × 13.5 inches.

PAGE 126 (bottom)—Pradeep Dalal, *Matter* (ASI/Lothal), 2013. Digital C Print, 34.5 × 22 inches.

WORK
IMAGE
SOURCE

NANCY SHAVER

MAXIMILIAN GOLDFARB

STERRETT SMITH

an enclosed space for displaying art...mocks [its] archival   enough

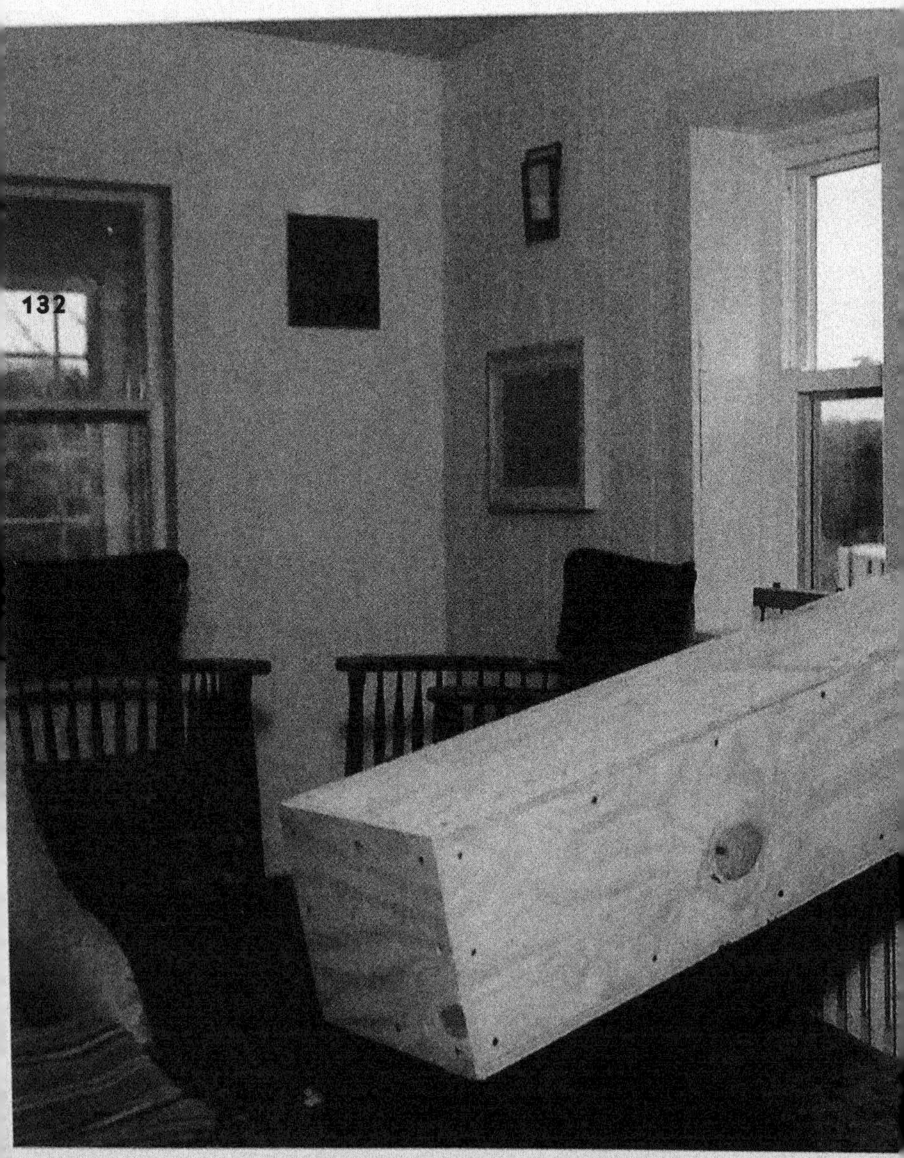

o a suitcase. He commissioned printers and

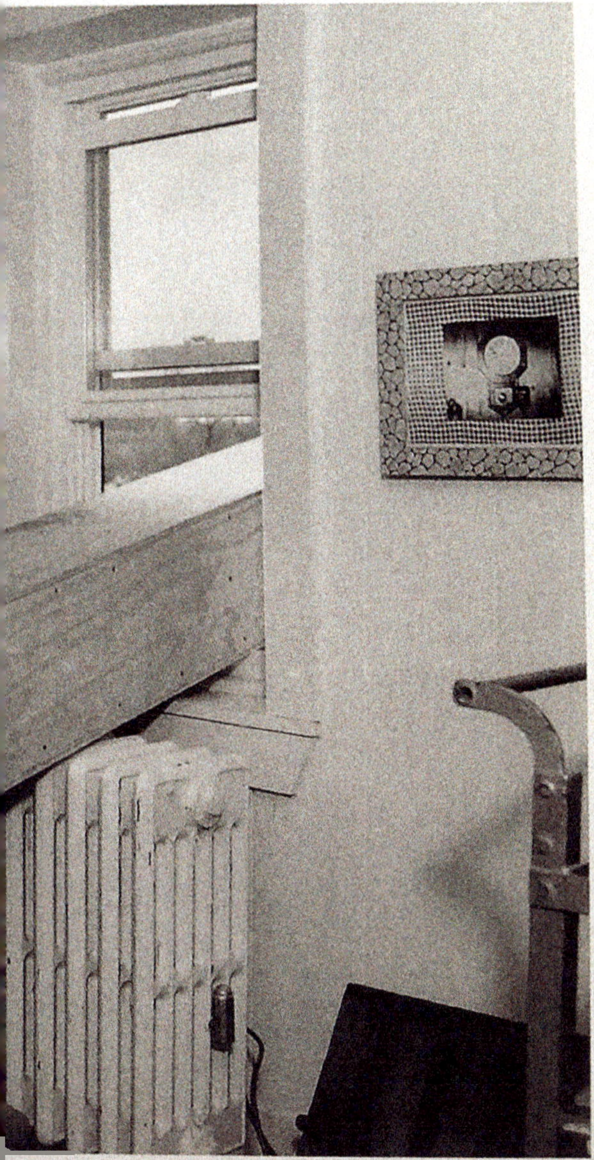

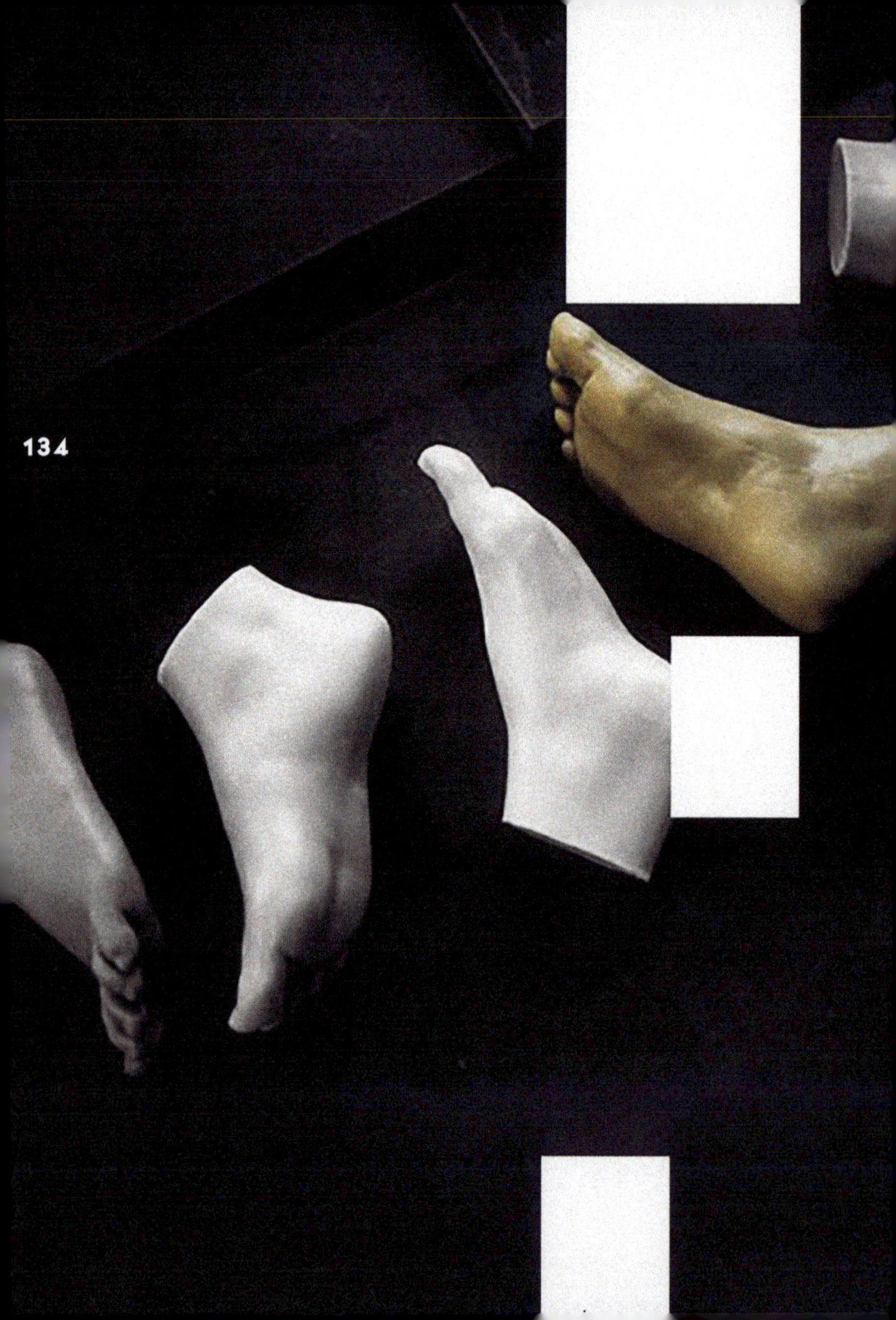

134

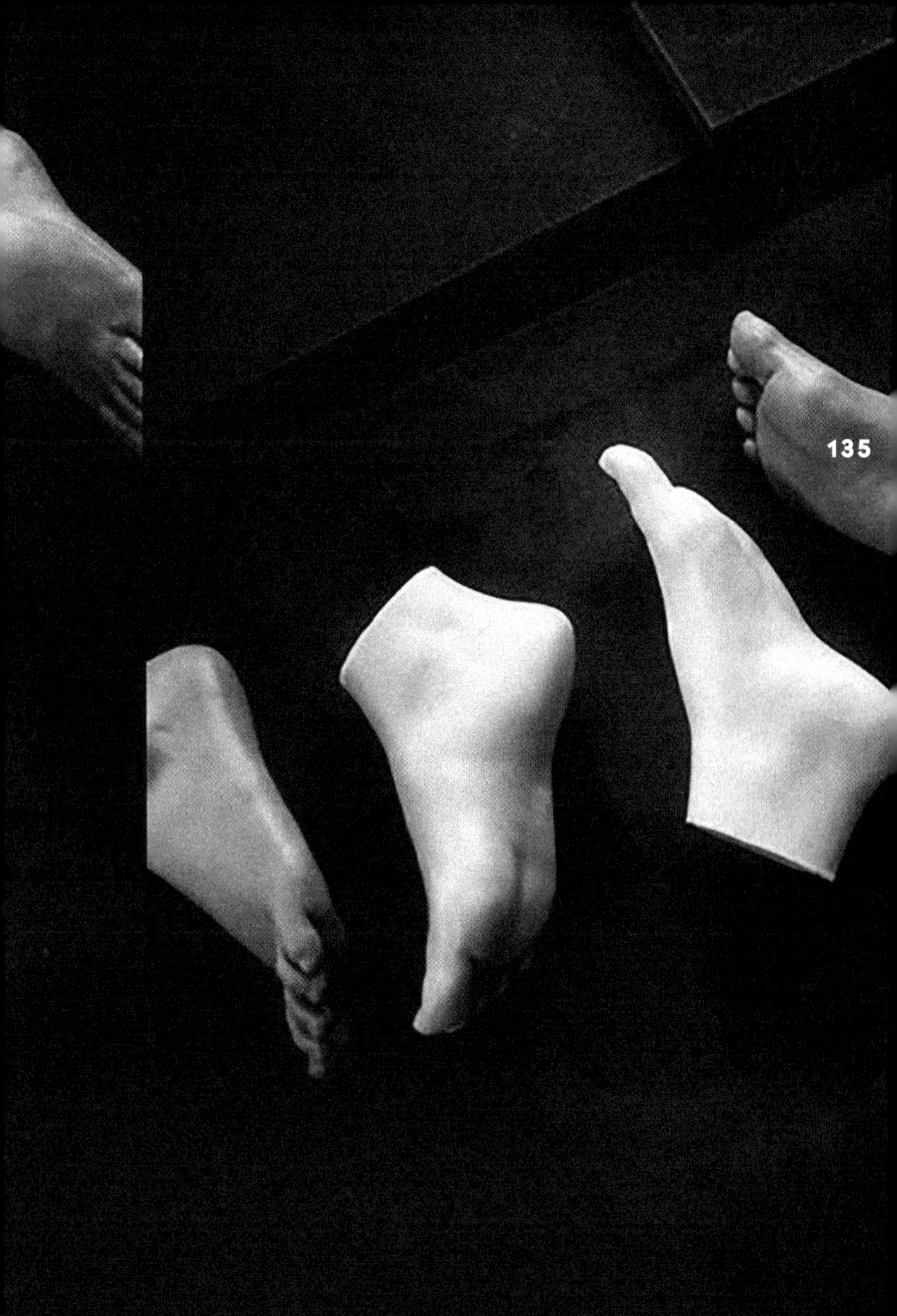

135

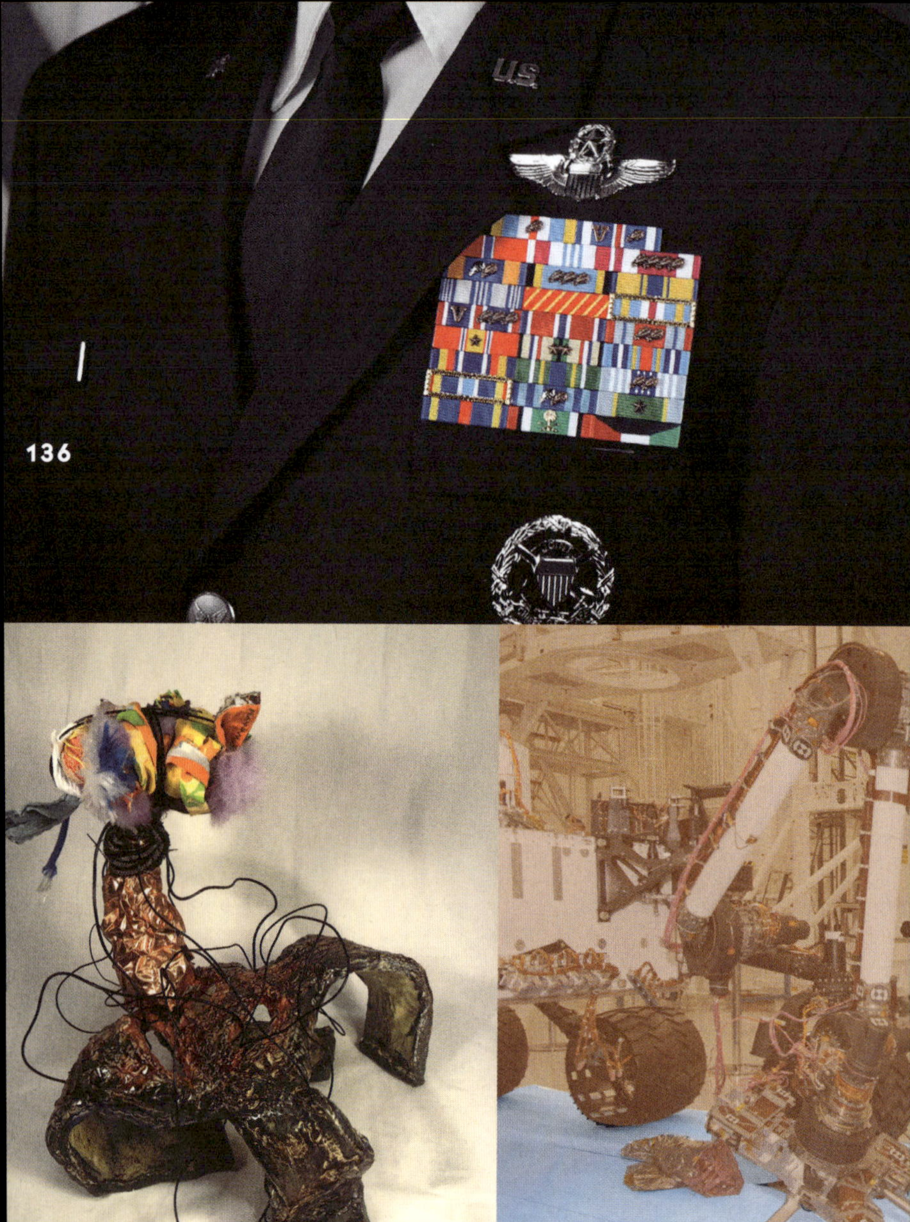

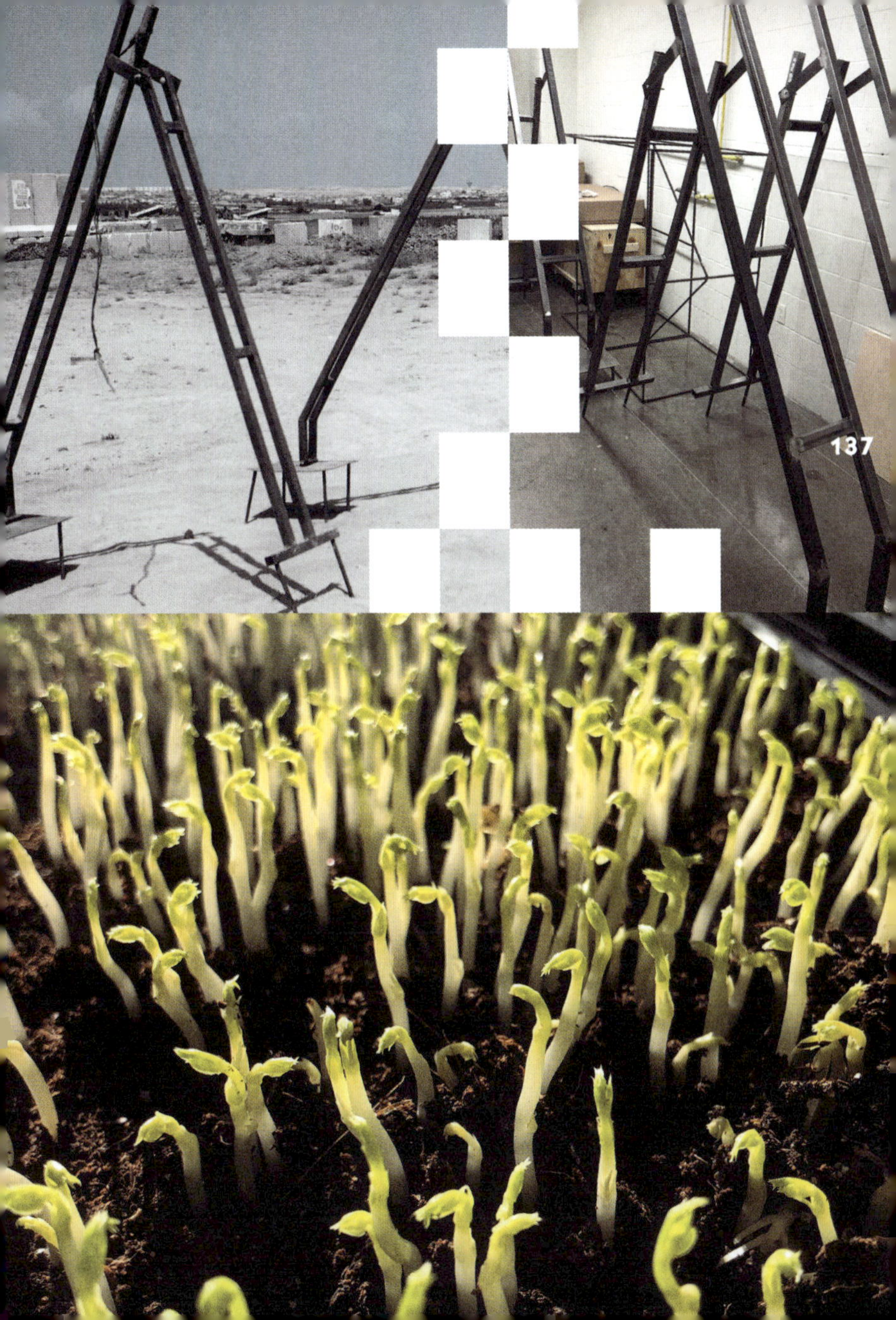

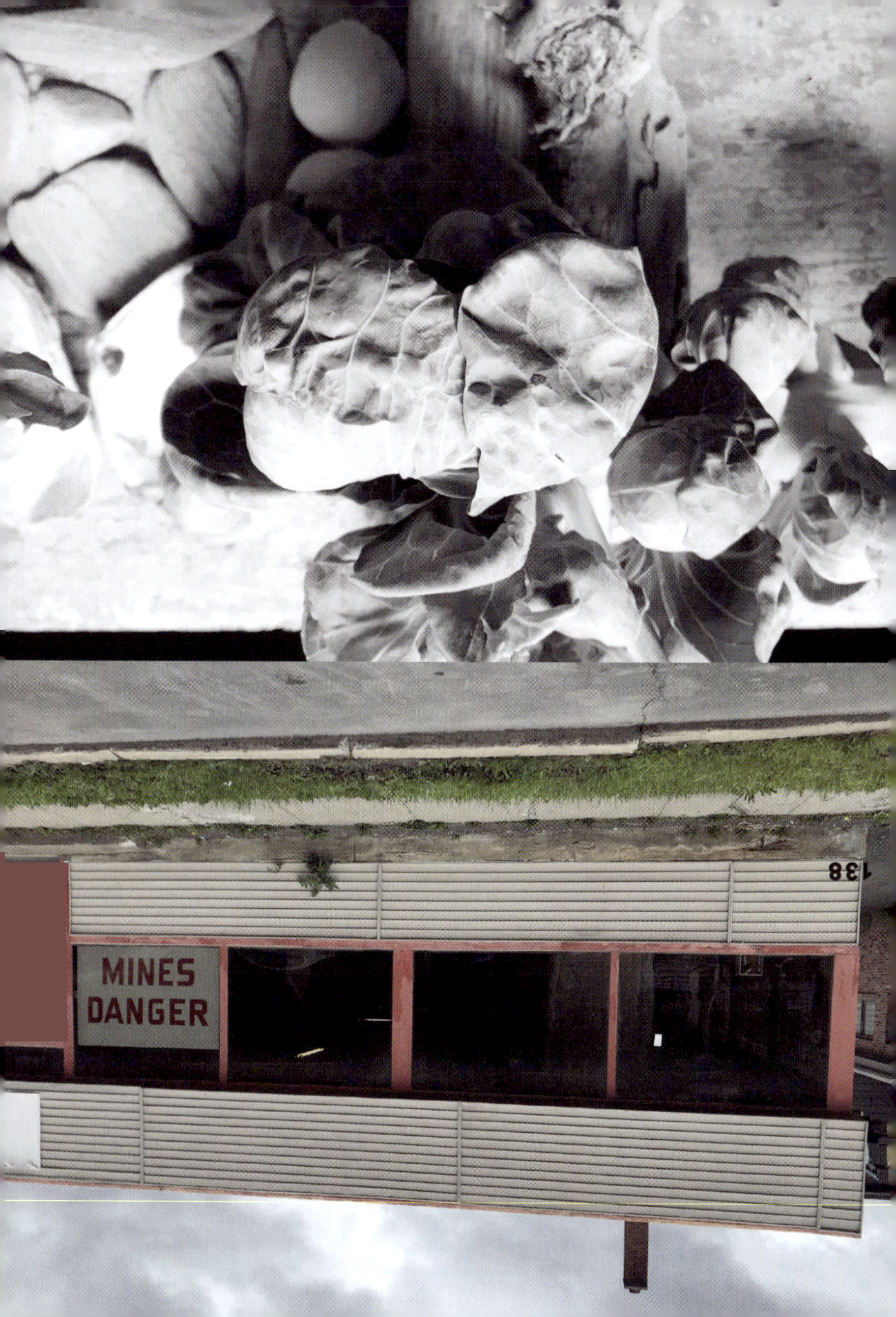
MINES
DANGER
138

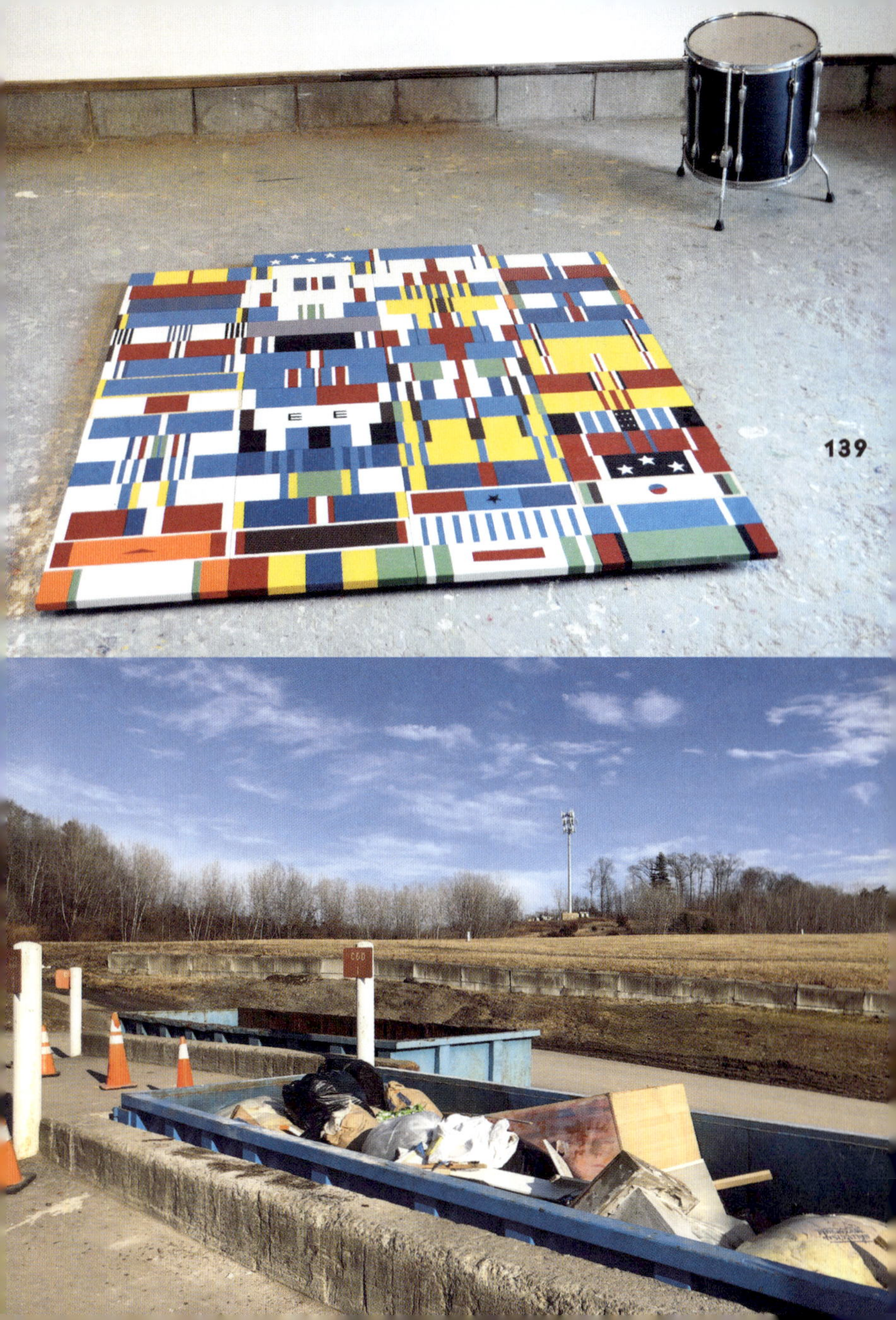

139

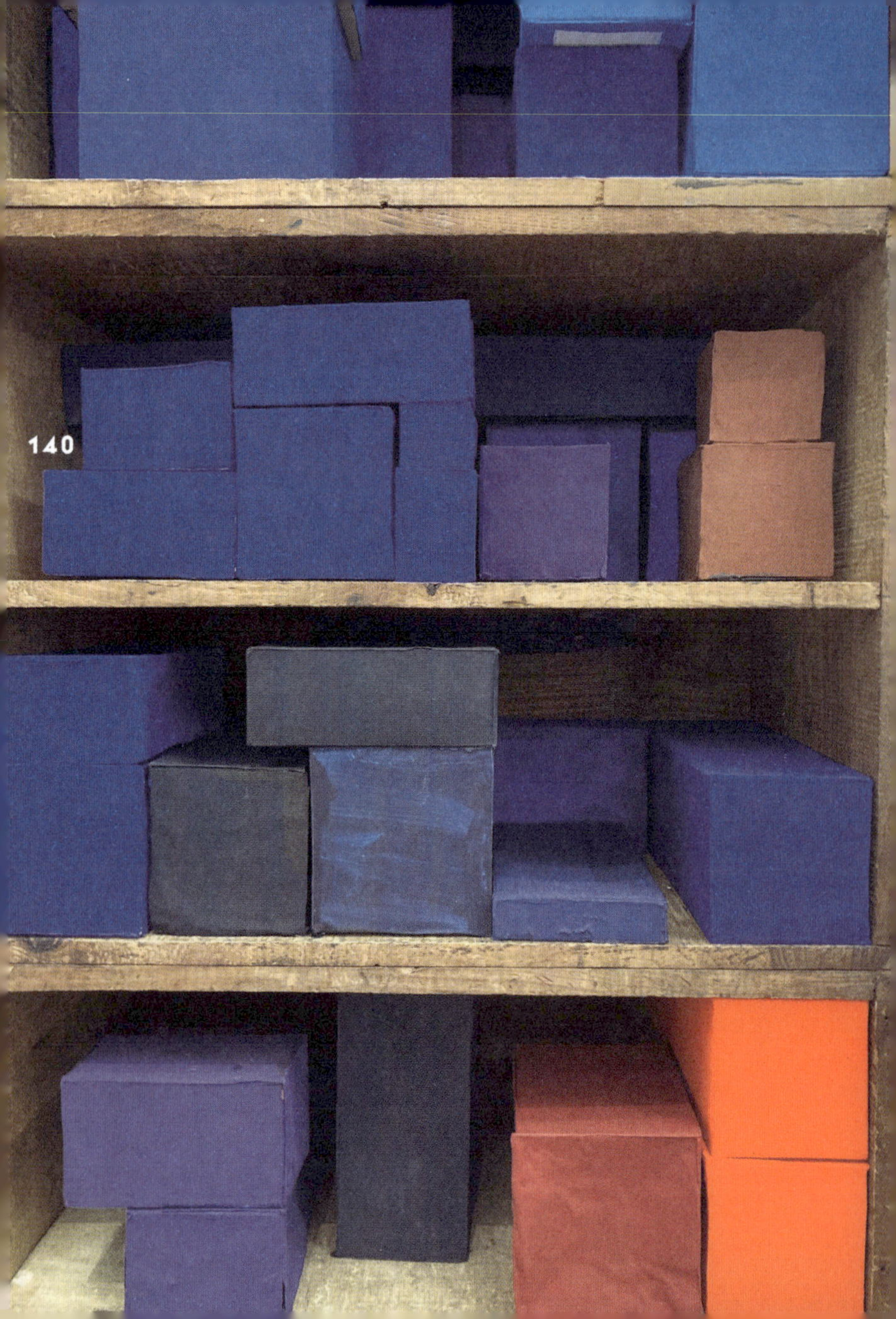
140

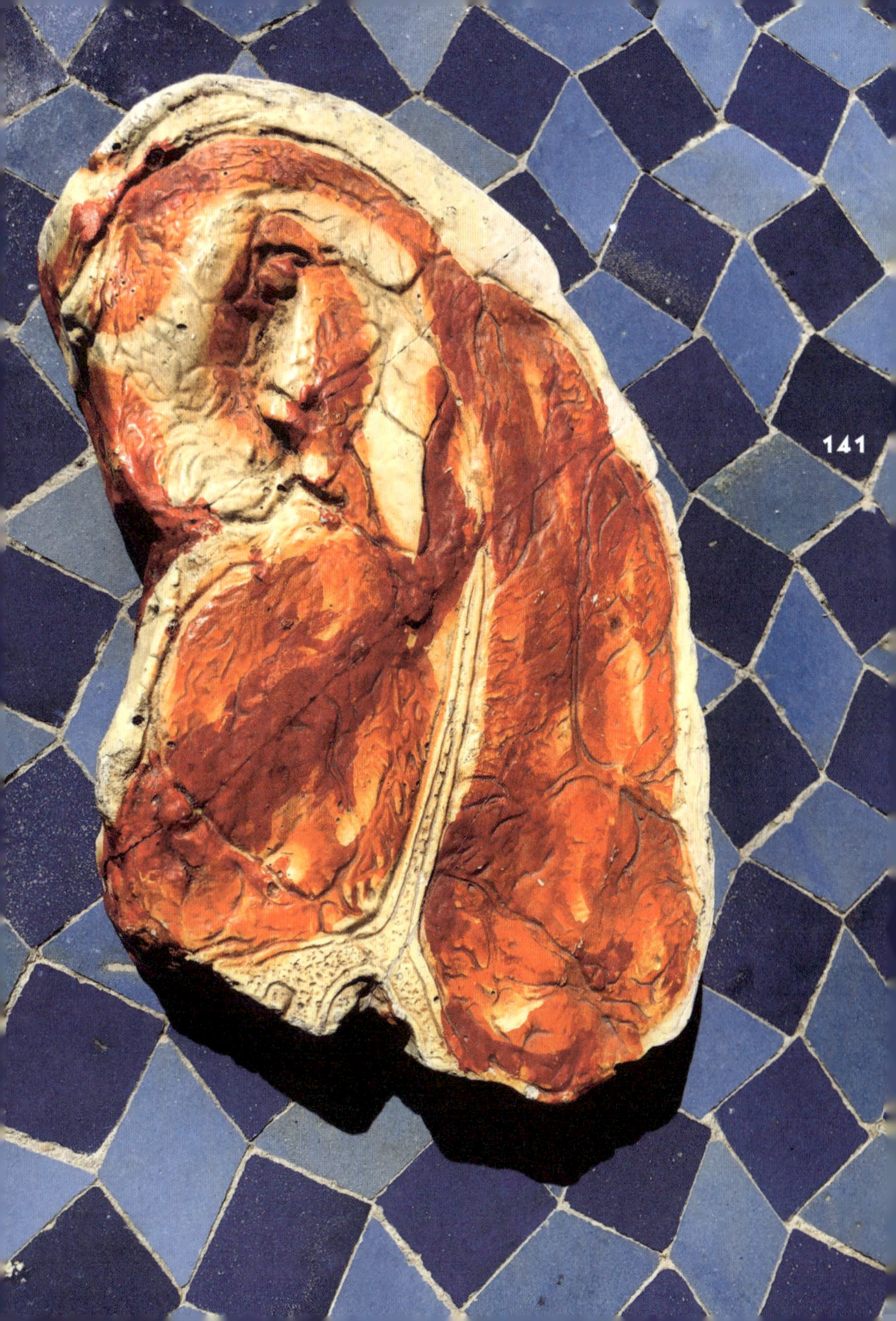

141

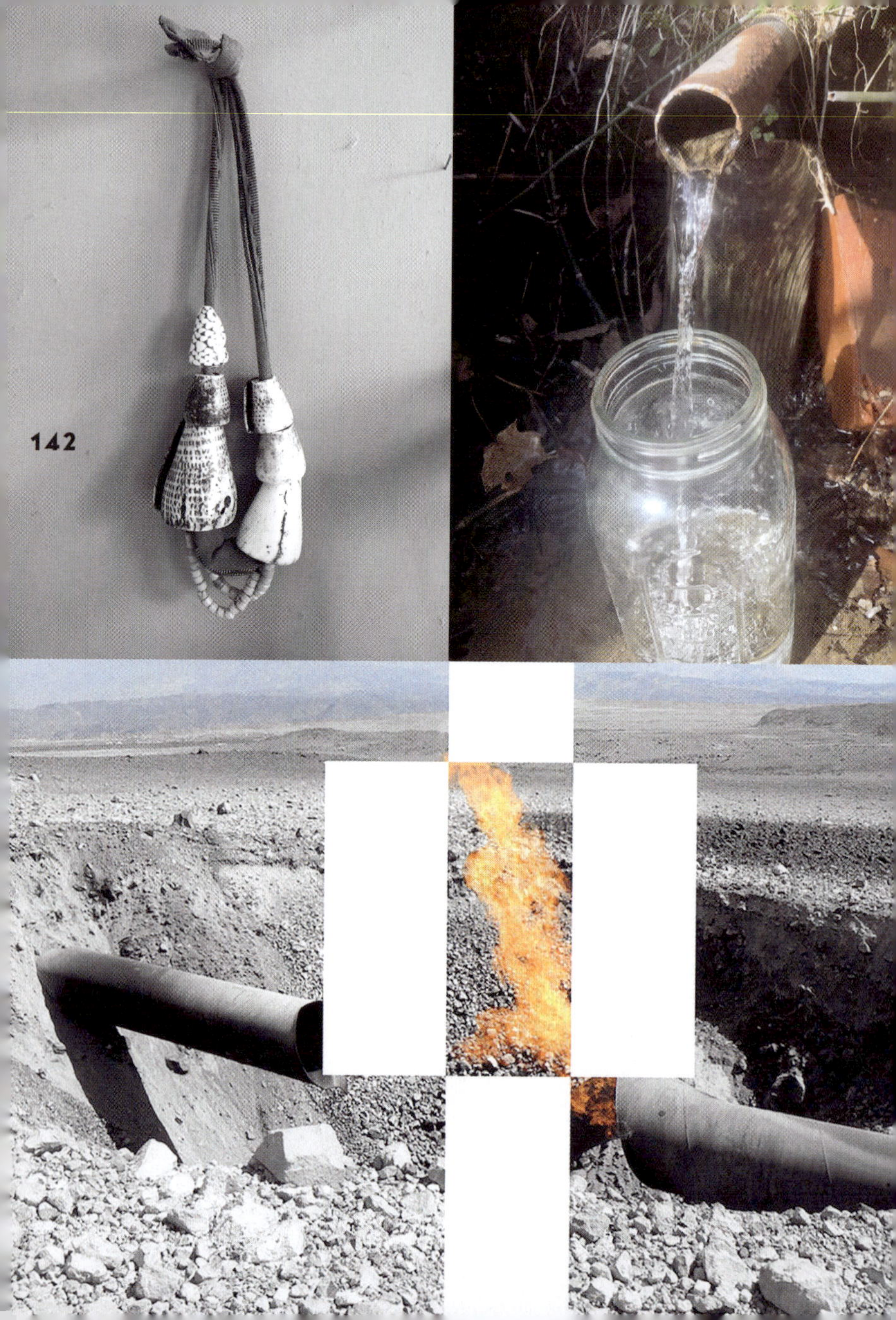
142

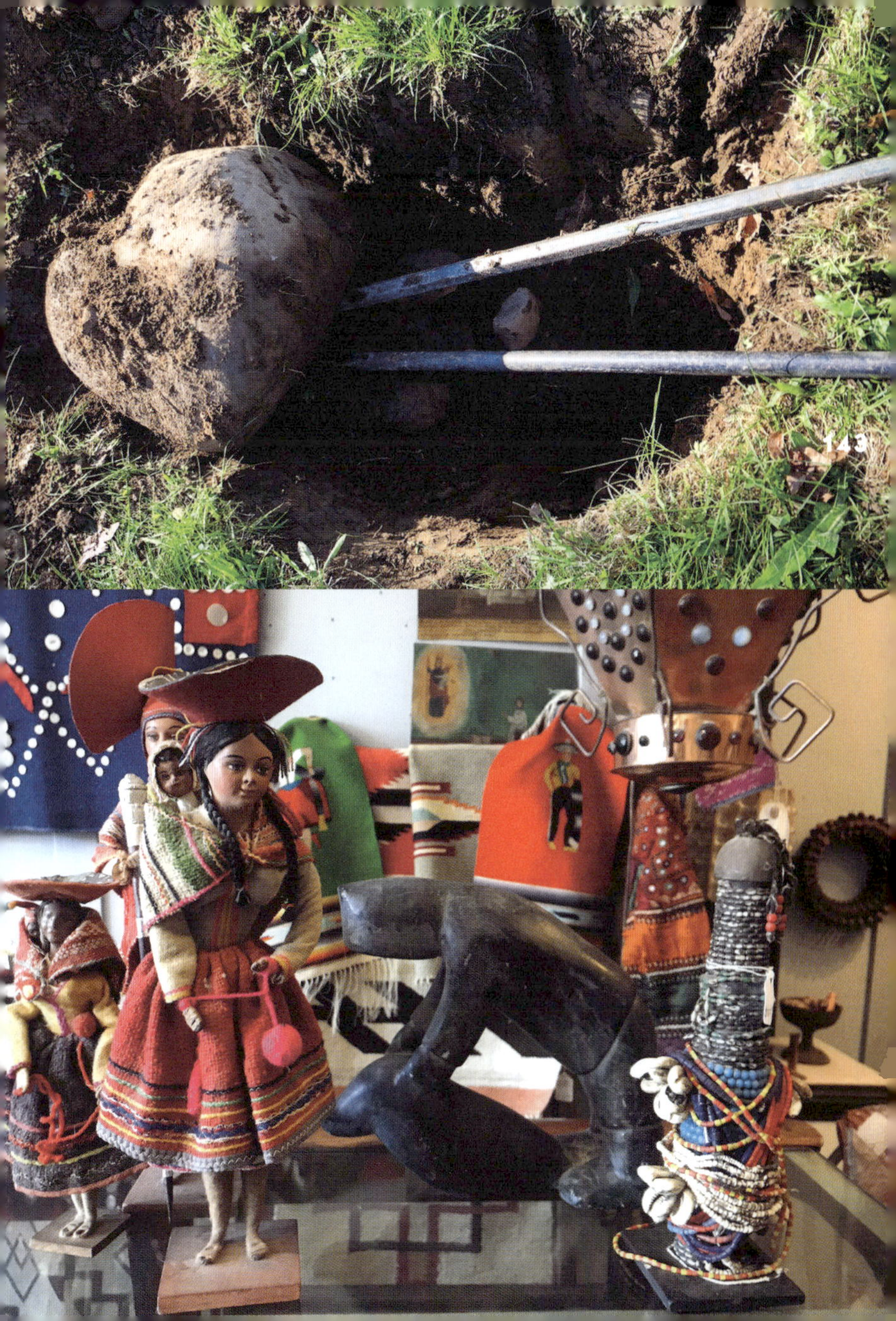

143

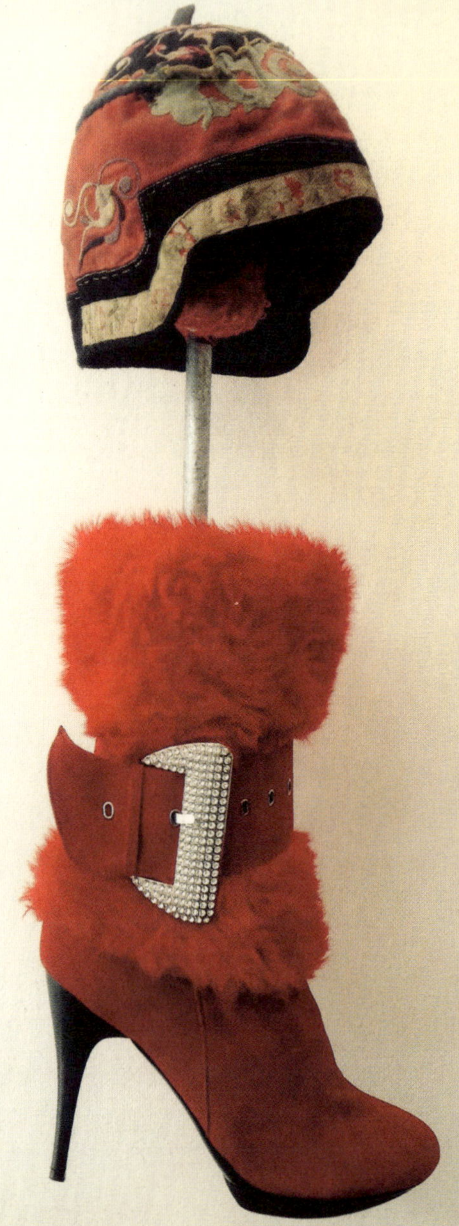

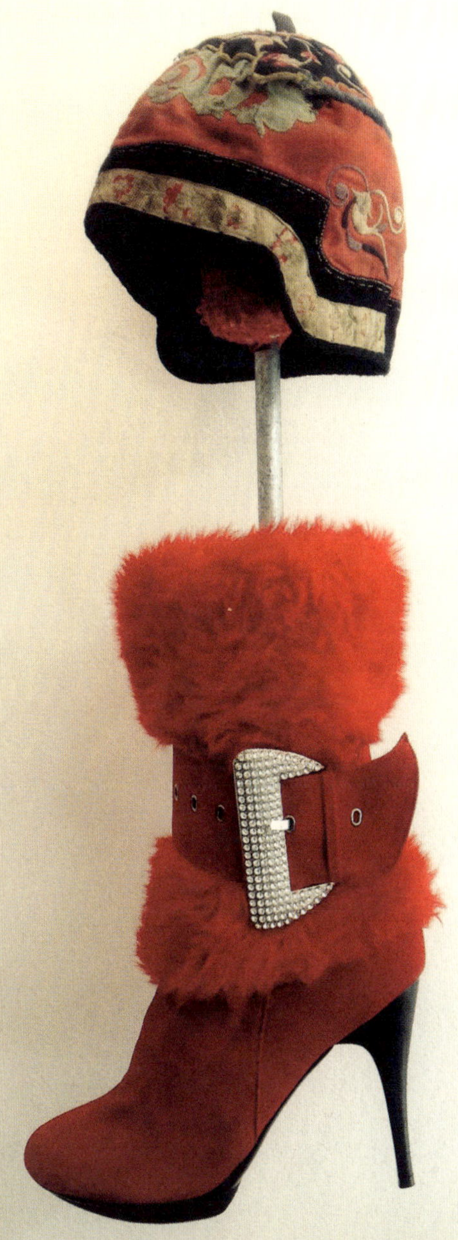

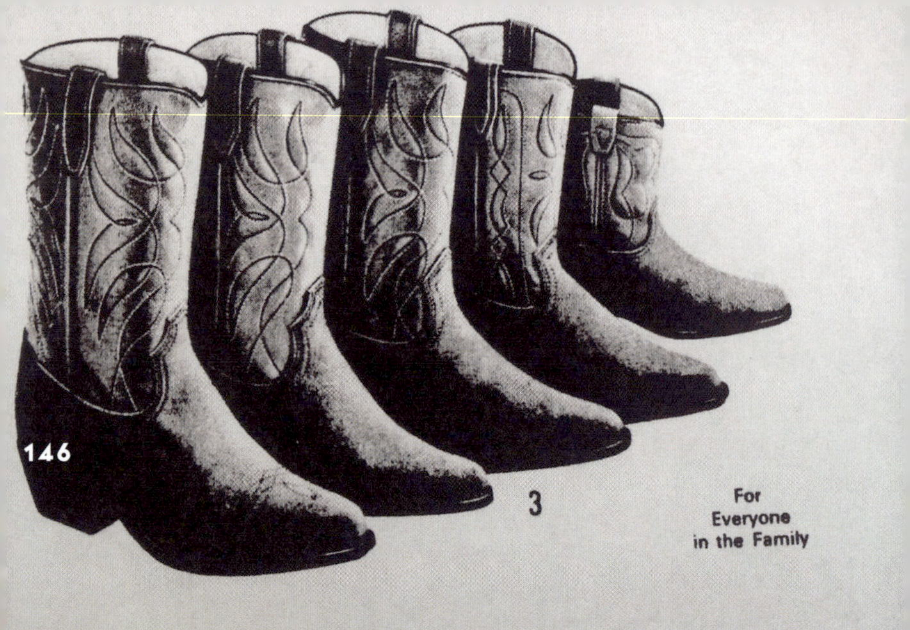

146
3
For
Everyone
in the Family

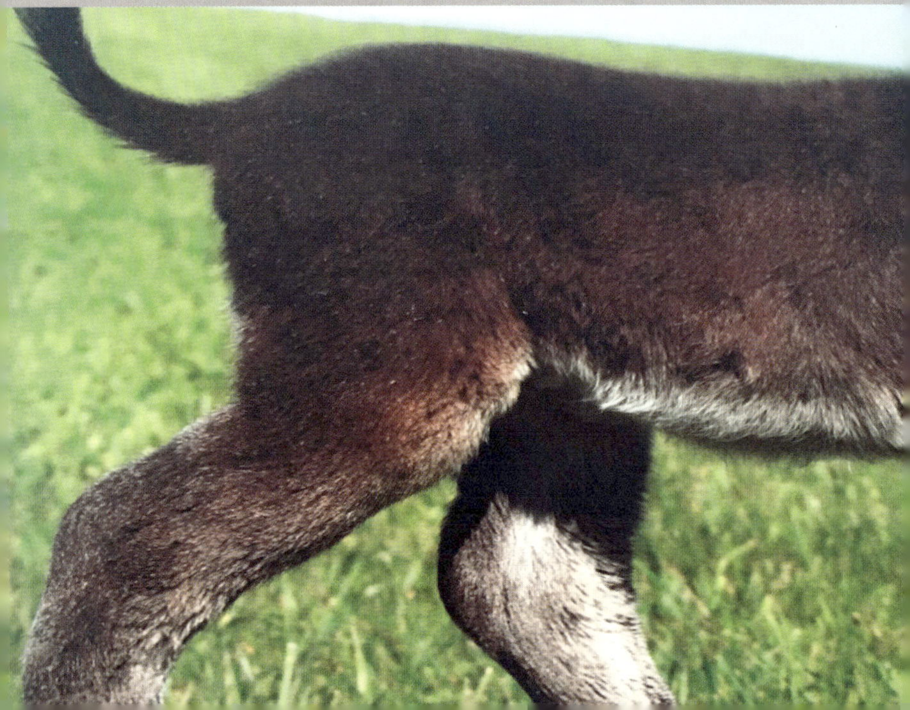

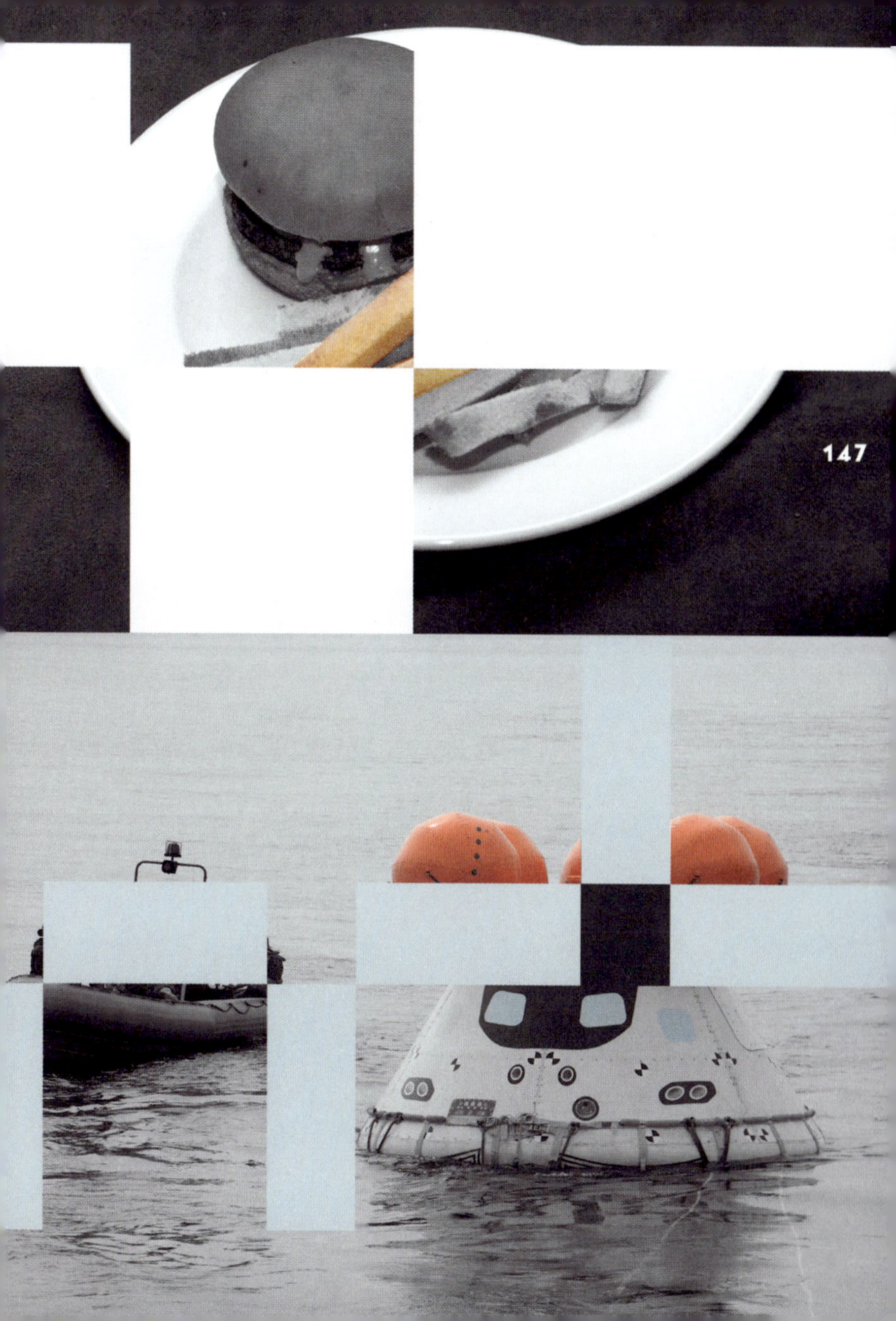

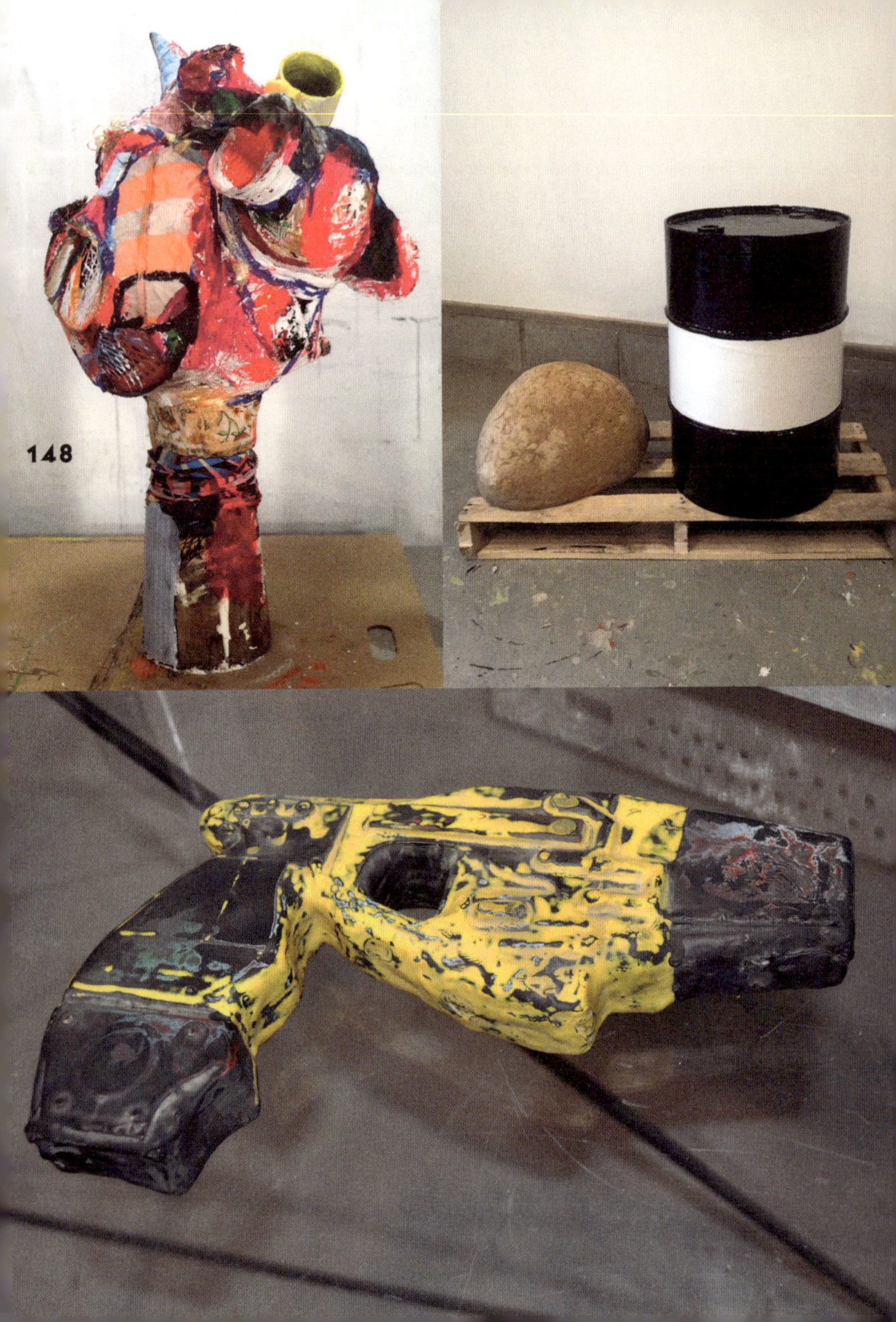

148

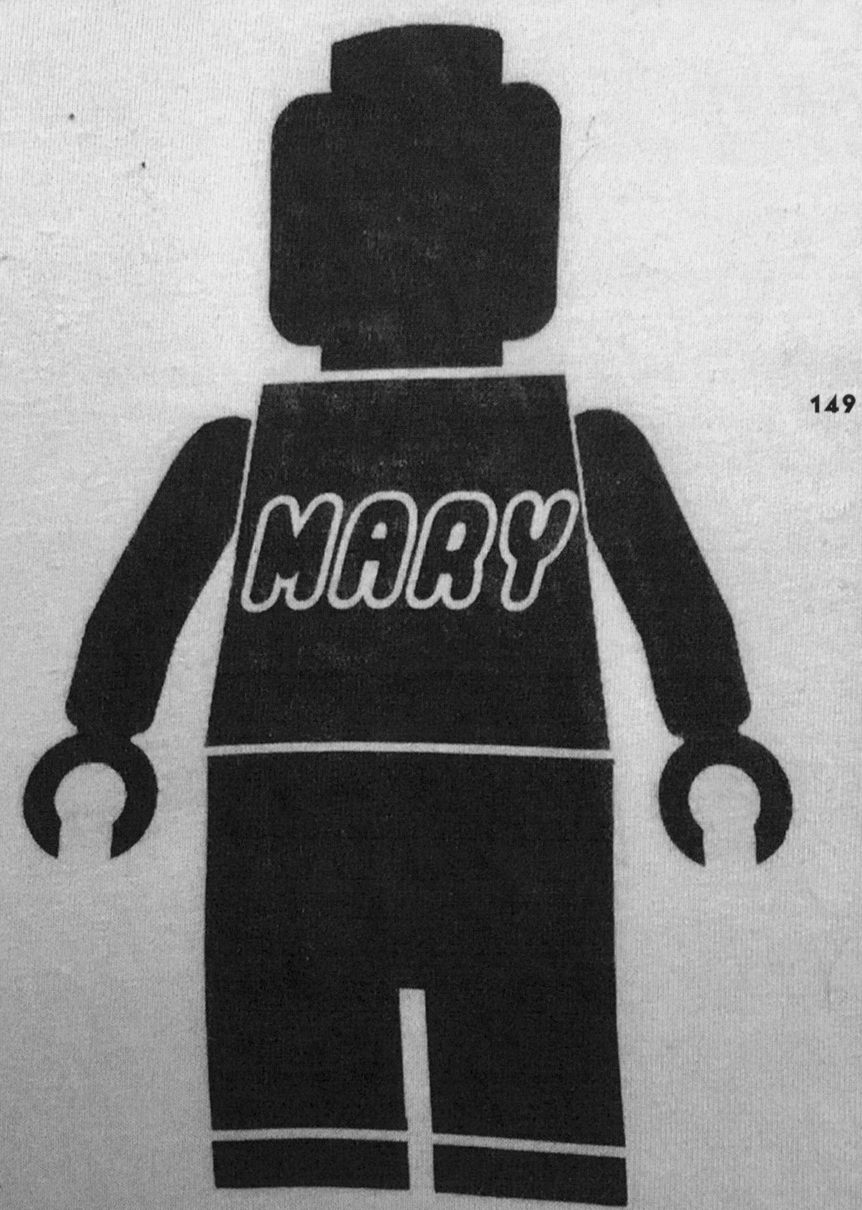
MARY

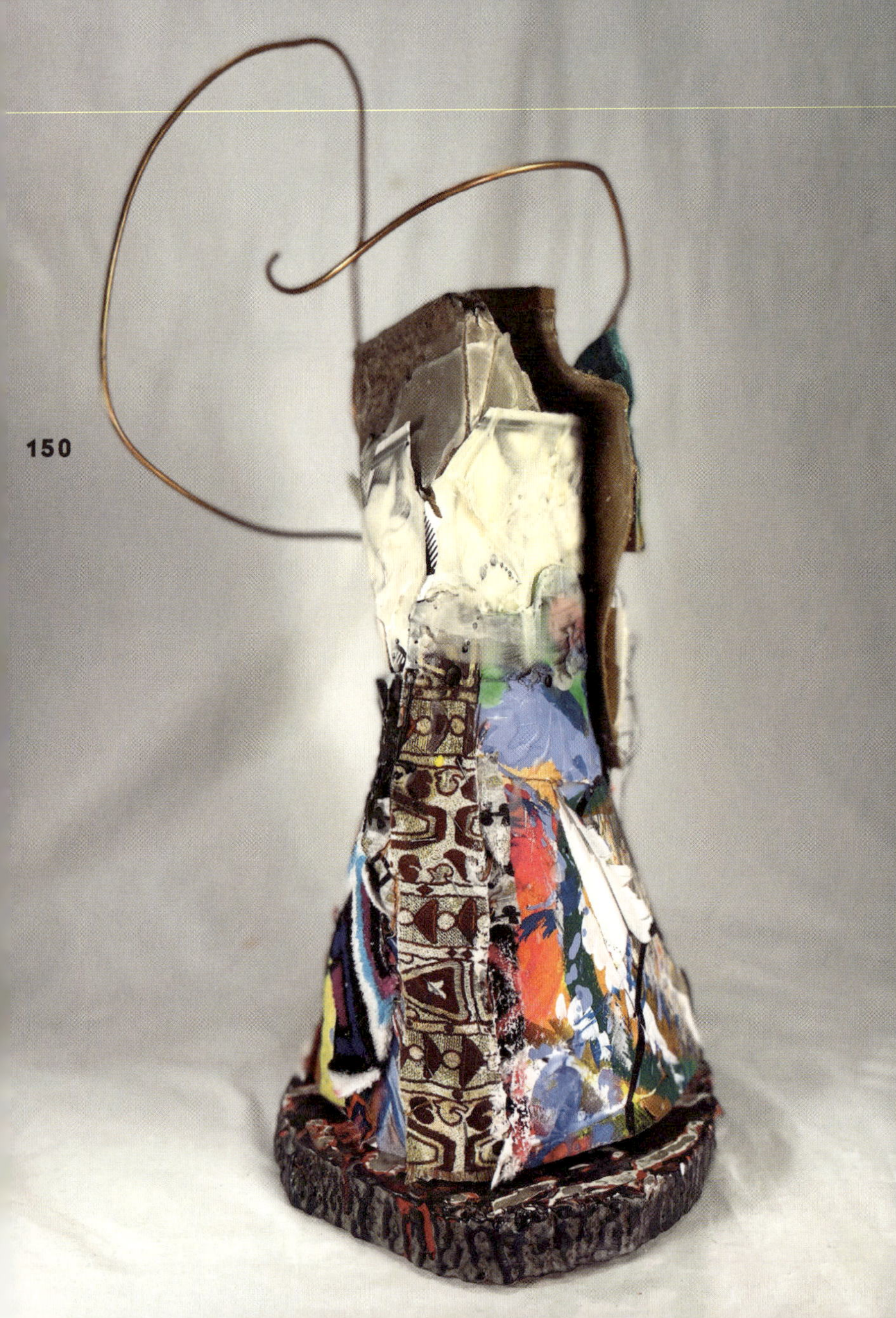

150

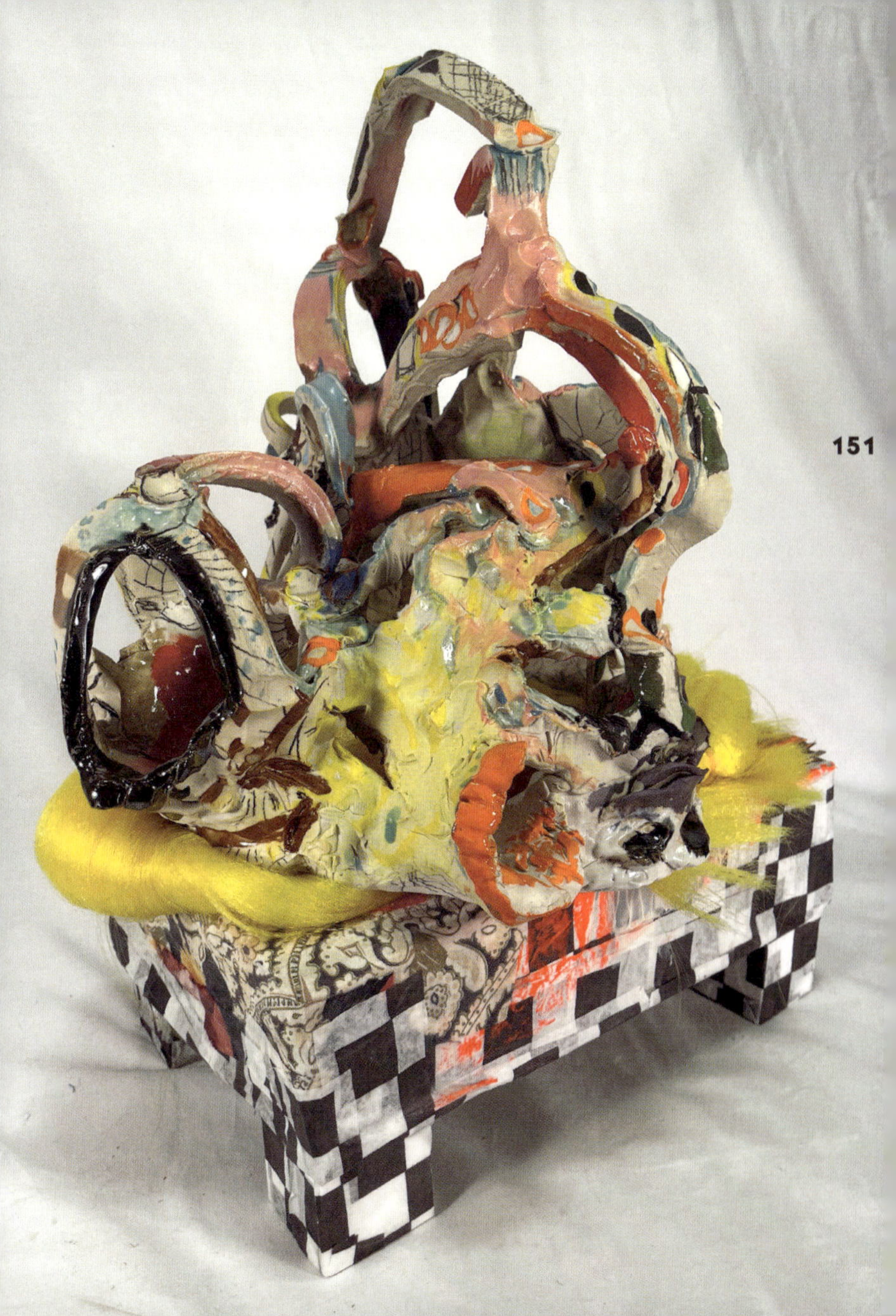

151

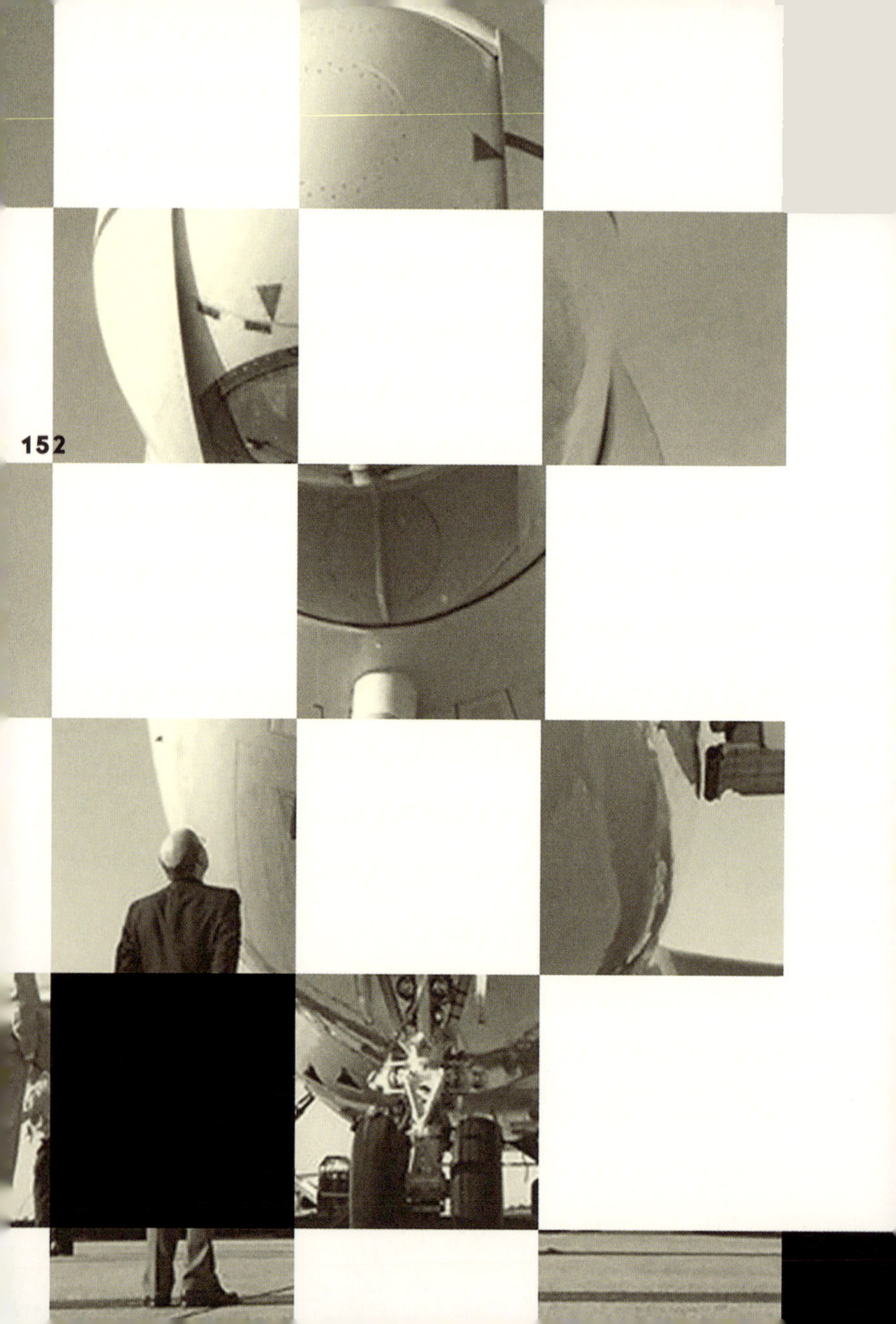
152

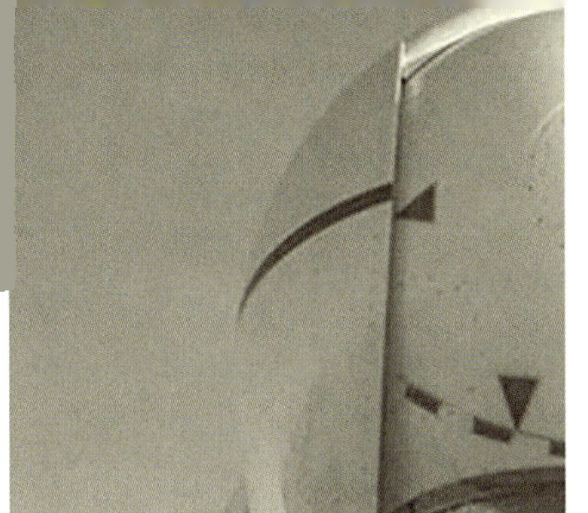

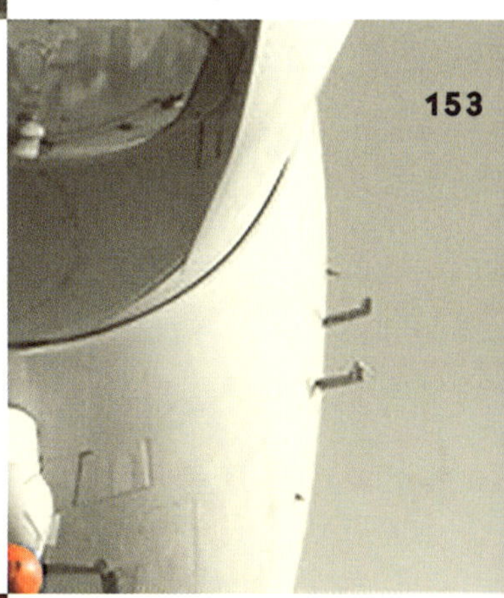

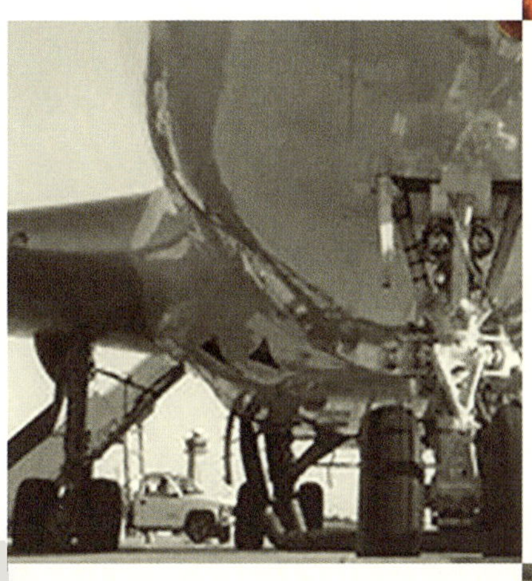

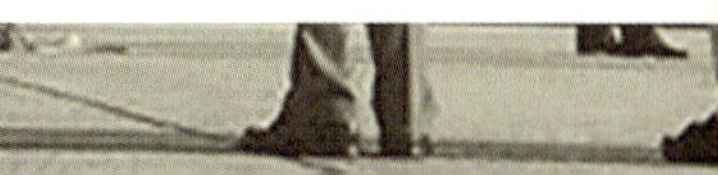

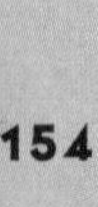

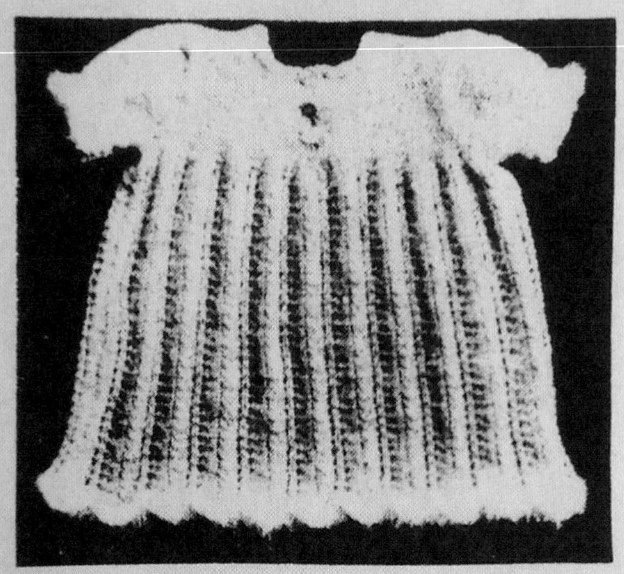

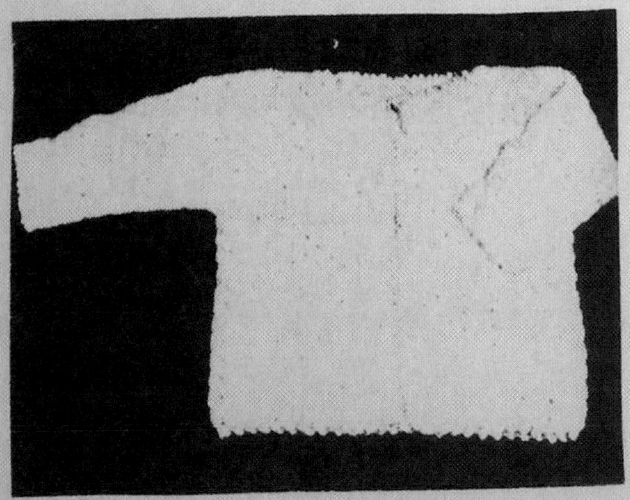

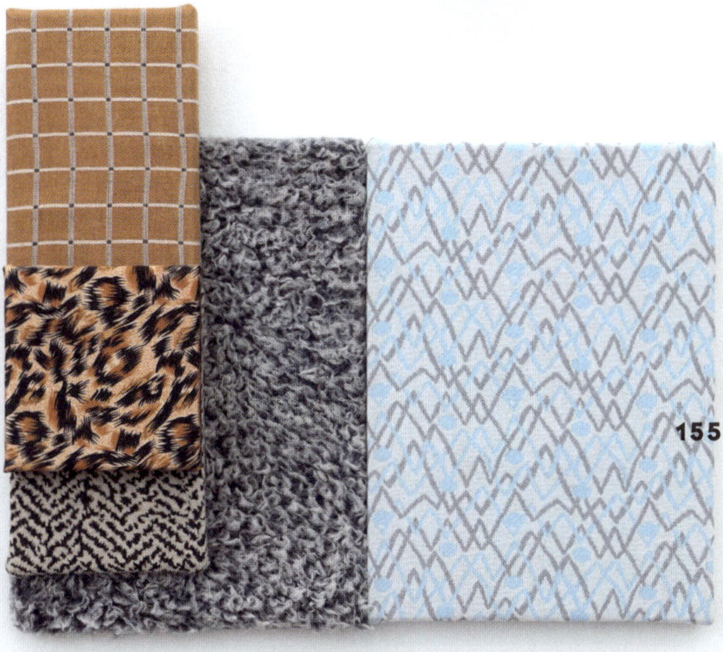

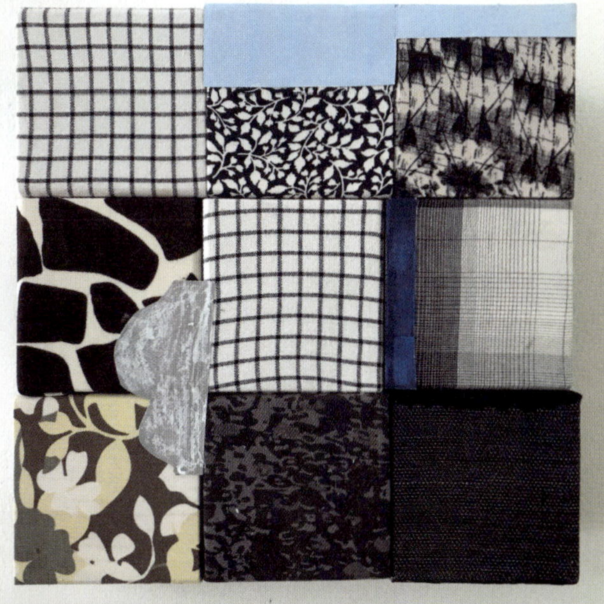

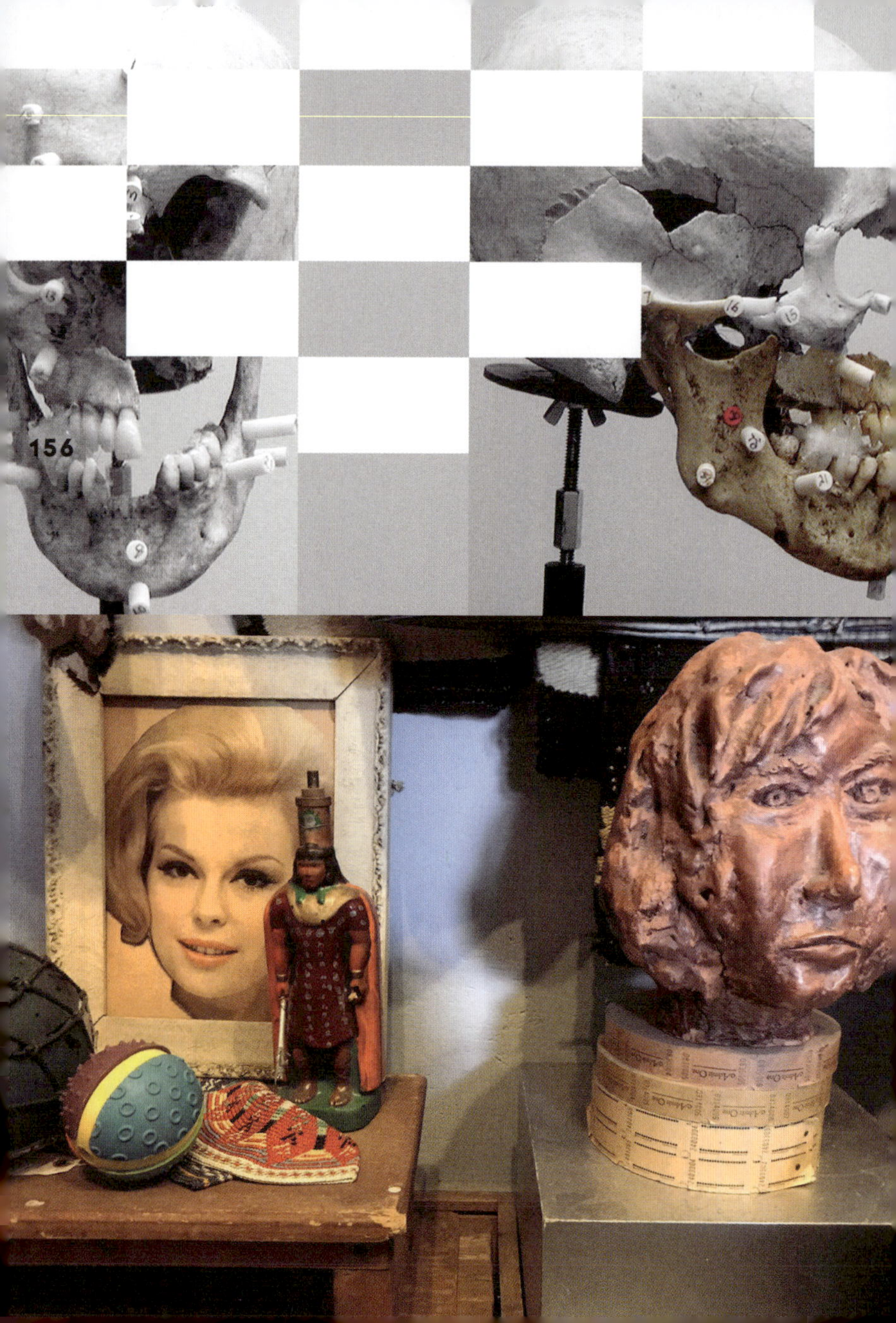

156

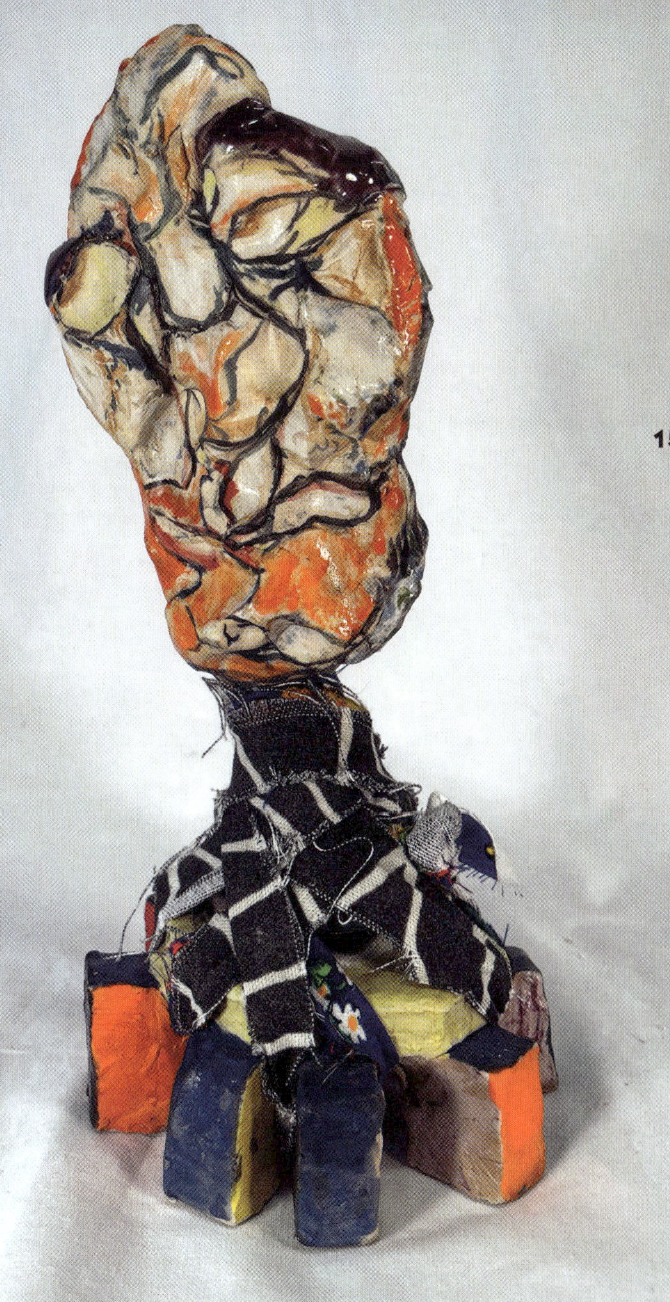

157

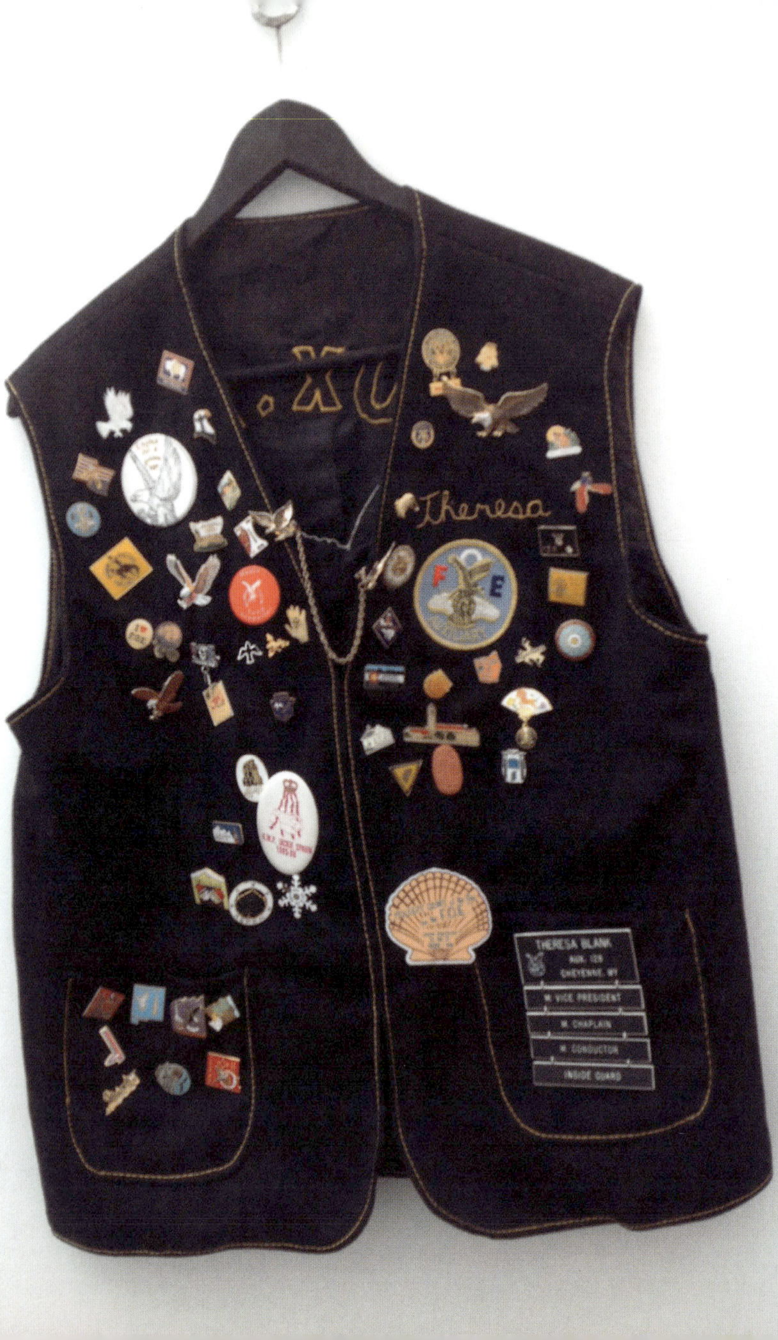

158
Theresa
THERESA BLANK
AUX. 128
CHEYENNE, WY
W VICE PRESIDENT
W CHAPLAIN
W CONDUCTOR
INSIDE GUARD

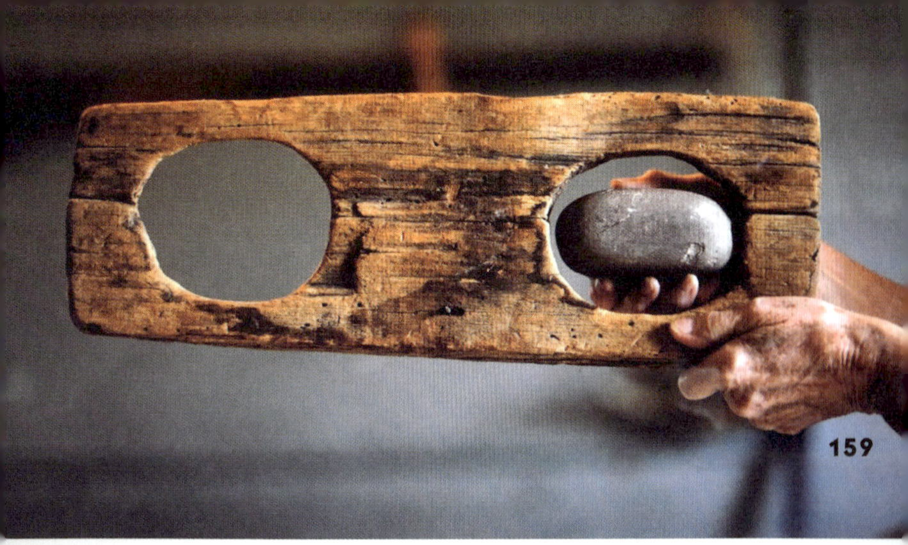

e sizer was used to keep or reject stones that were too large to be included in the makeup of the structure.

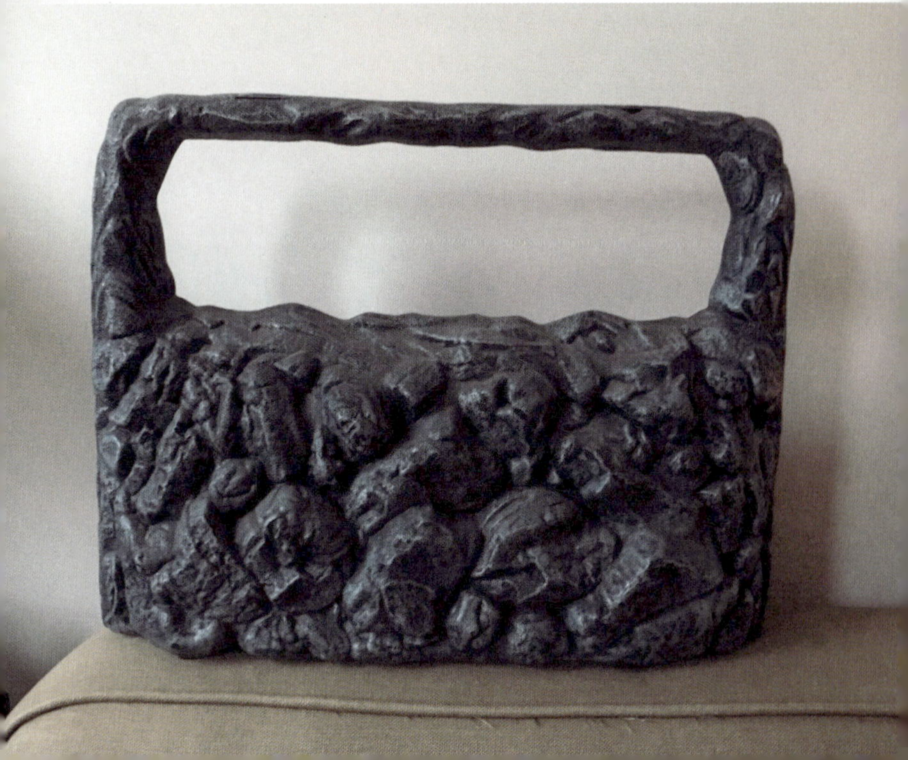

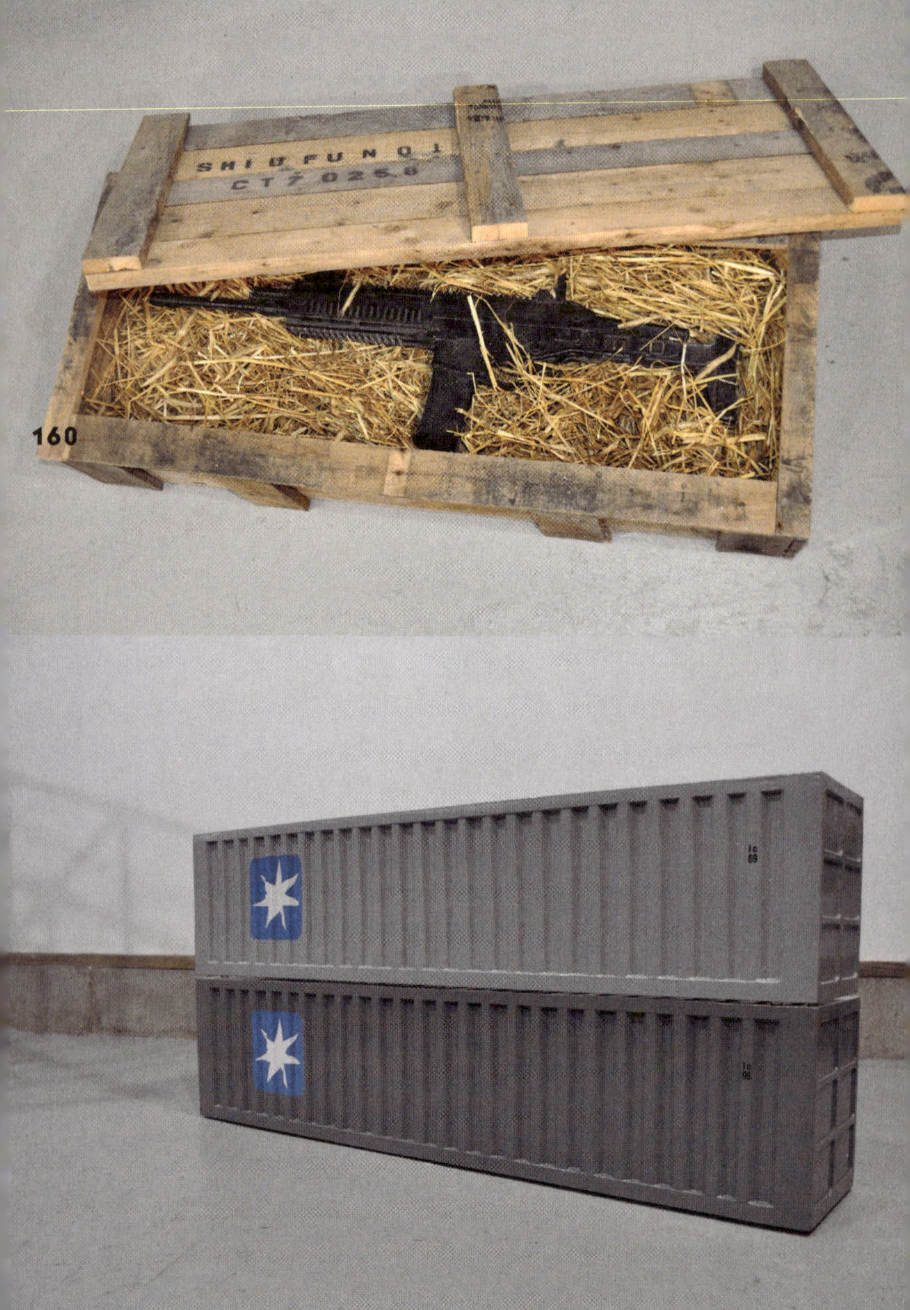
160
SHI UFU N 01
CT 7 025.8

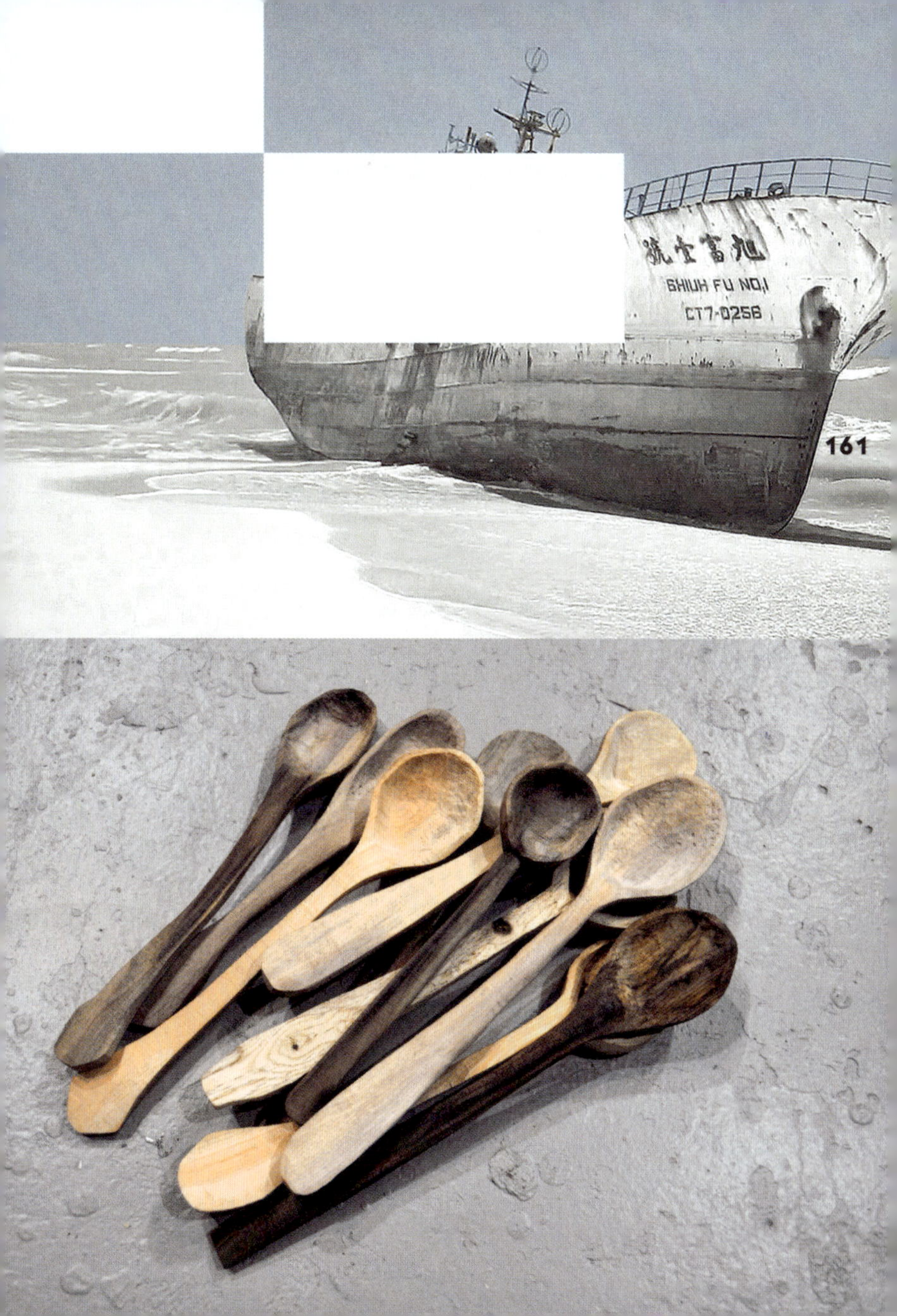
旭富寶號
SHIUH FU NO.I
CT7-0256
161

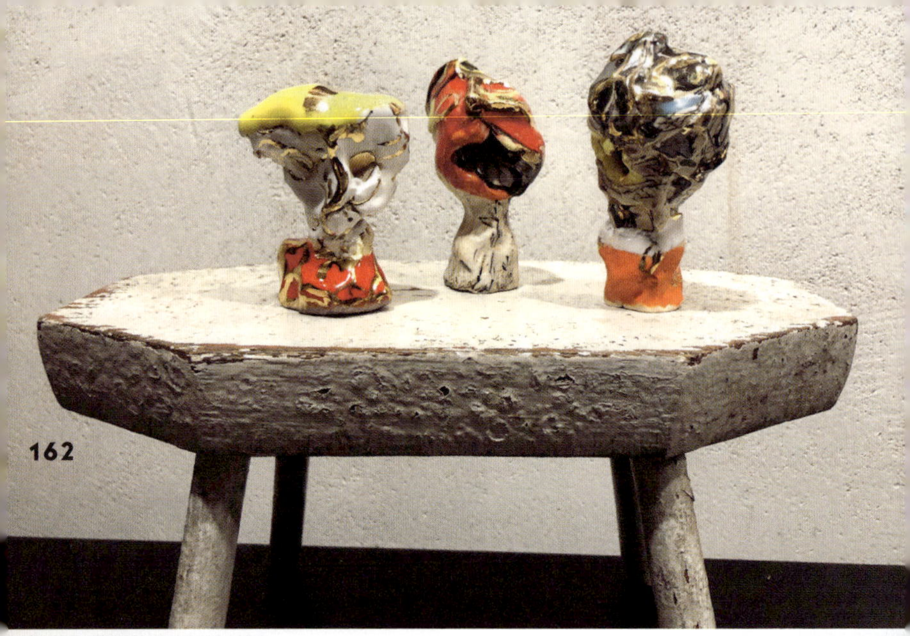

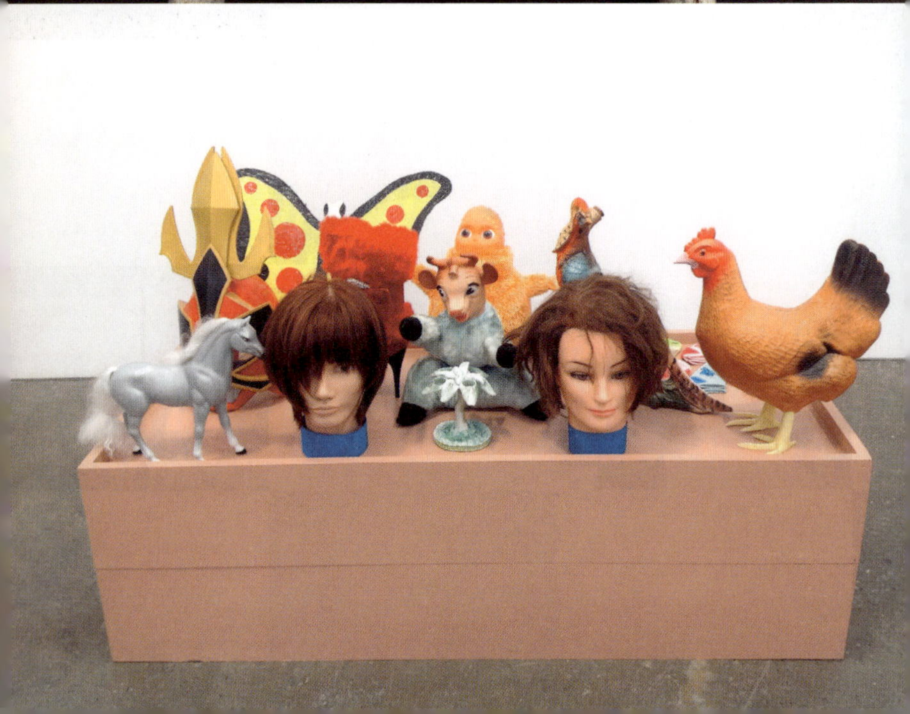

162

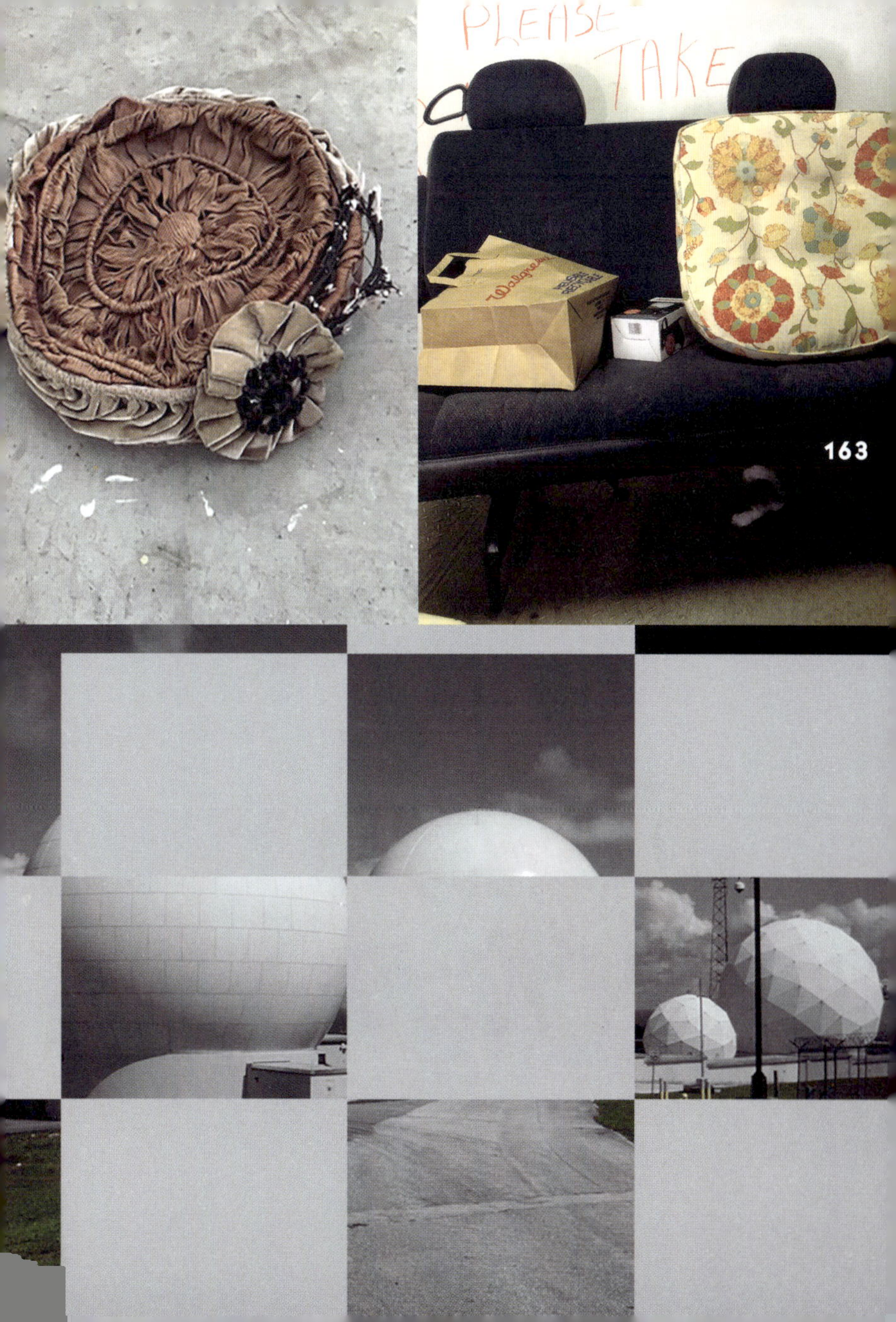
PLEASE
TAKE
163

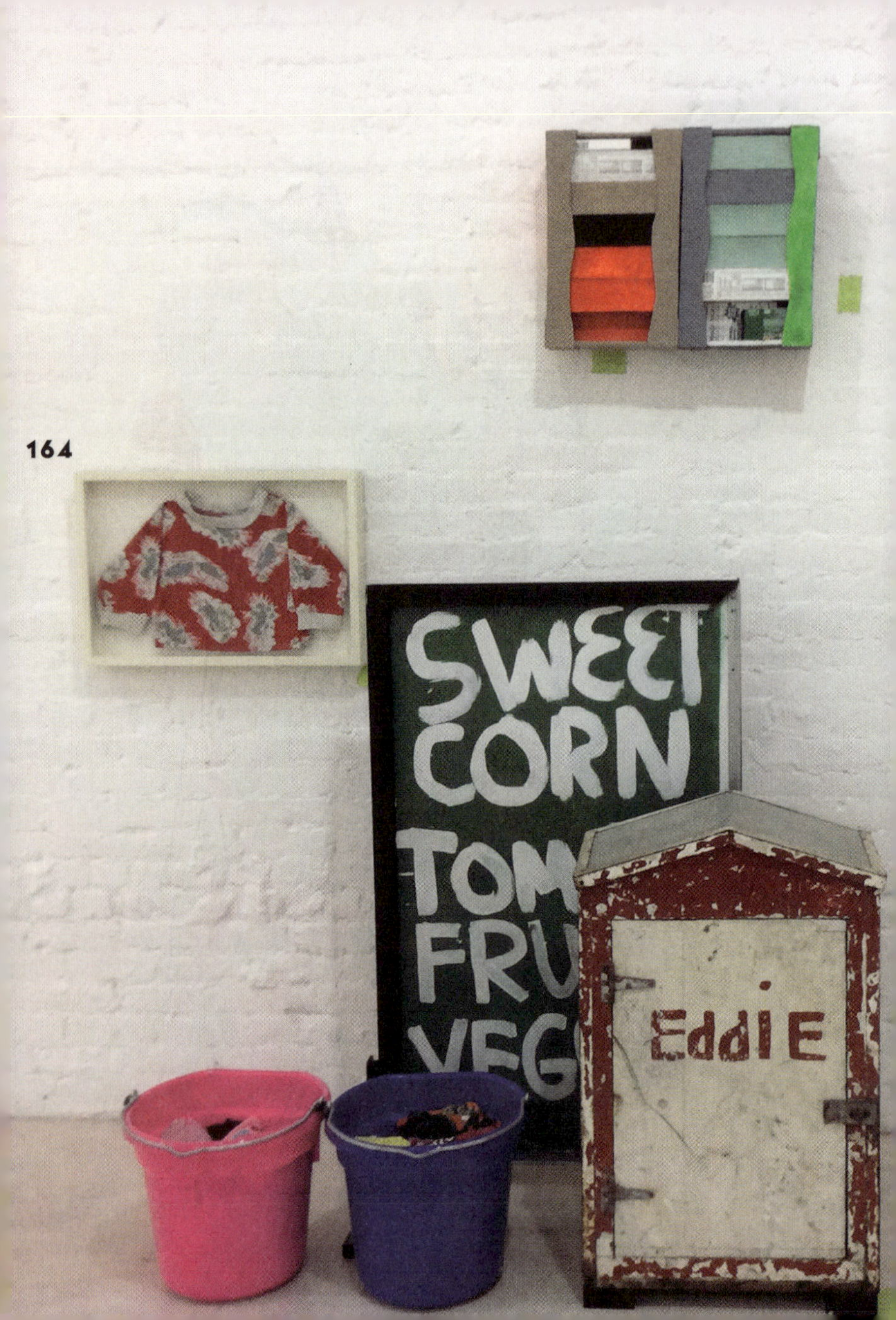

164

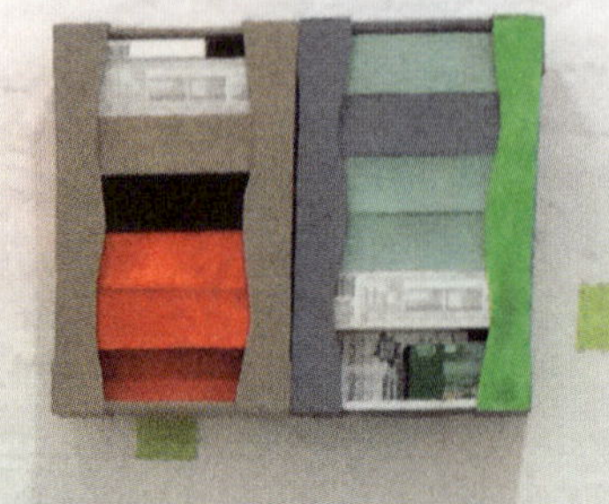

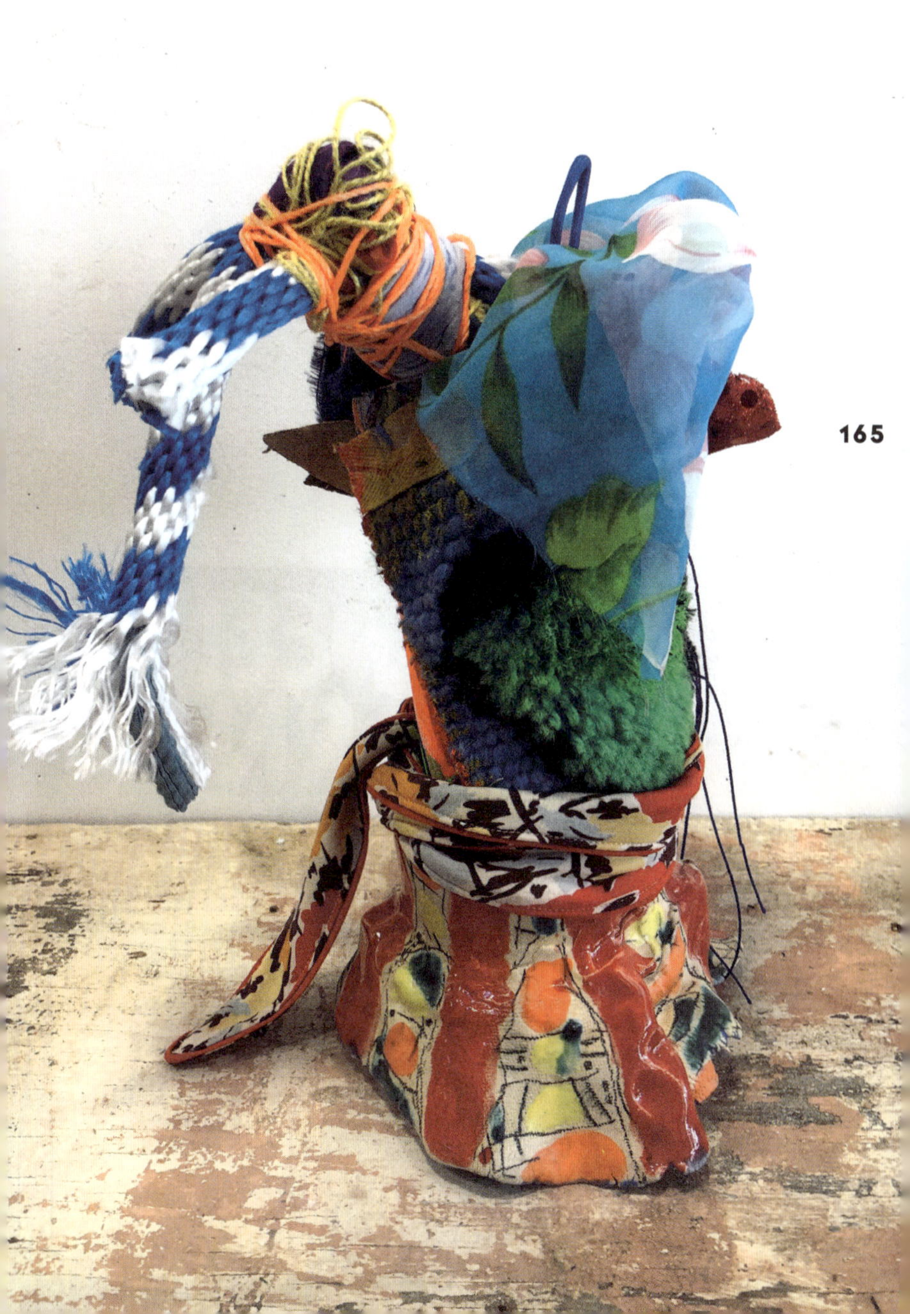

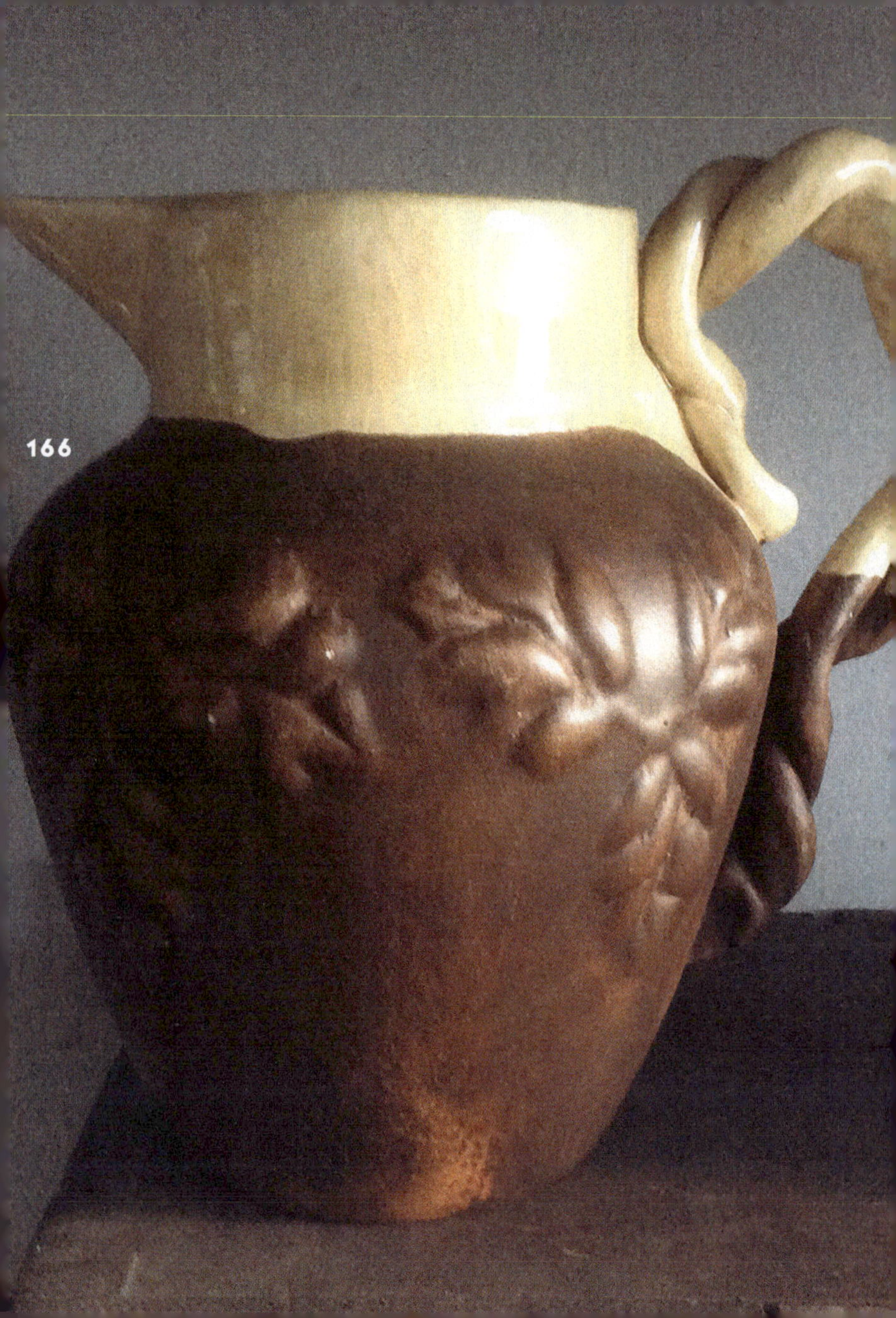
166

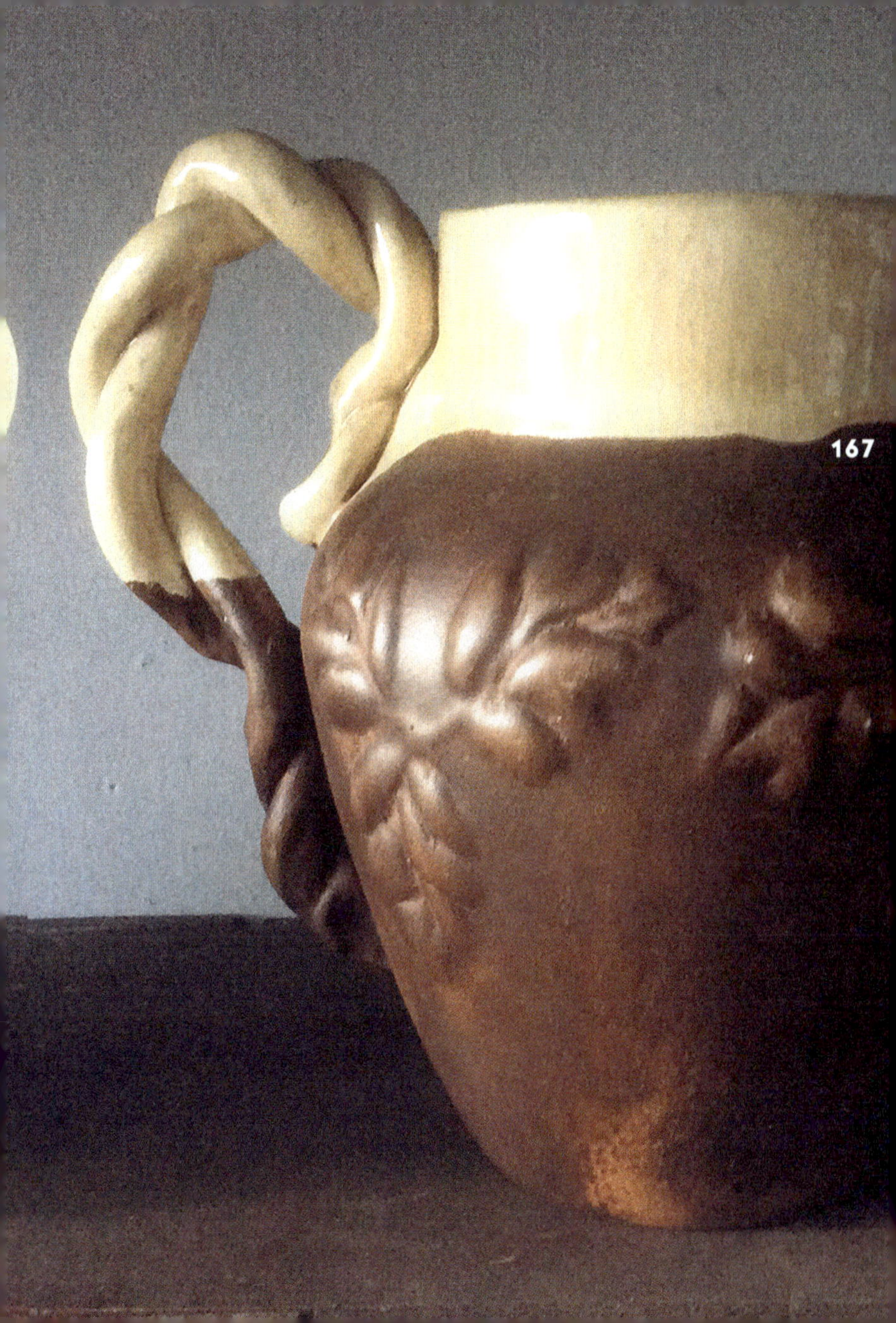
167

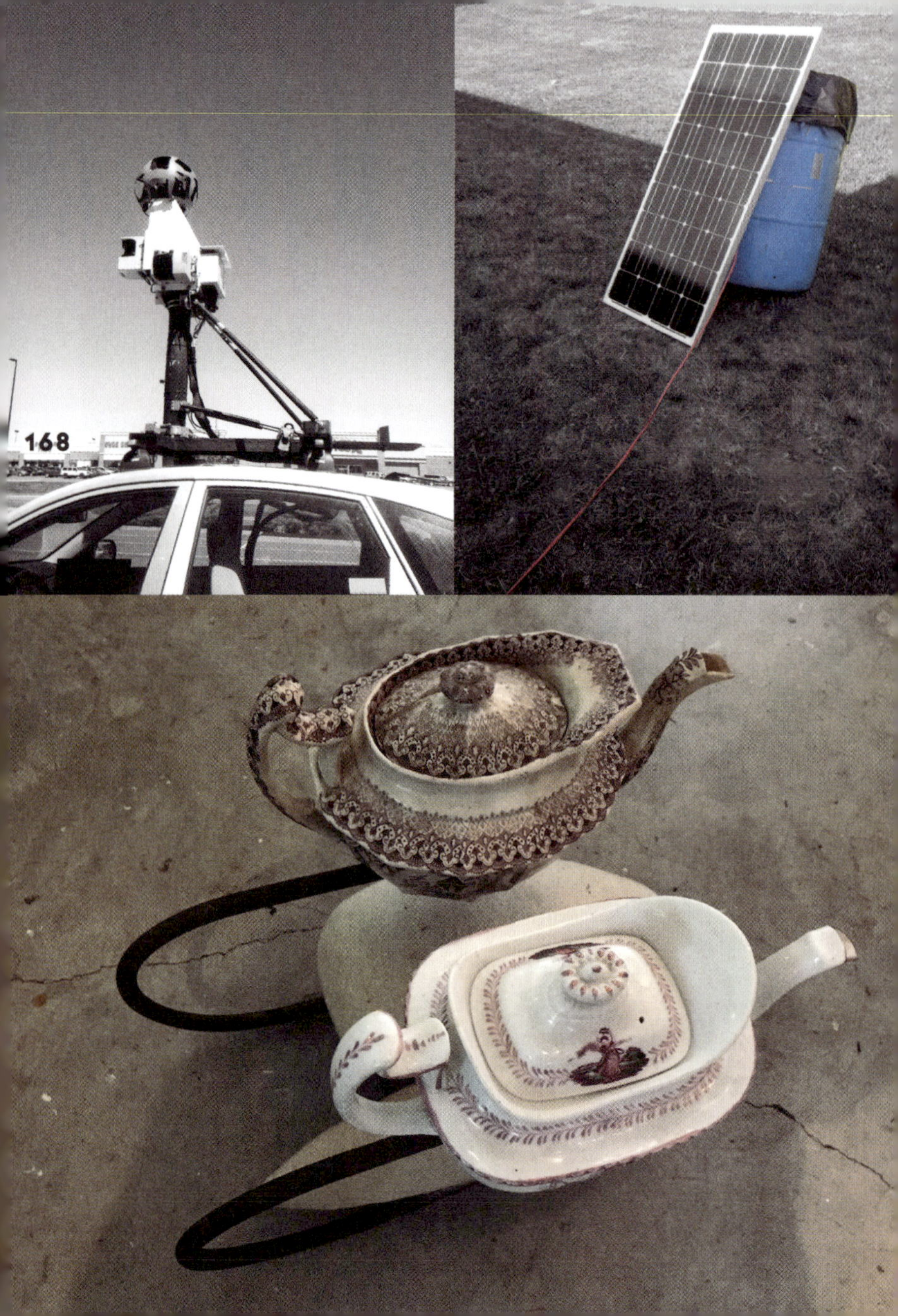

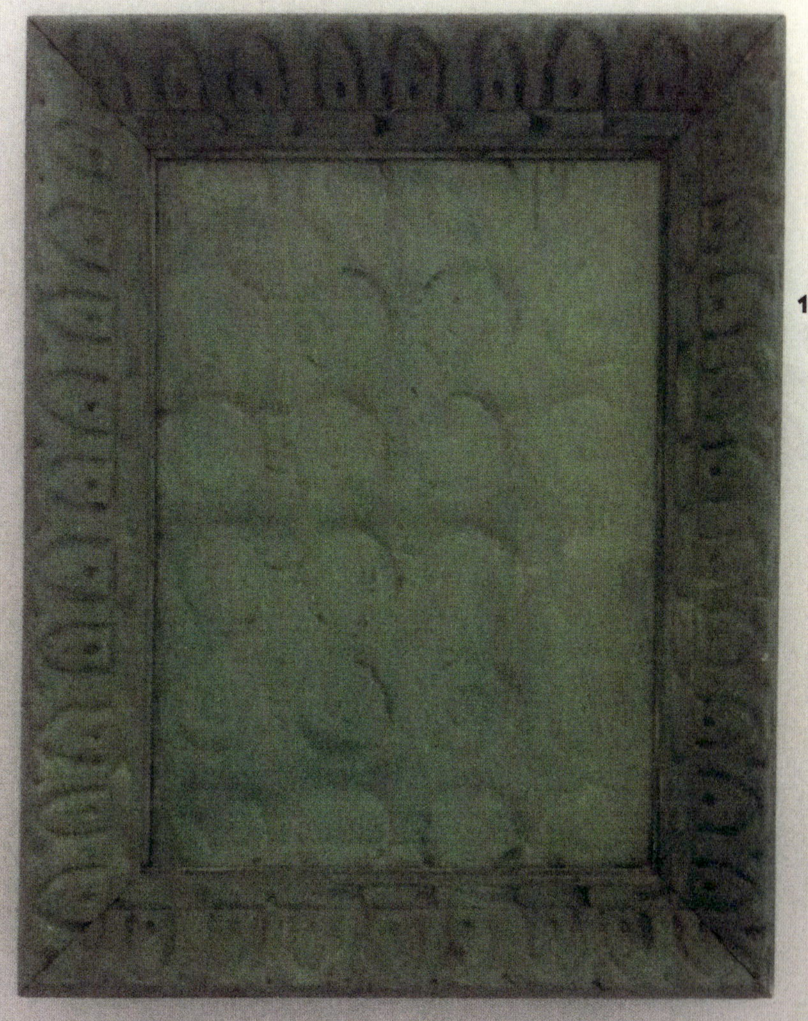

169

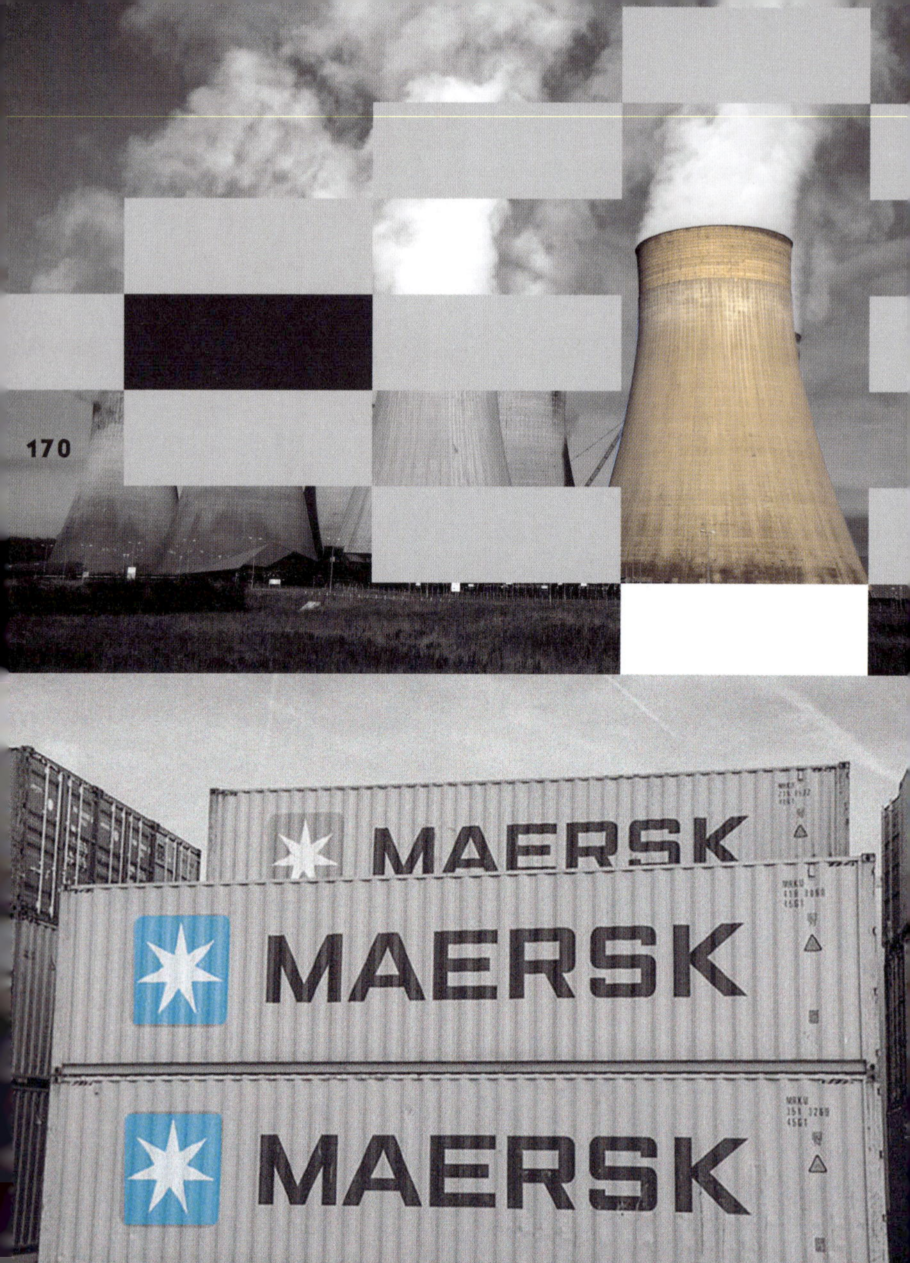

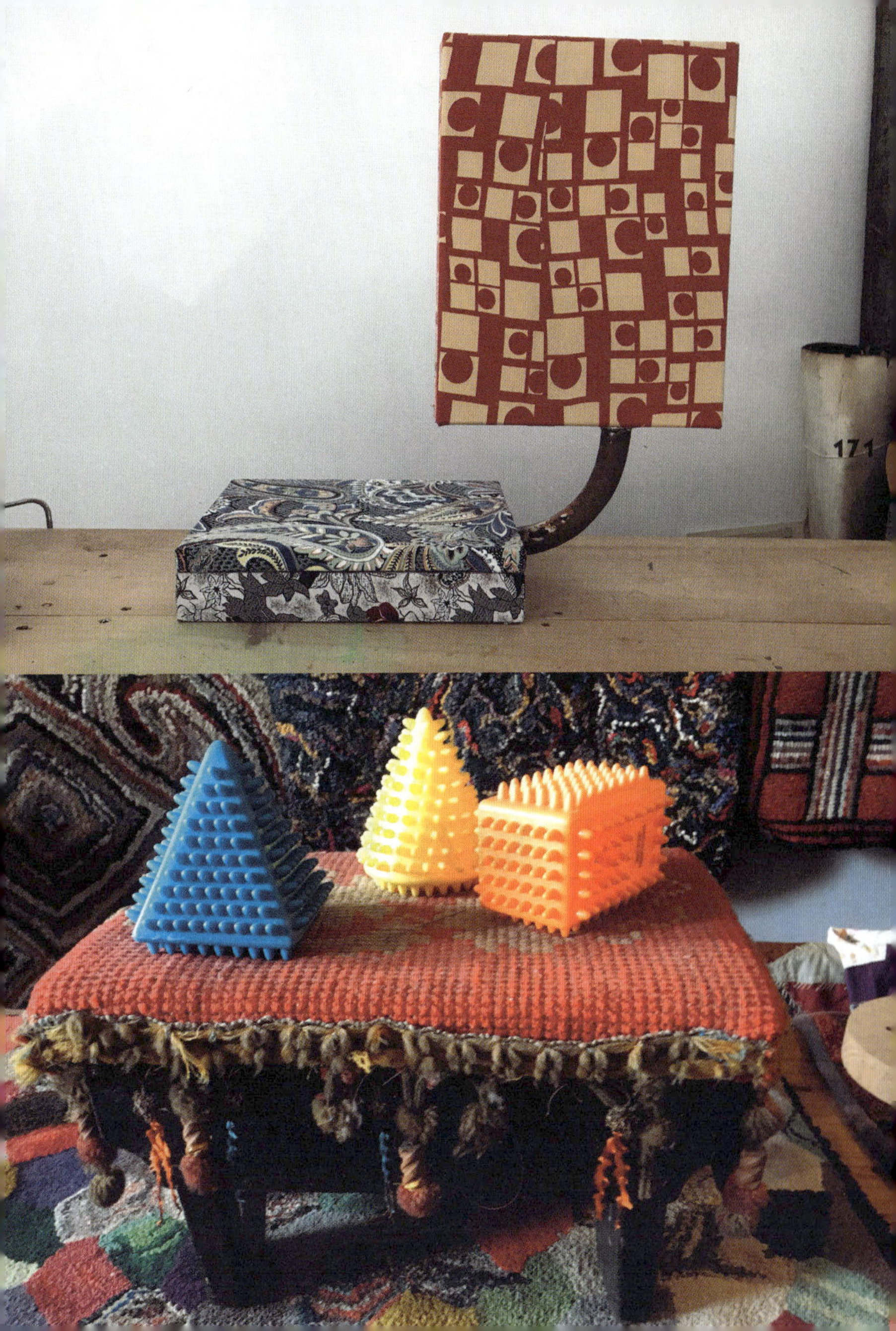

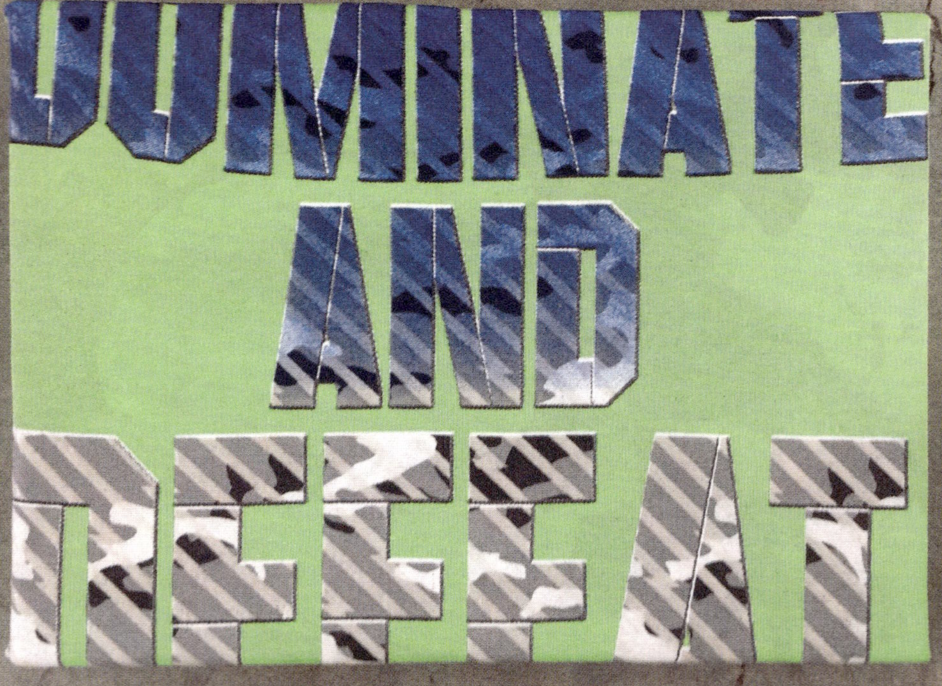

DOMINATE
AND
REPEAT

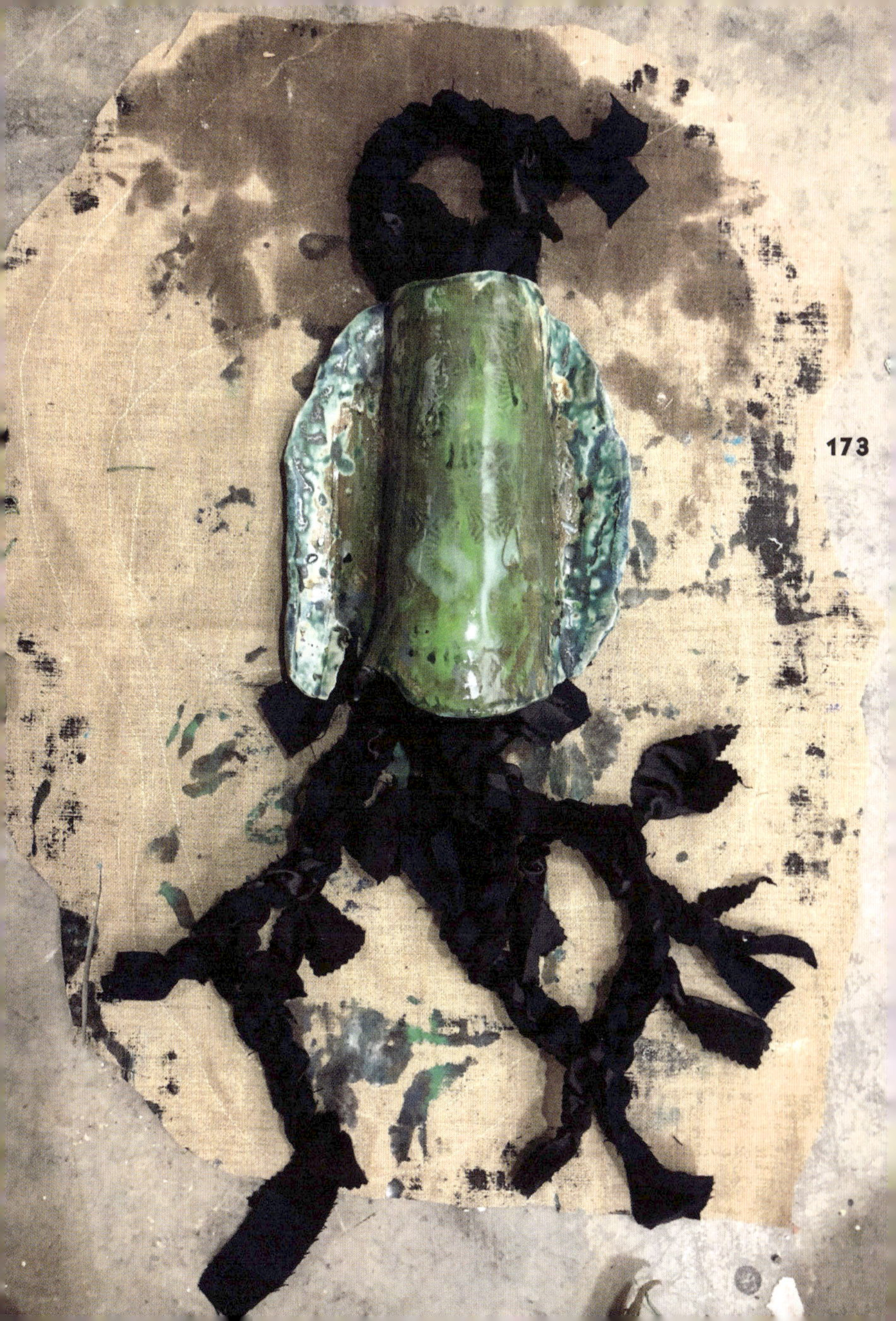

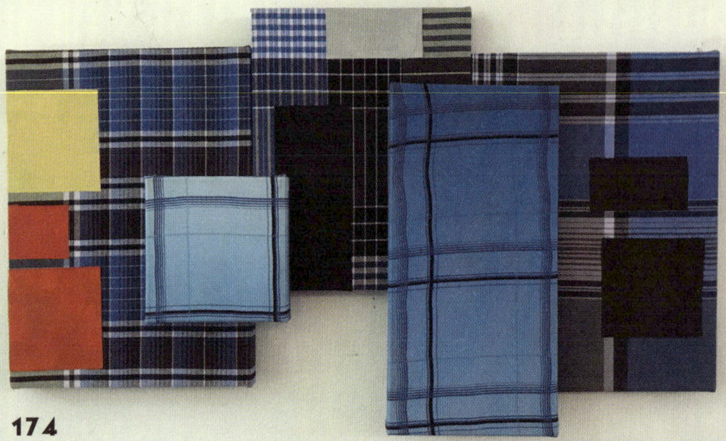

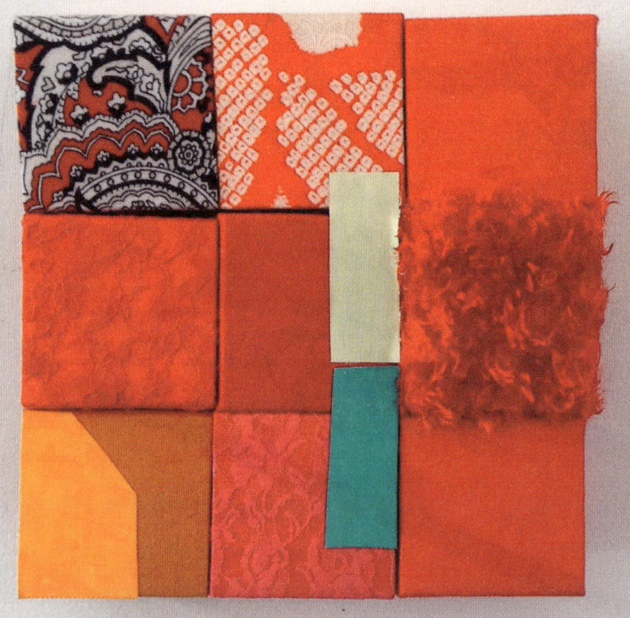

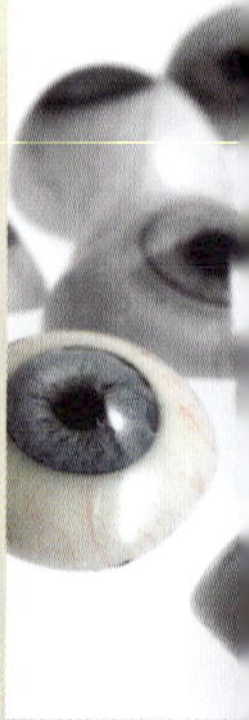

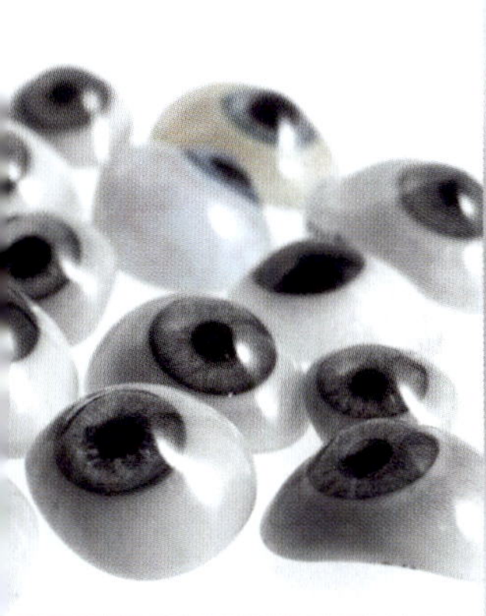

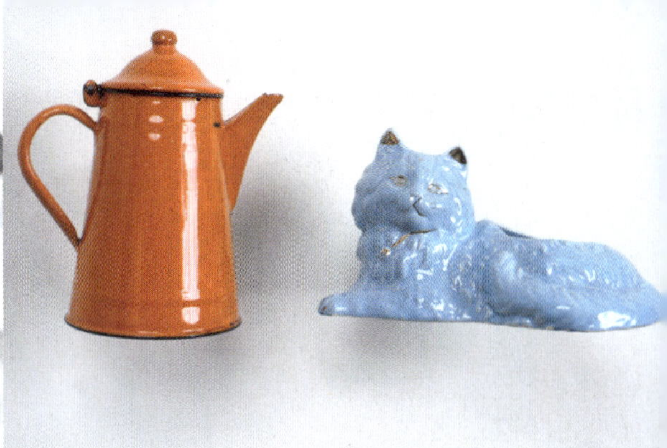

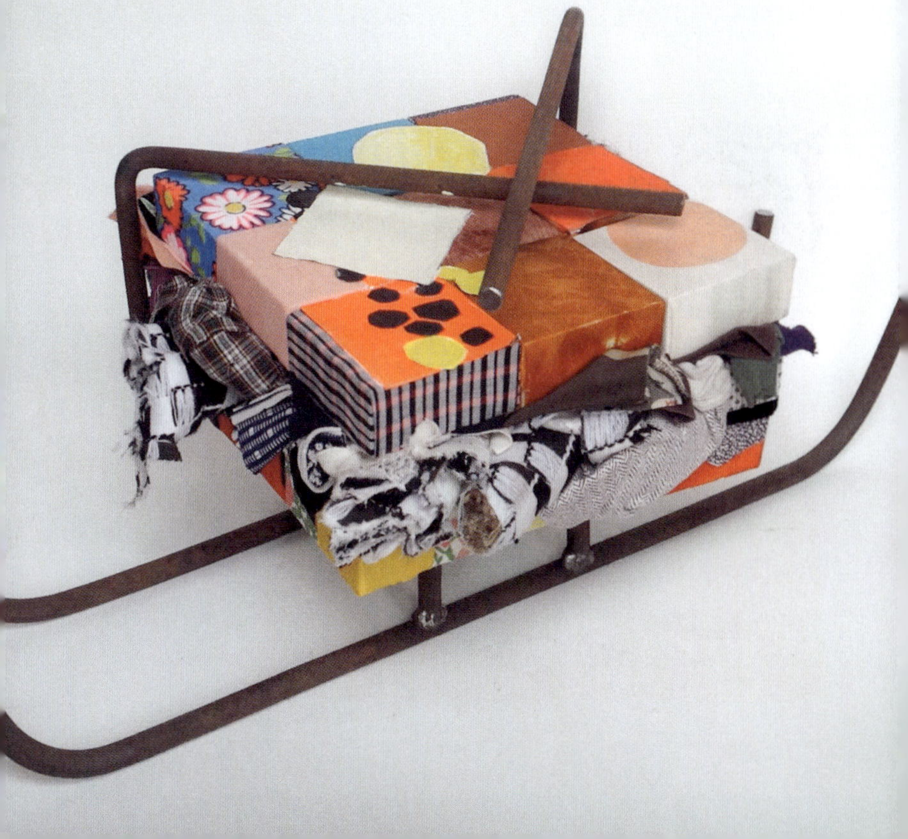

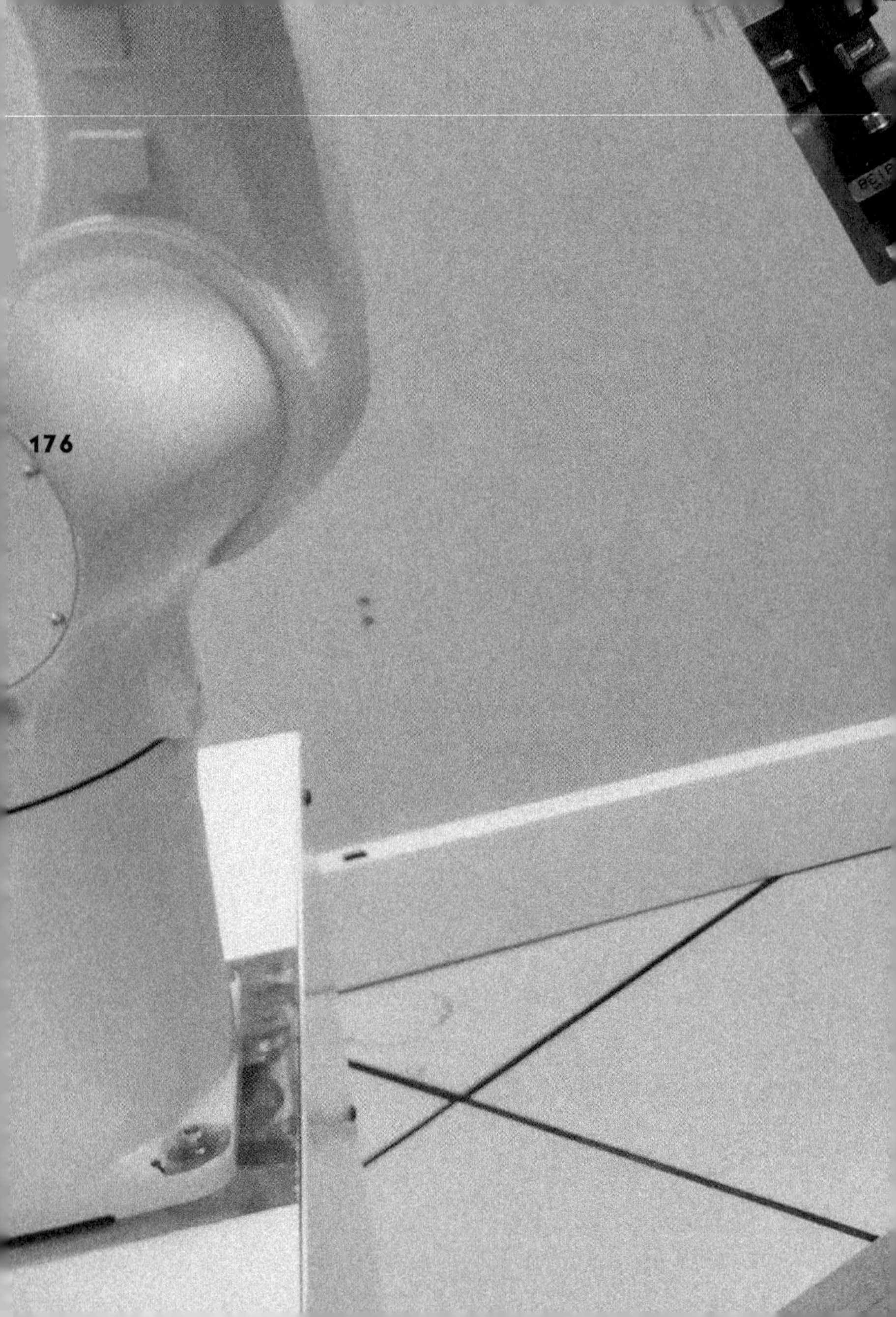
176

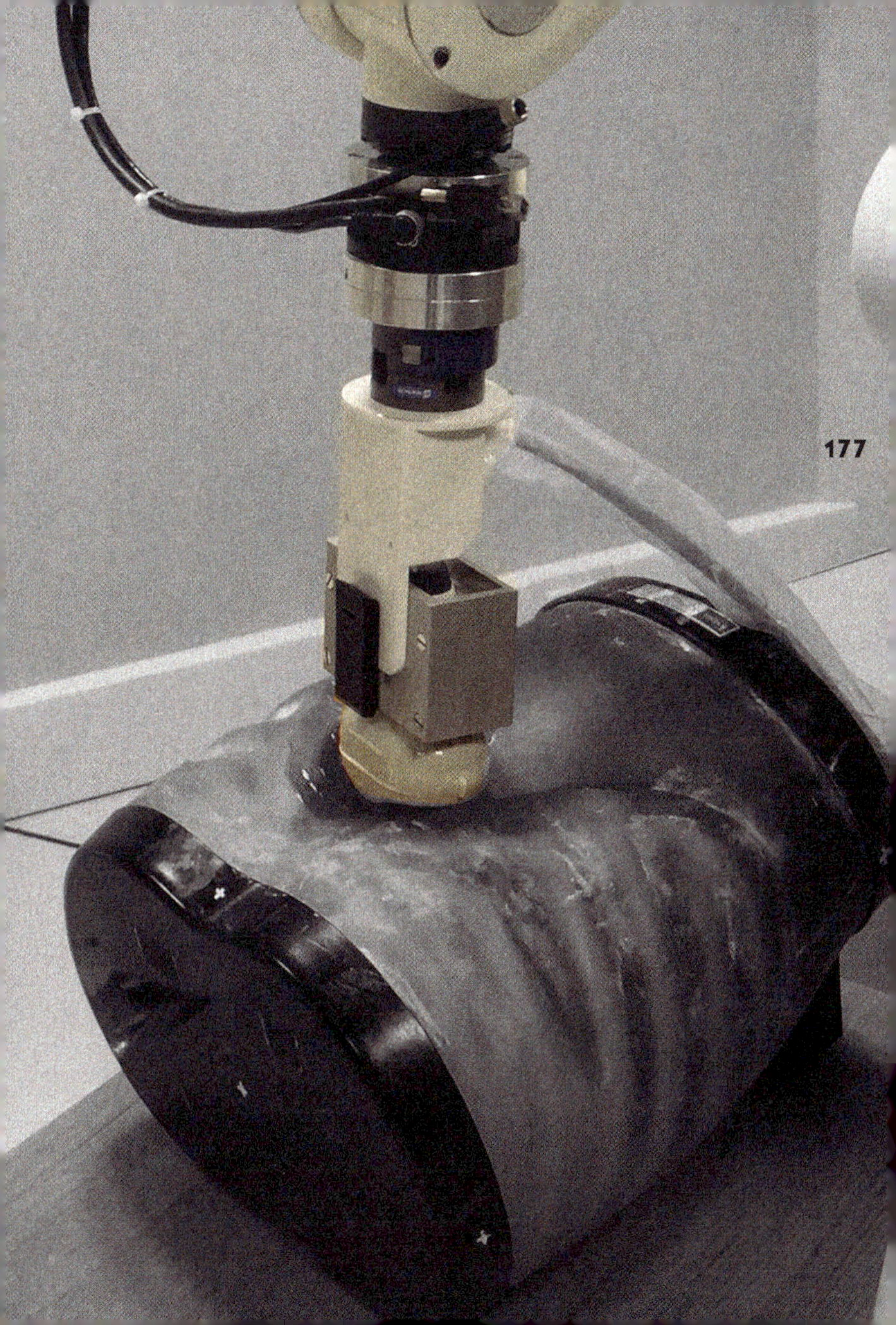

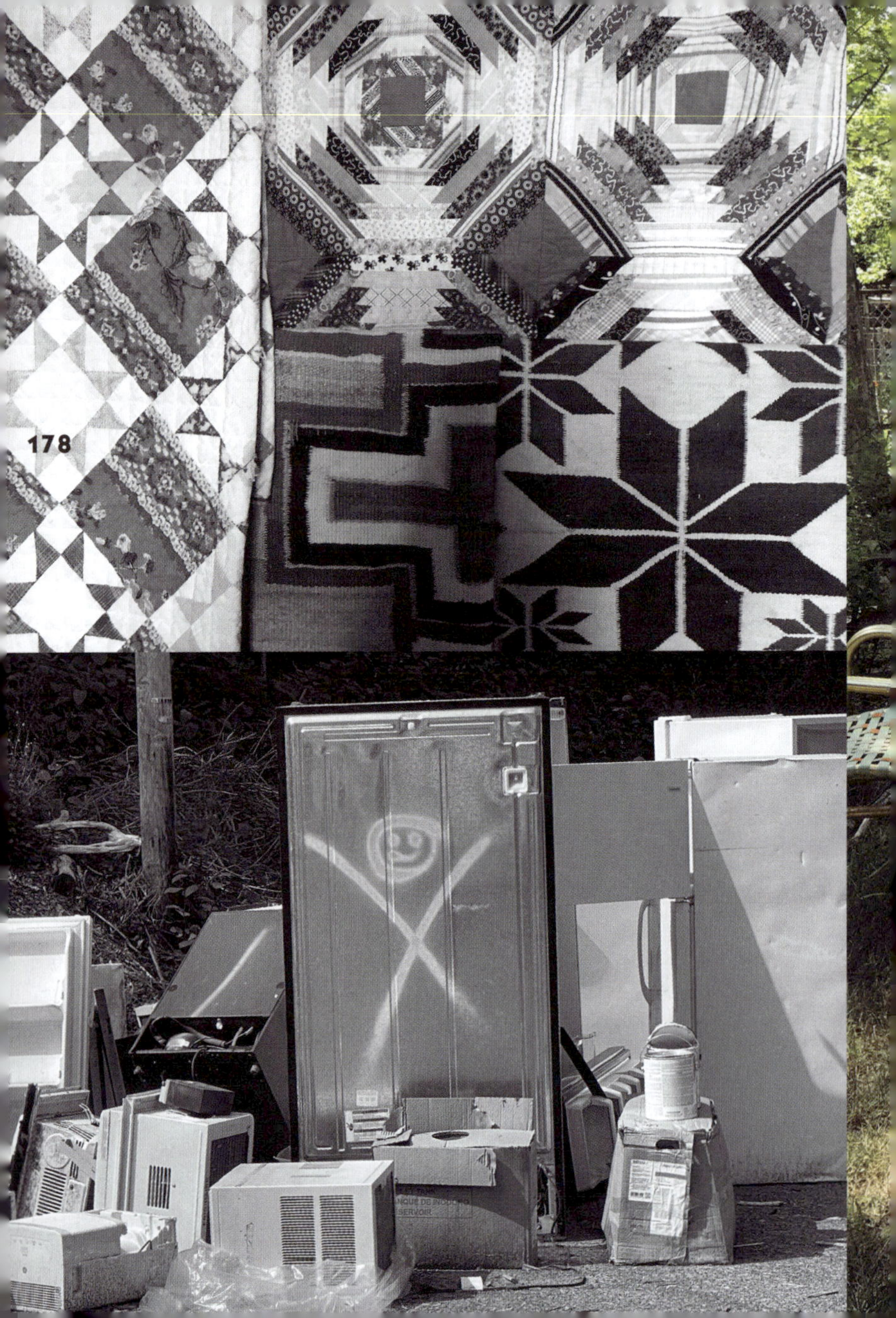
178

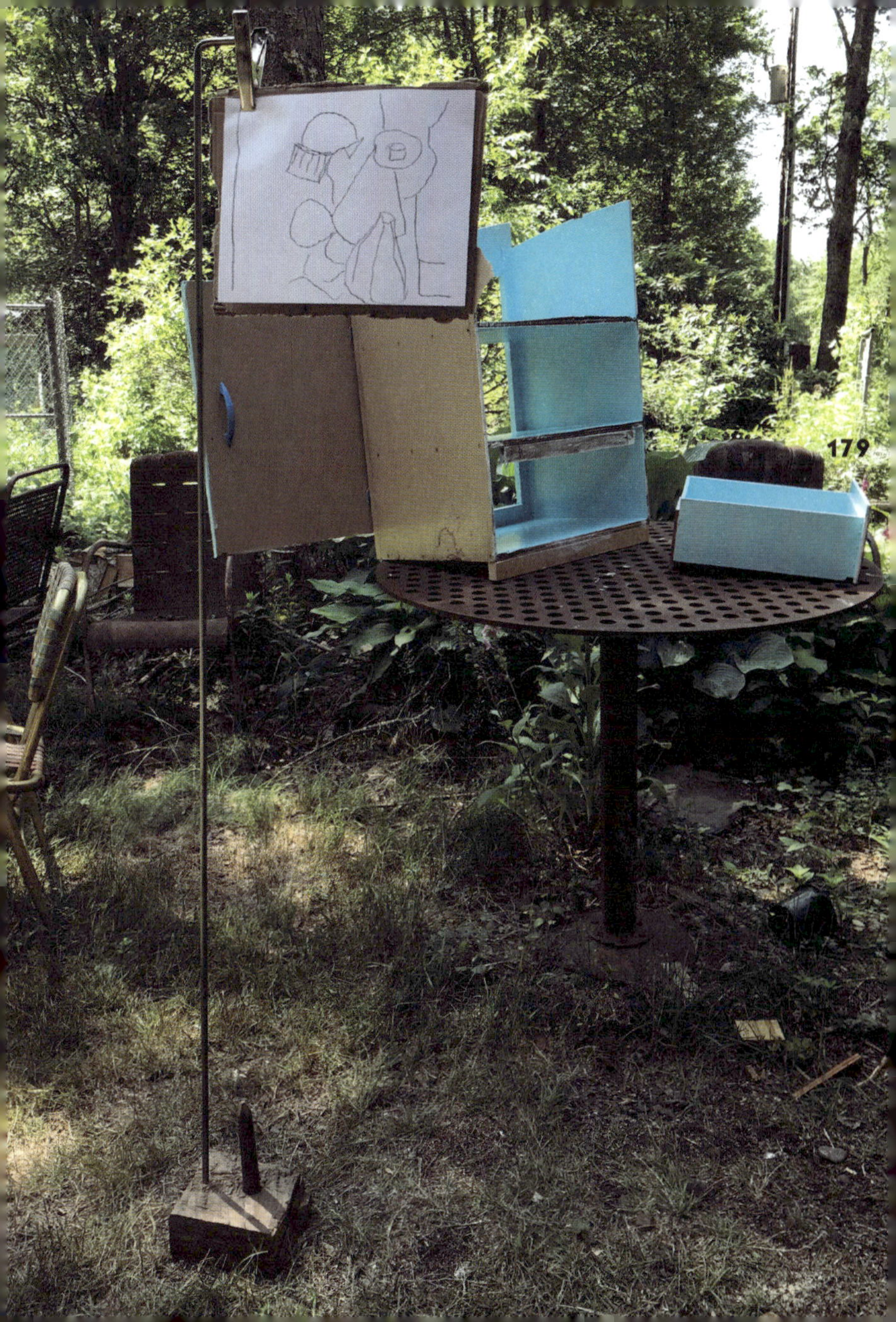
179

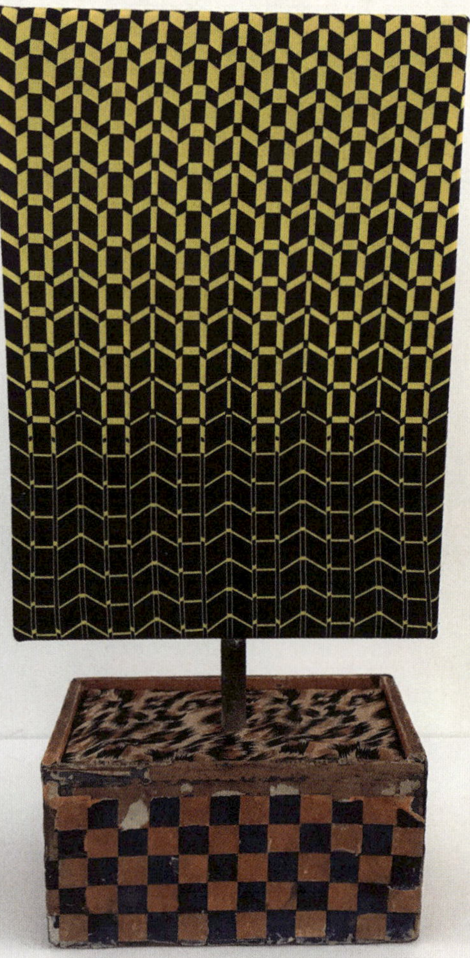

180

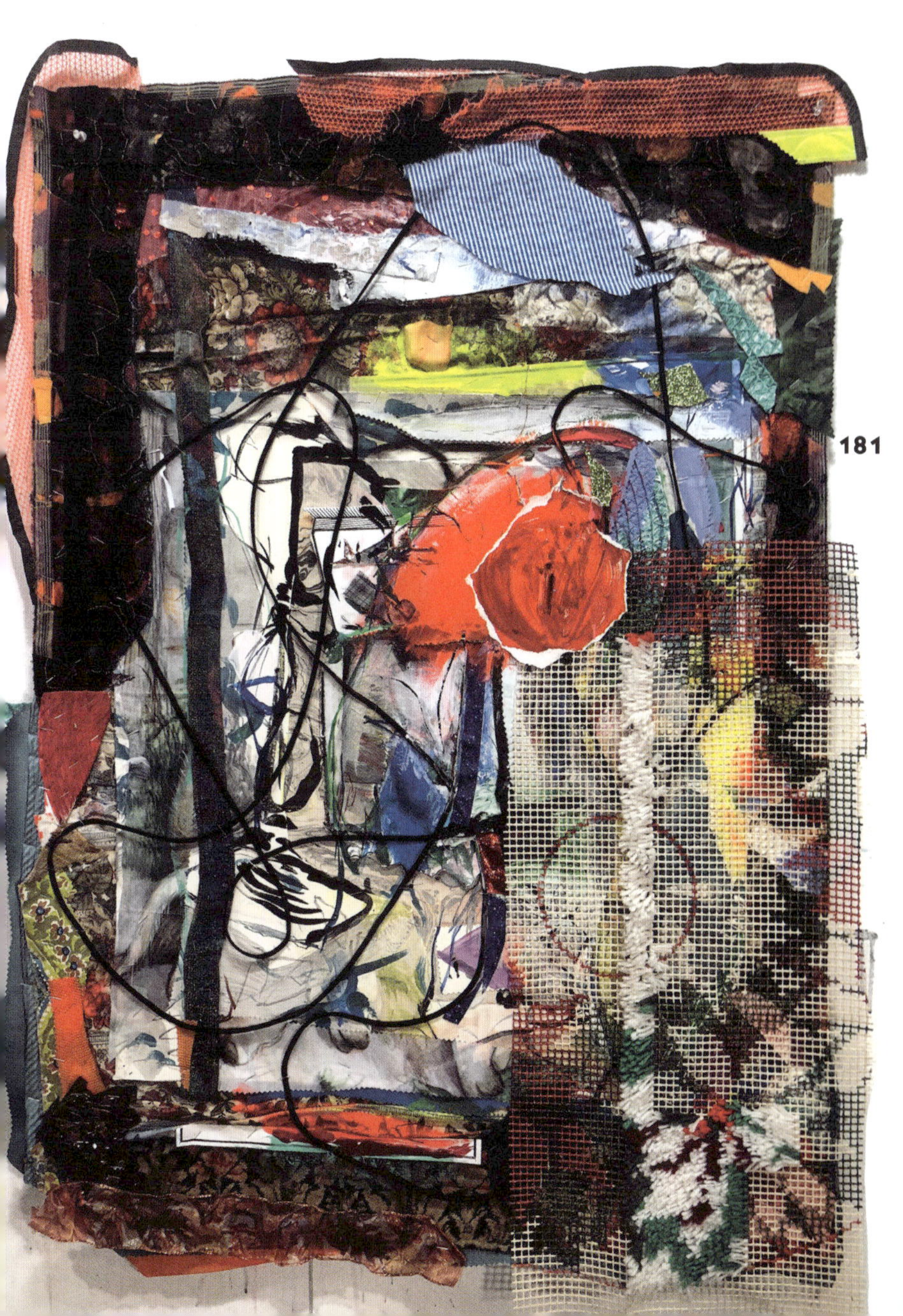

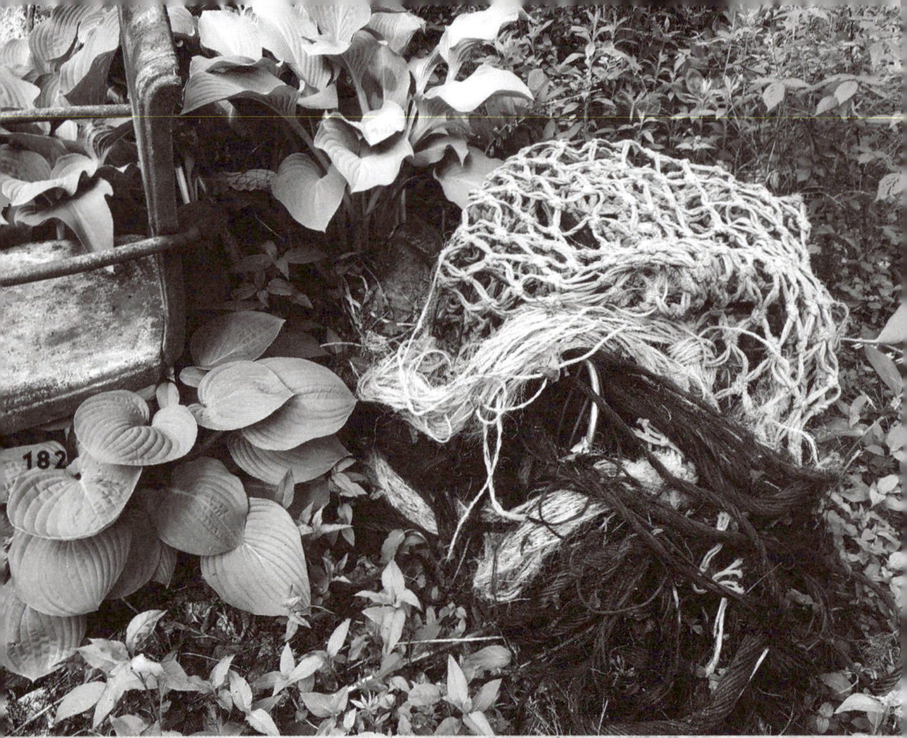

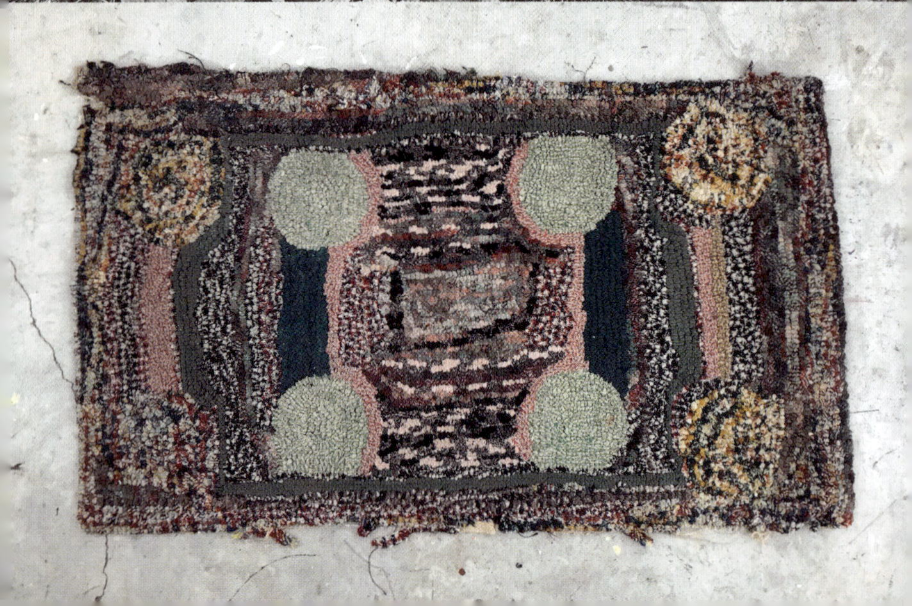

182

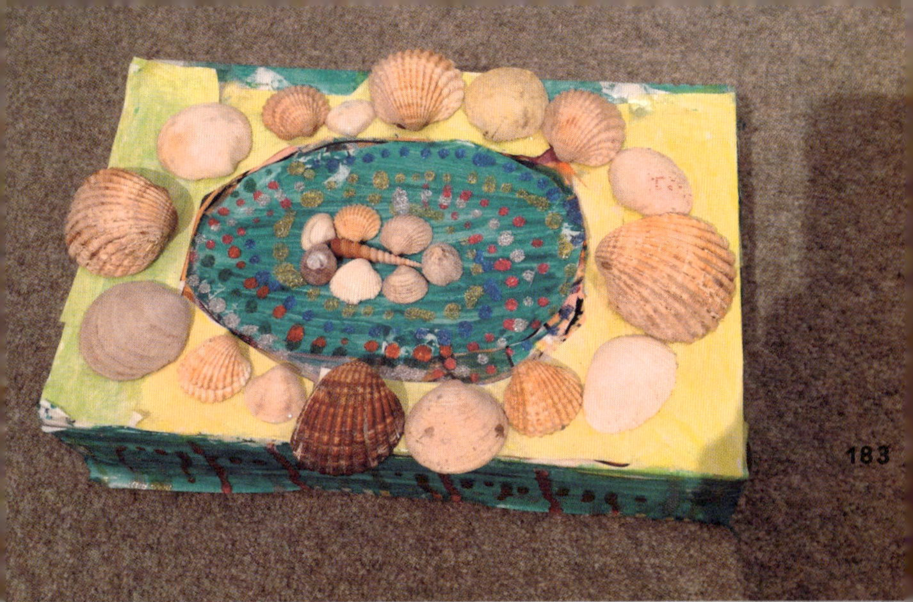

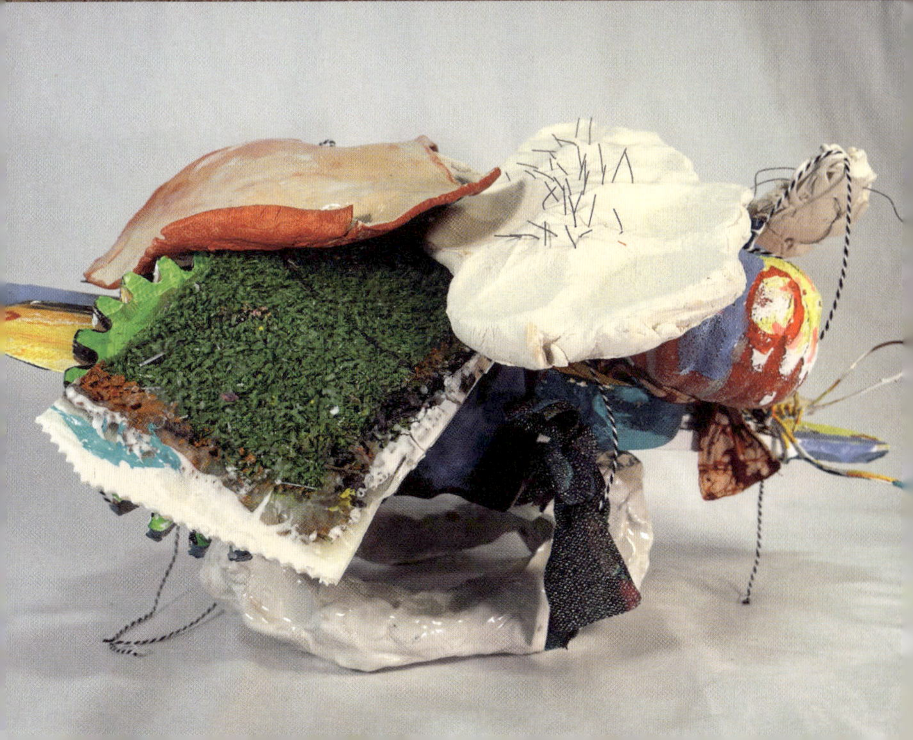

183

184

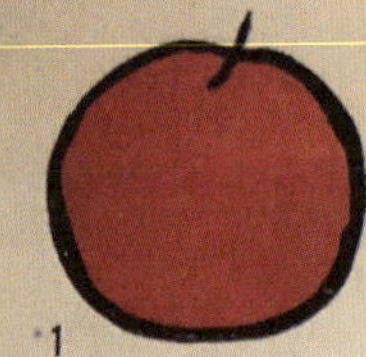

1

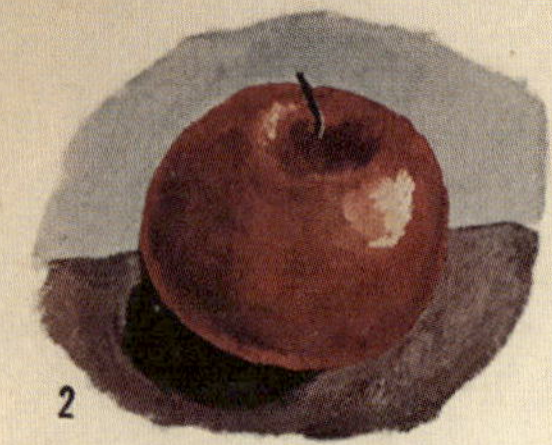

2

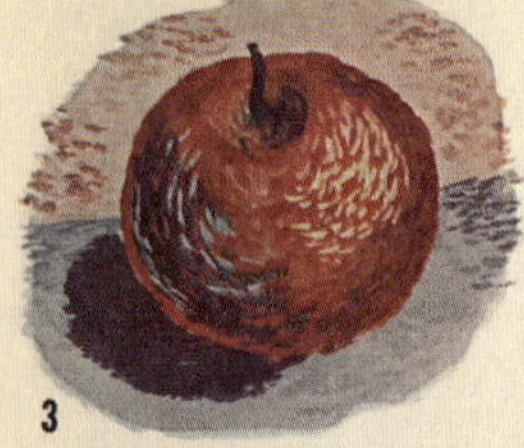

3

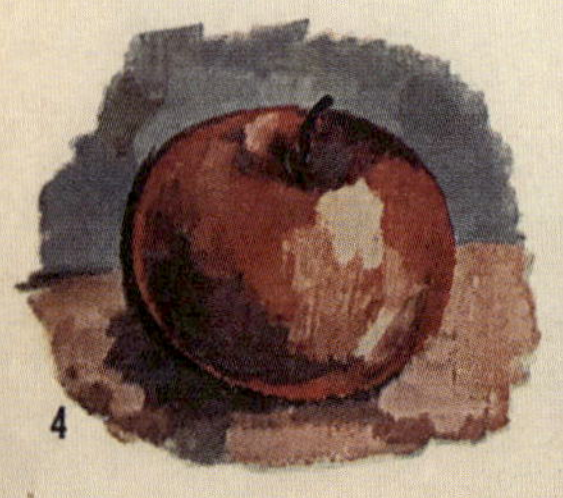

4

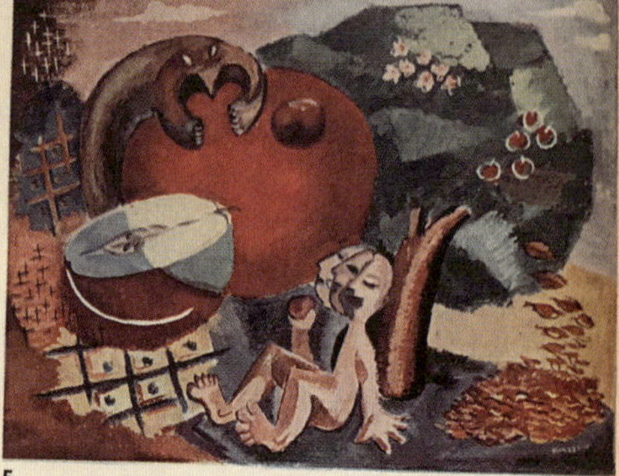

5

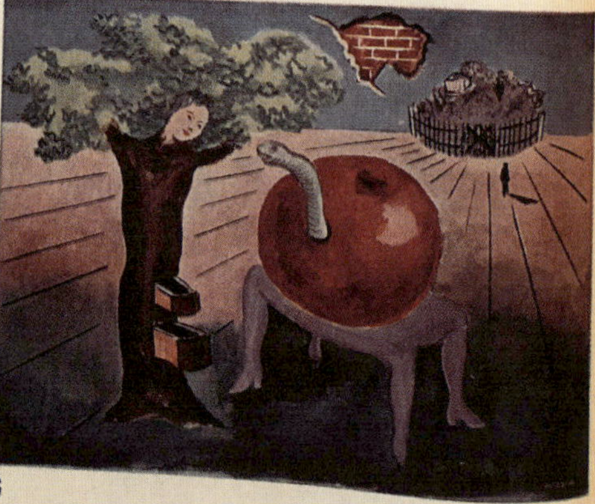

6

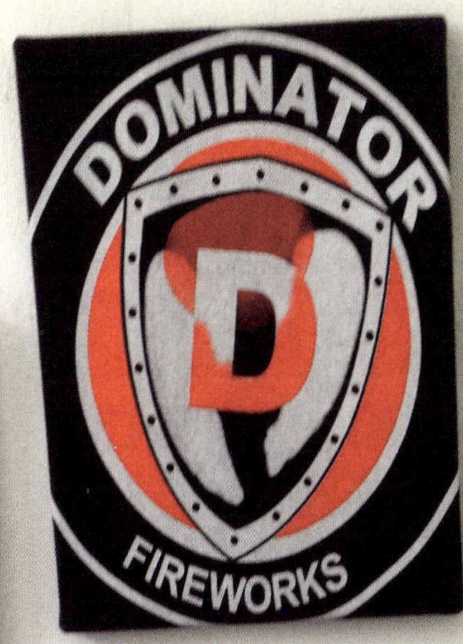

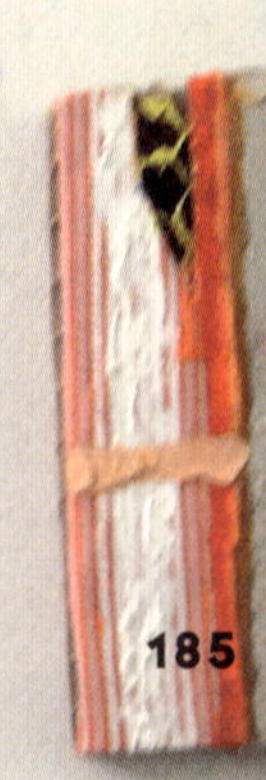

185

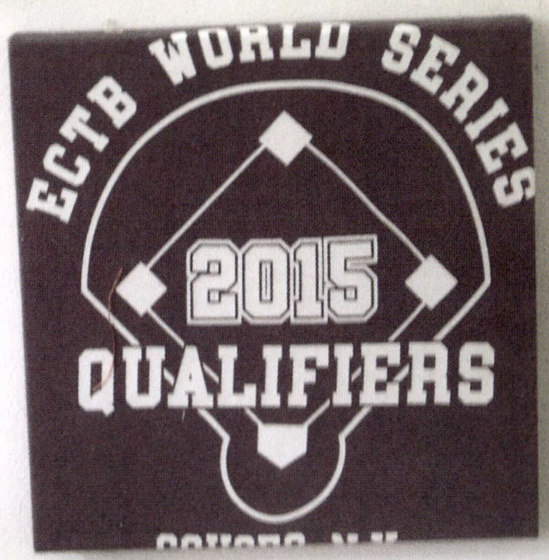

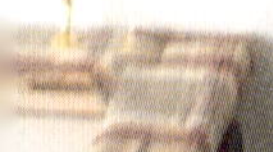

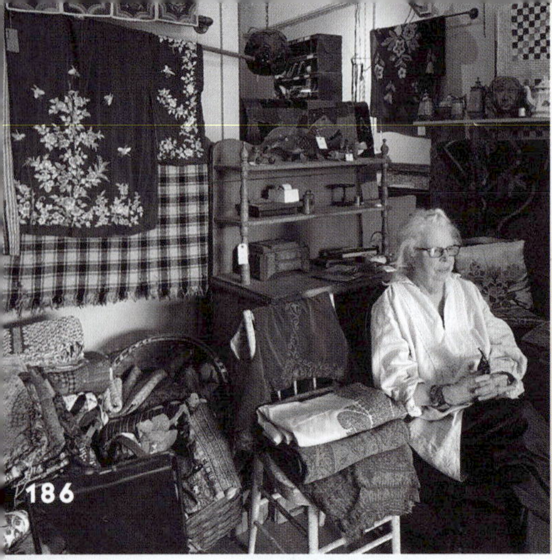

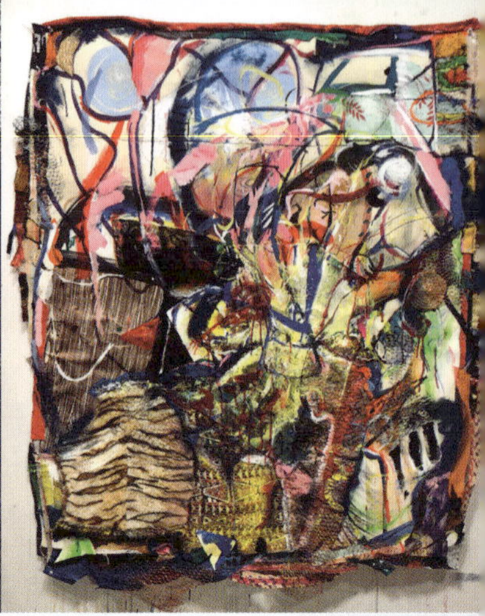

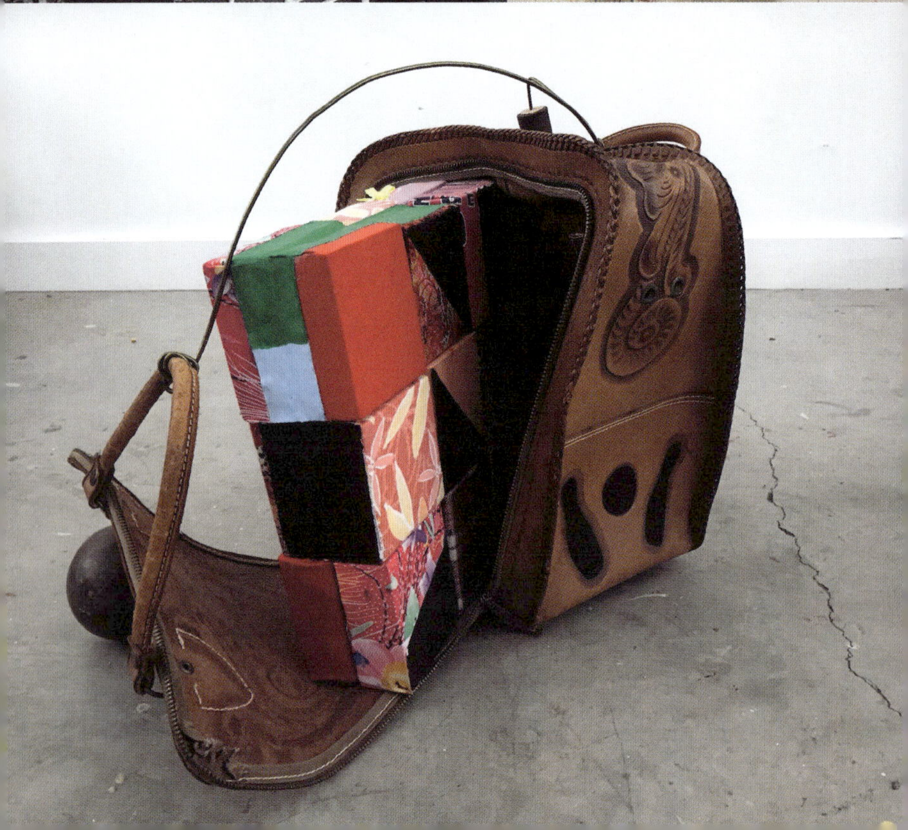

186

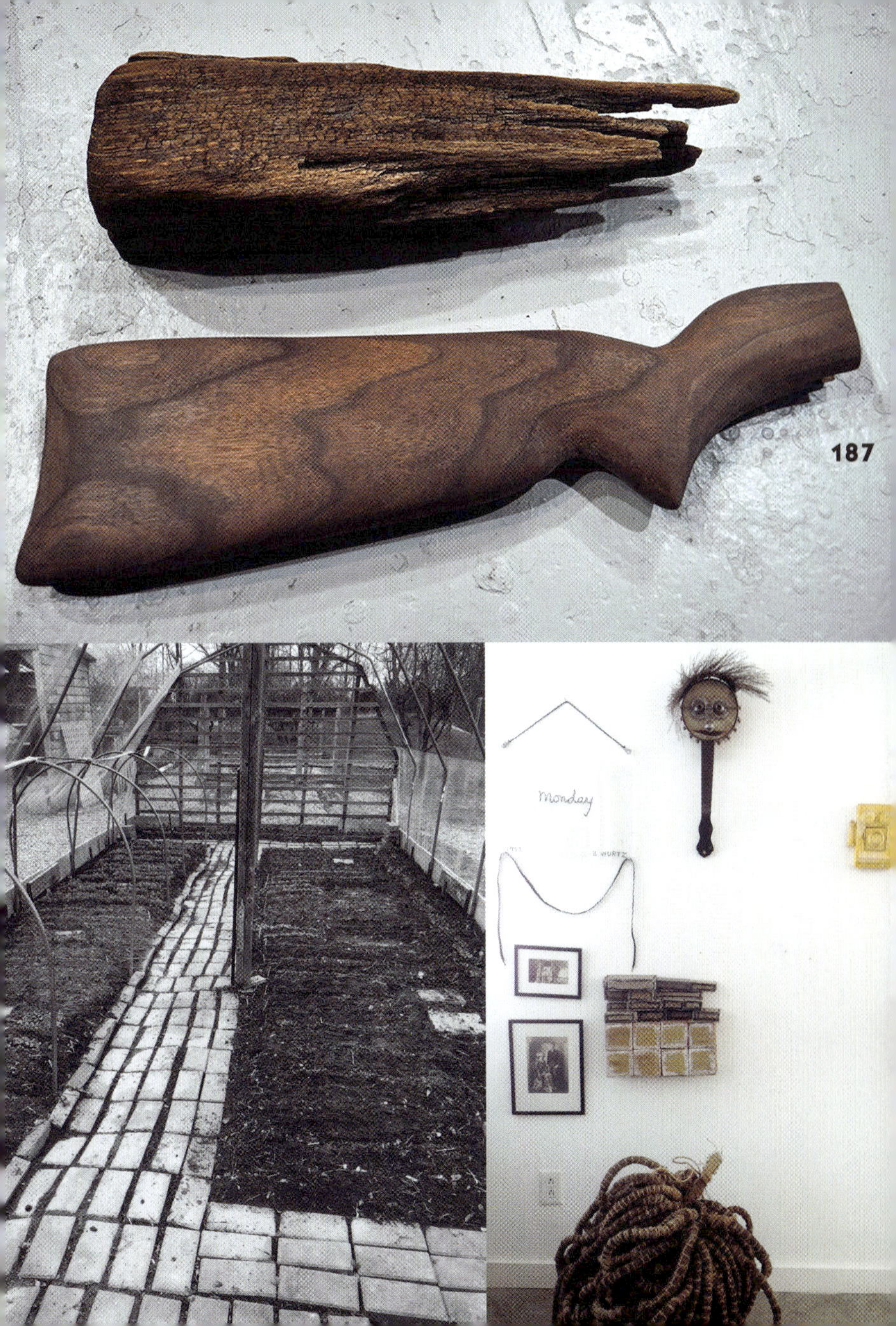

187

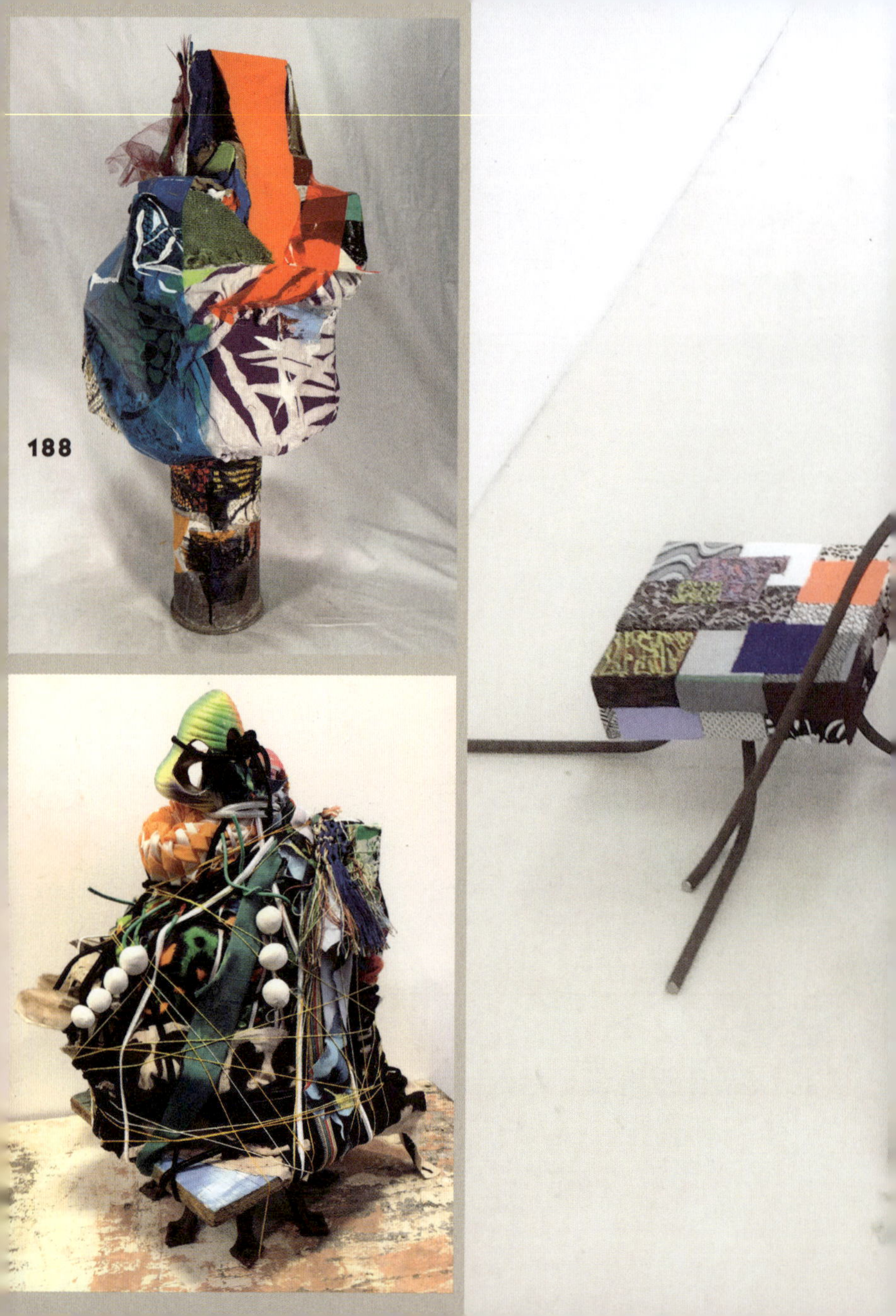

188

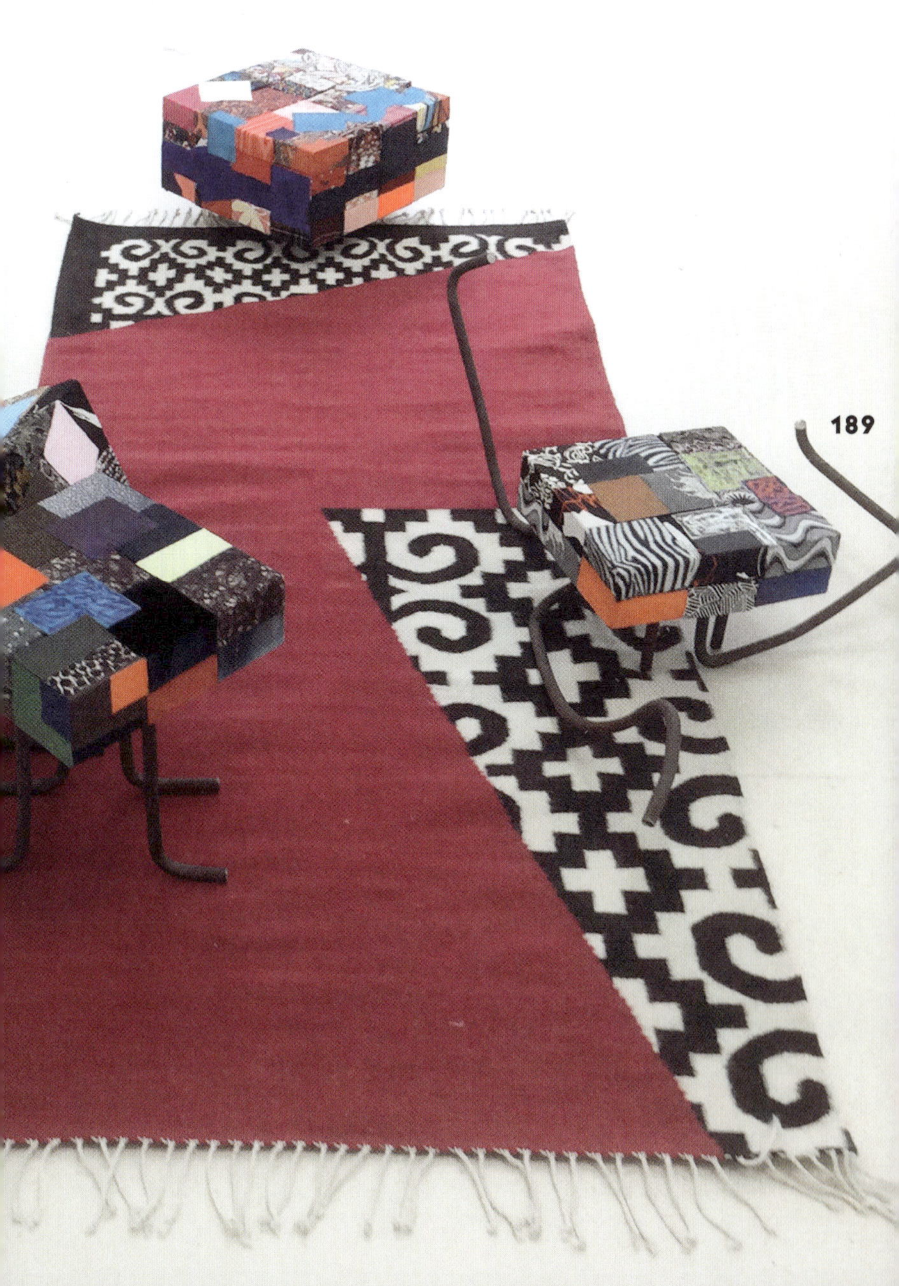

189

190

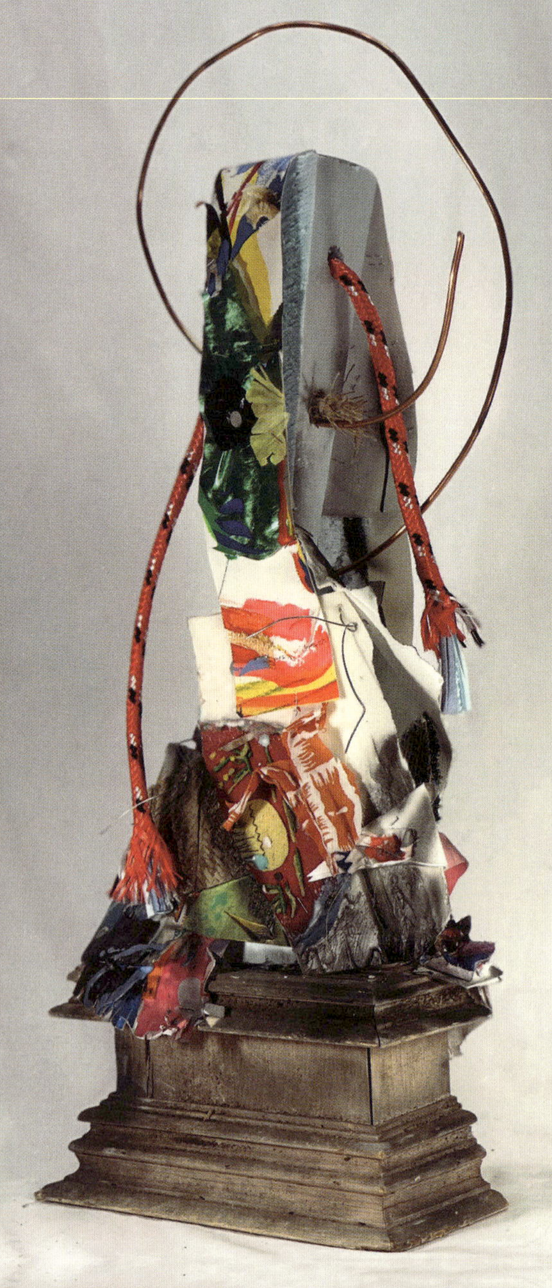

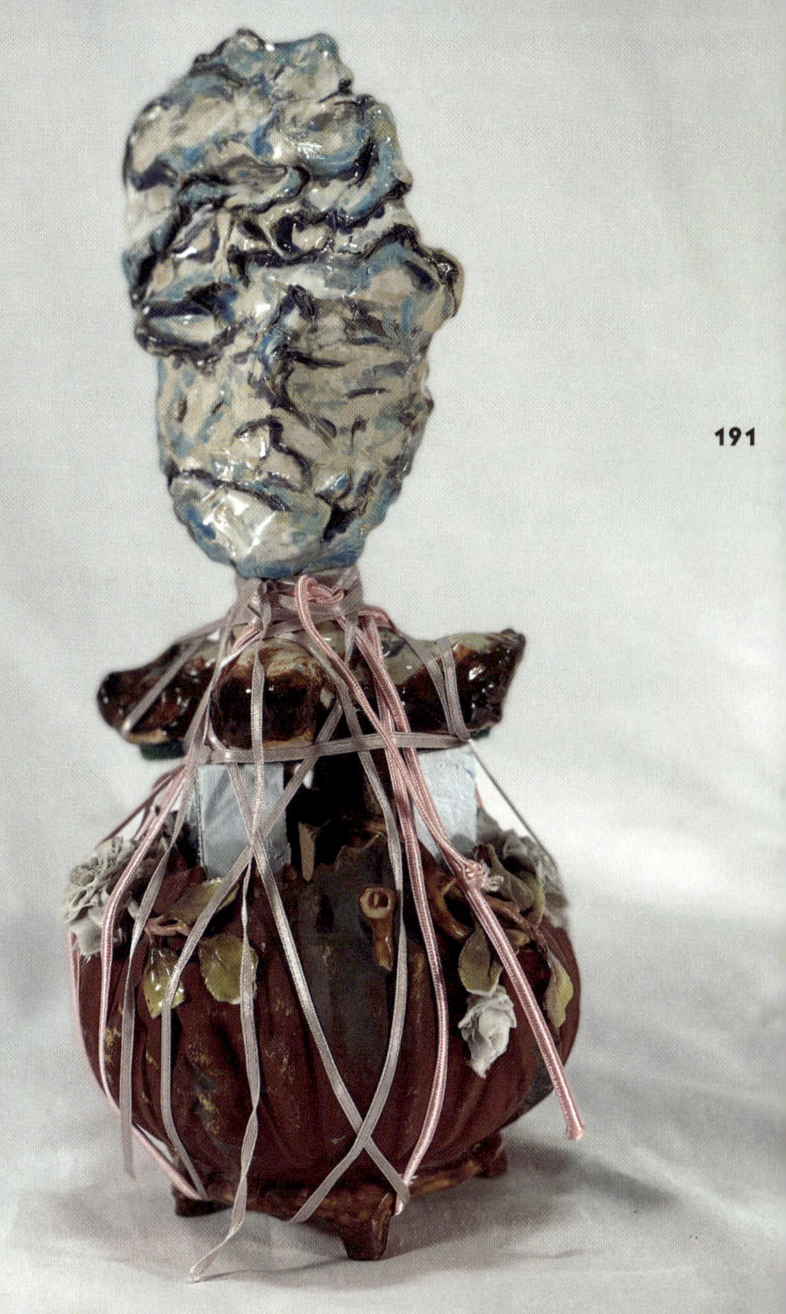

191

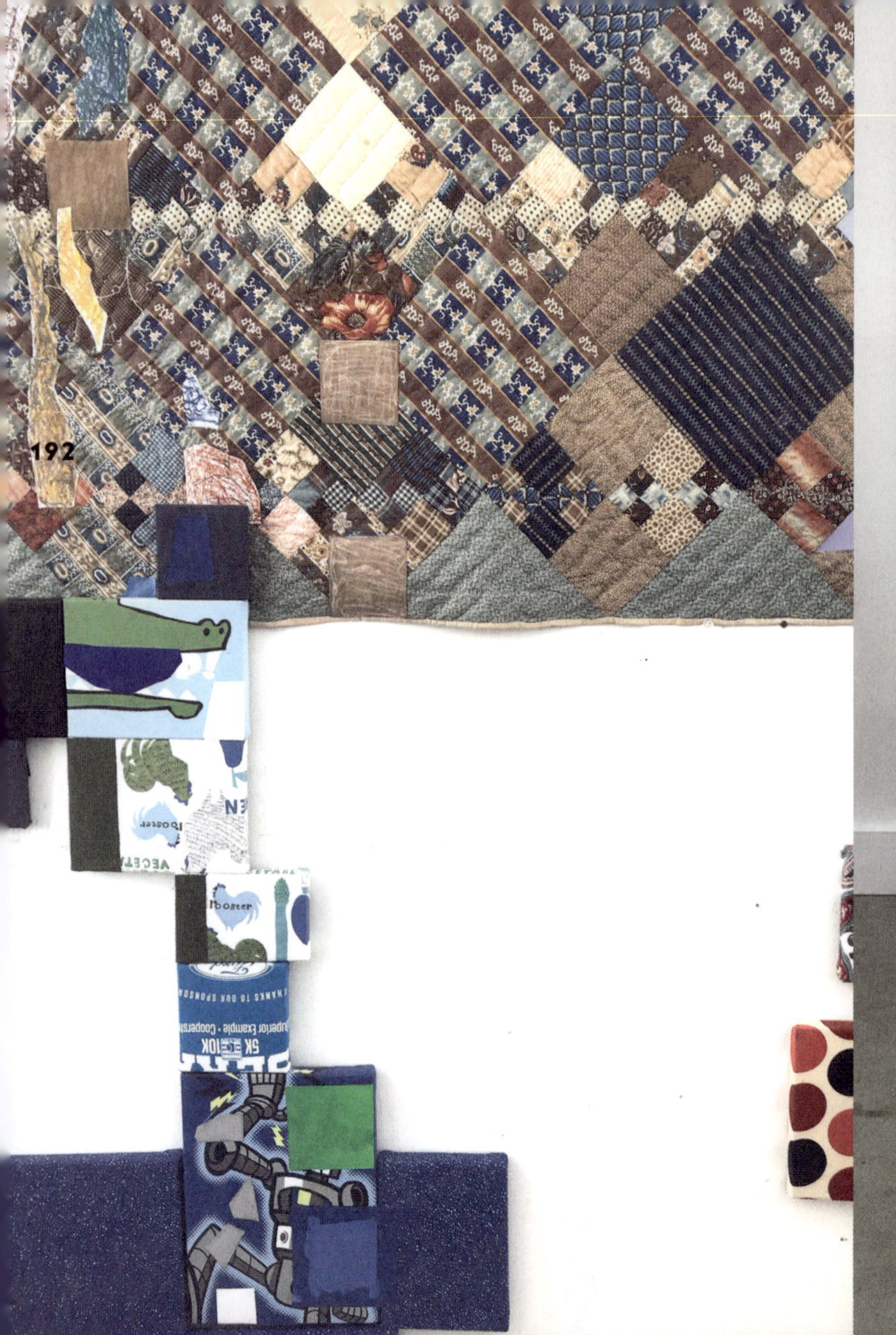

192
Rooster
VEGET
Rooster
THANKS TO OUR SPONSOR
Superior Example · Cooperst

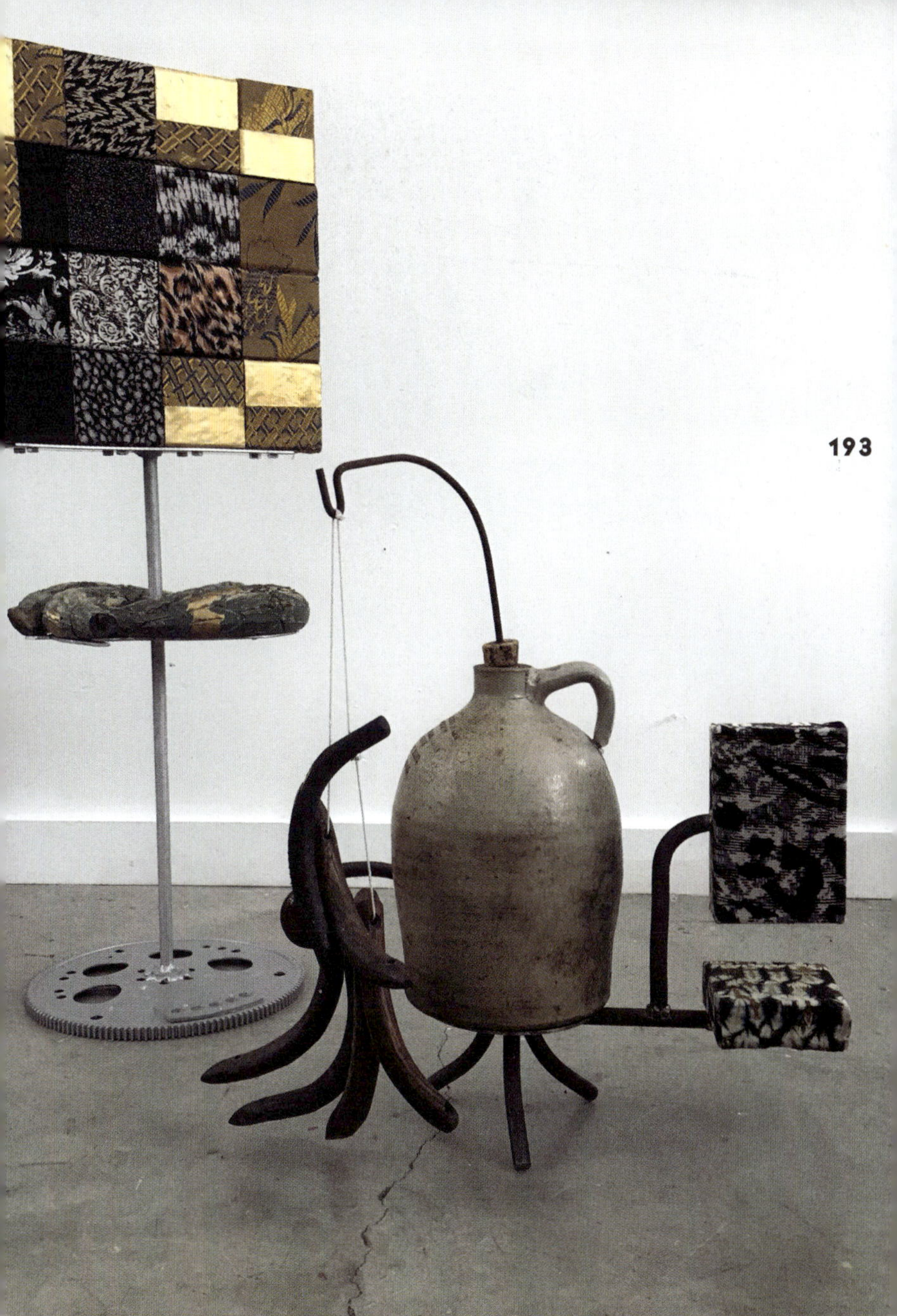

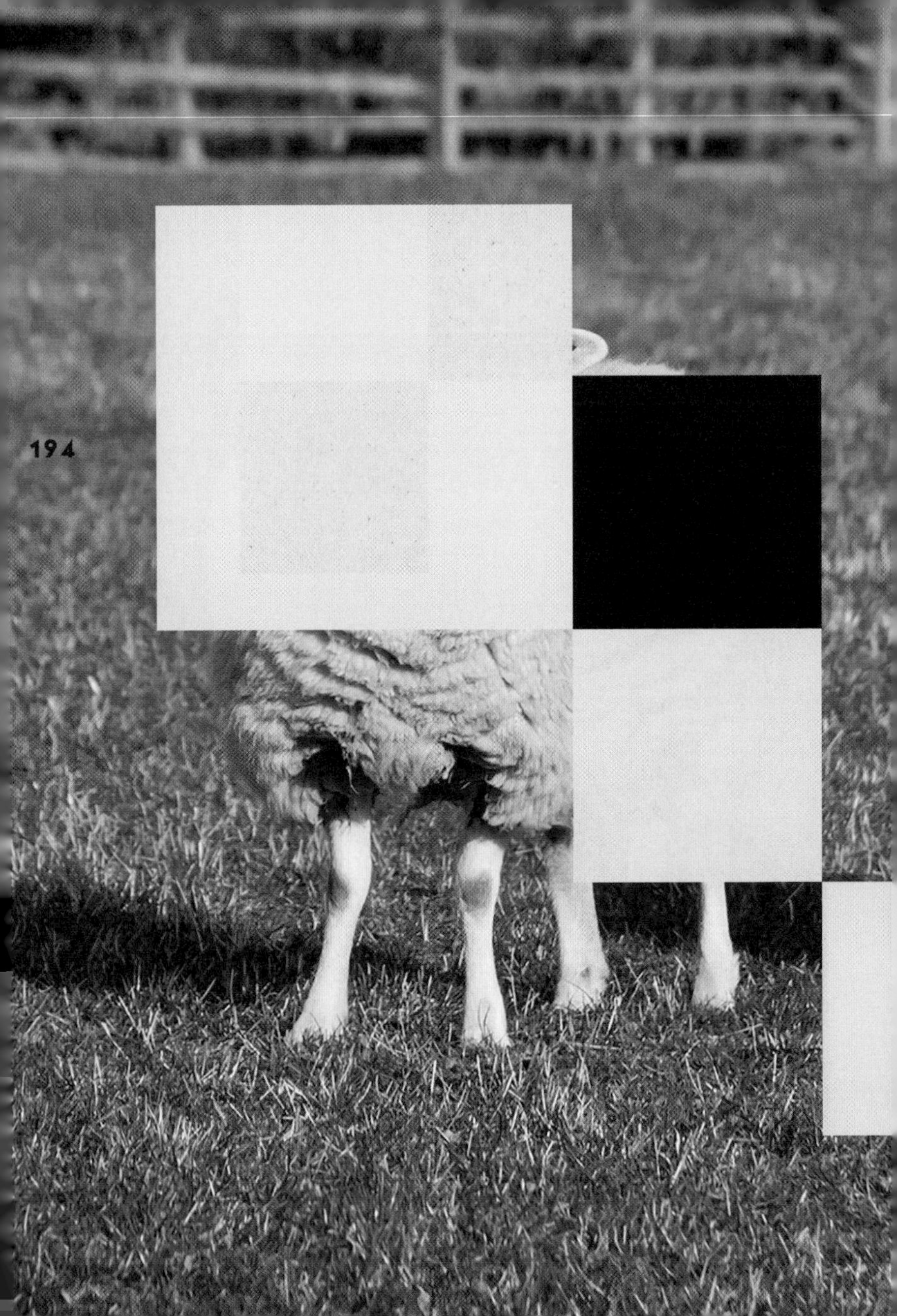

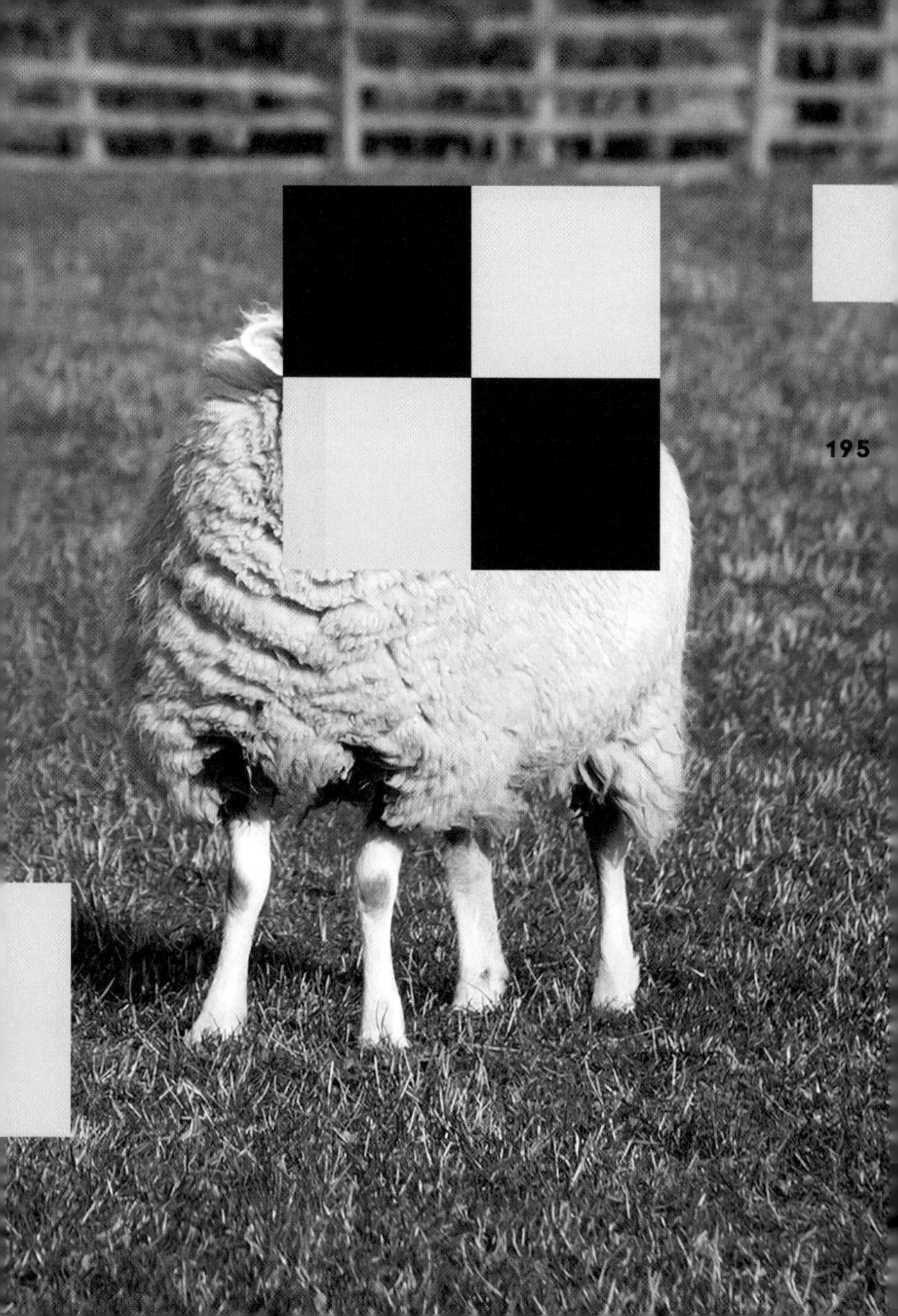

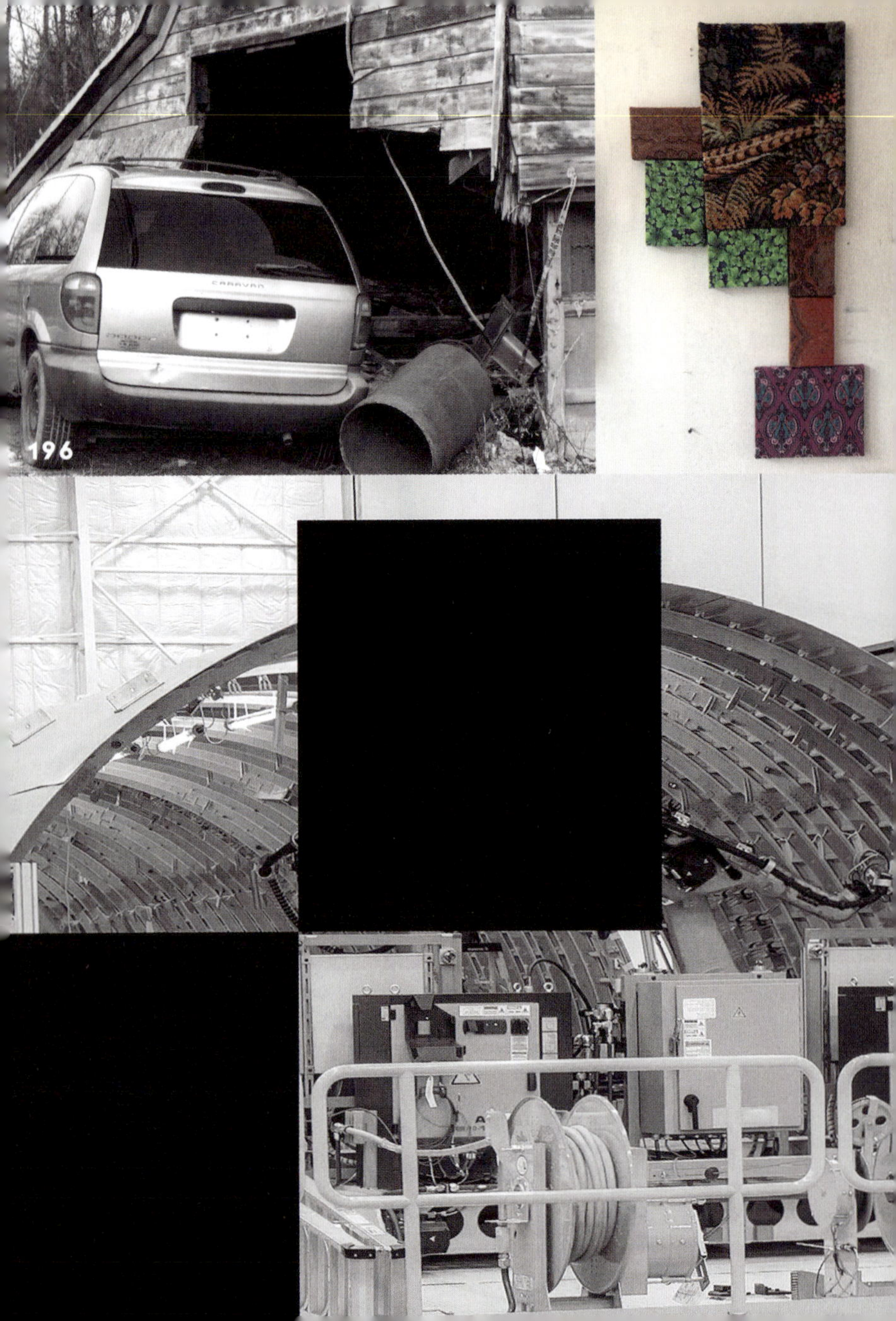
196

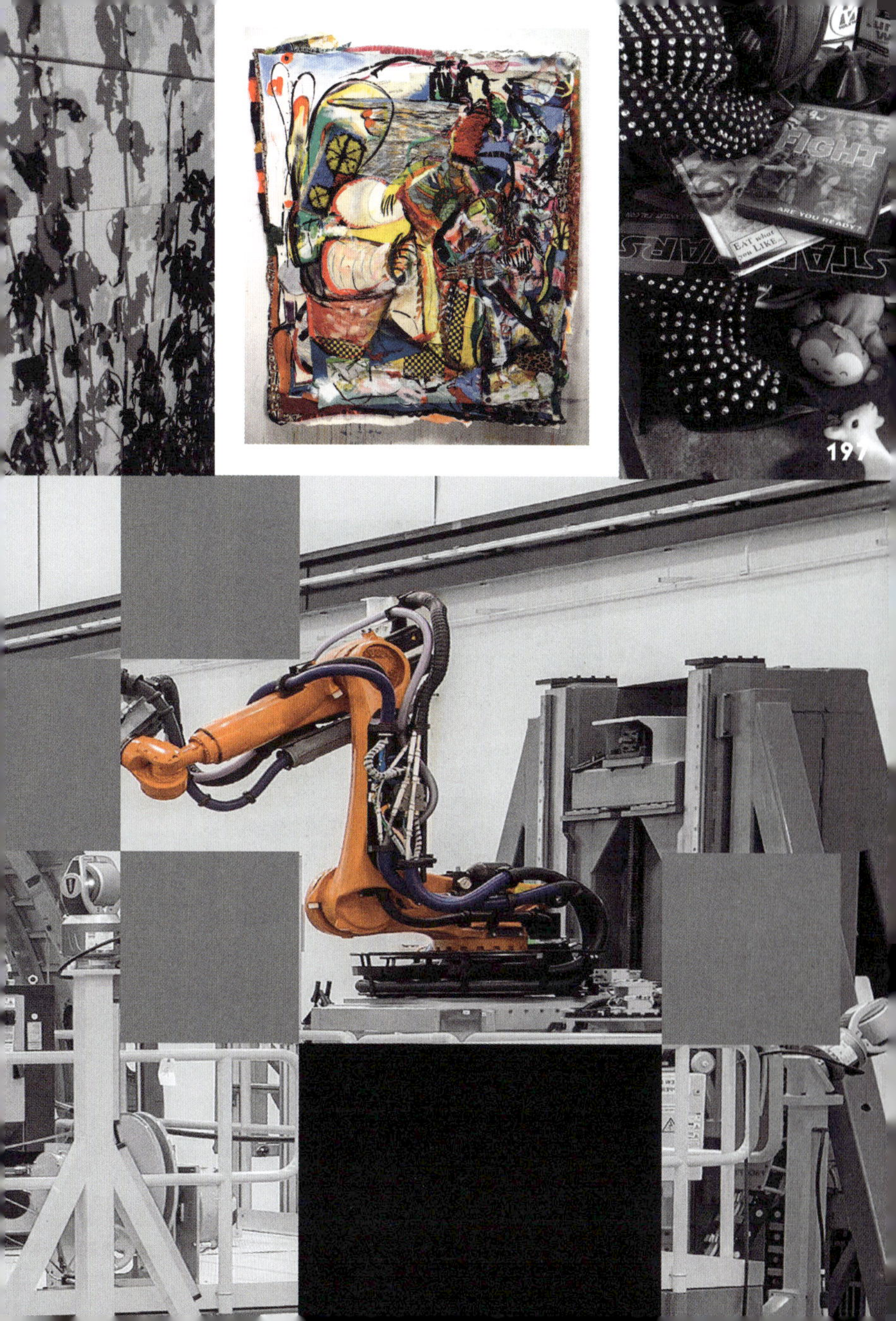

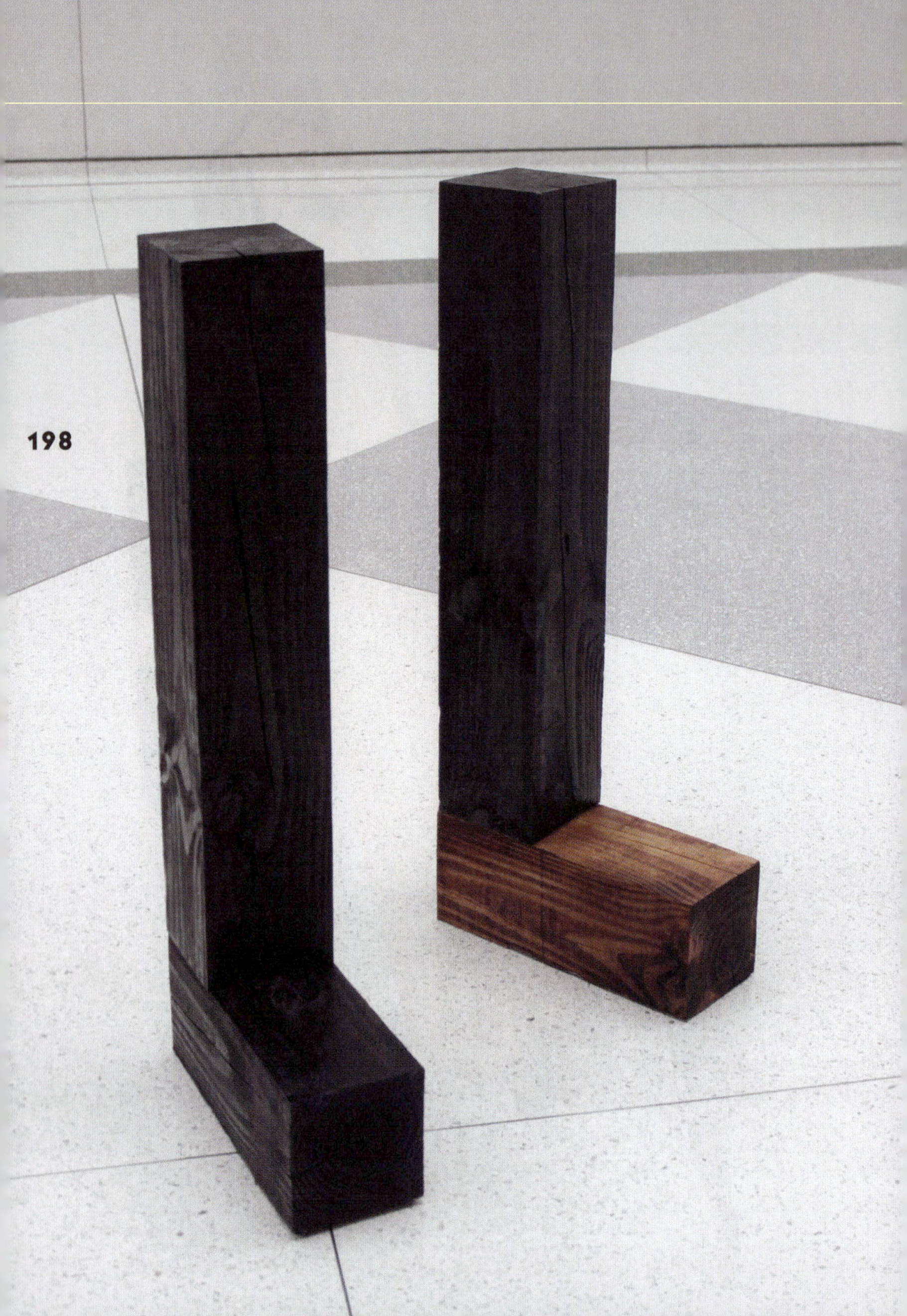

198

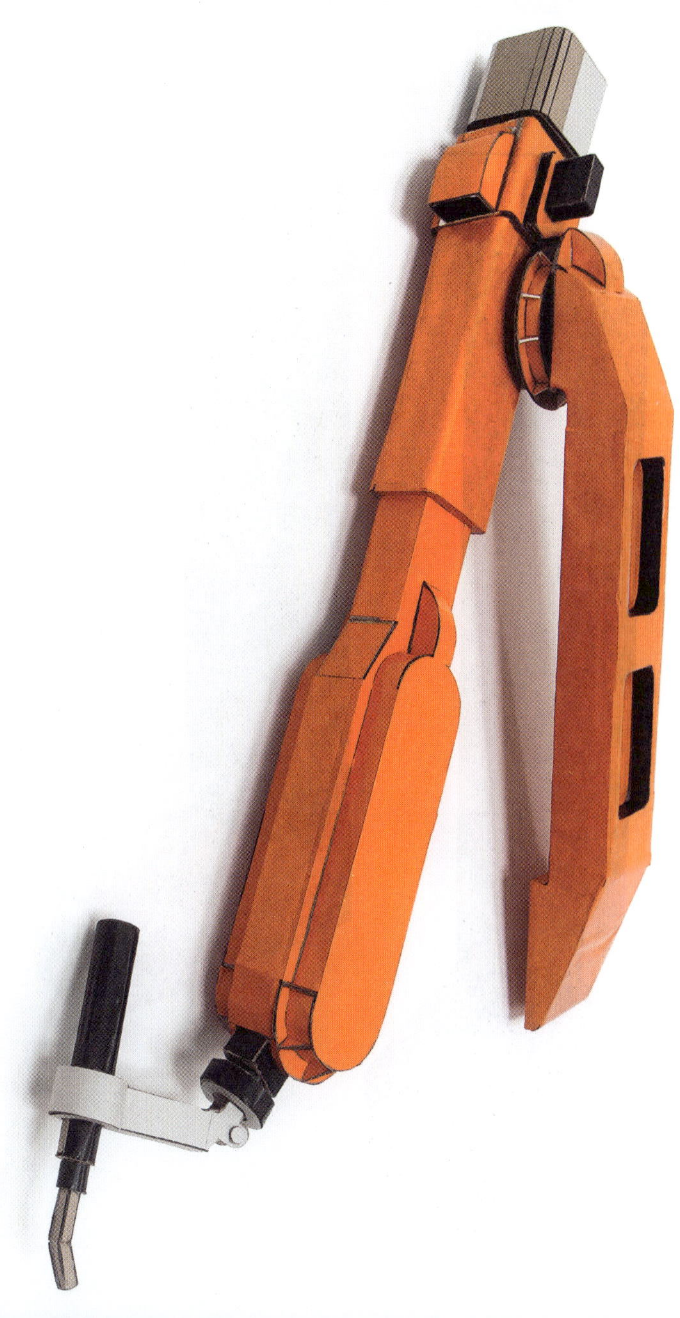

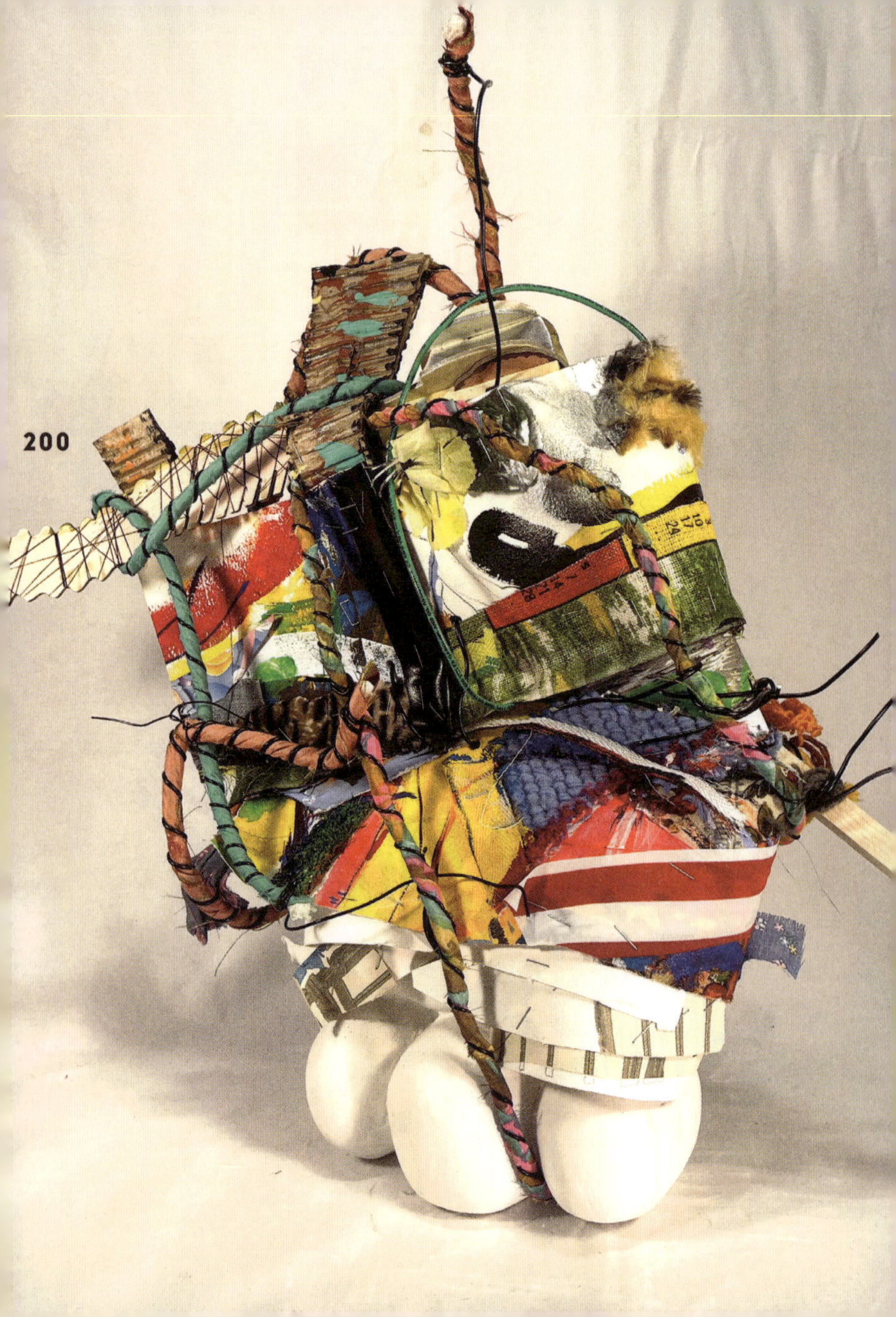

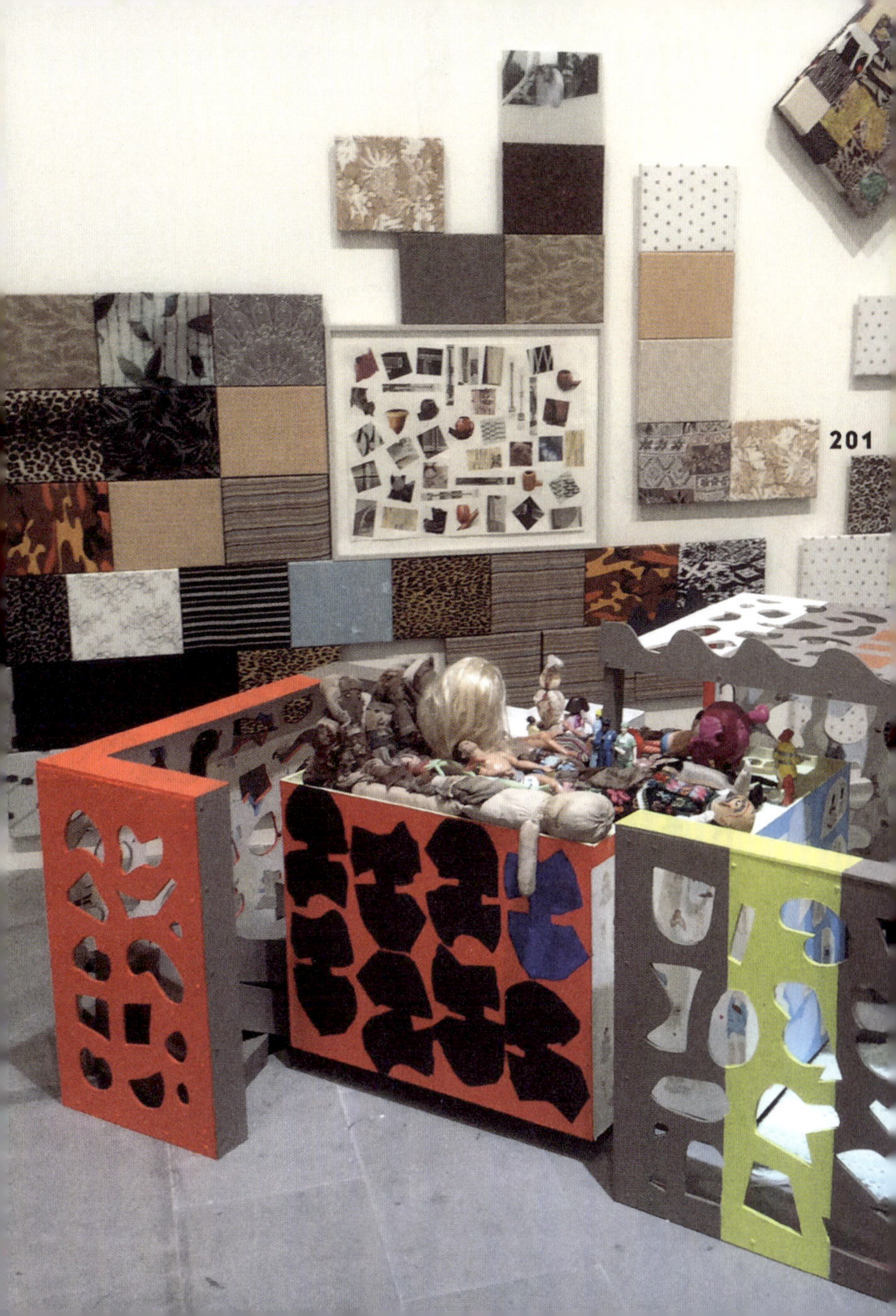
201

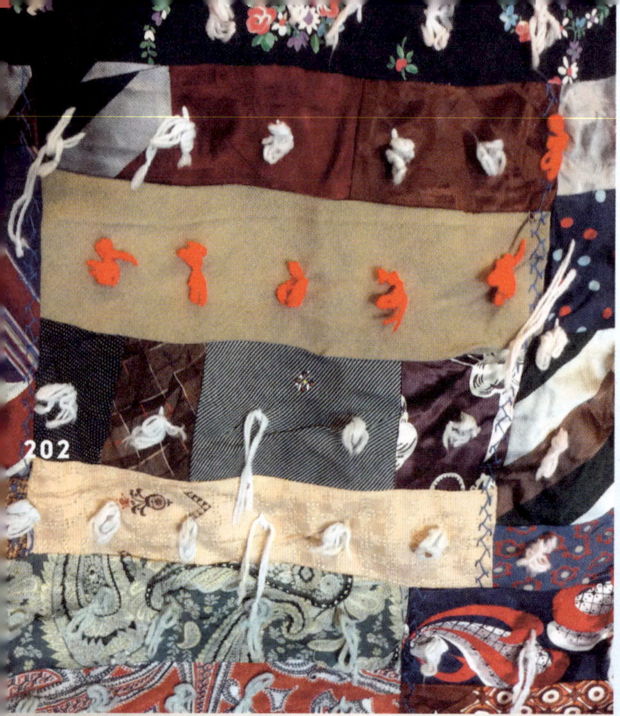

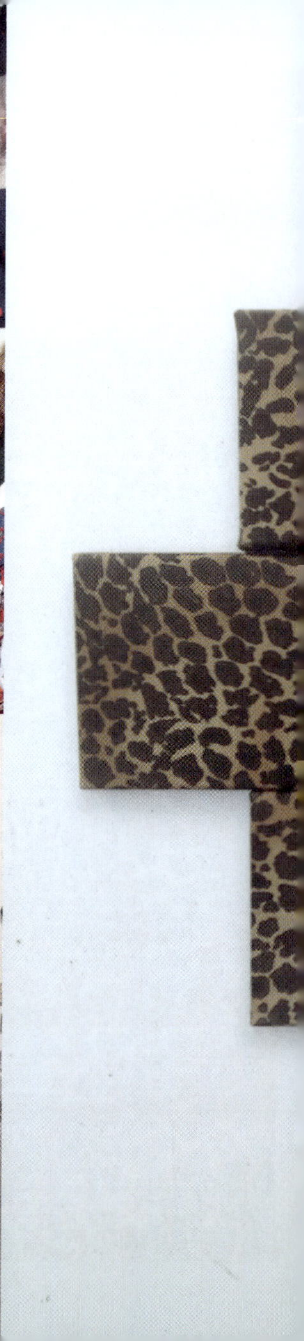

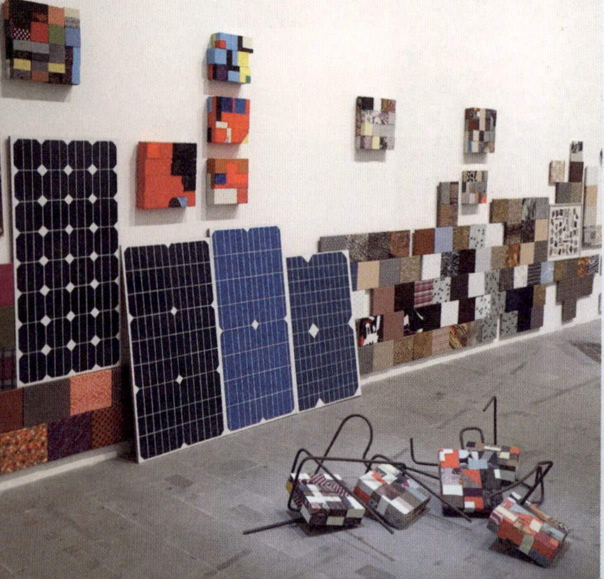
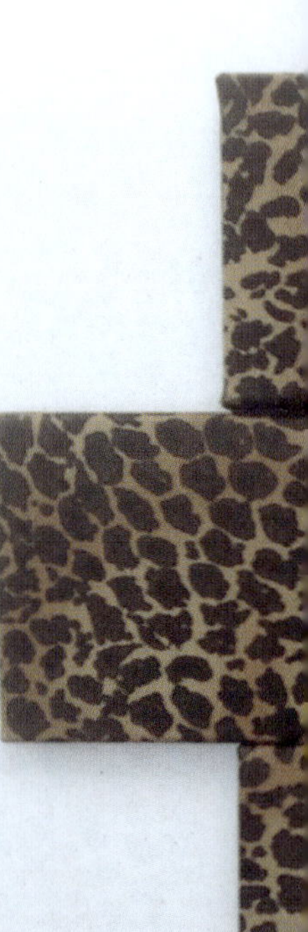

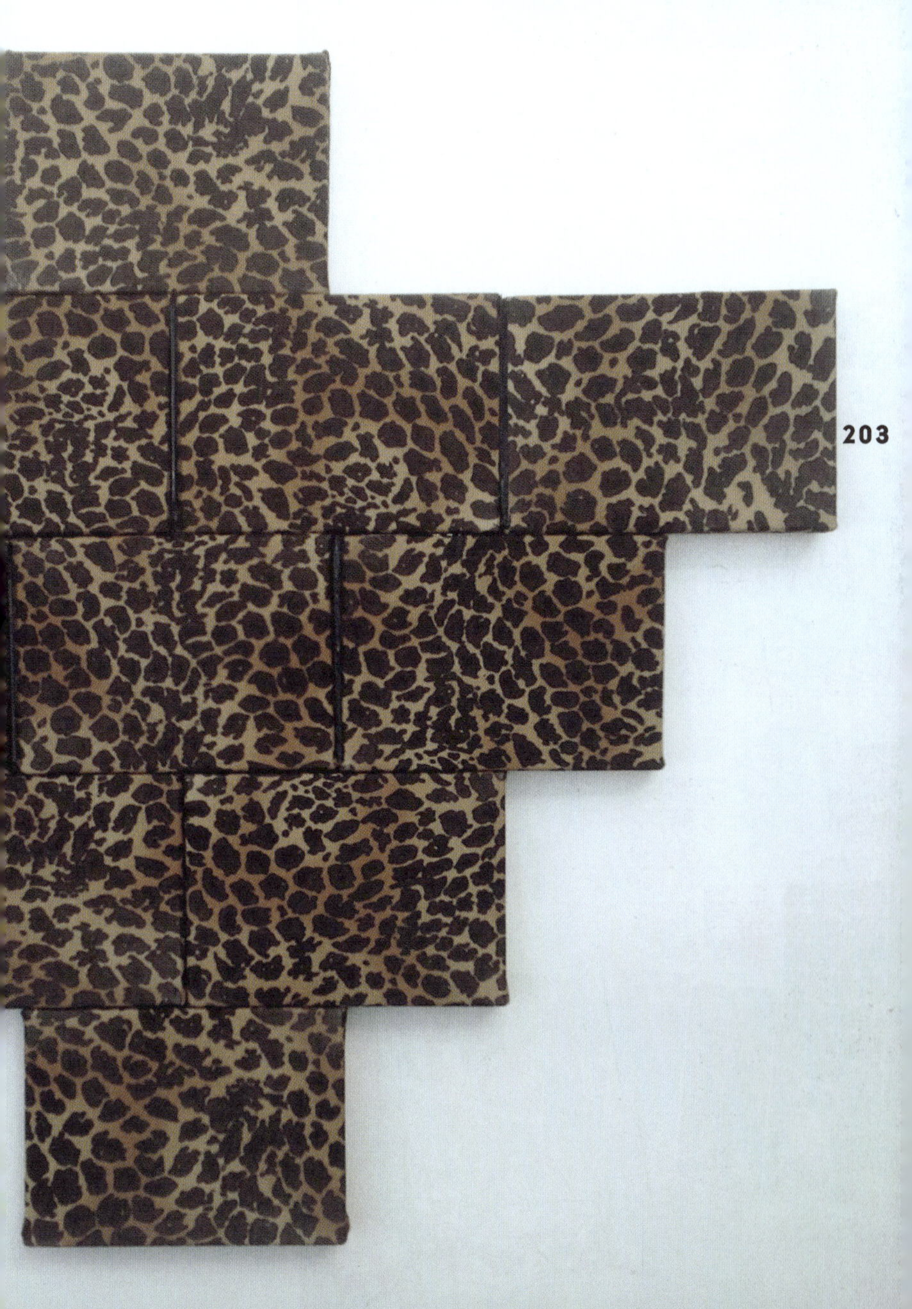
203

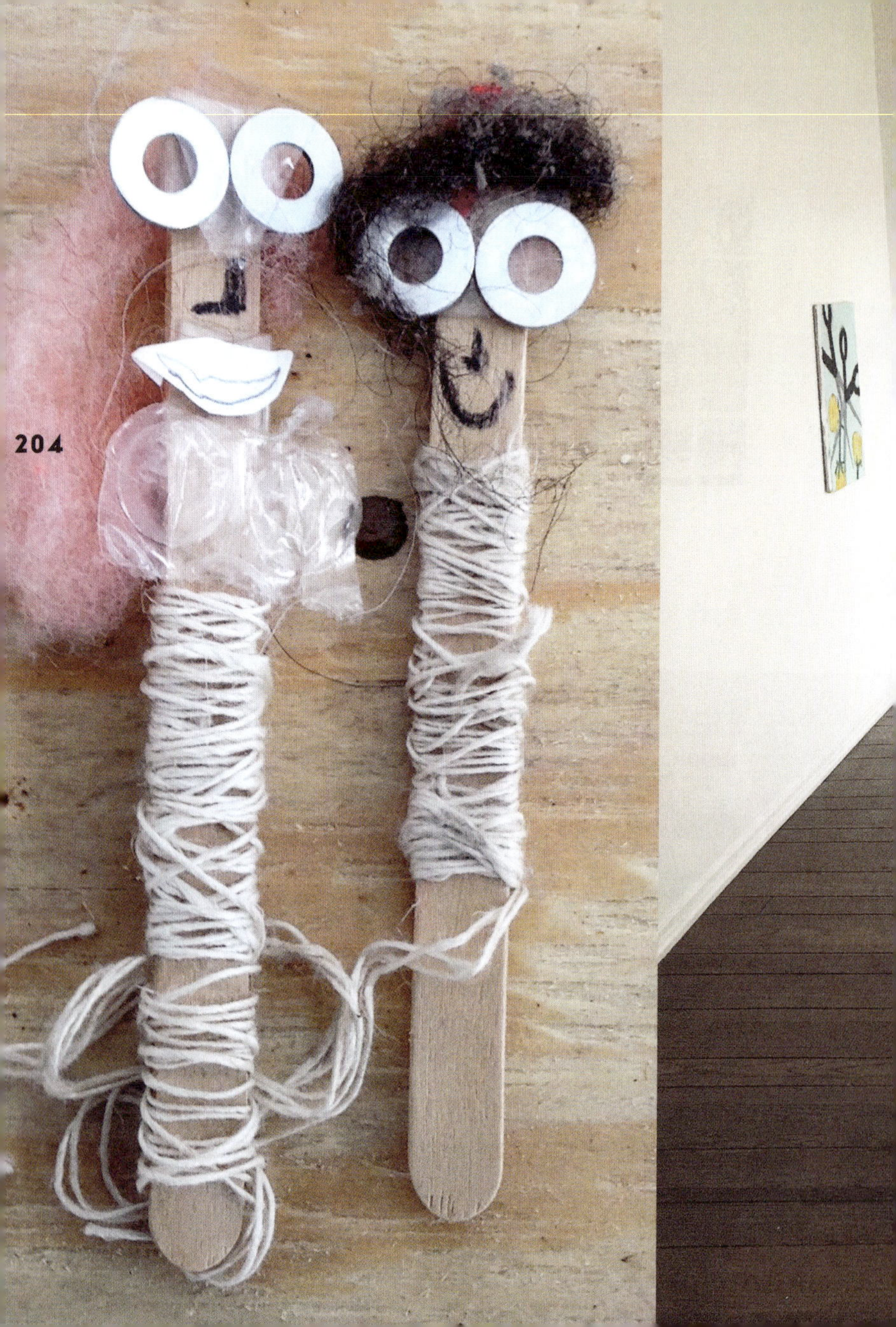

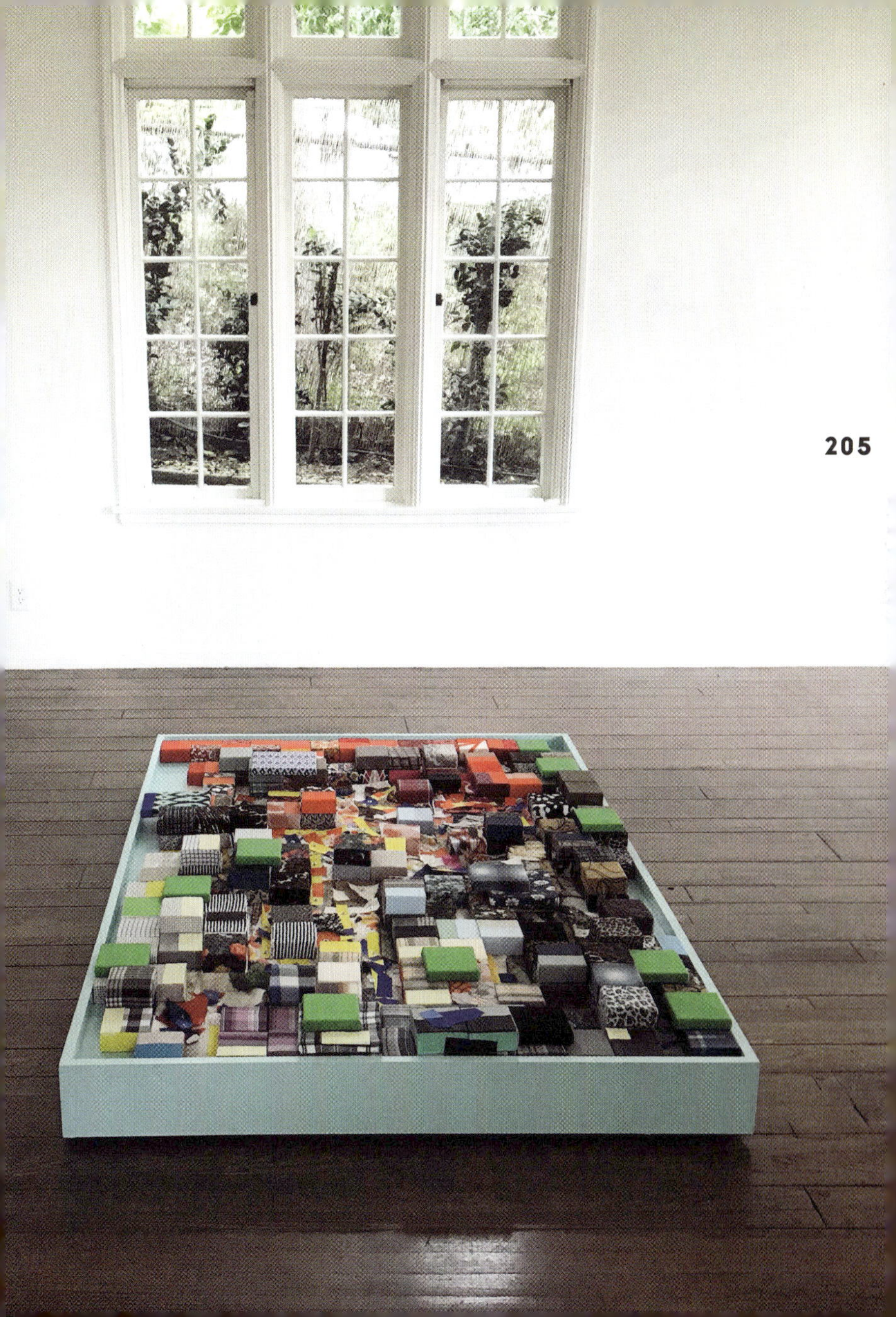

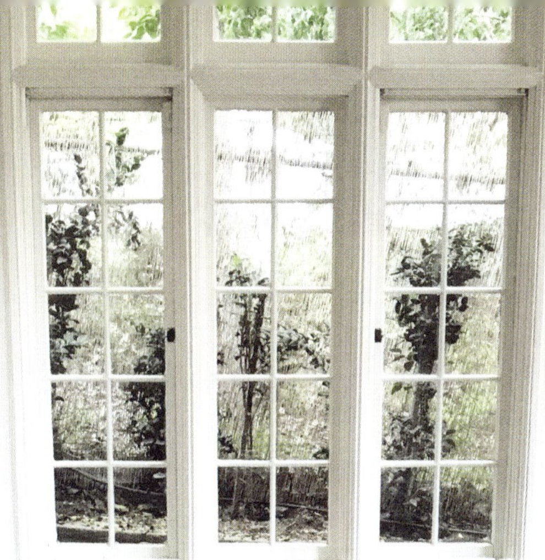

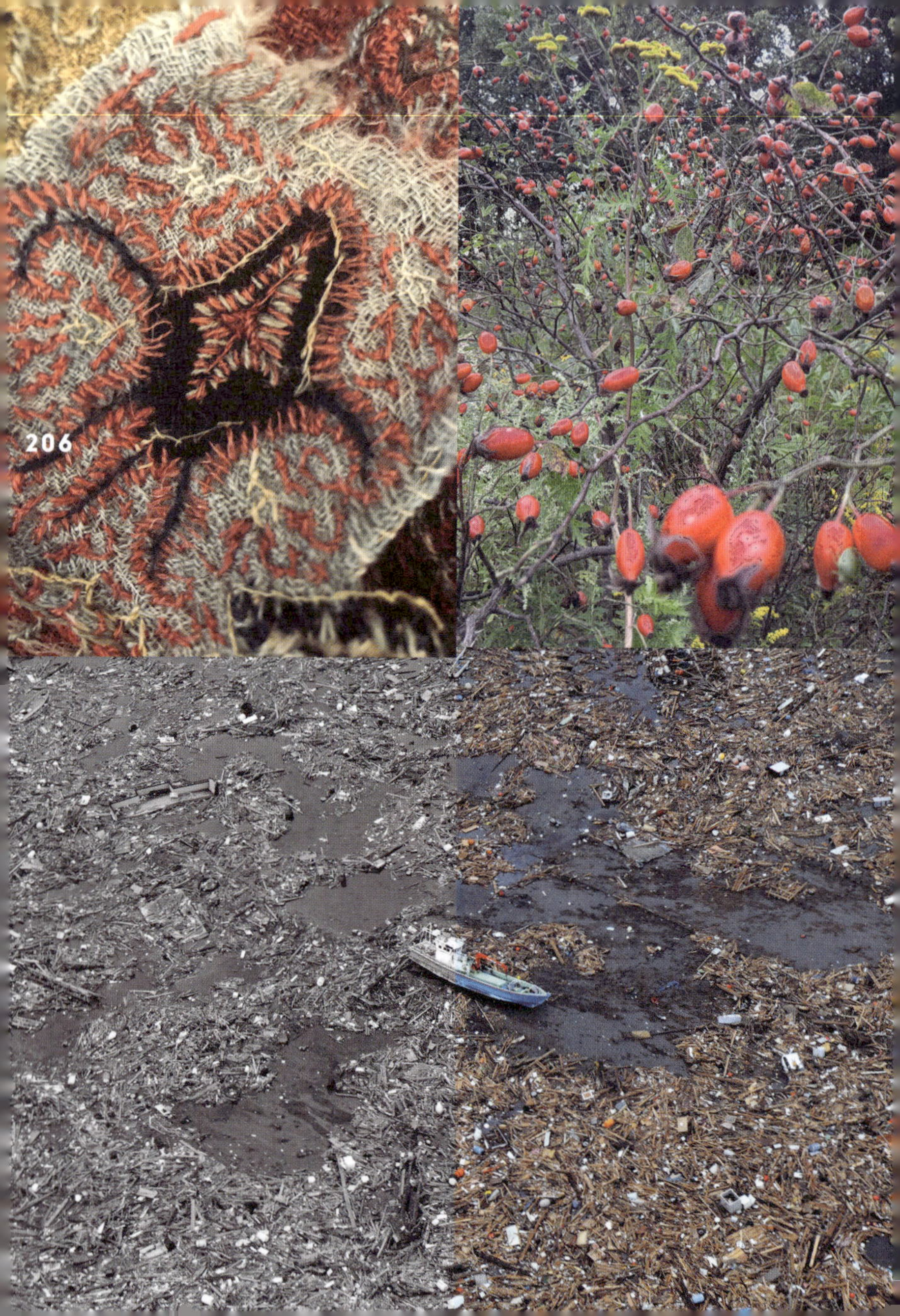
206

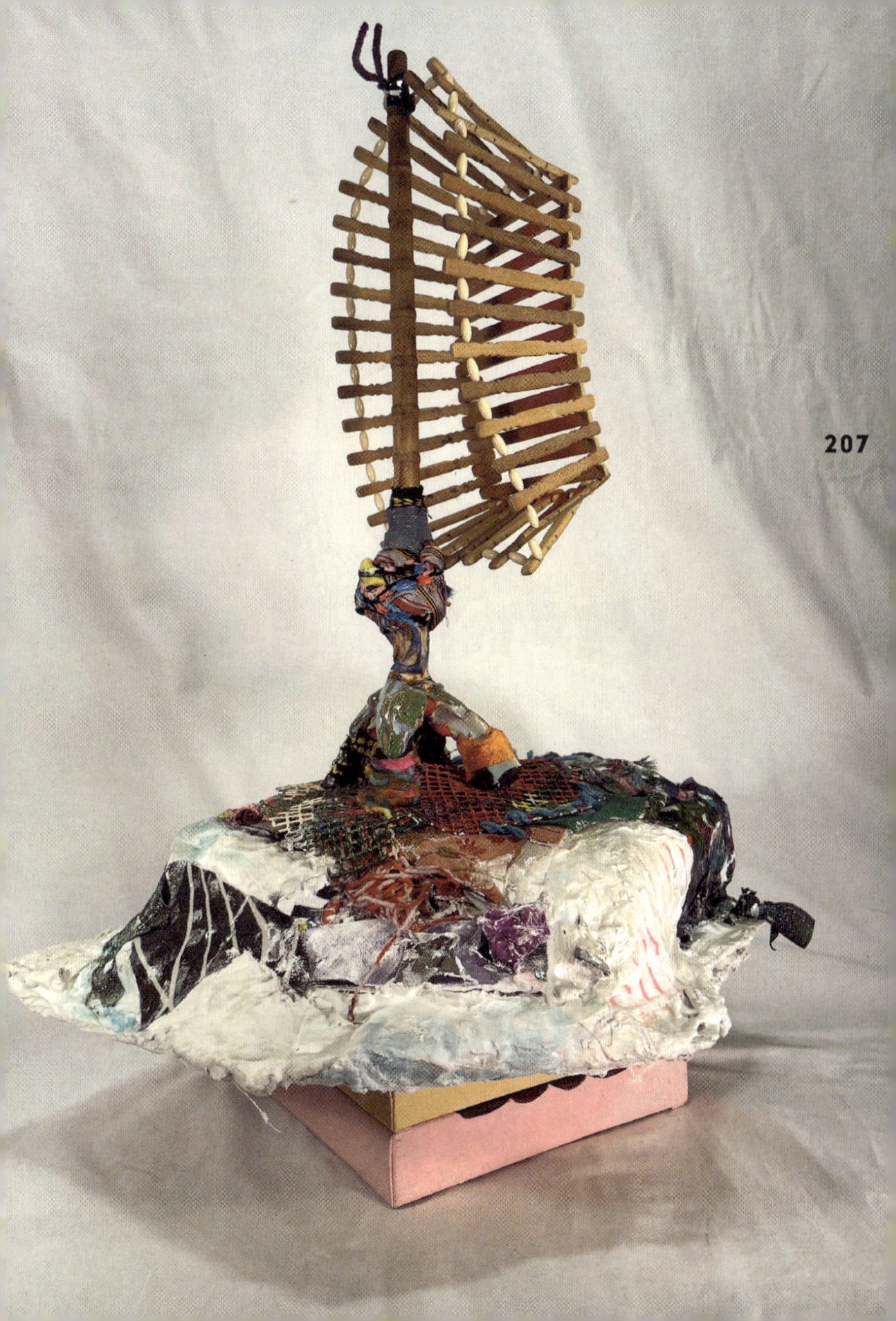

207

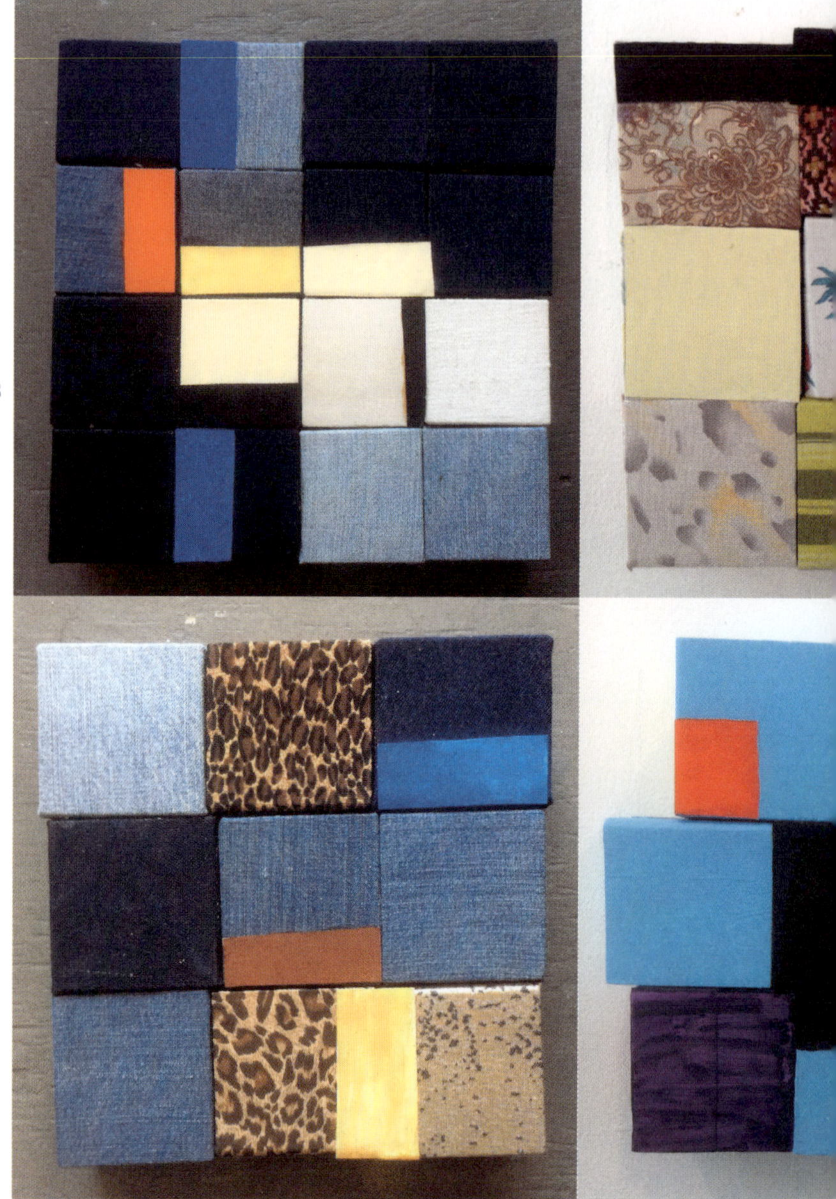

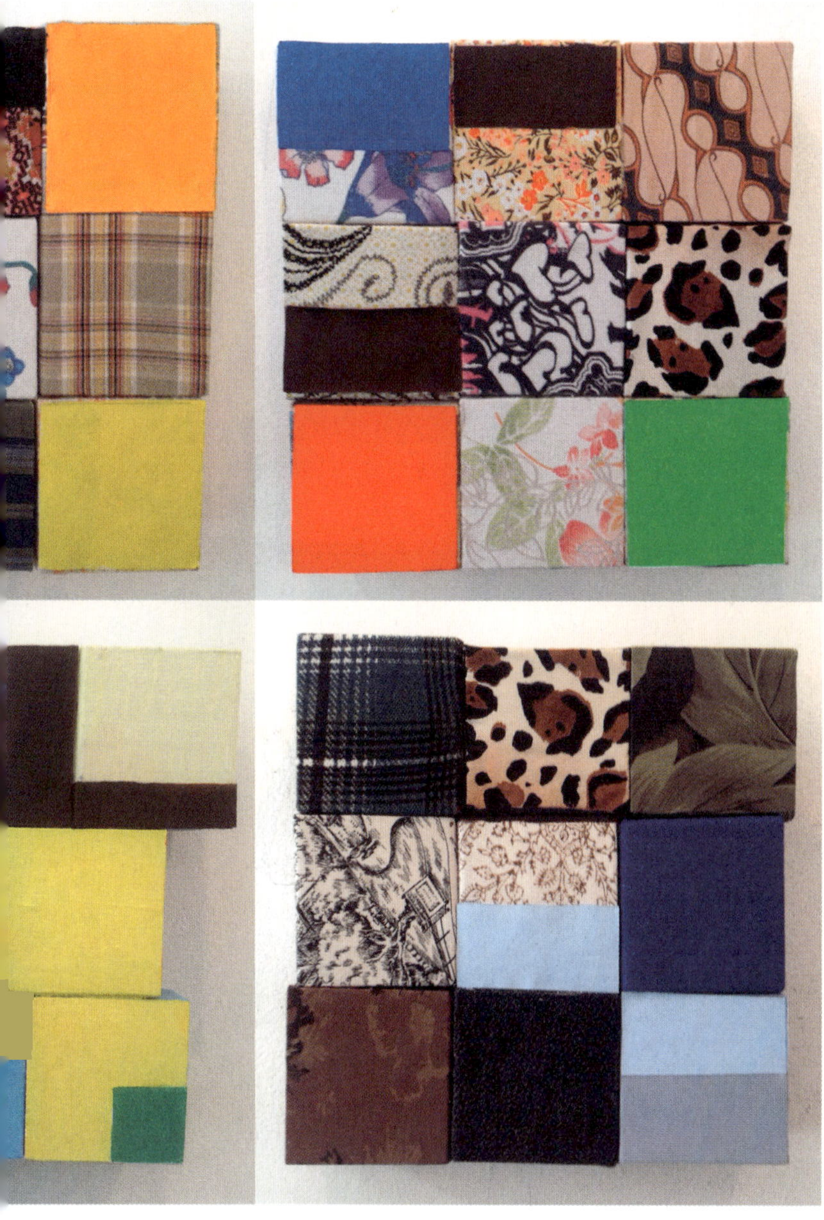

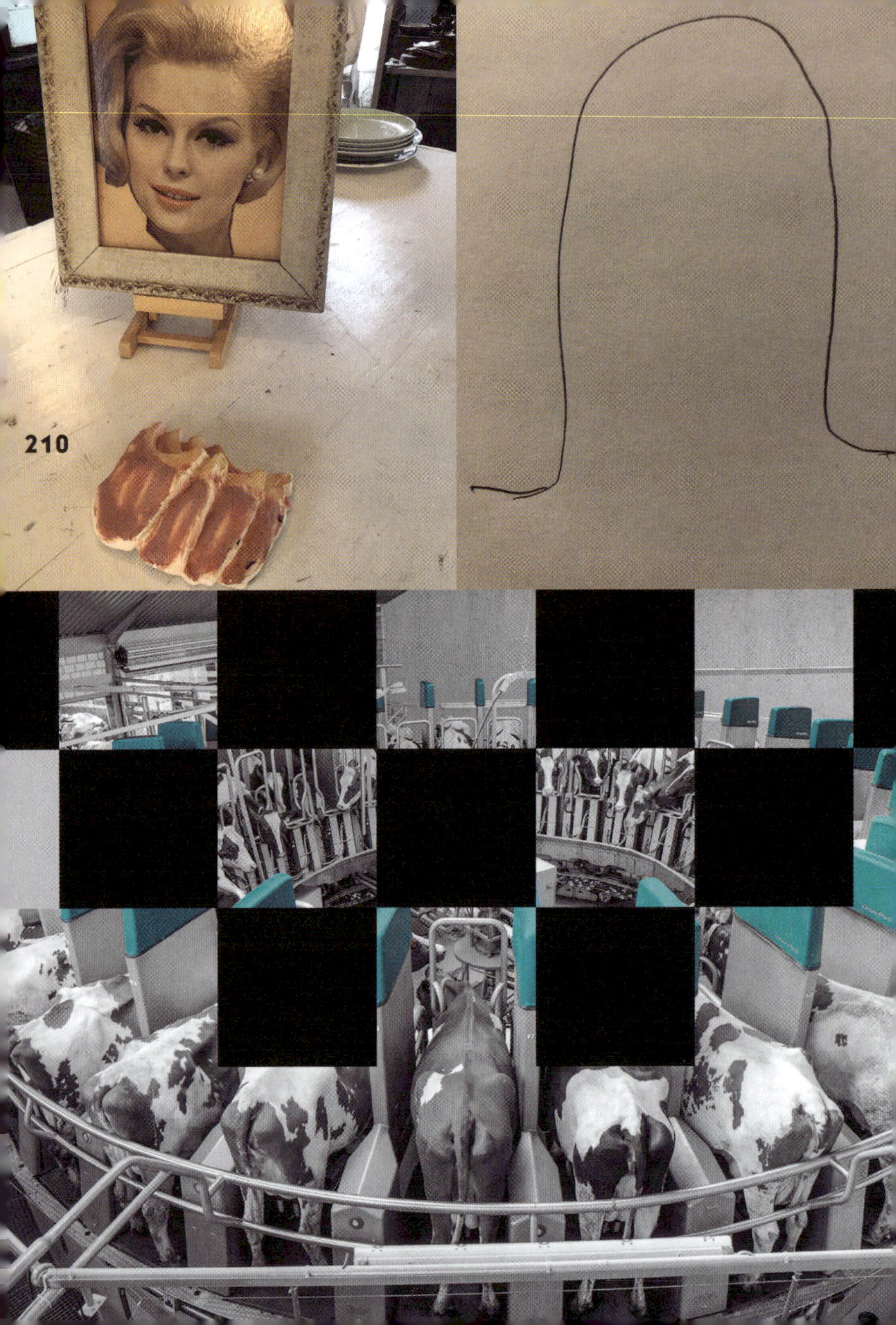
210

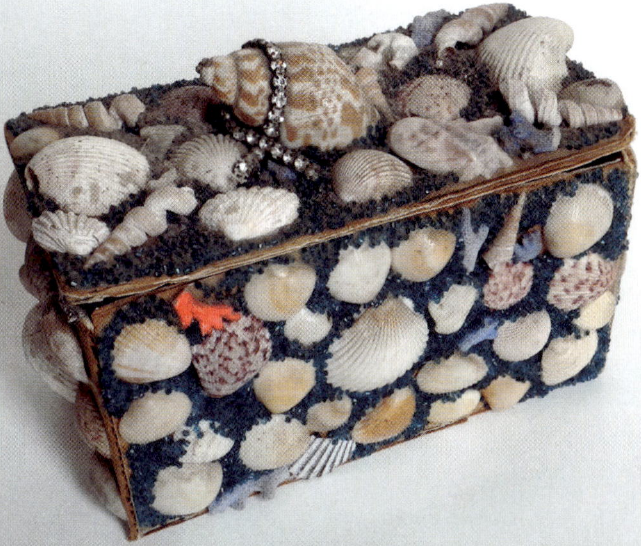

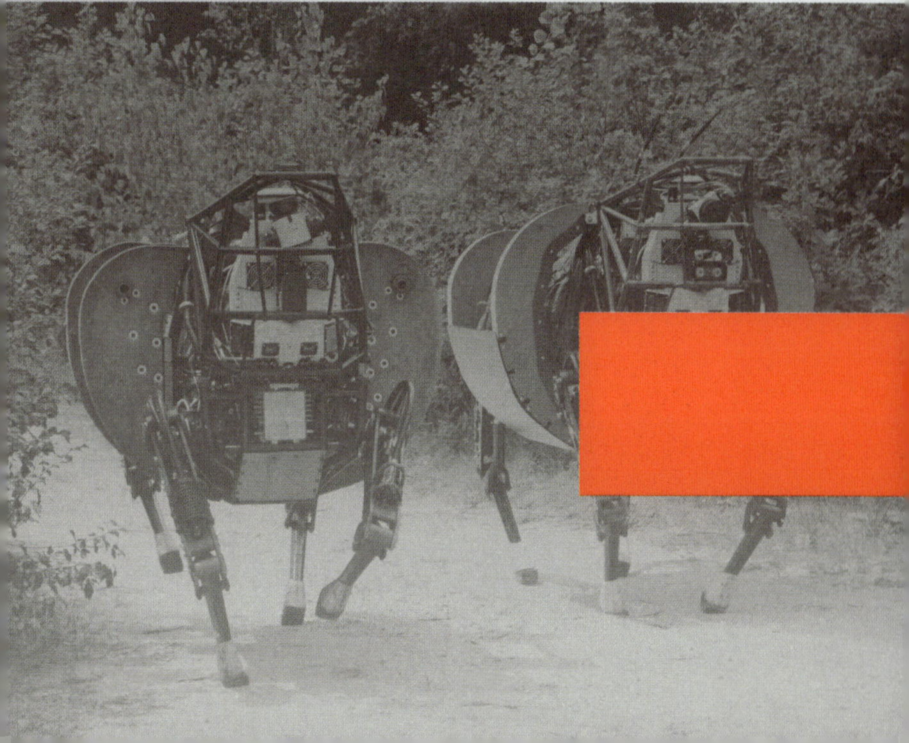

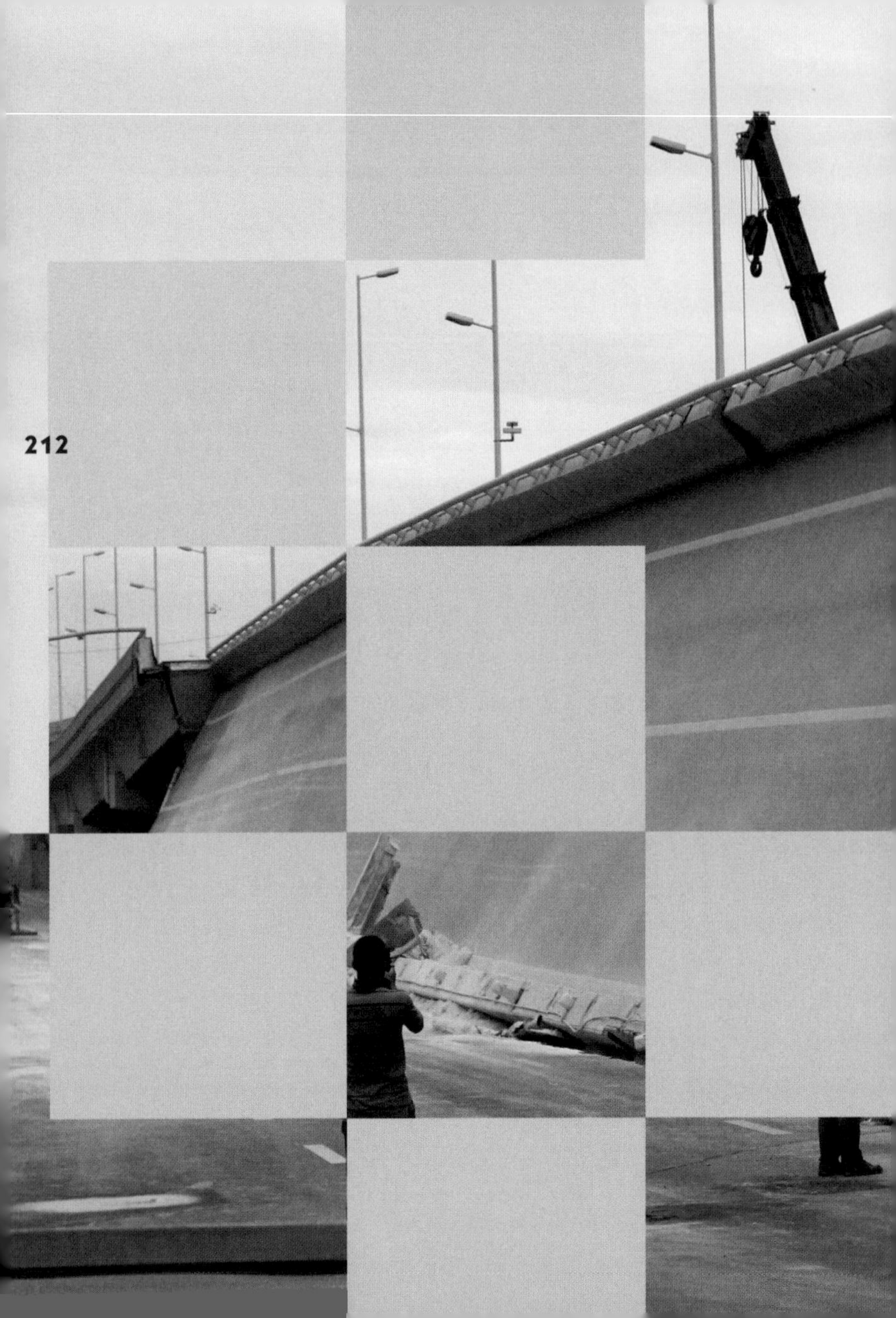

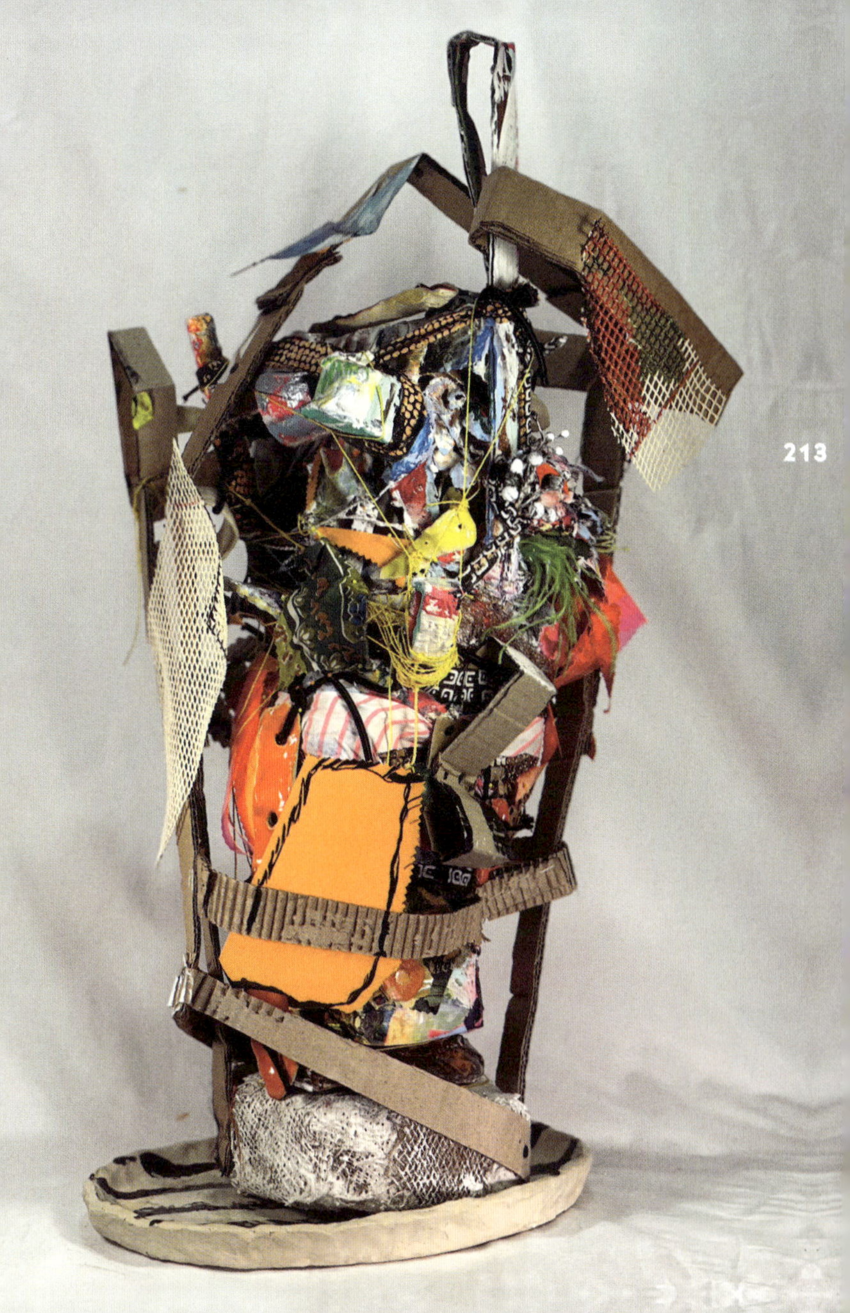

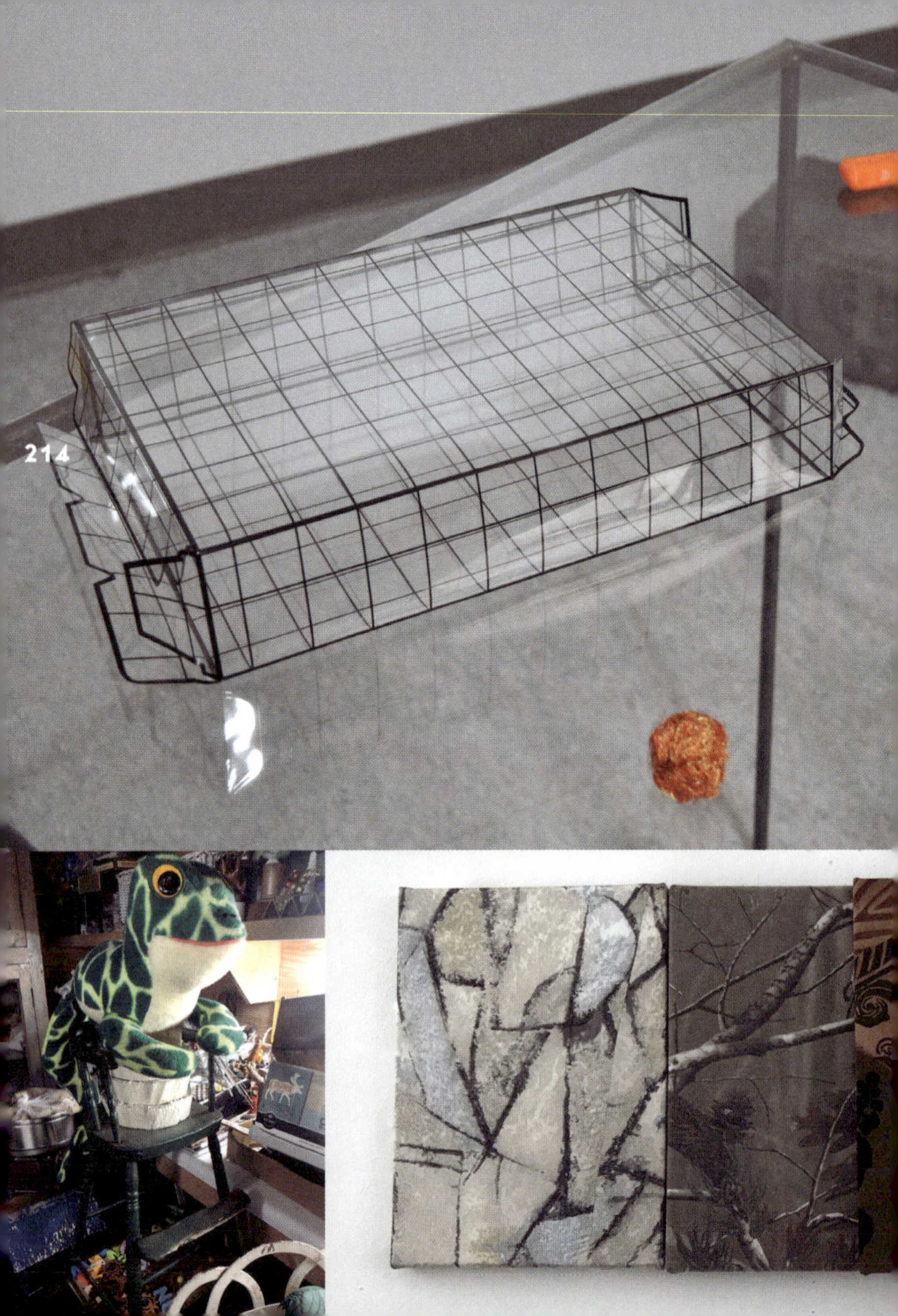
214

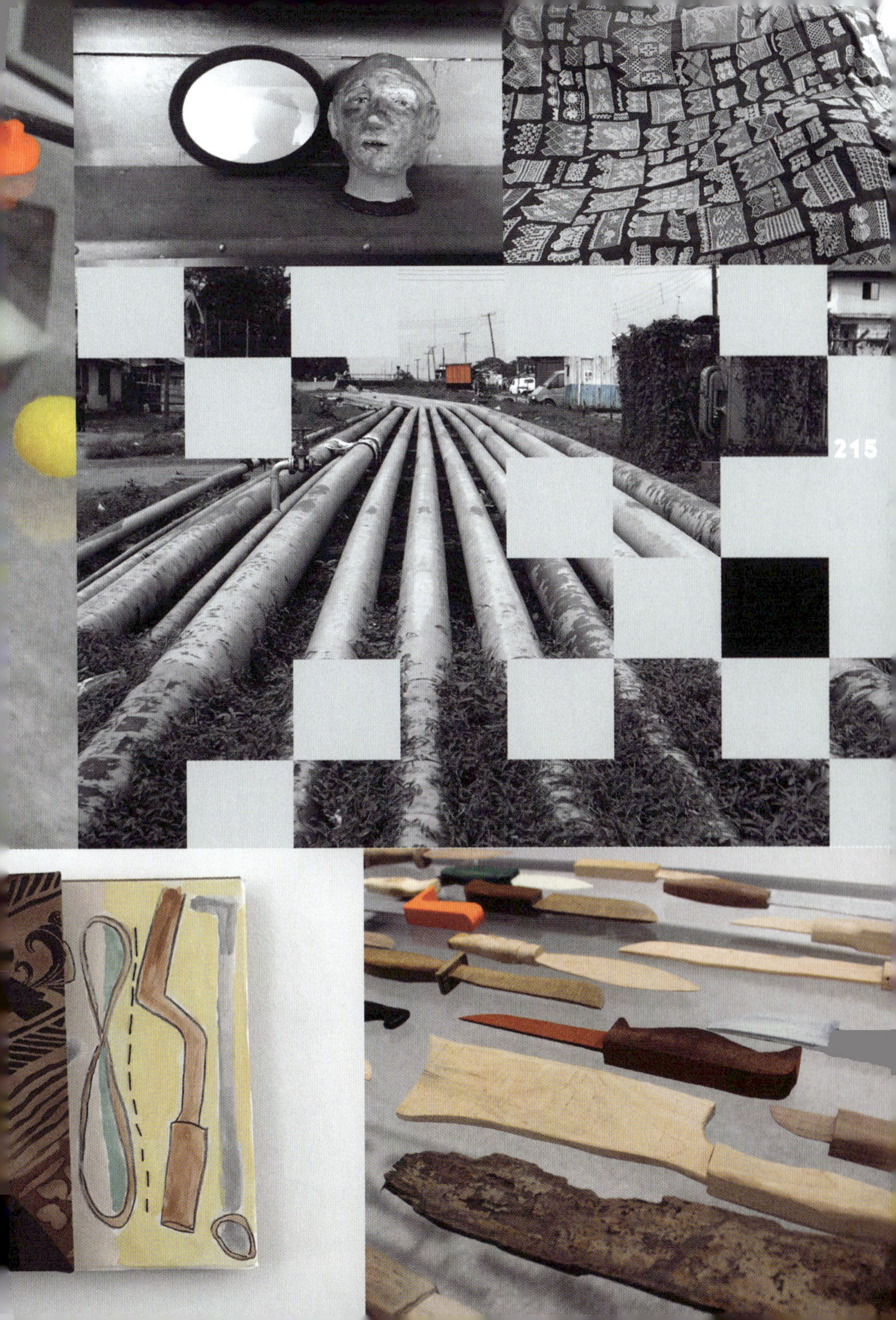

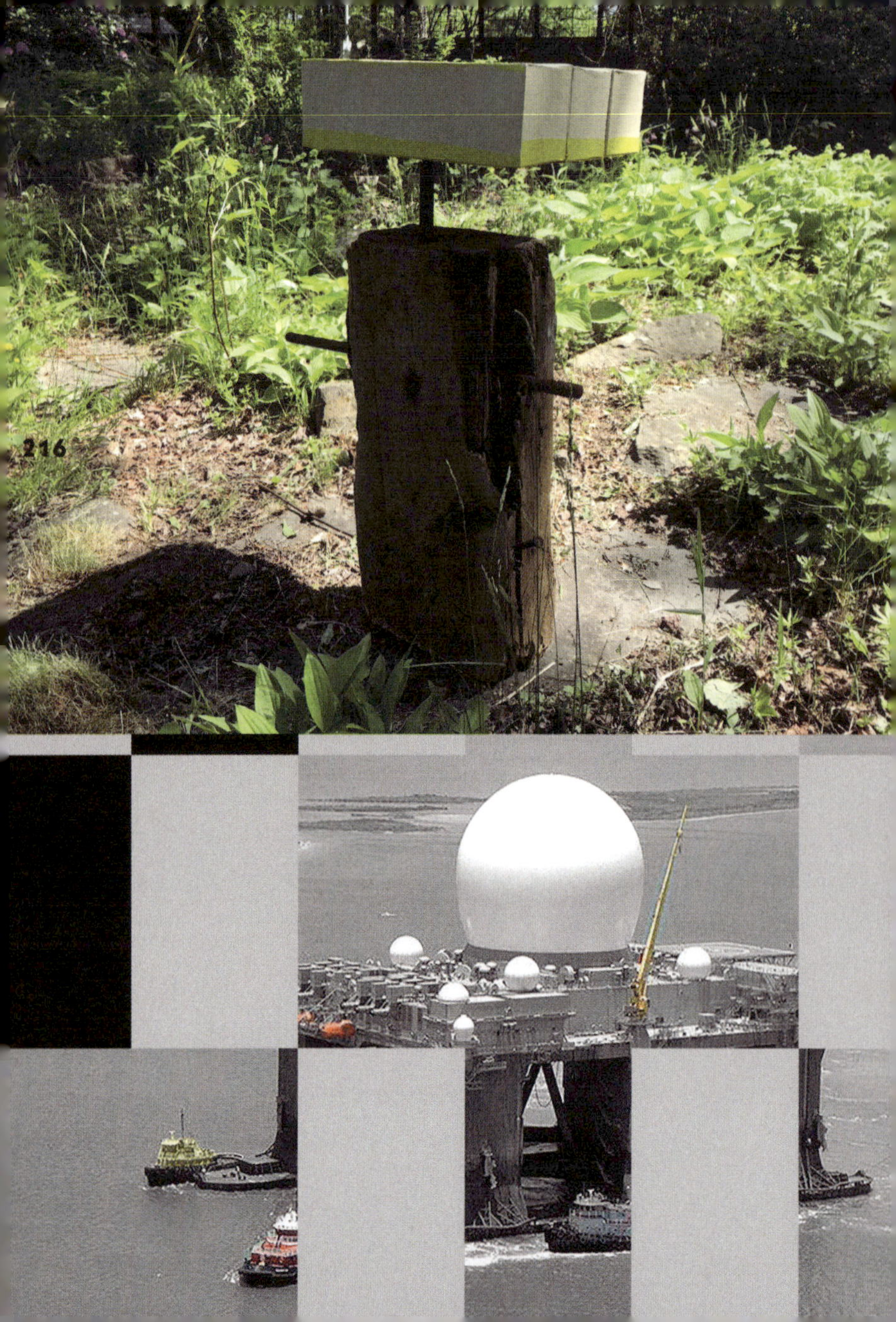
216

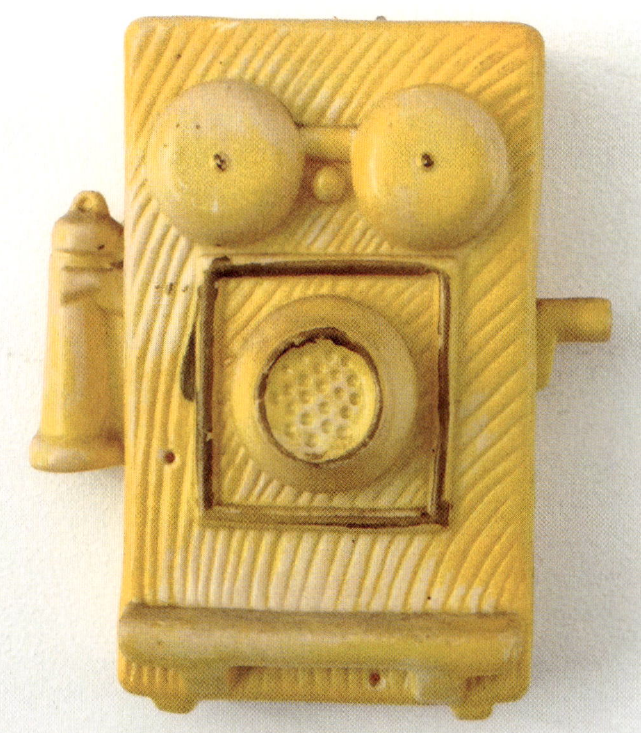

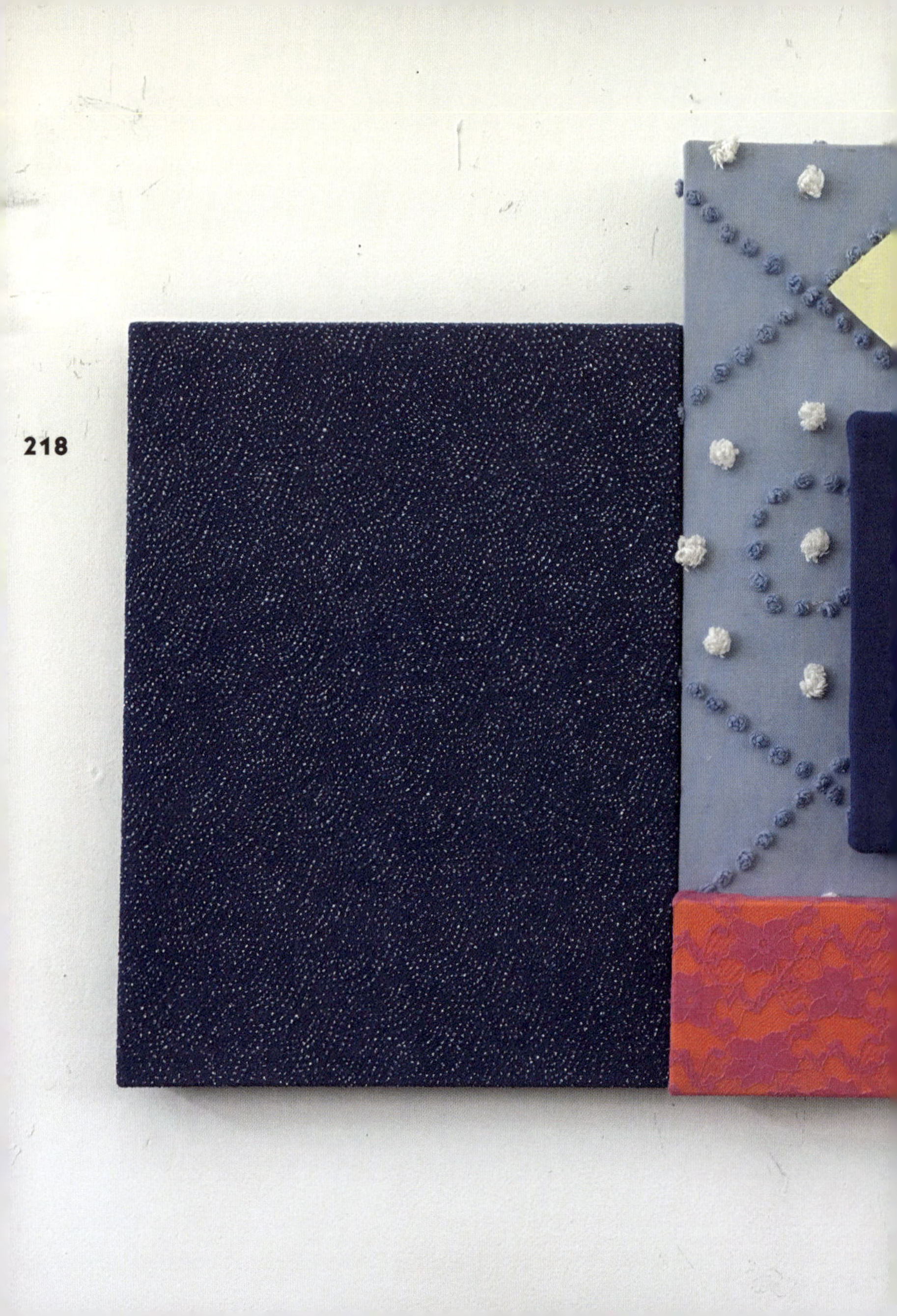

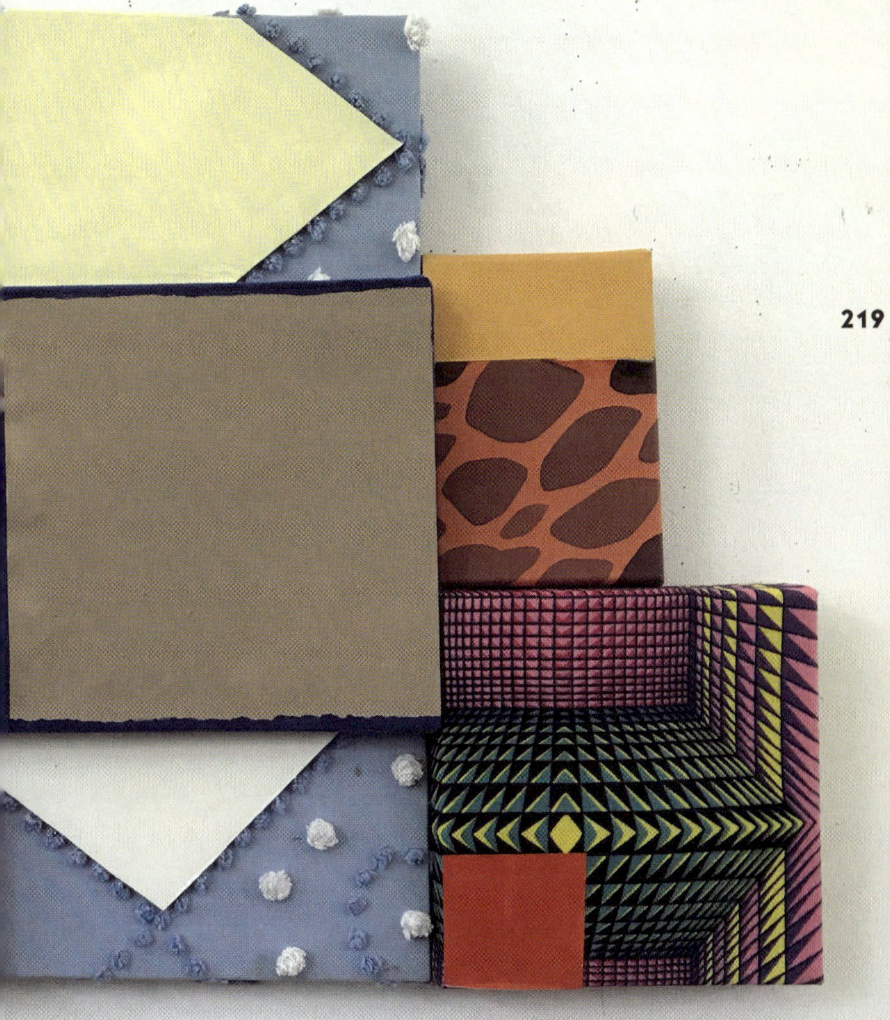

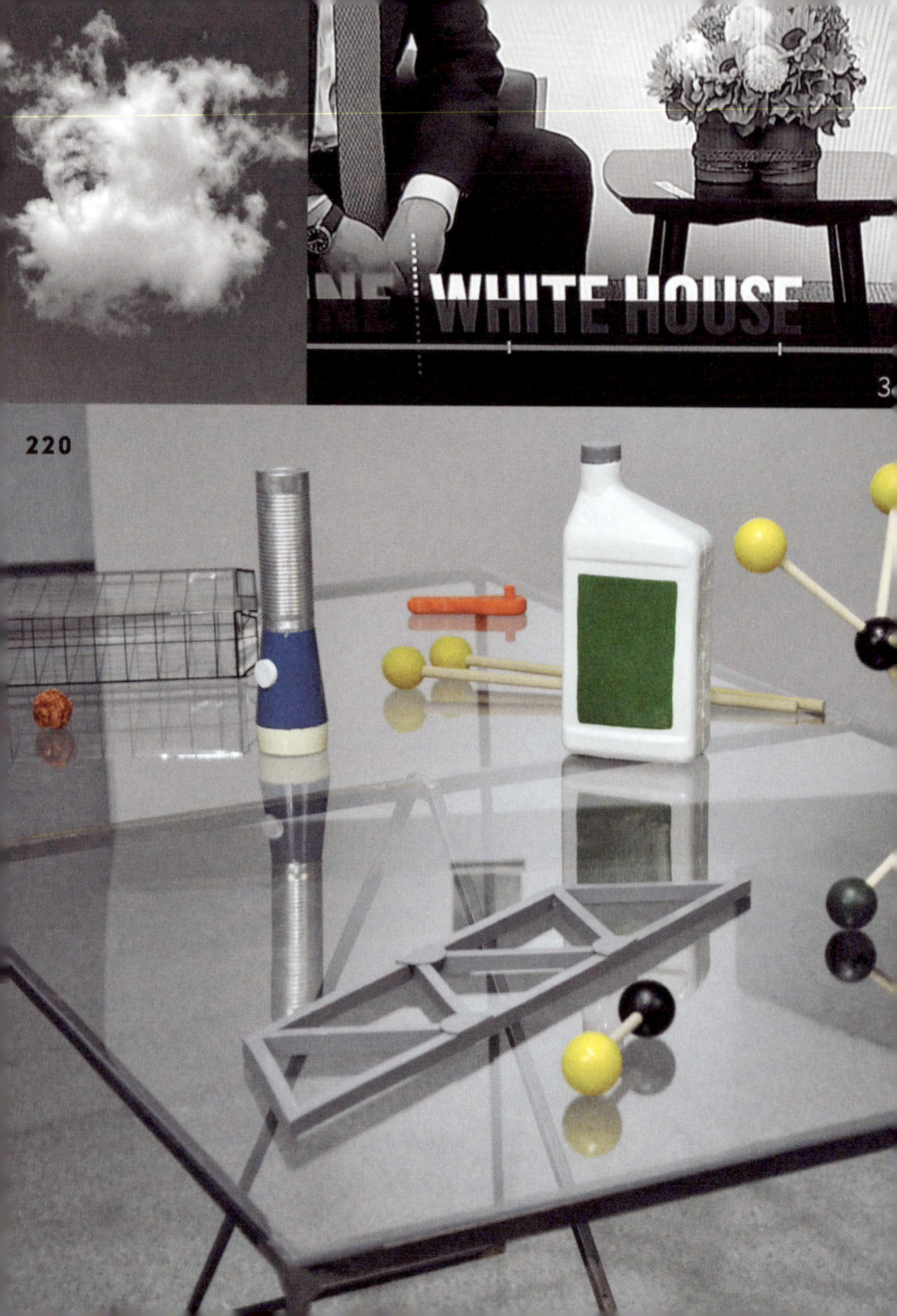
220
WHITE HOUSE

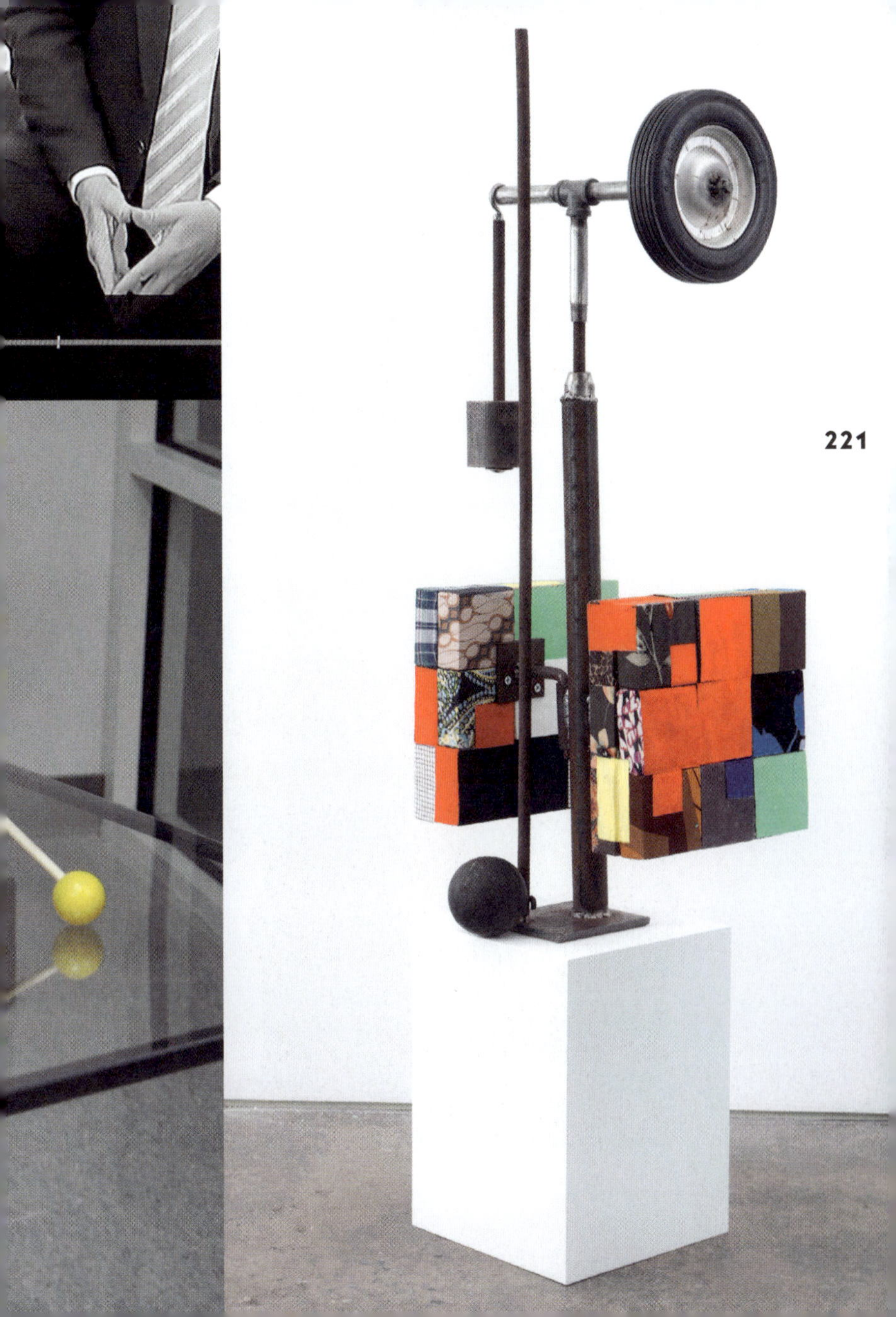

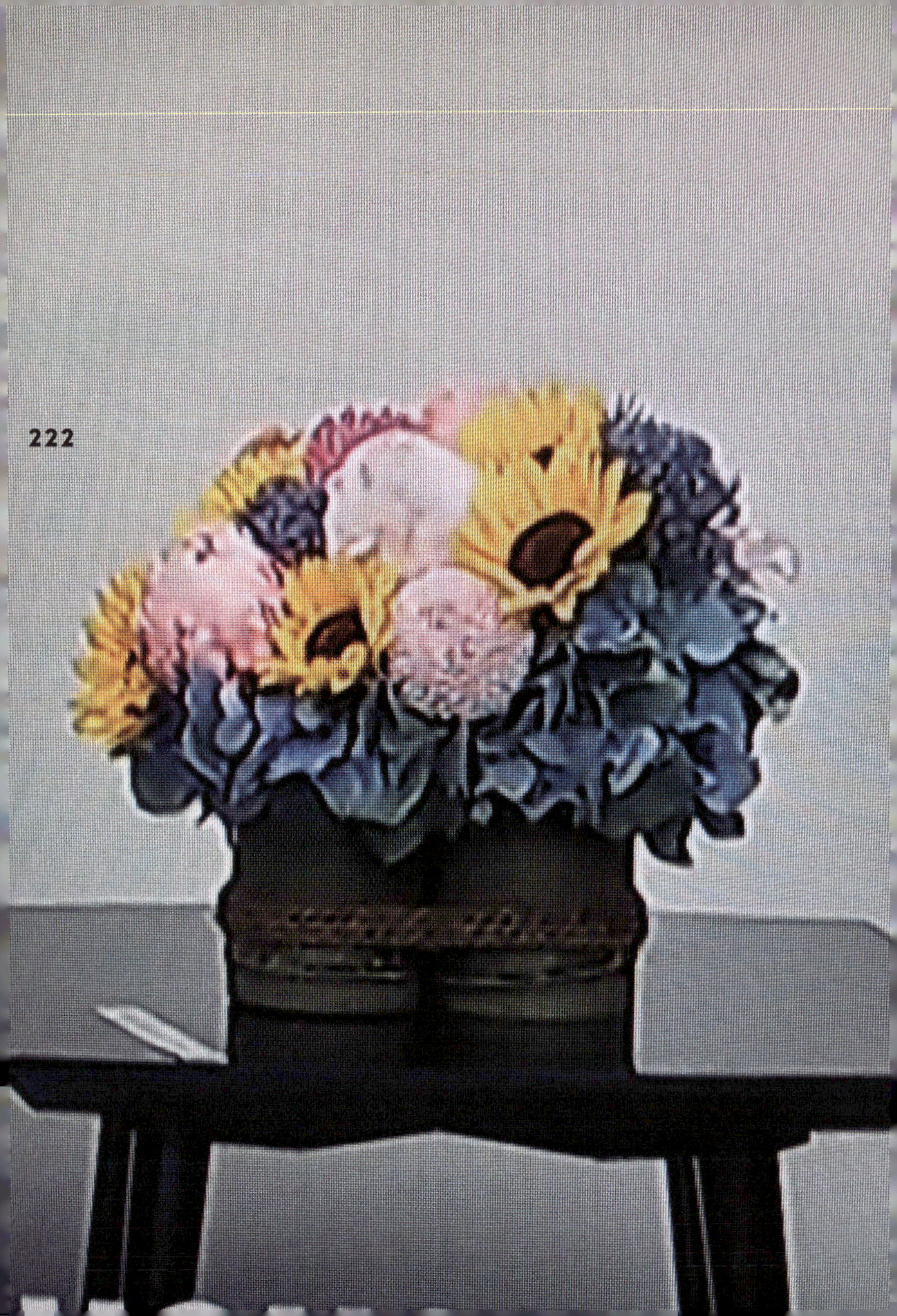

222

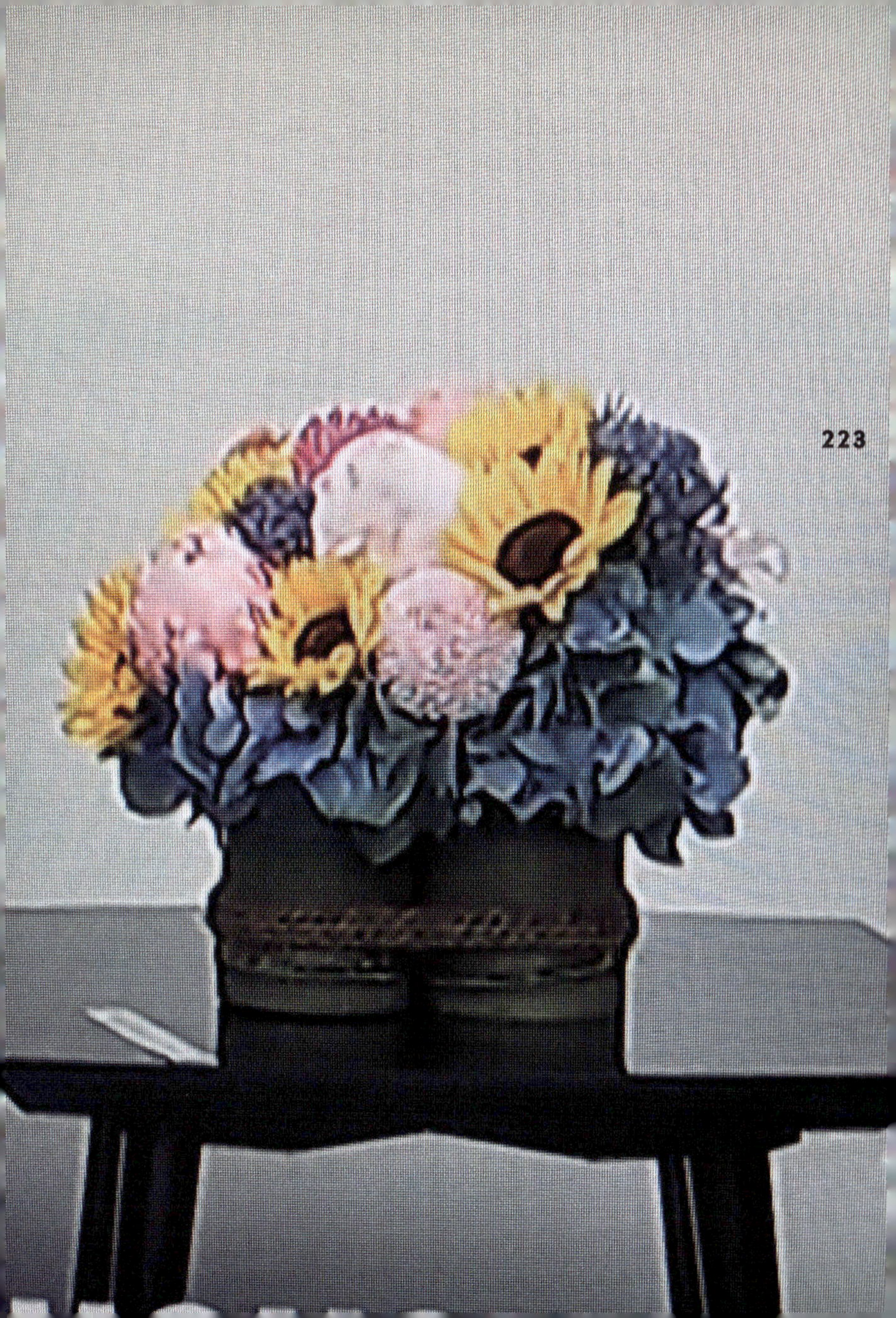

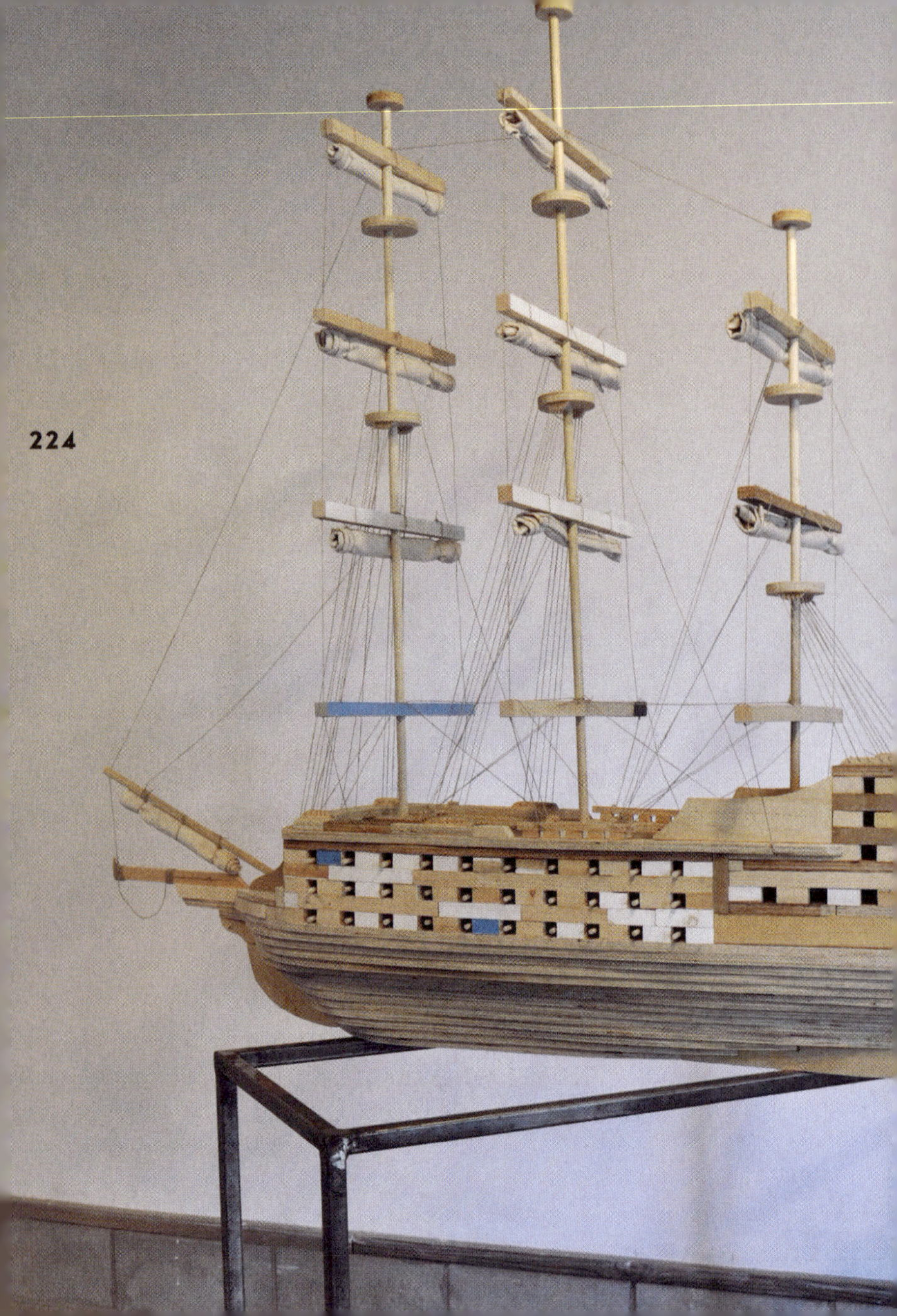
224

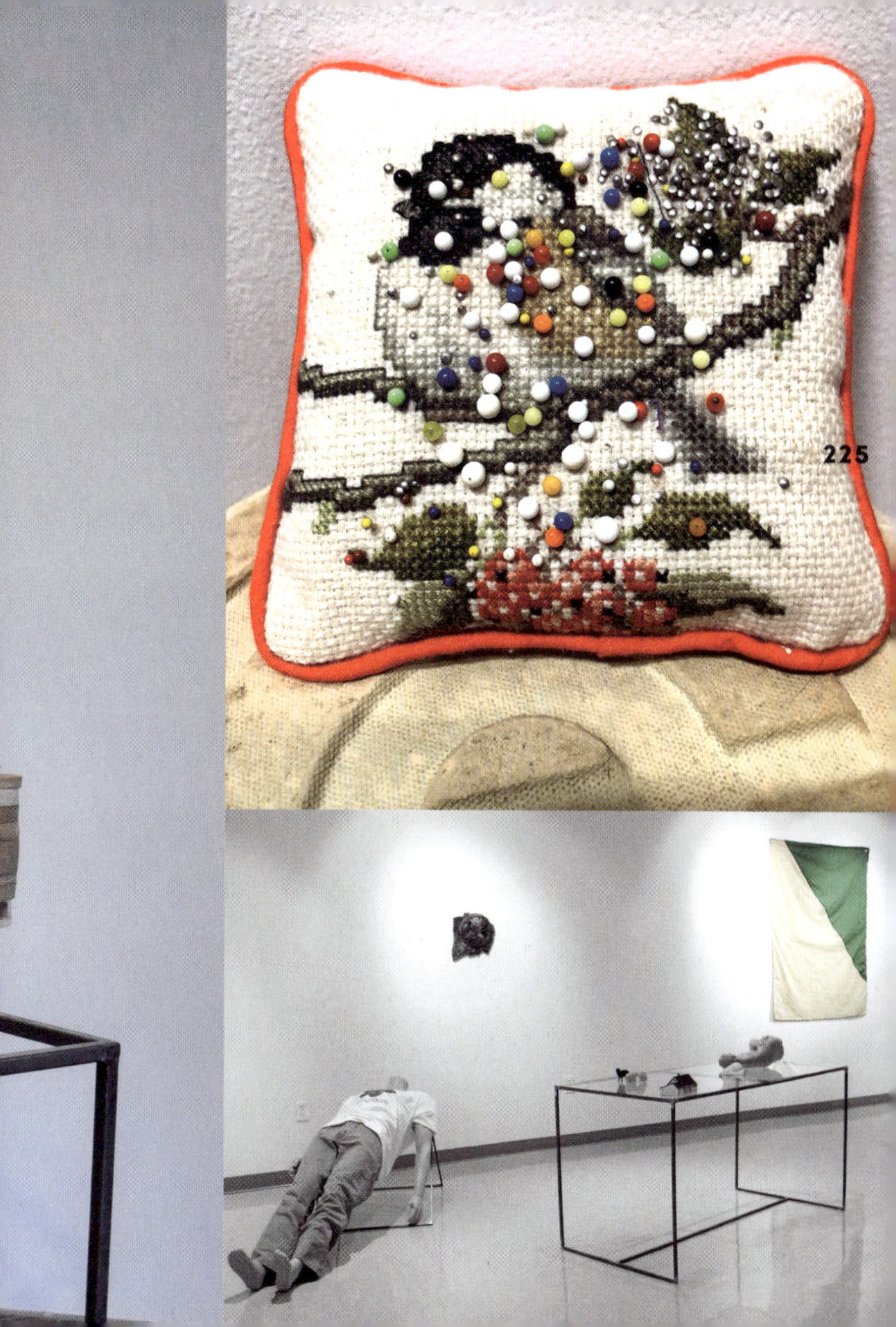

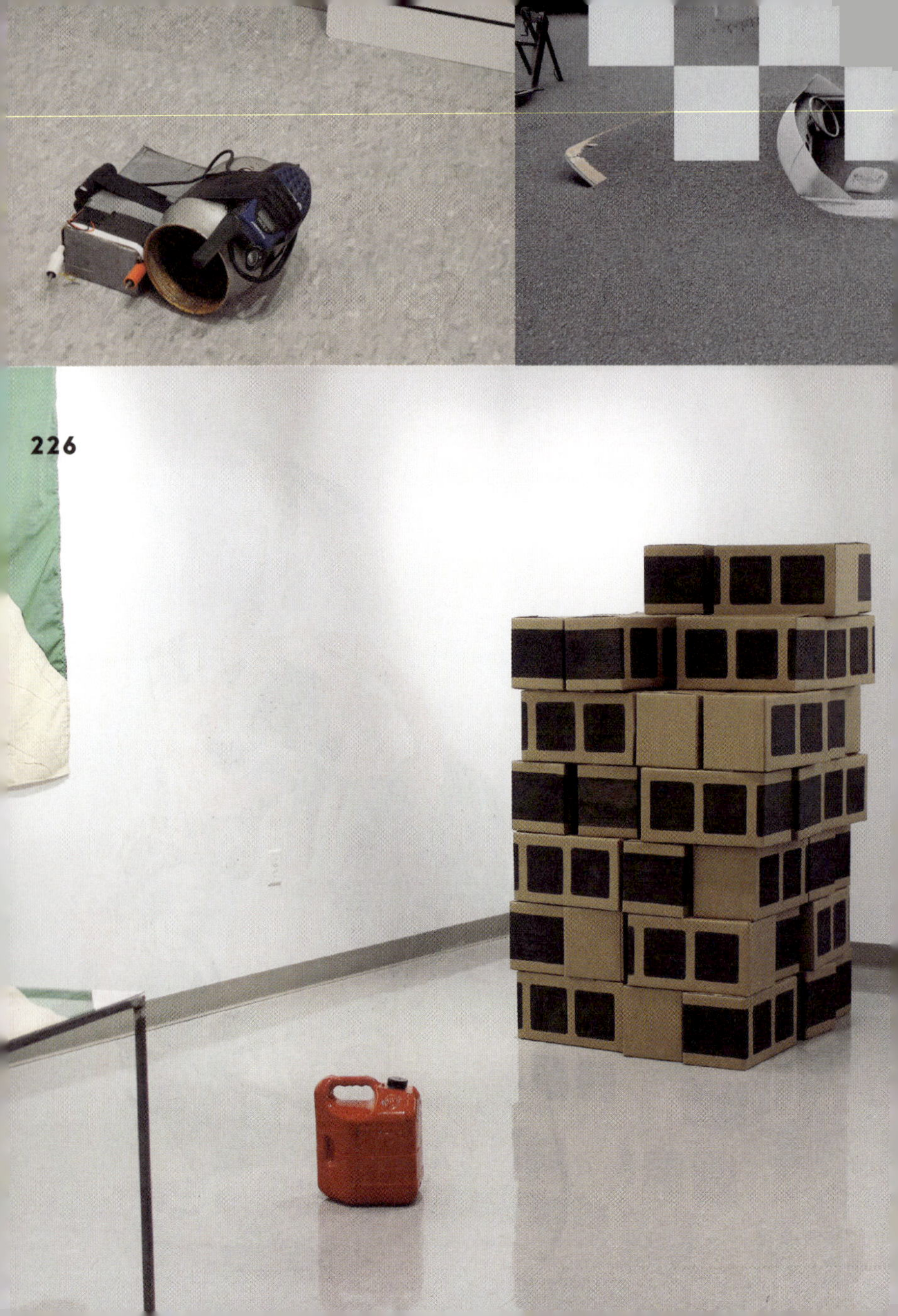

226

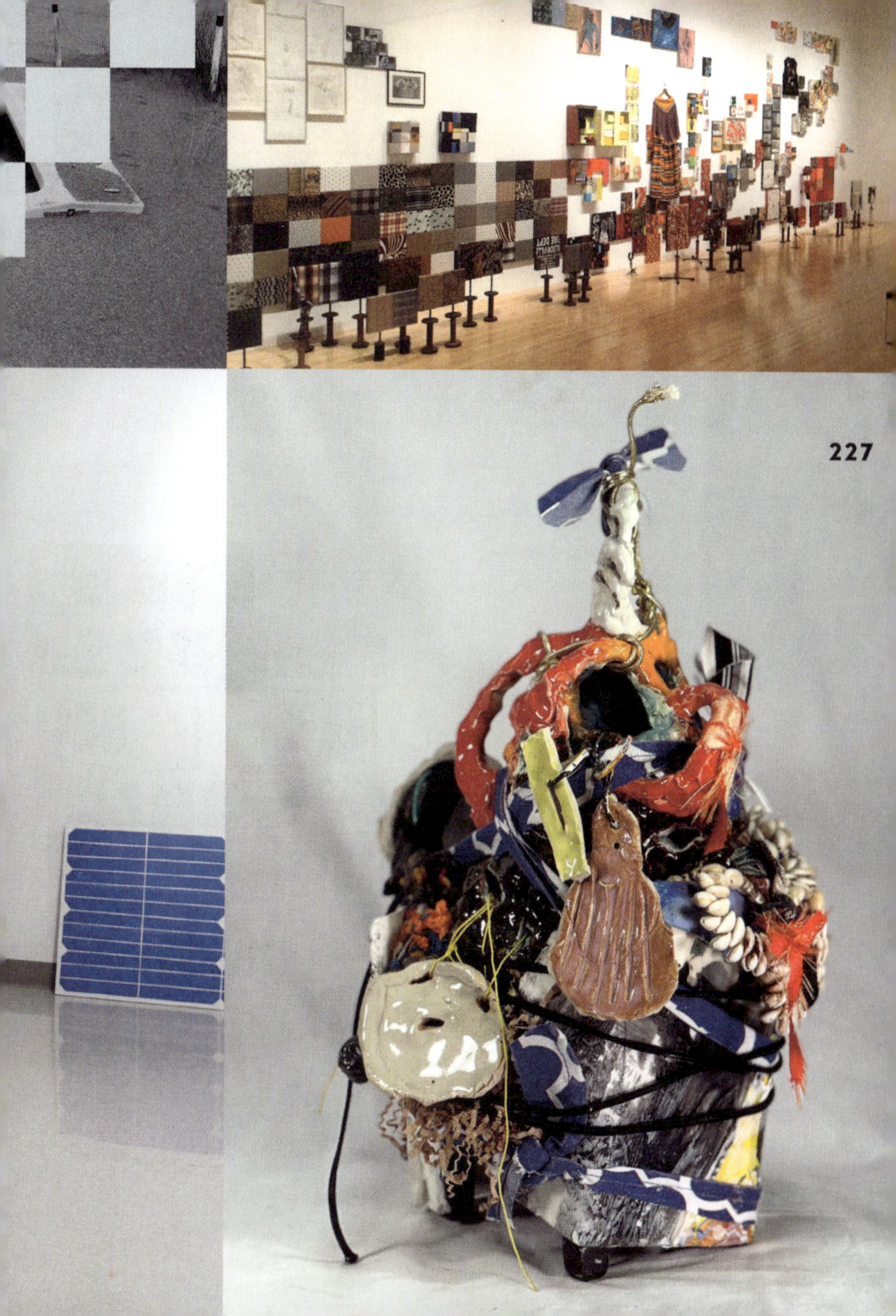

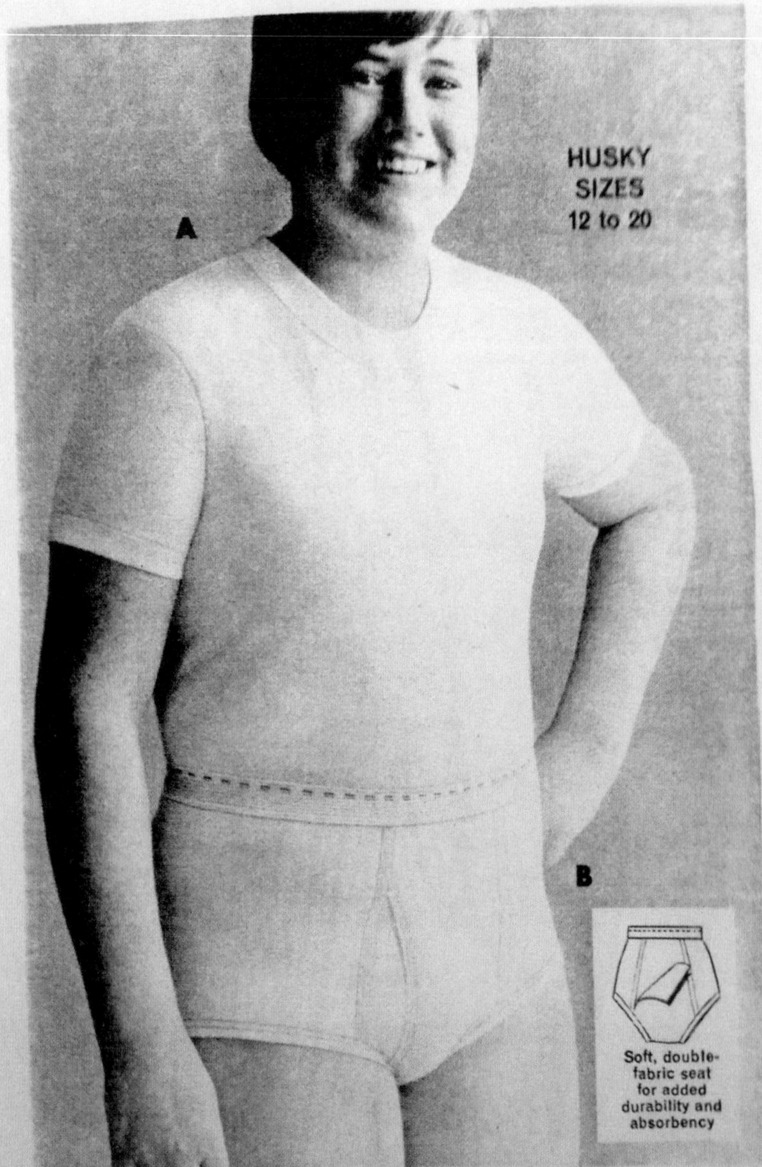
A
228
HUSKY
SIZES
12 to 20
B
Soft, double-
fabric seat
for added
durability and
absorbency

A
HUSKY
SIZES
12 to 20
B
Soft, double-
fabric seat
for added
durability and
absorbency

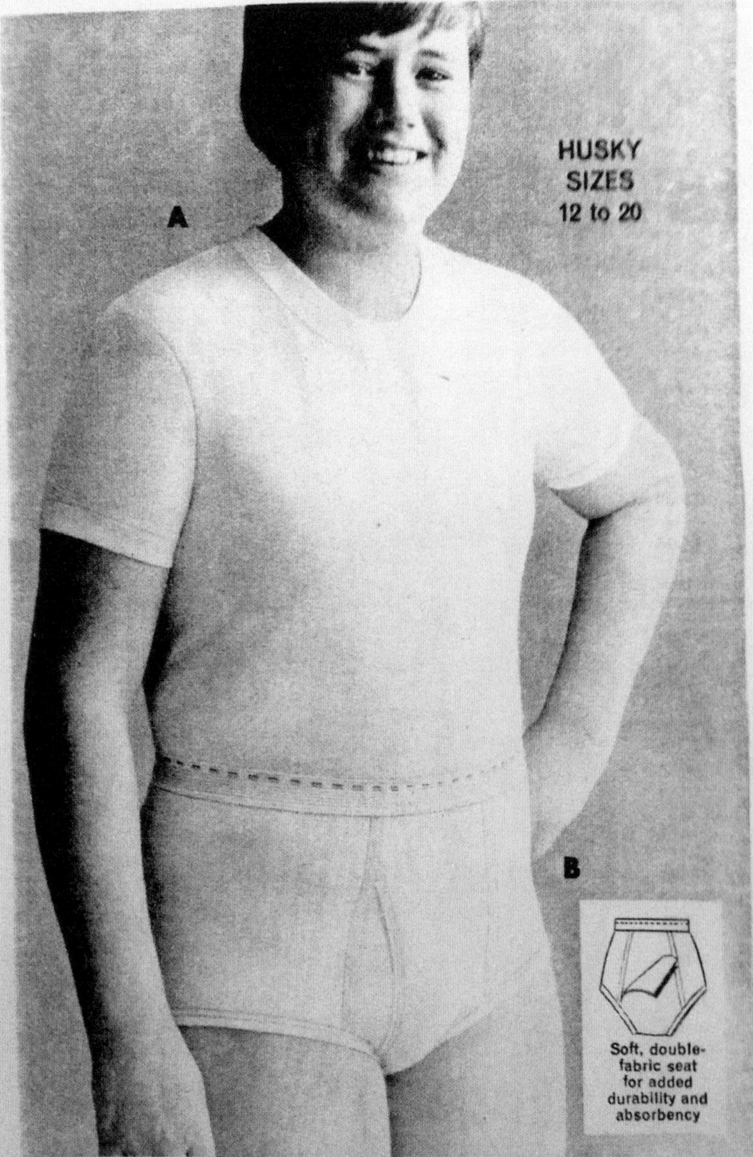

229

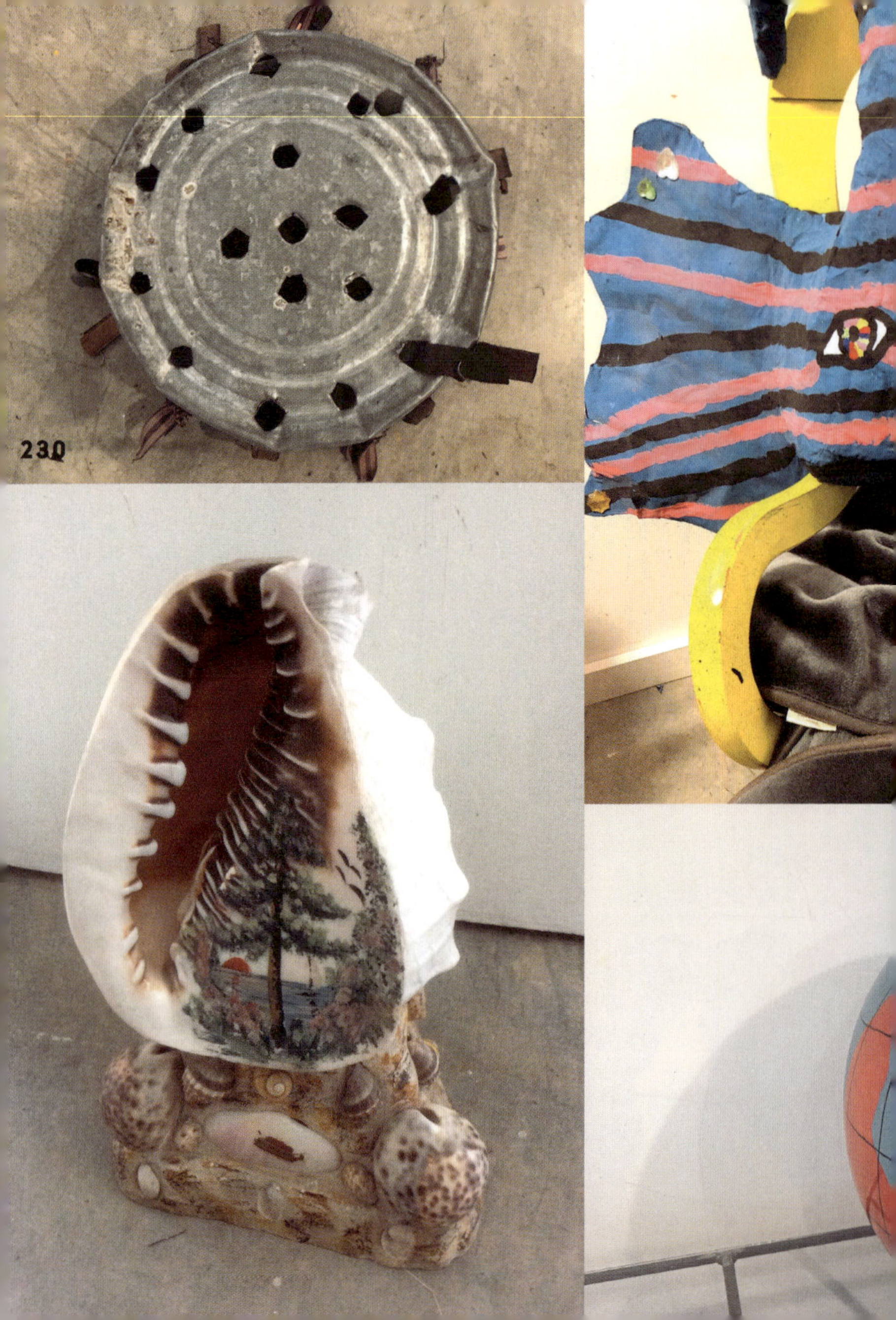
230

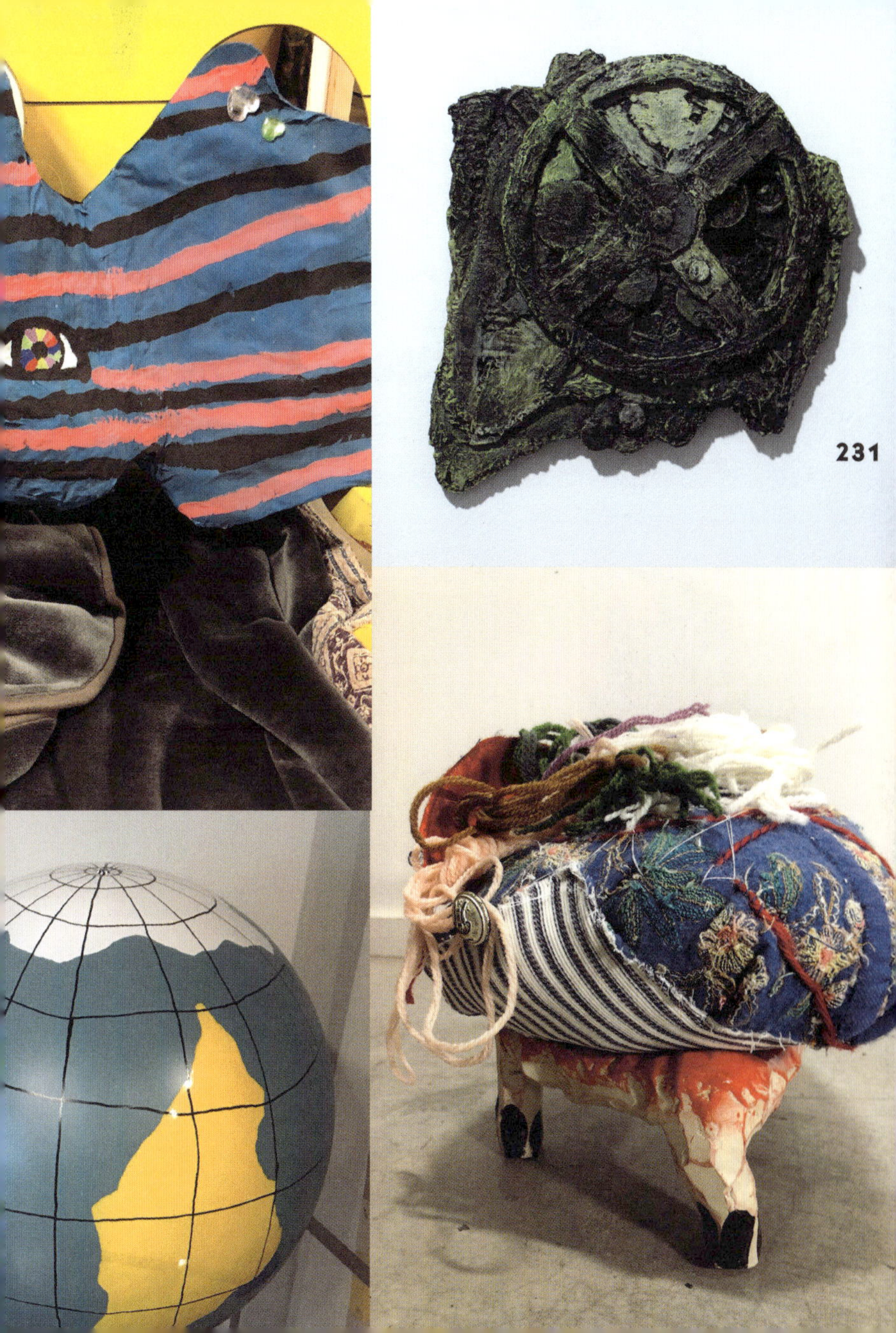
231

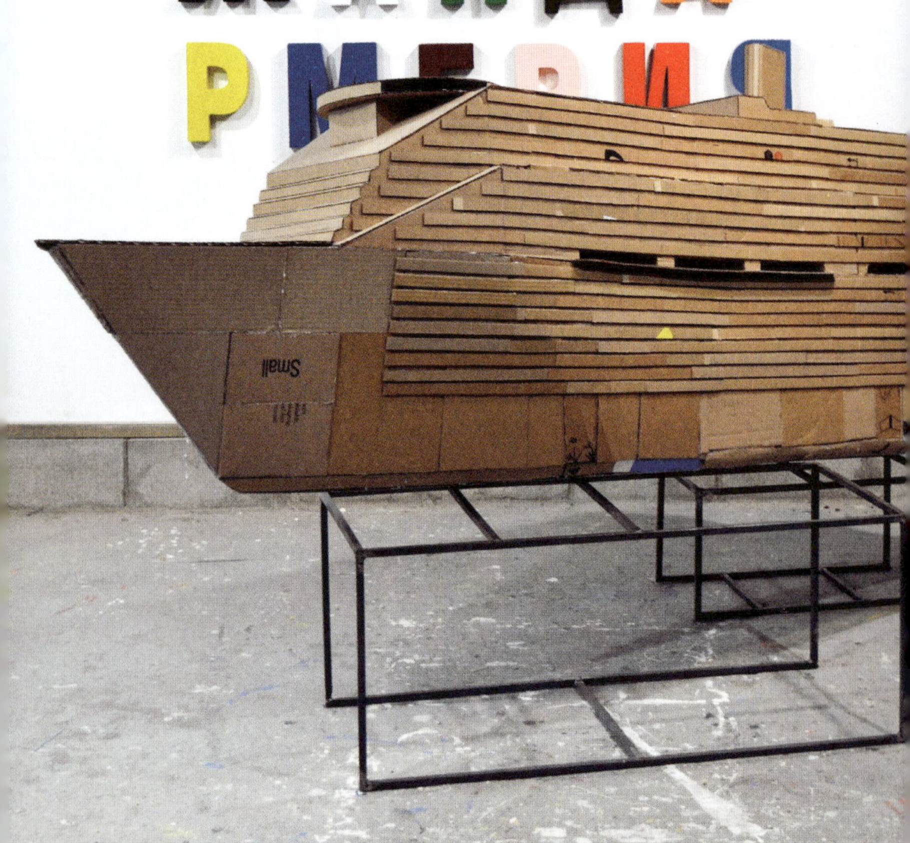
GENDA
RMERIE
ЖАНДА
РМЕРИЯ
Small

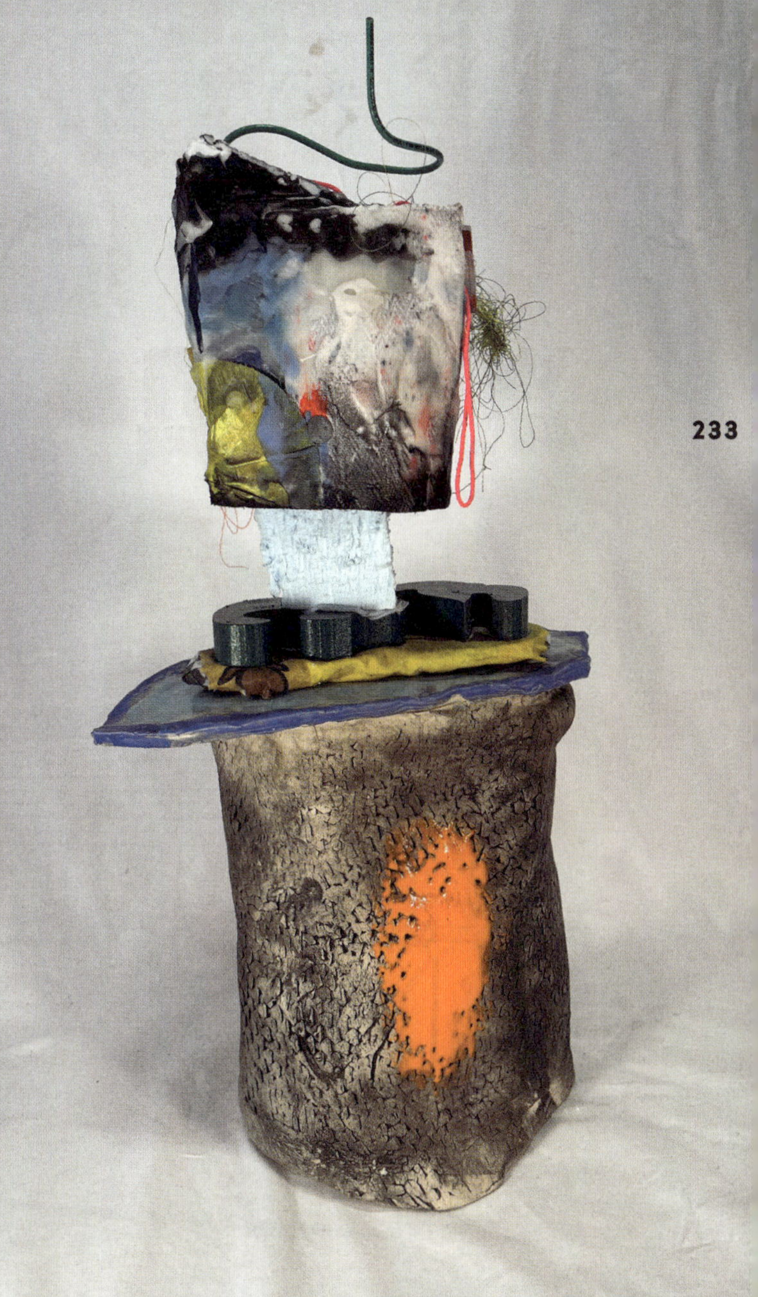

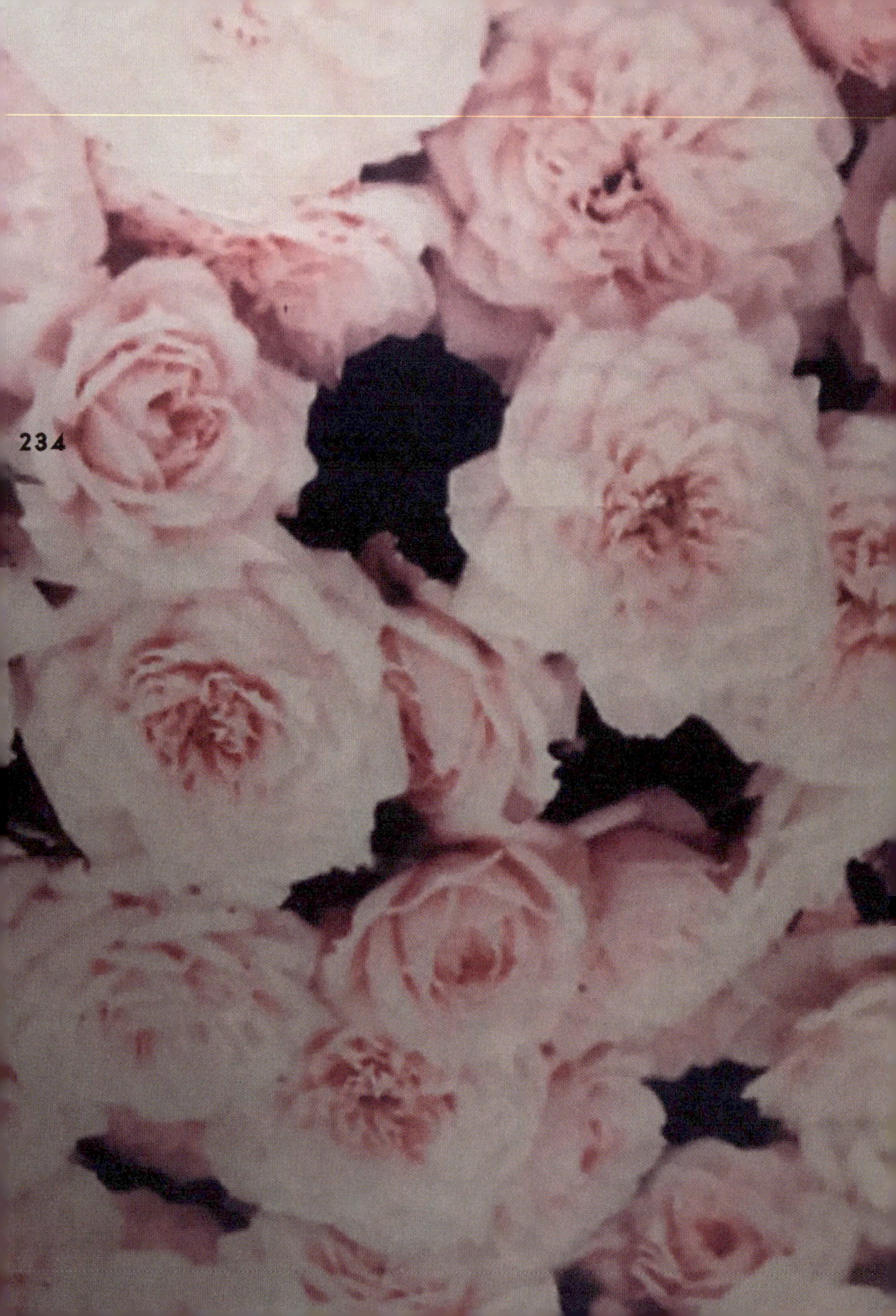

234

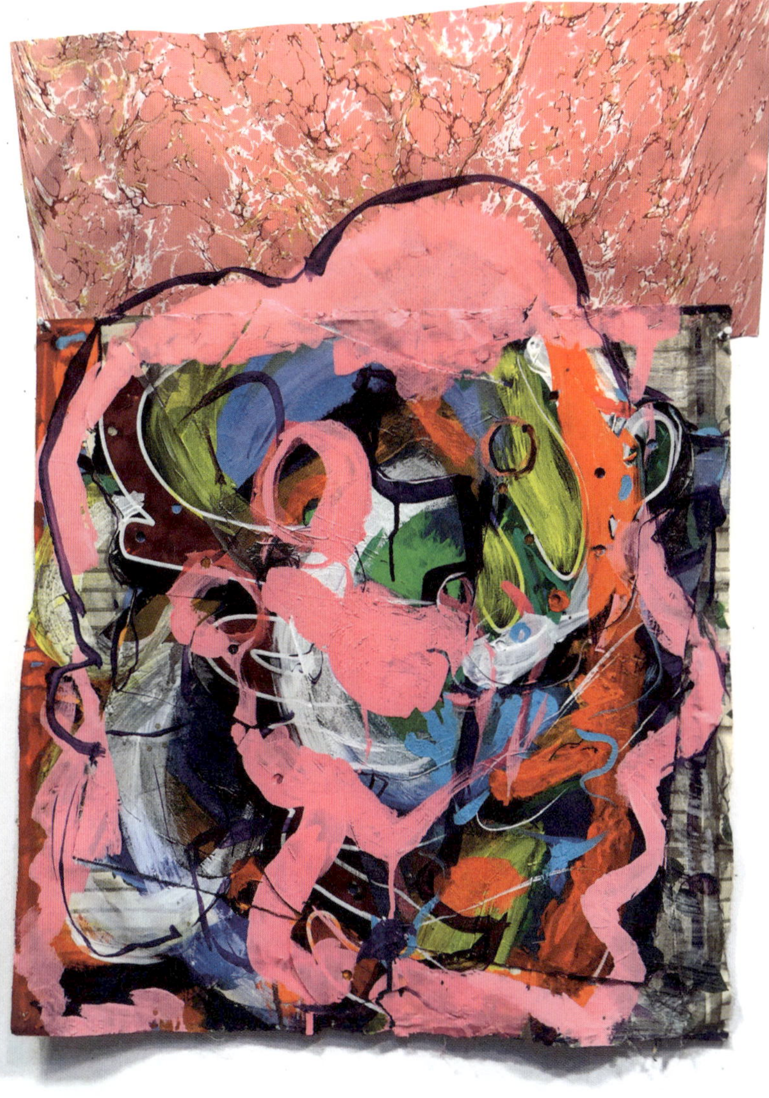

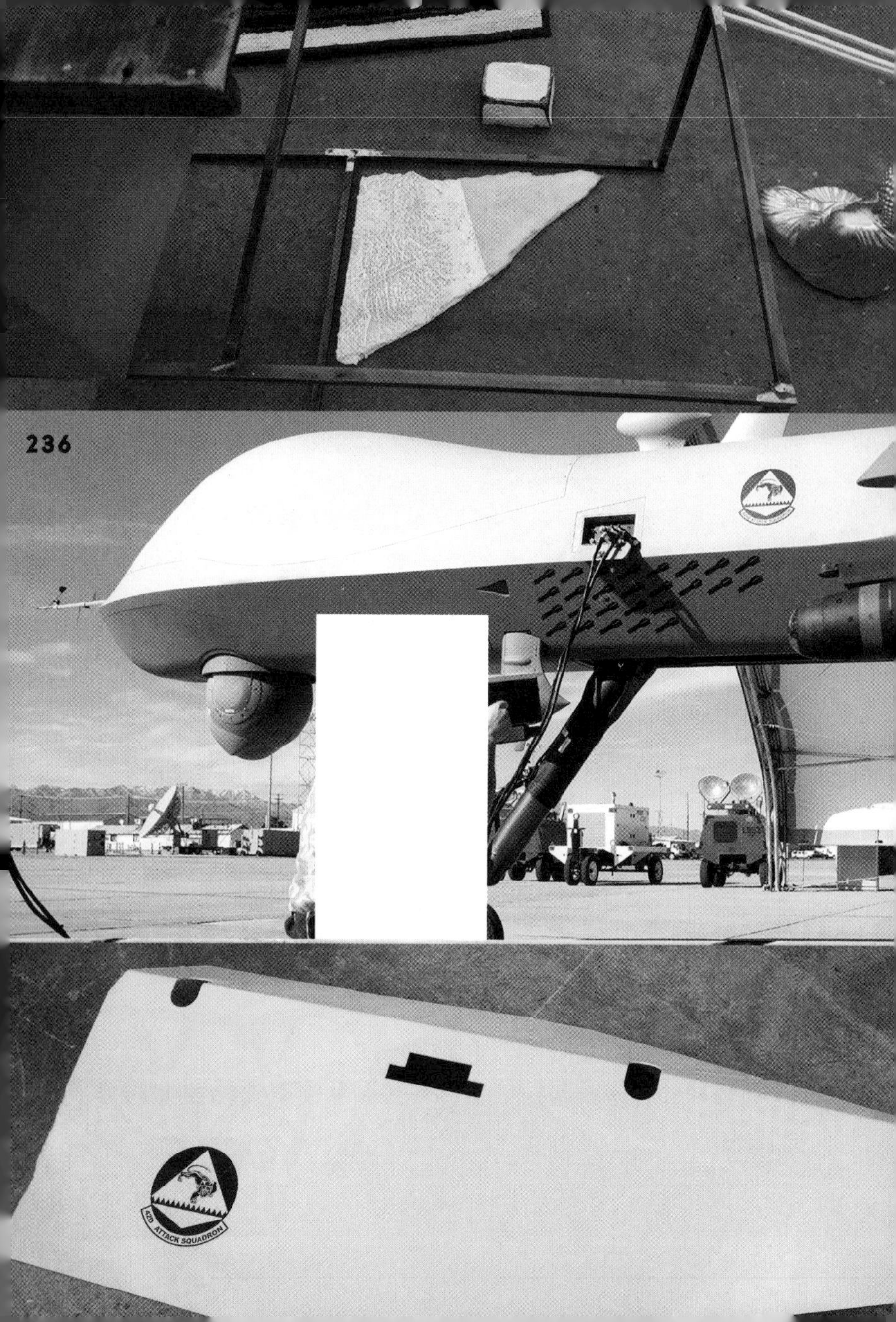

236
42D ATTACK SQUADRON

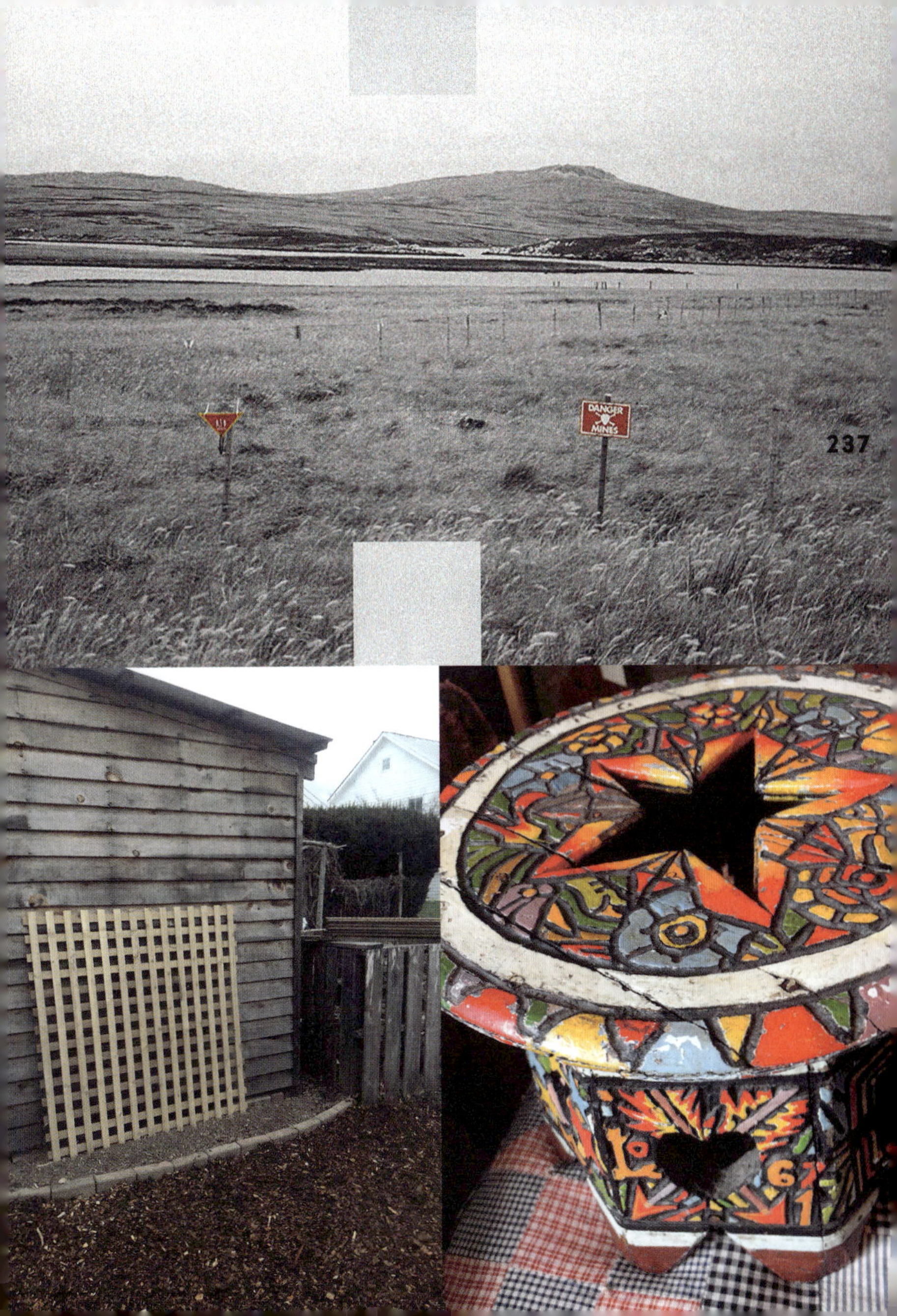
DANGER
MINES

238

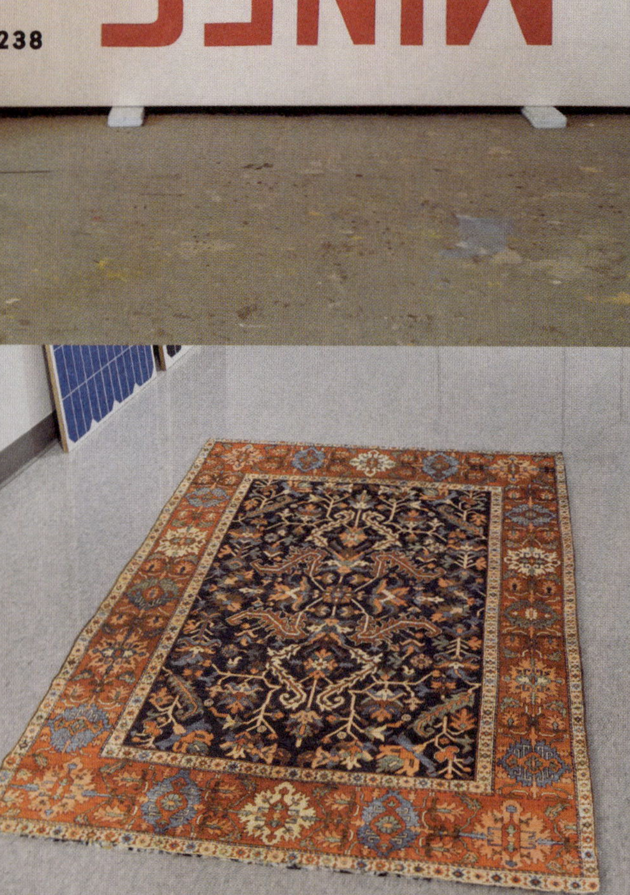

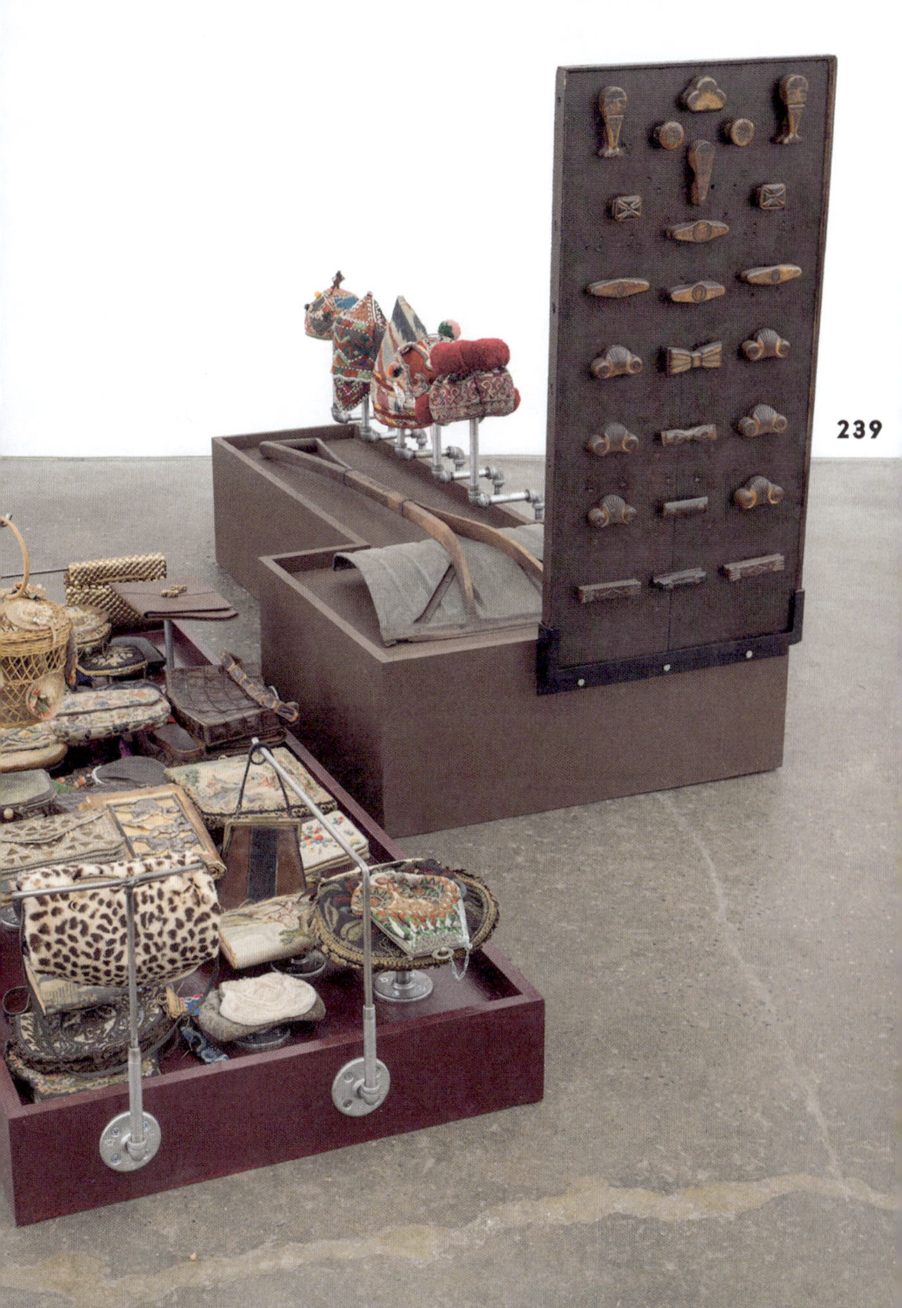

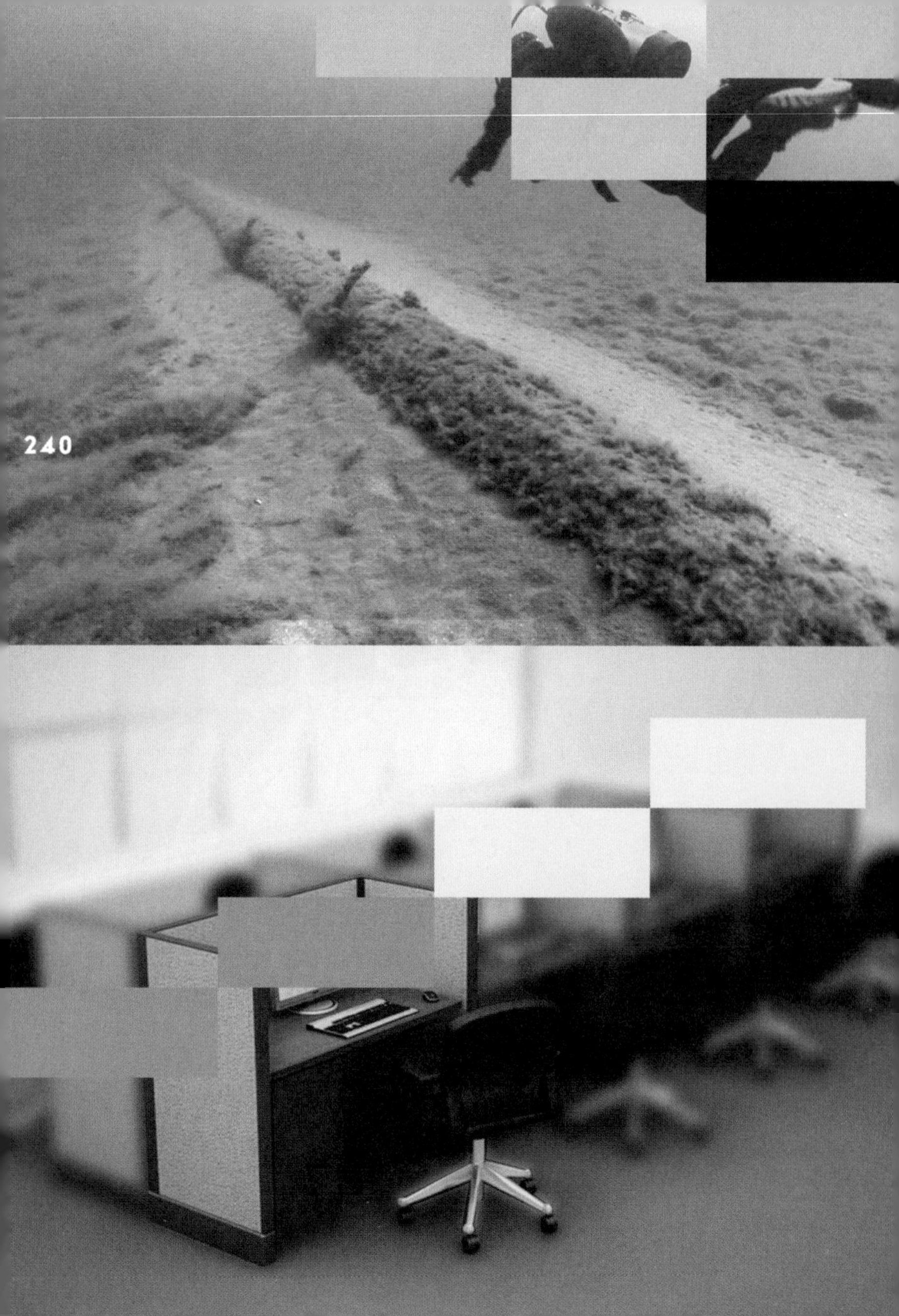

240

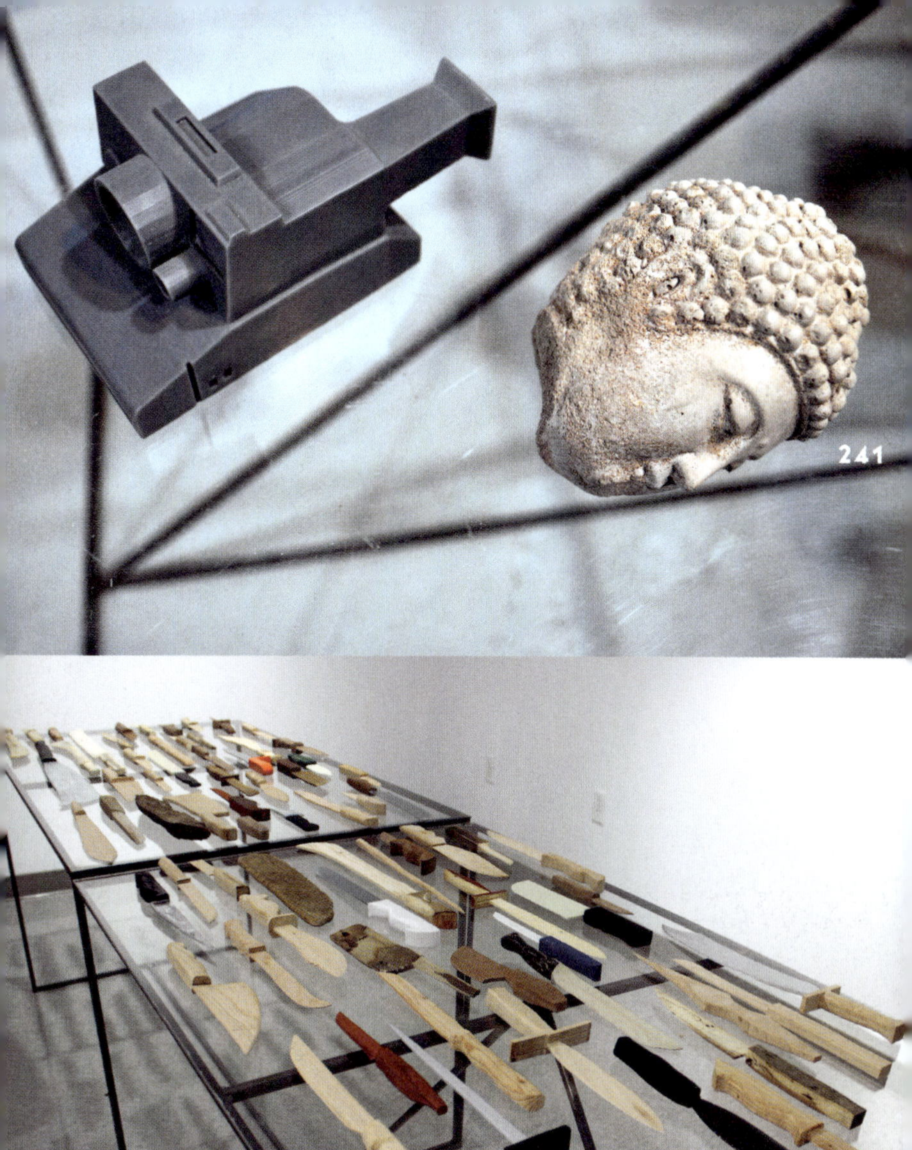

241

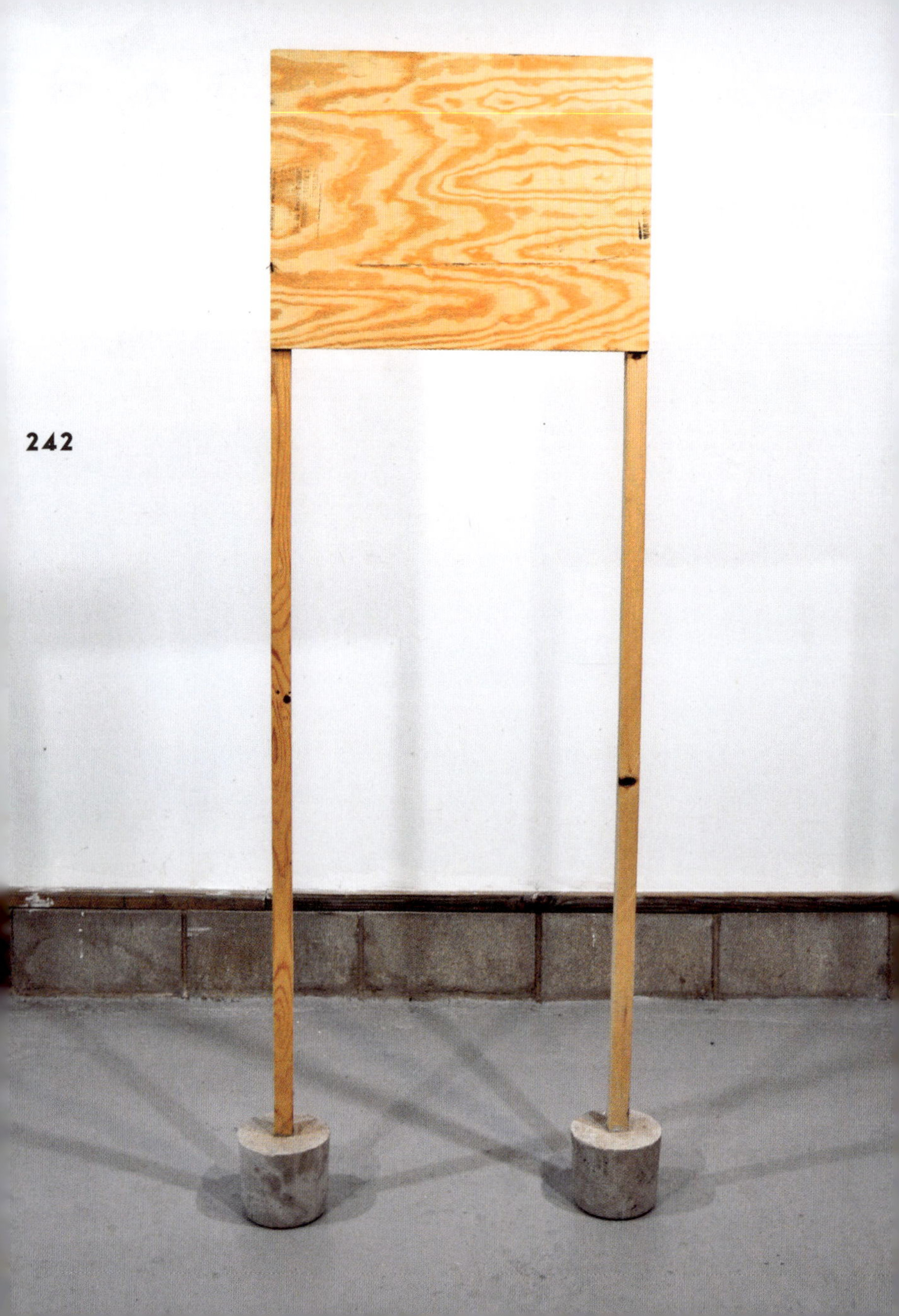
242

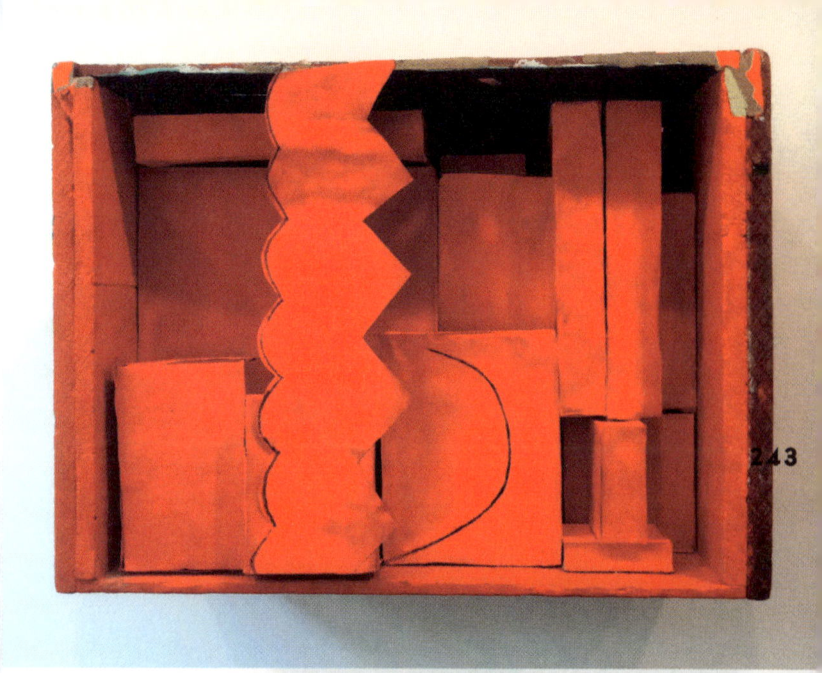

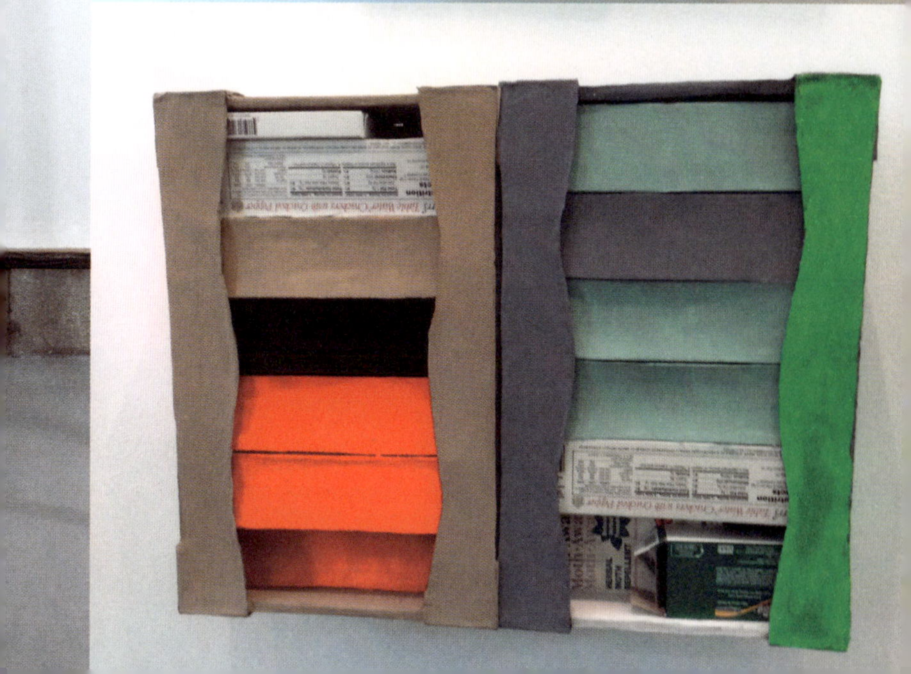

243

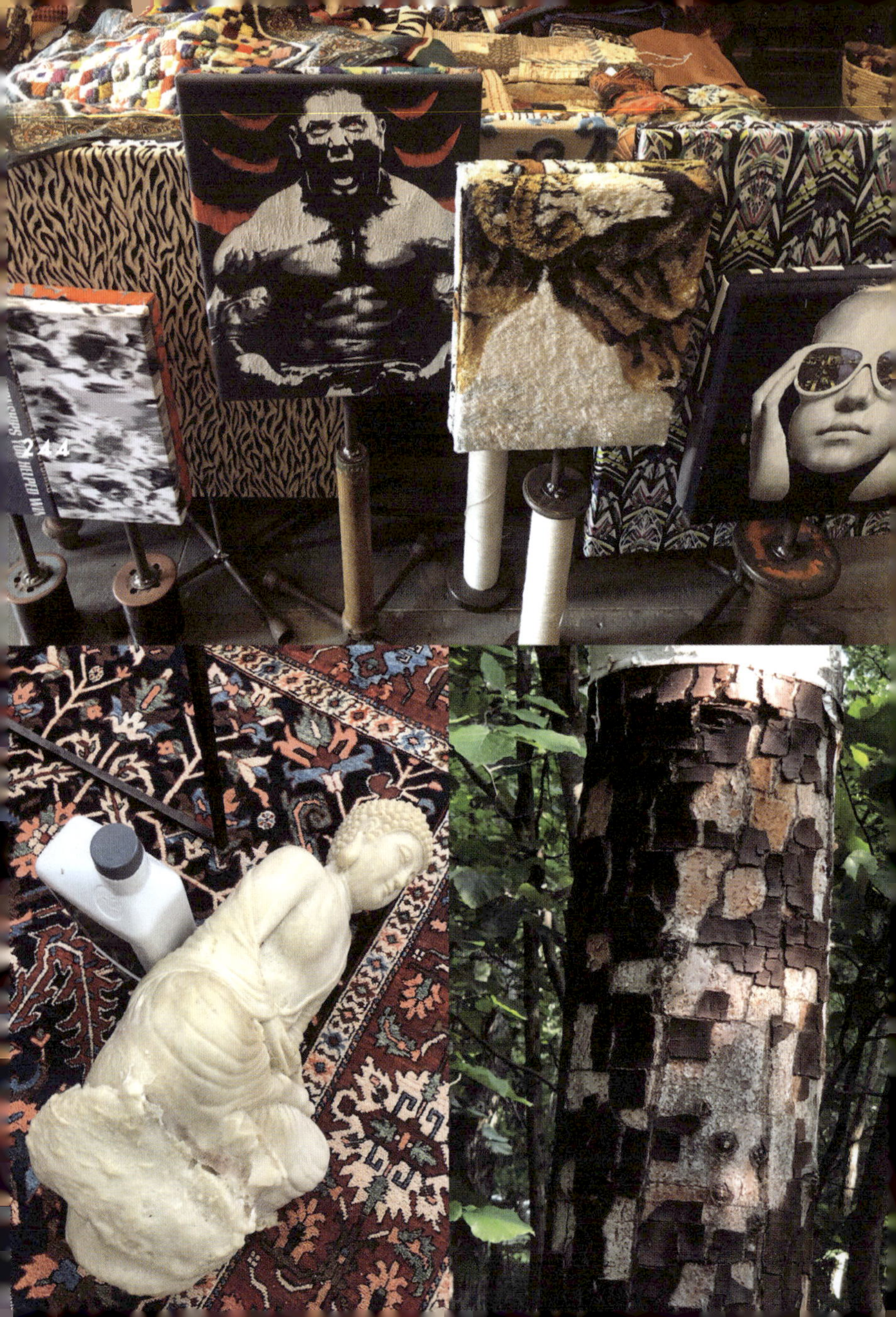

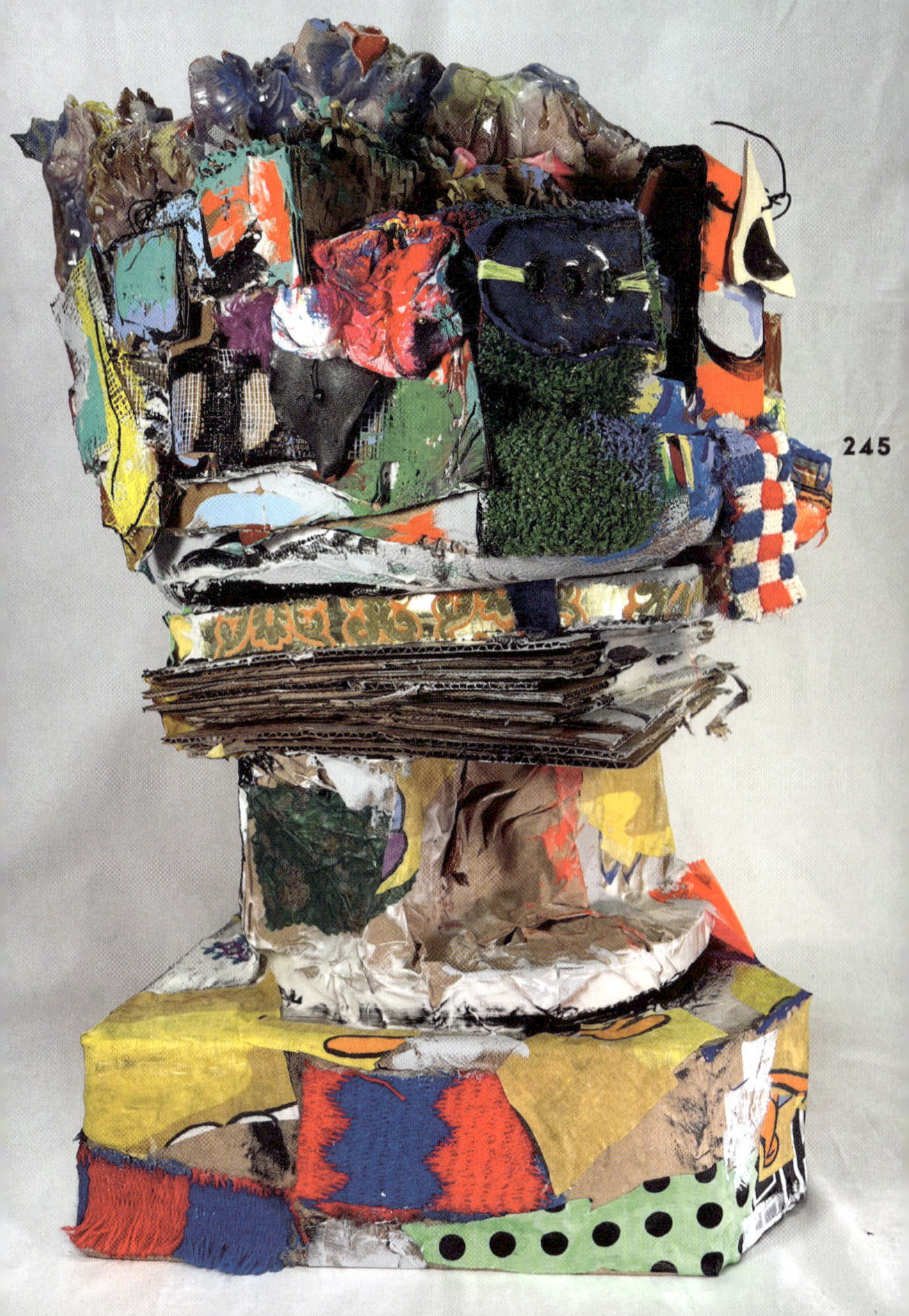

245

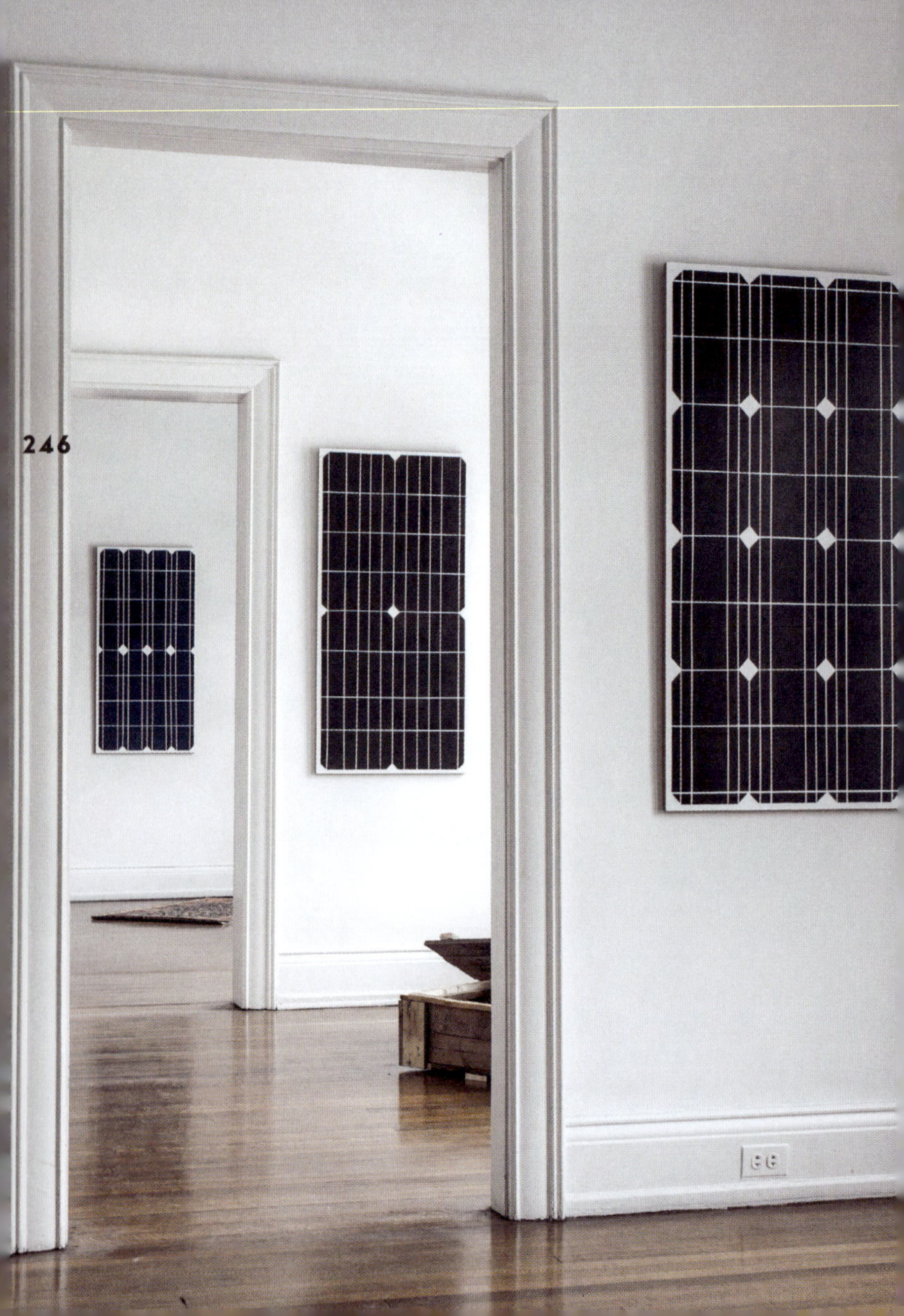
246

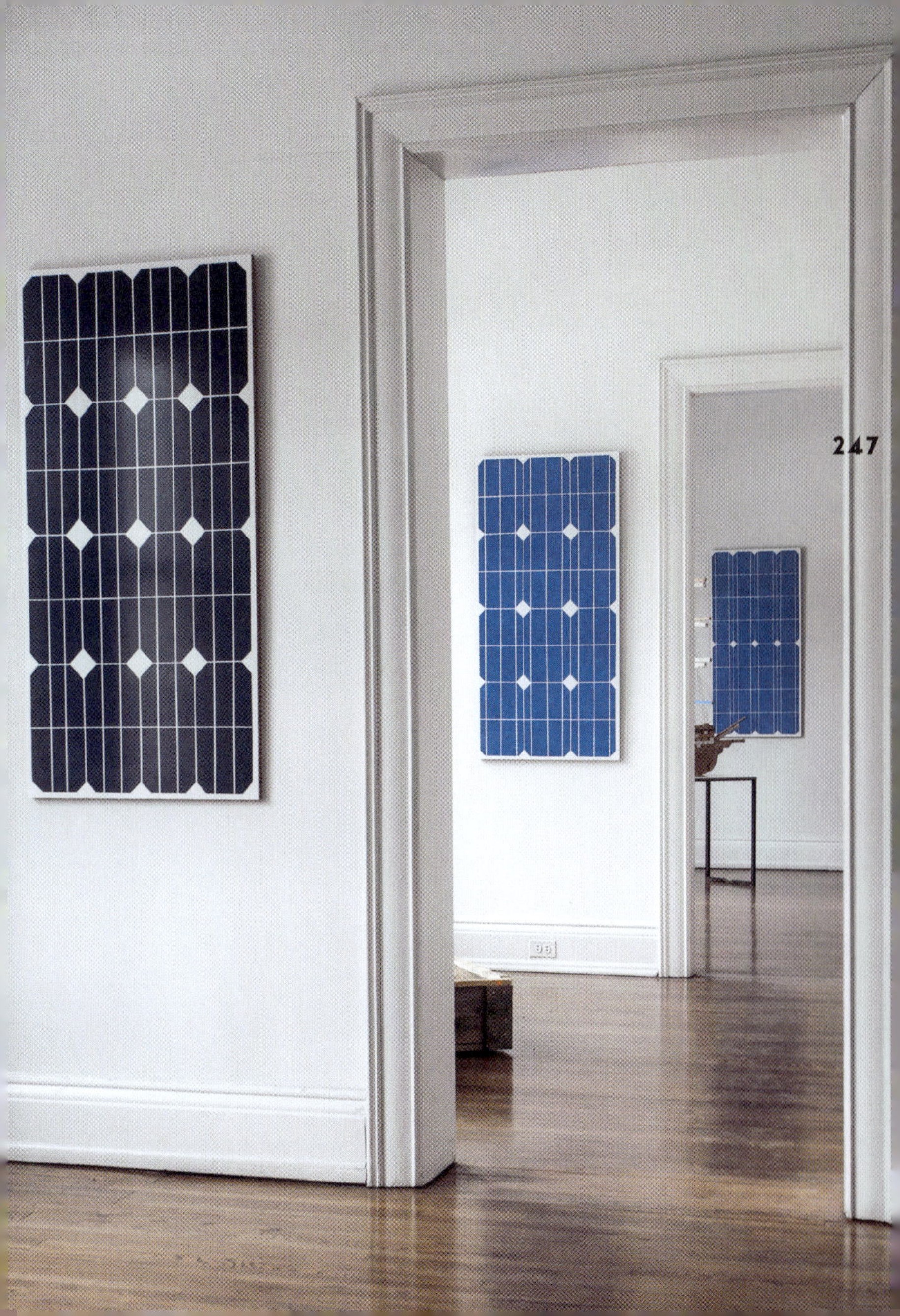

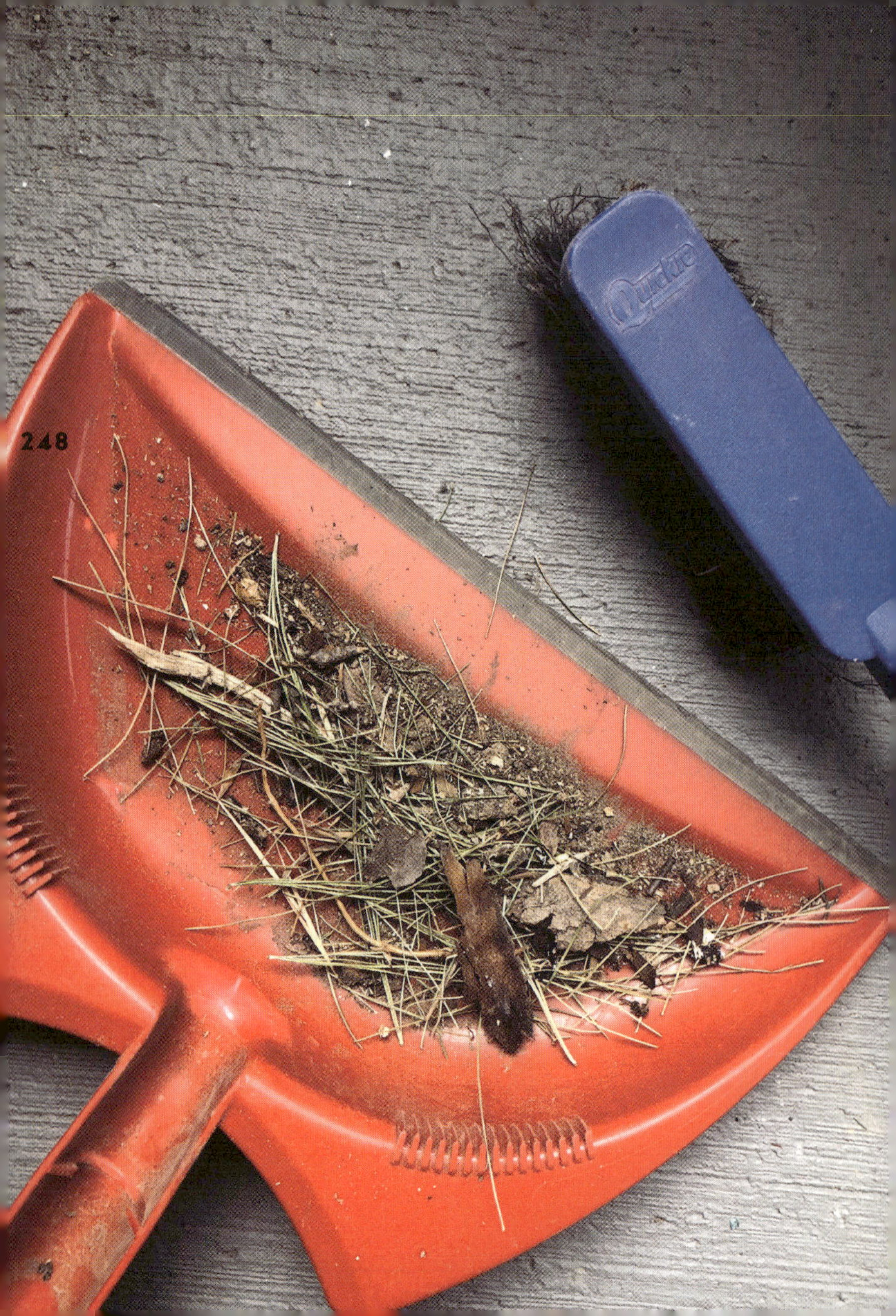

248

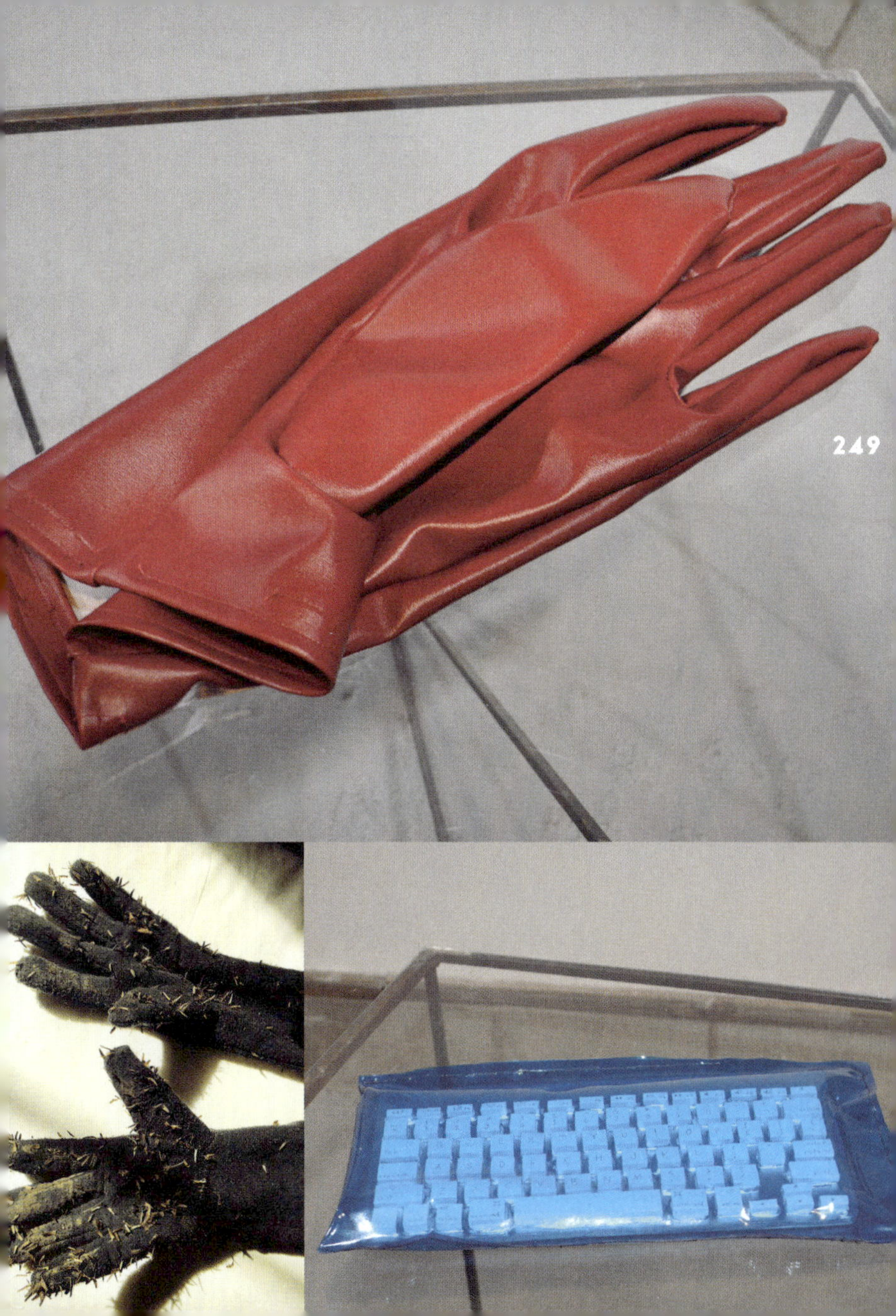
249

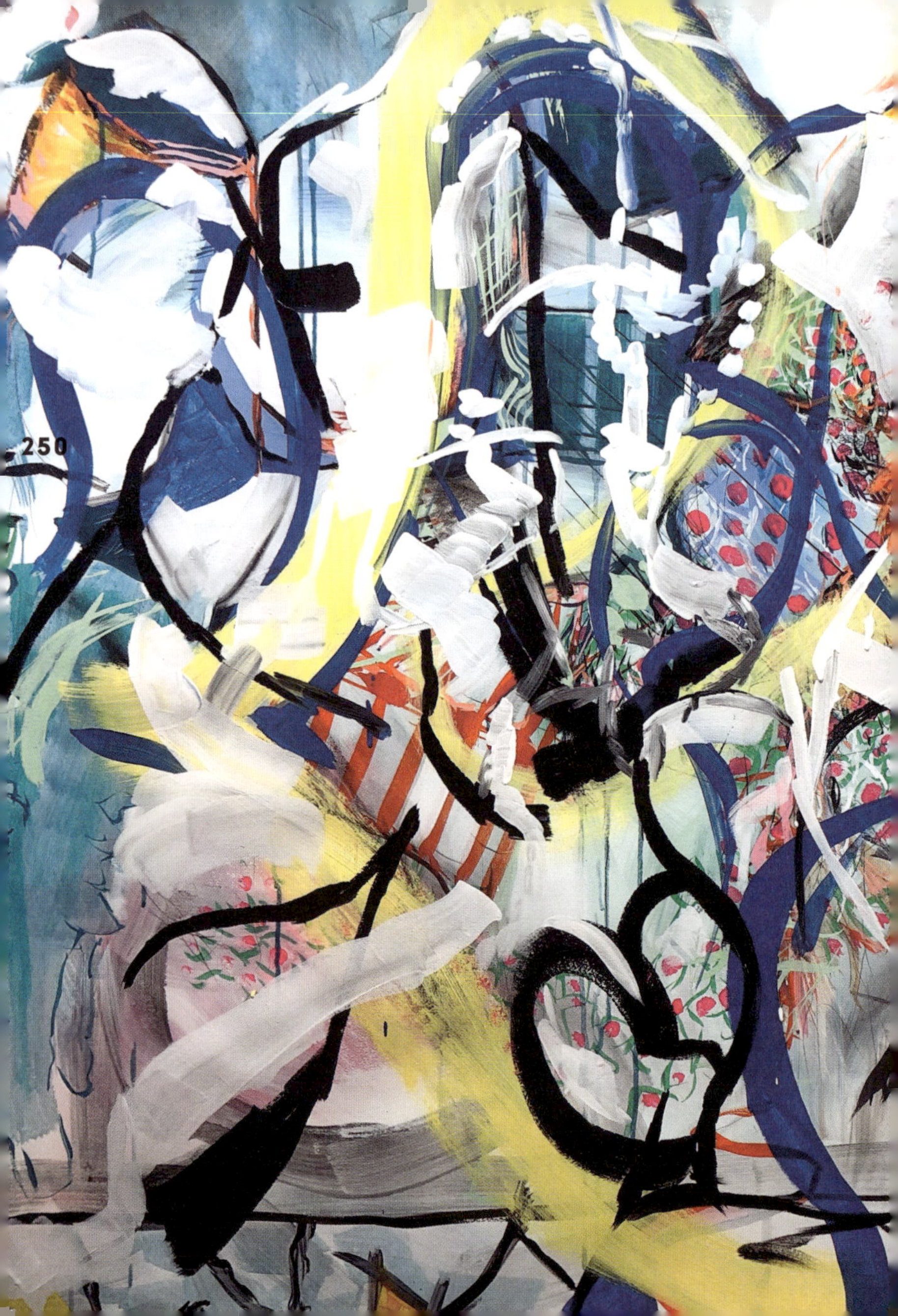
250

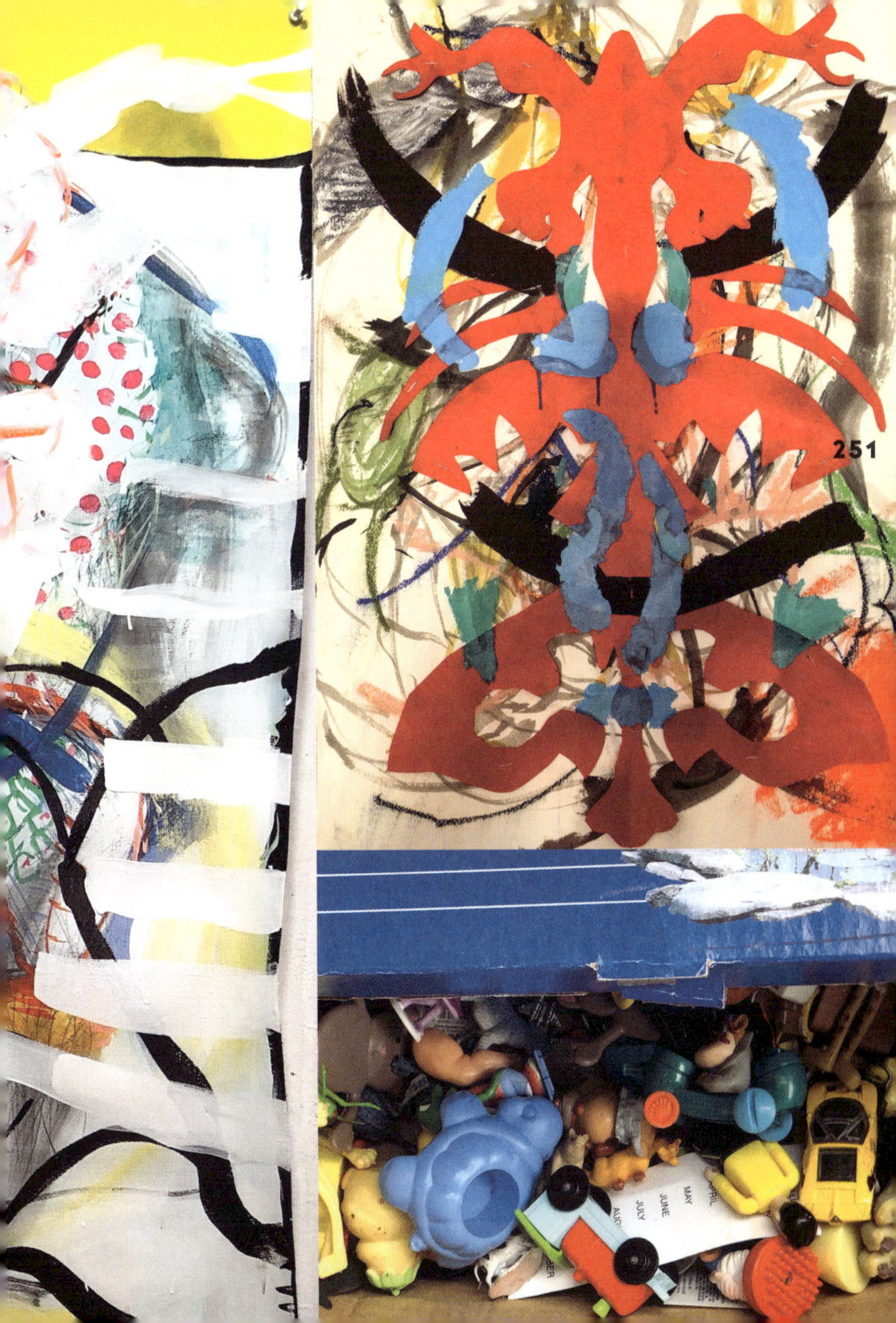
251

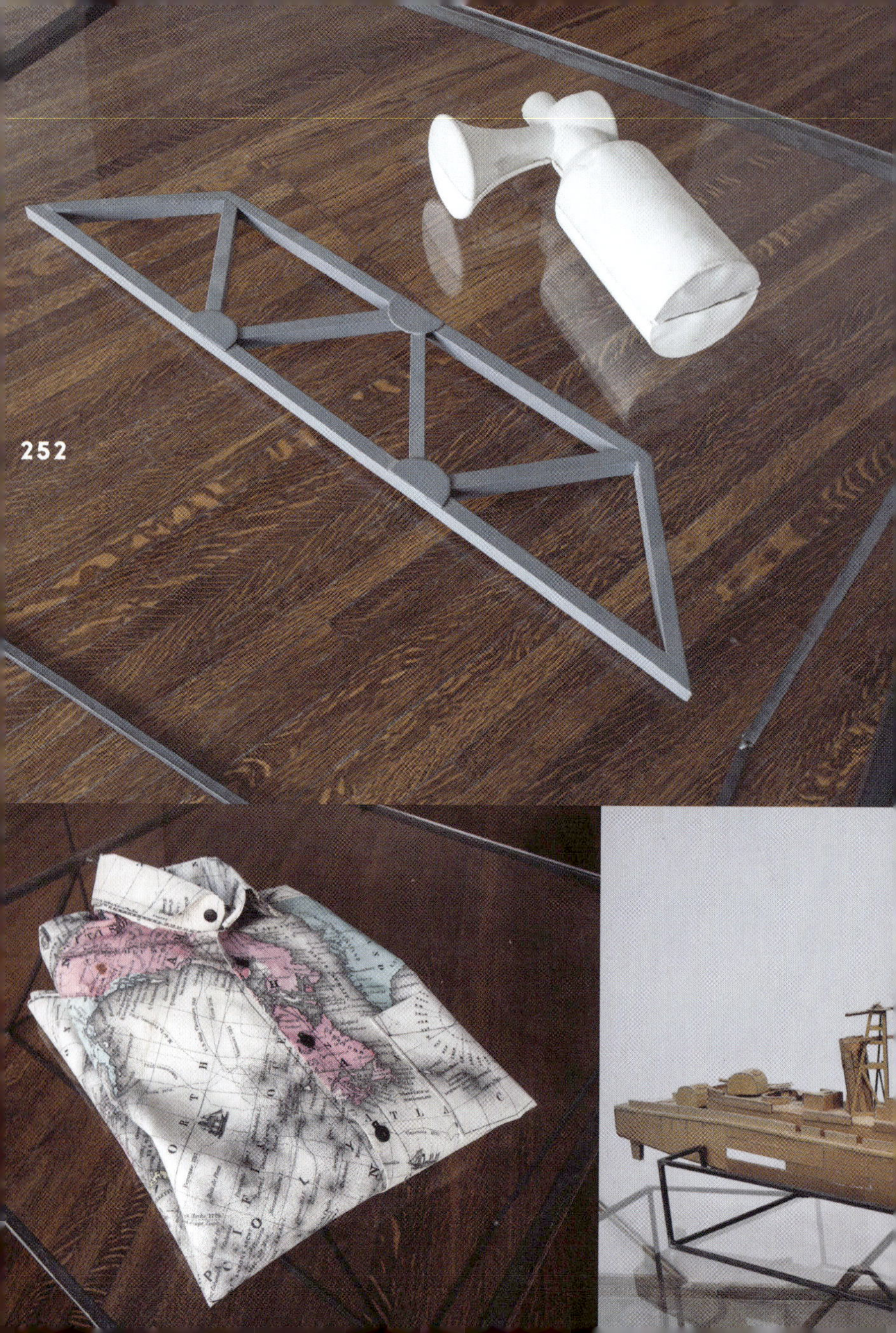

252

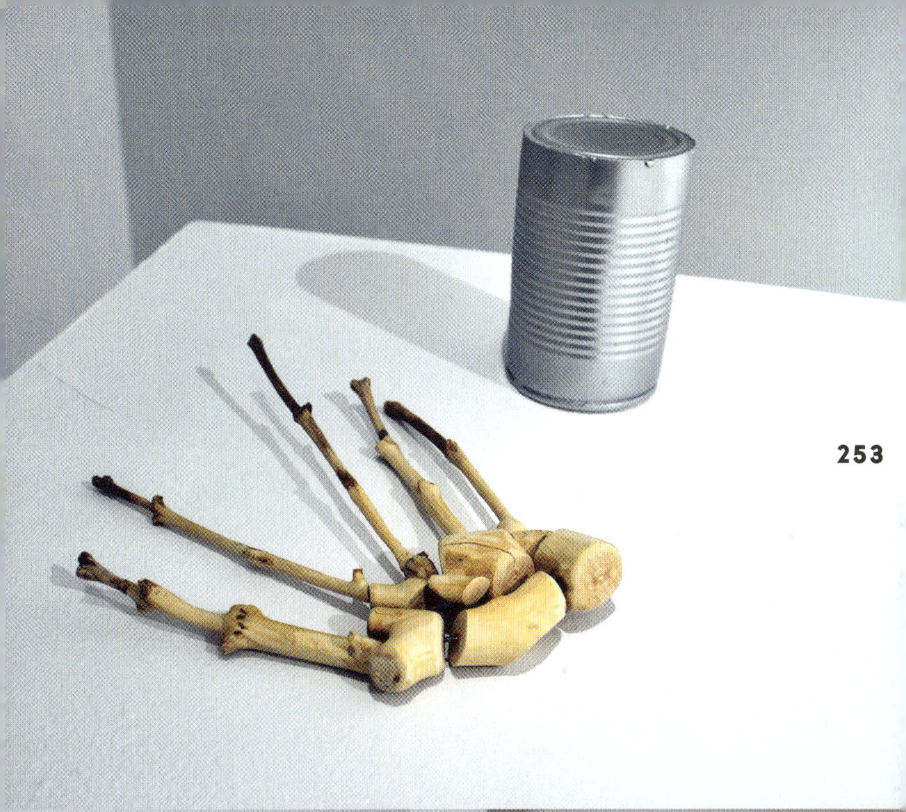

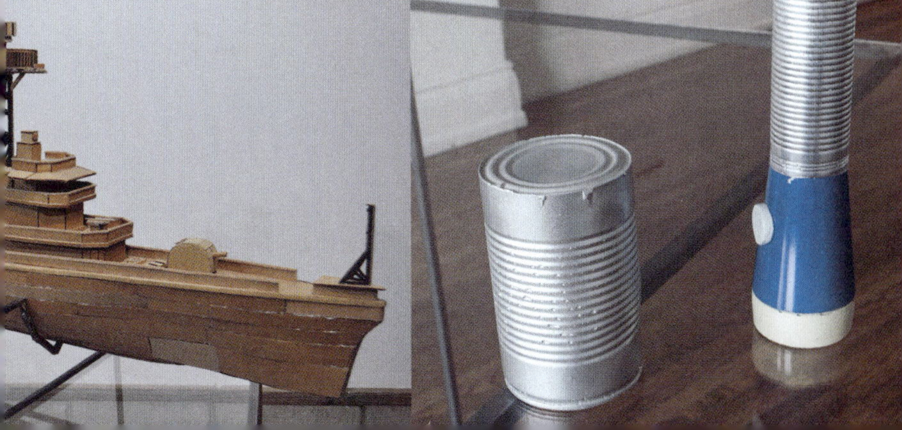

253

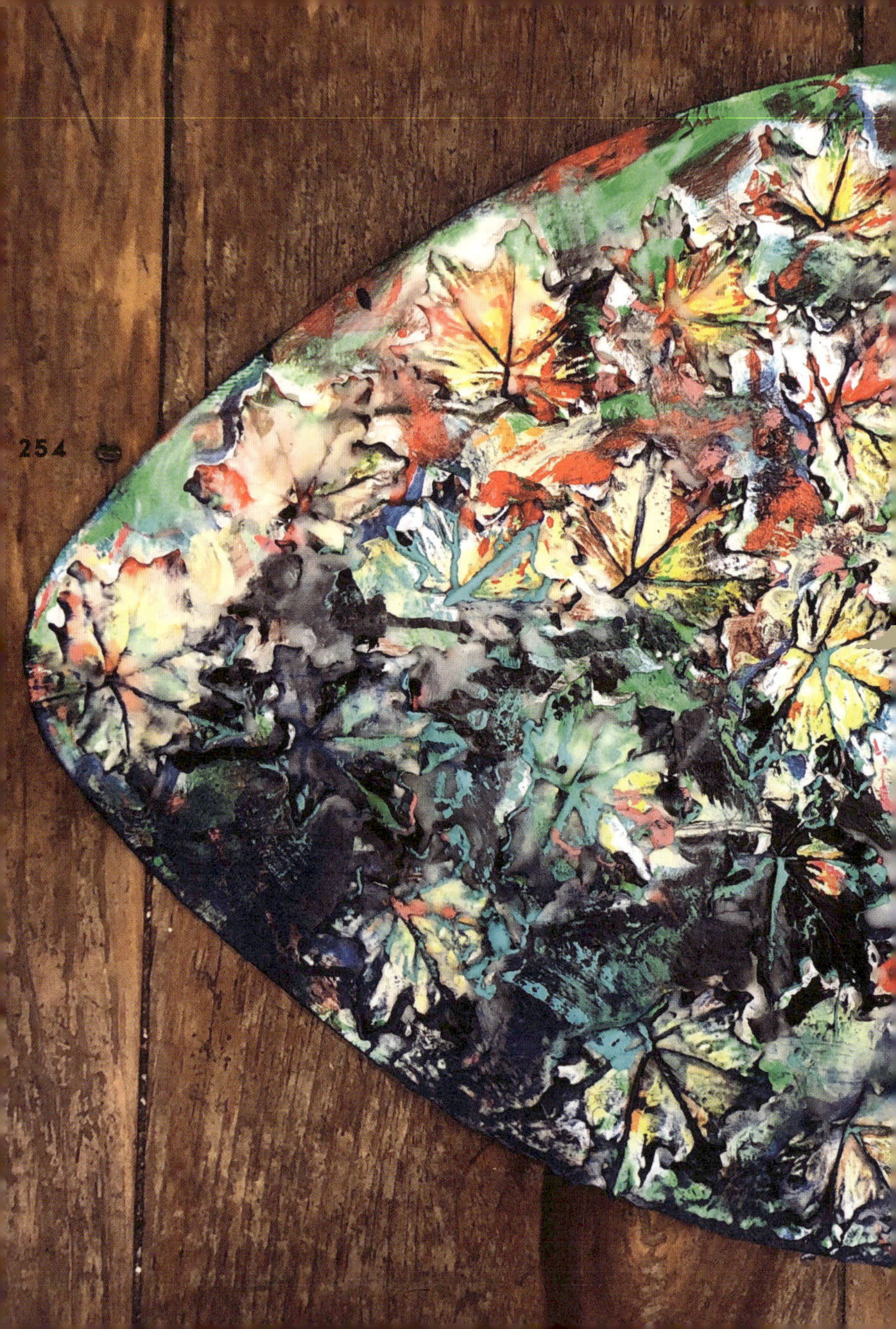

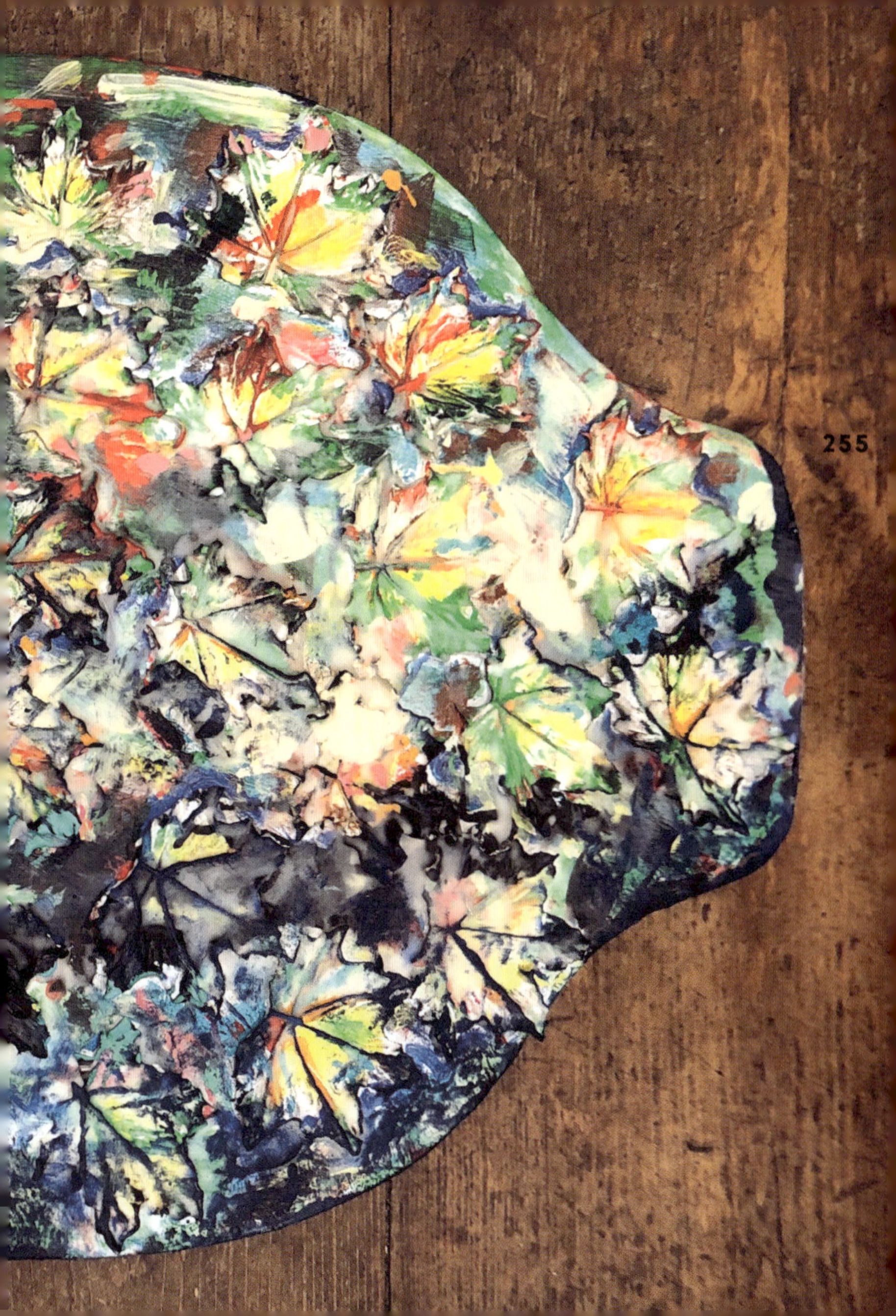
255

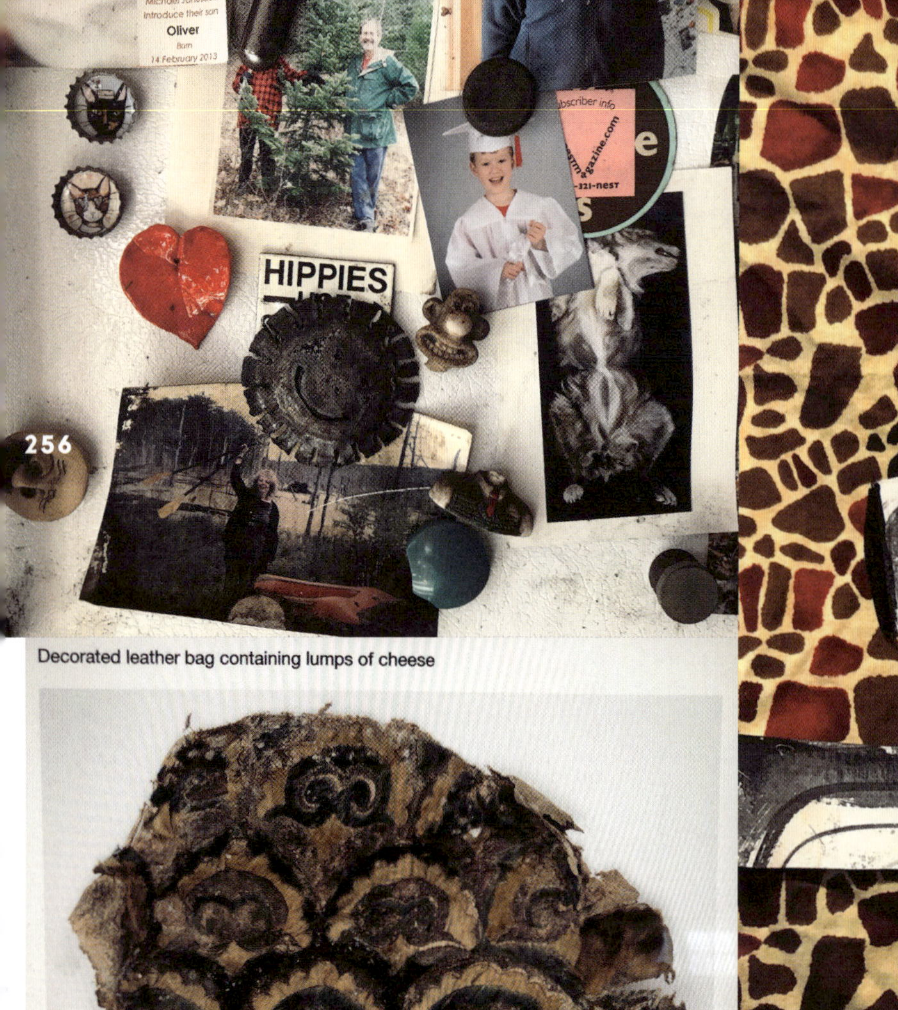

Decorated leather bag containing lumps of cheese

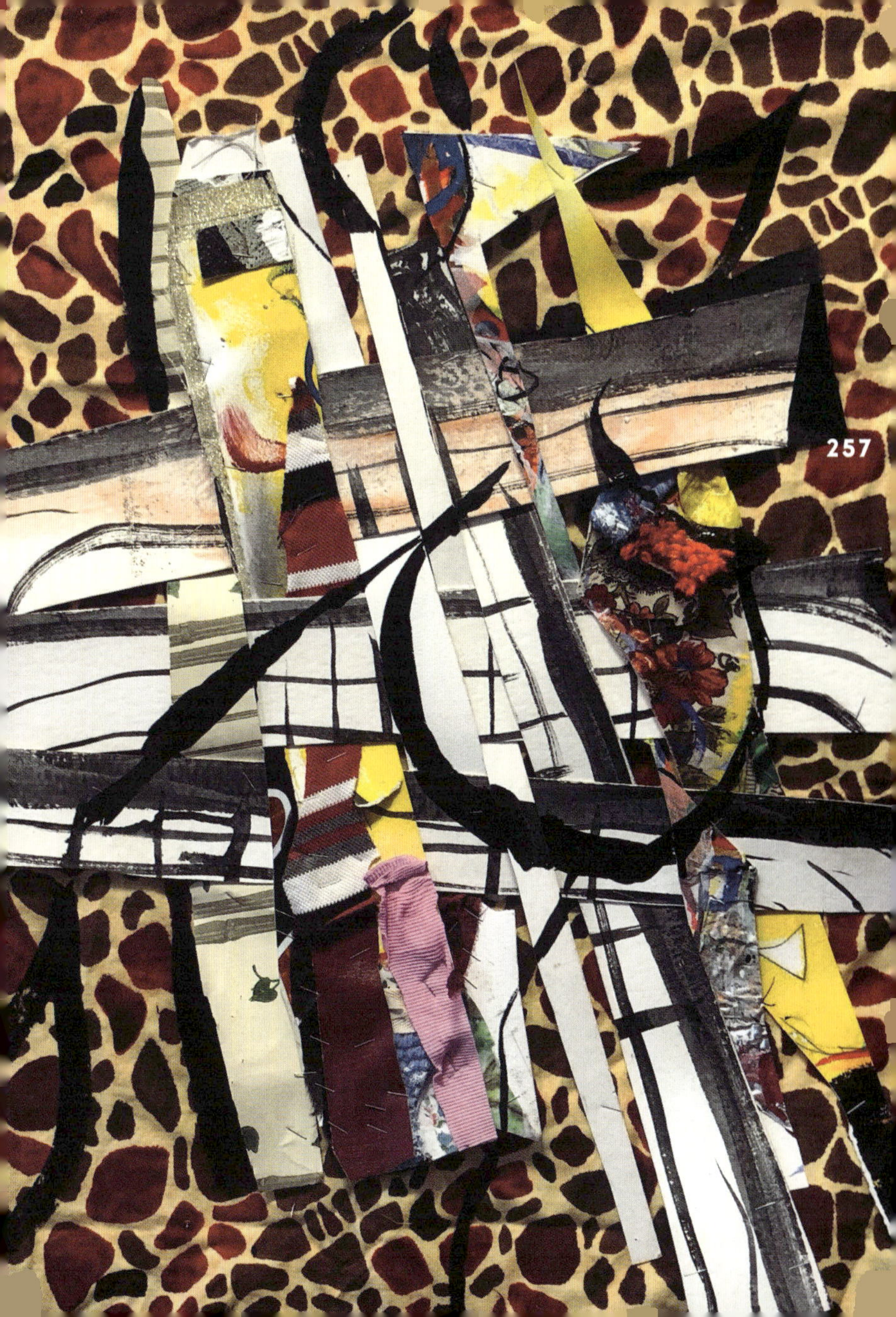
257

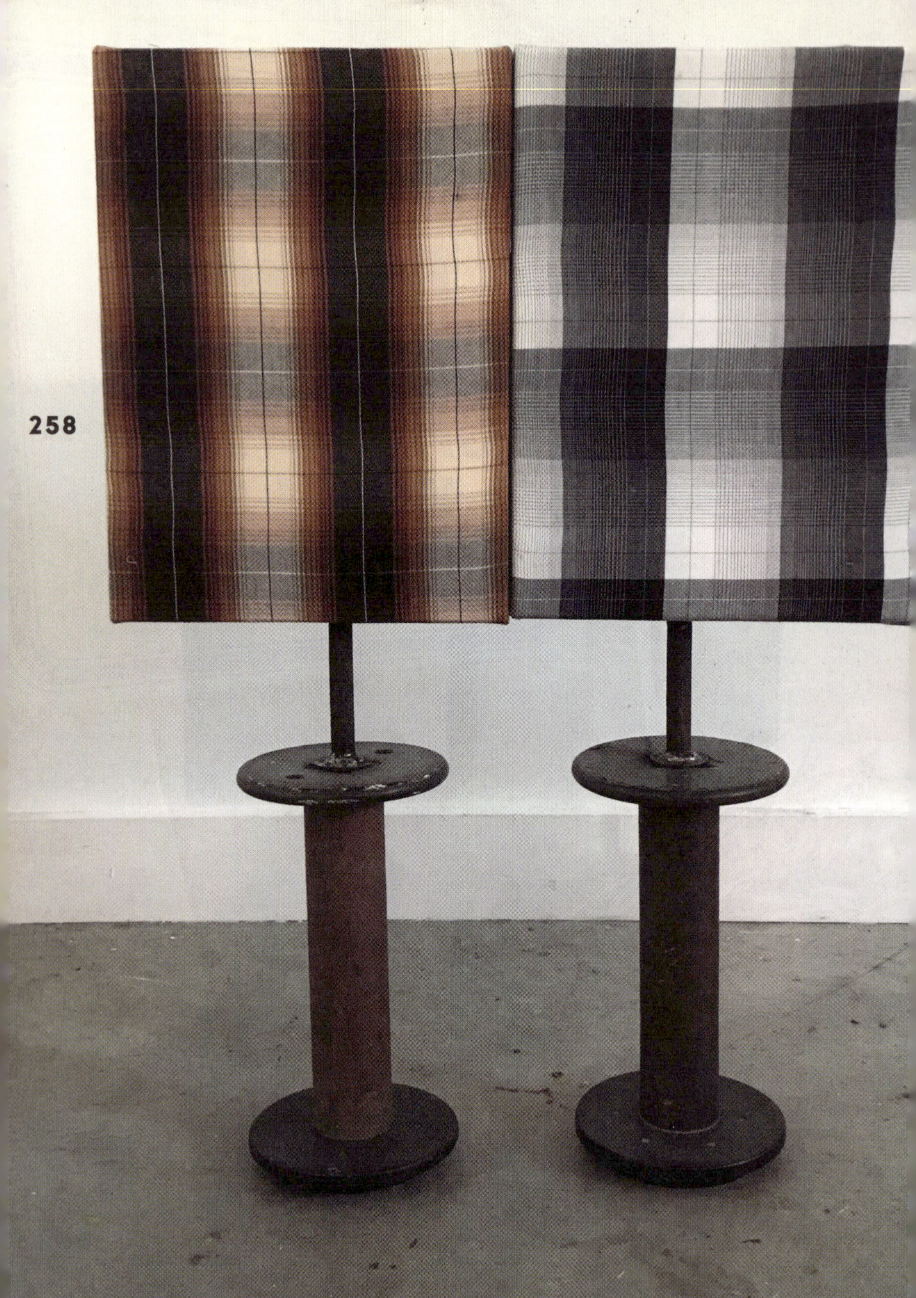

258

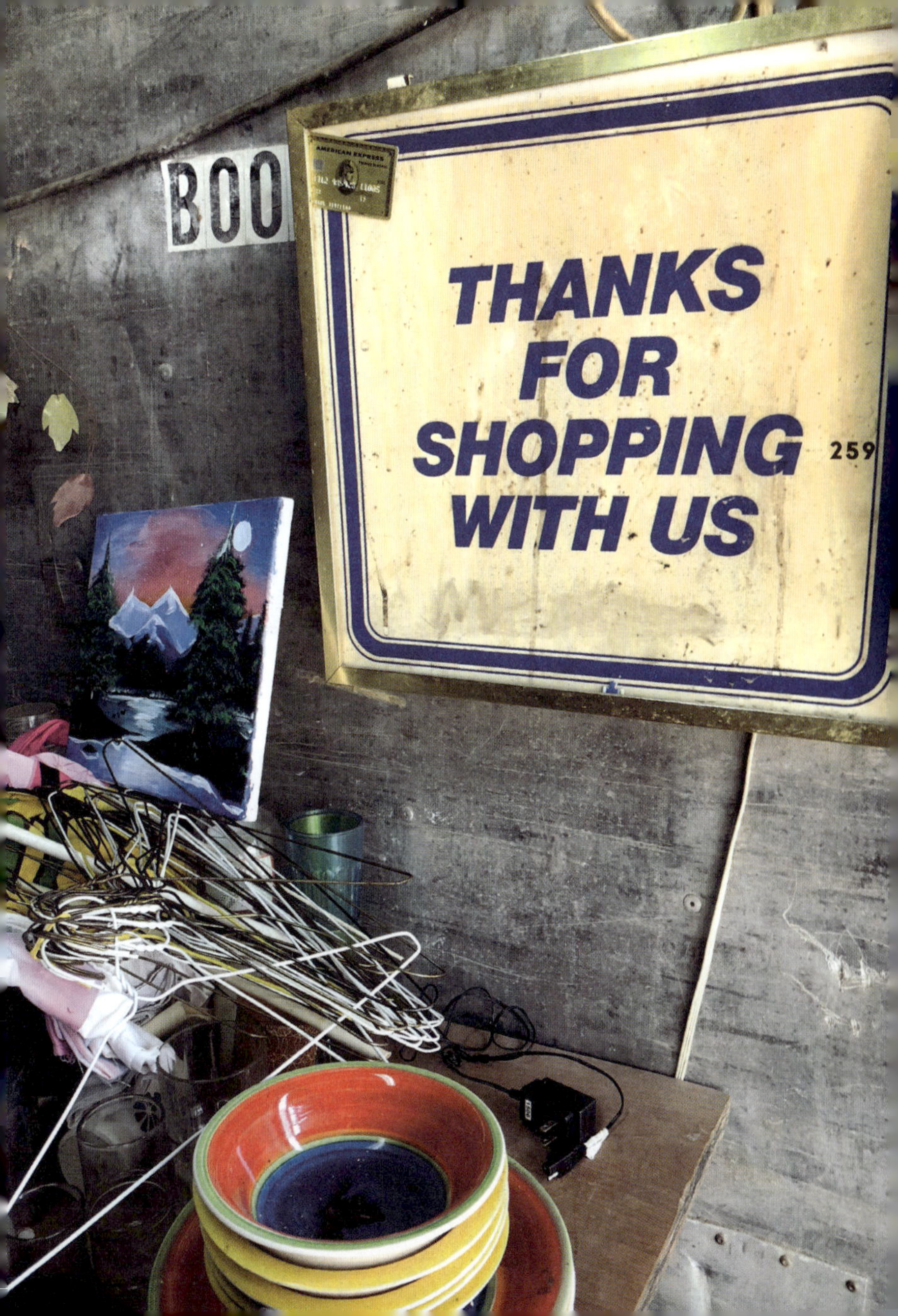
BOO
AMERICAN EXPRESS
THANKS
FOR
SHOPPING
WITH US
259

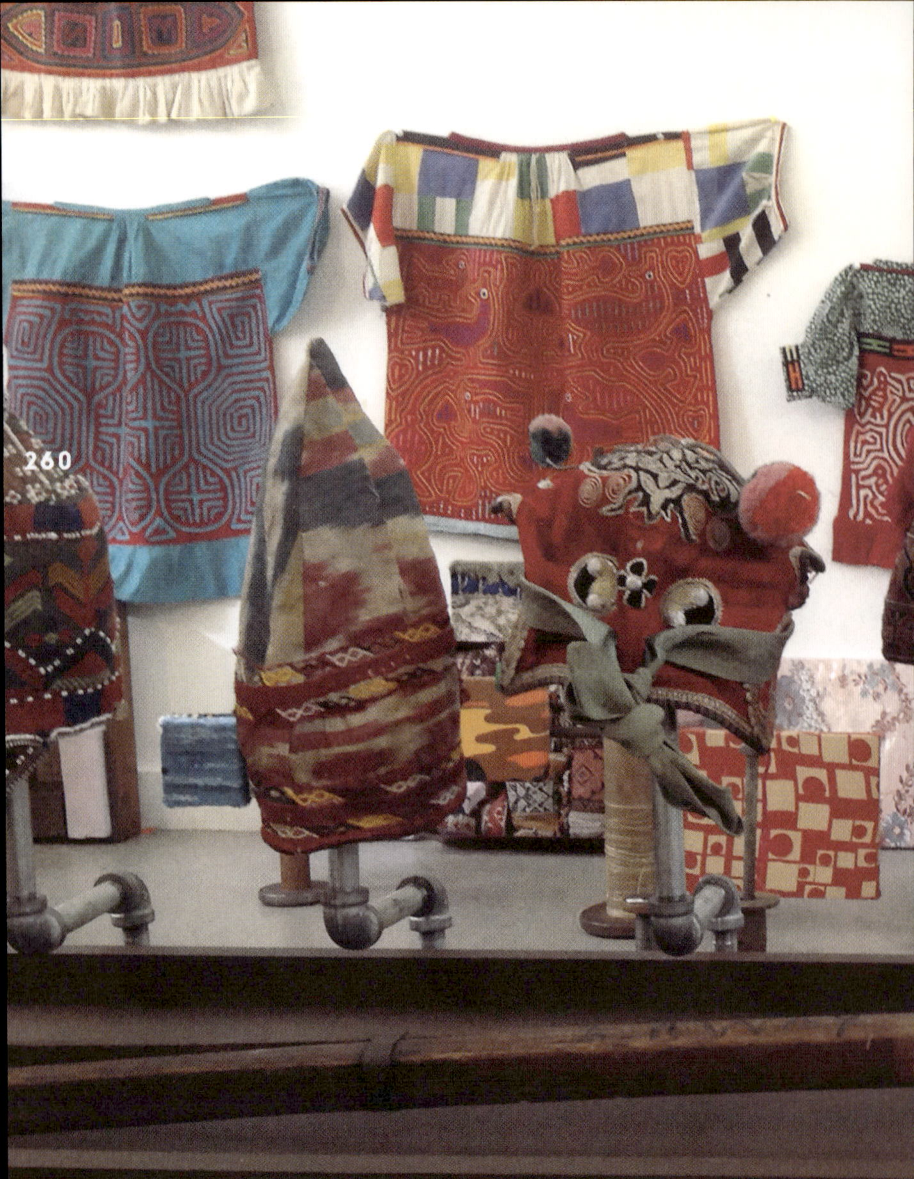
260

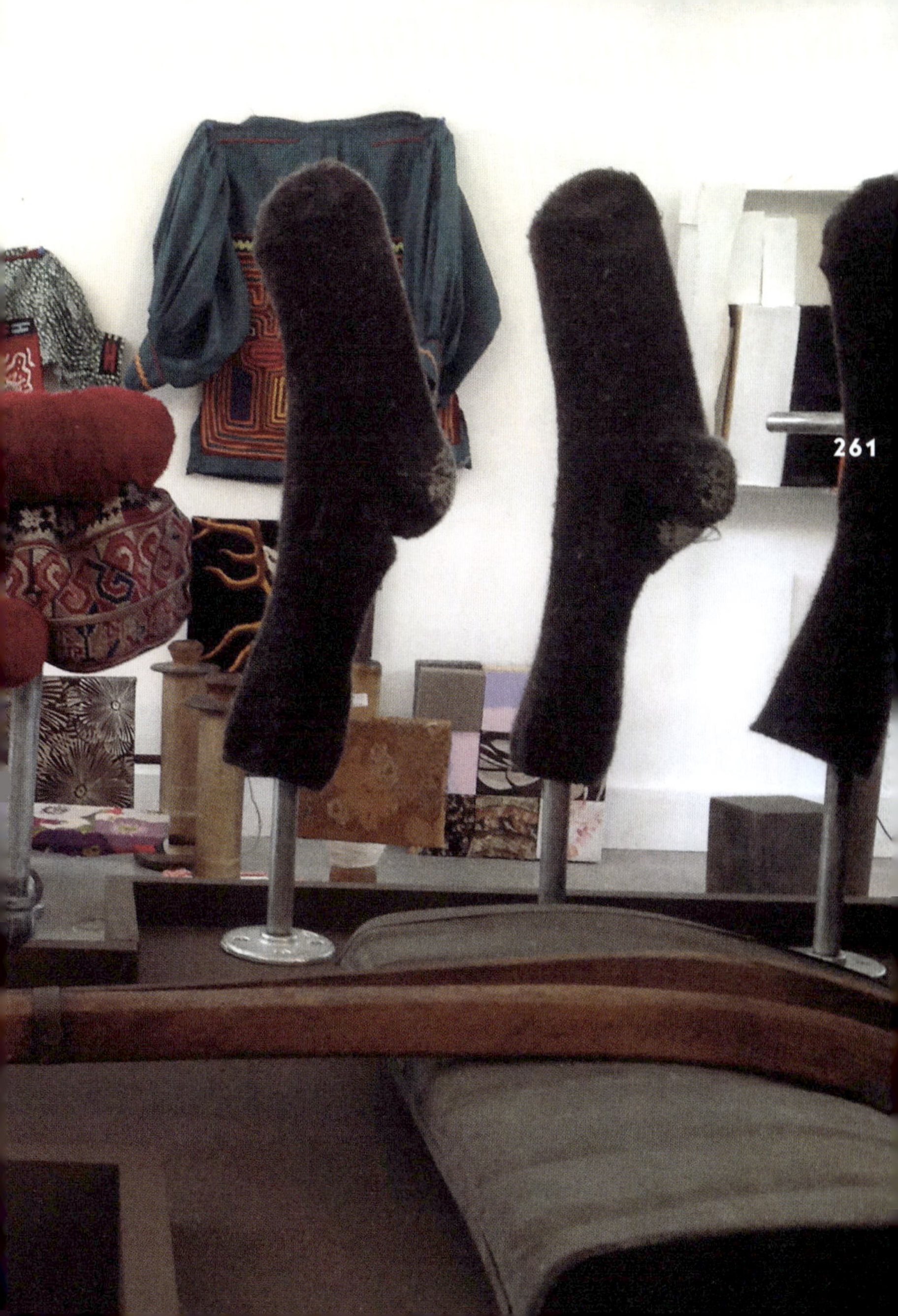
261

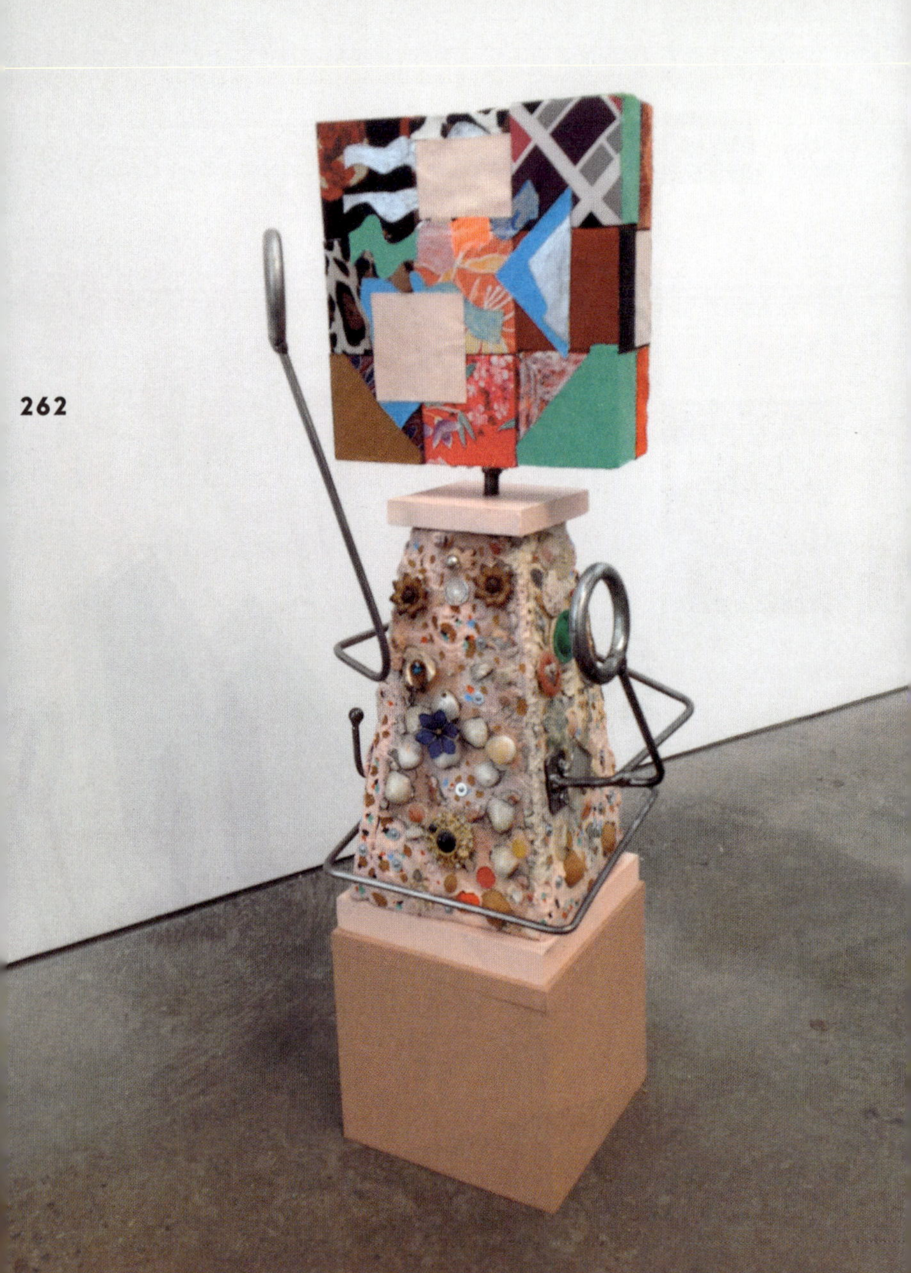

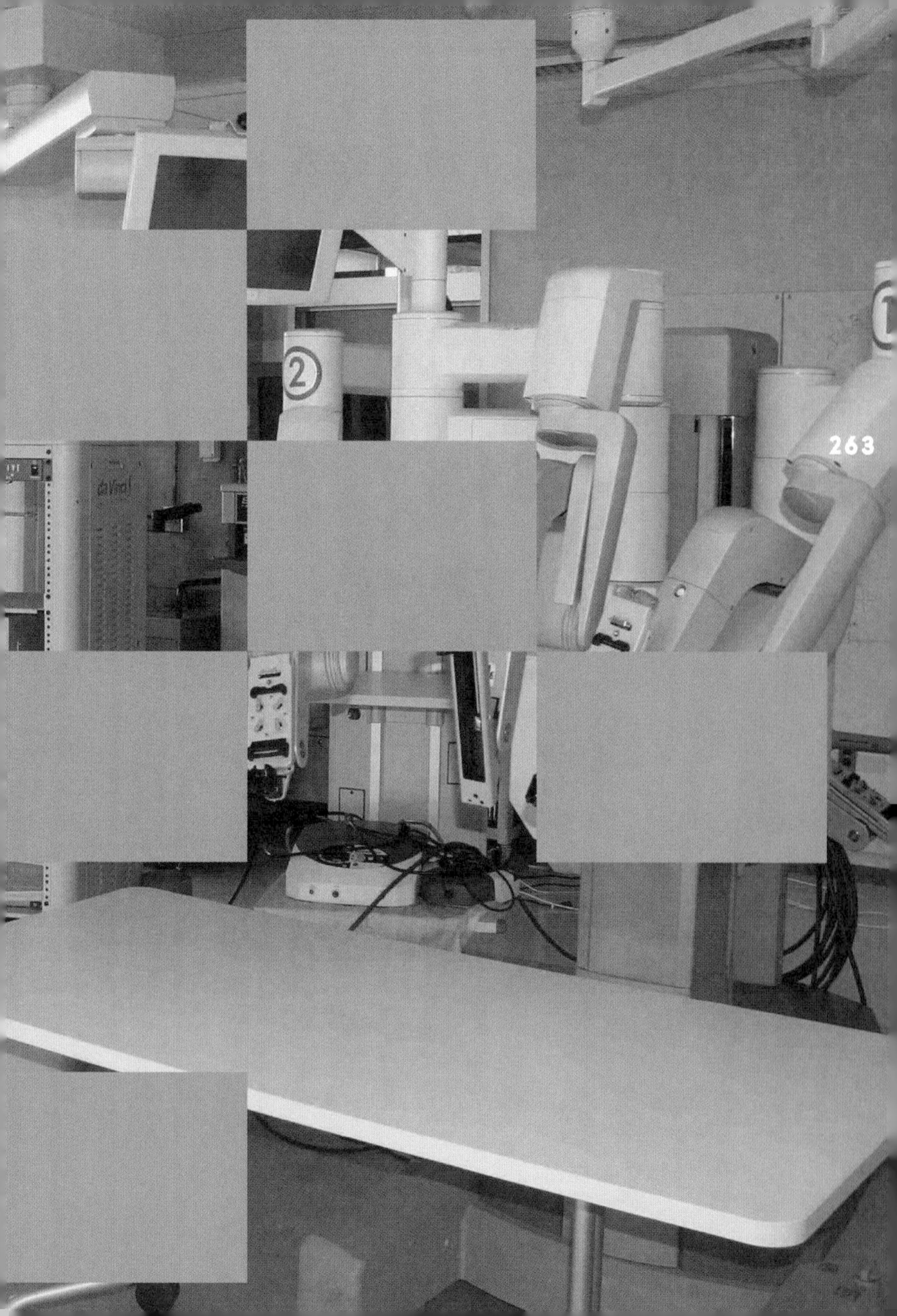
2
1
263
da Vinci

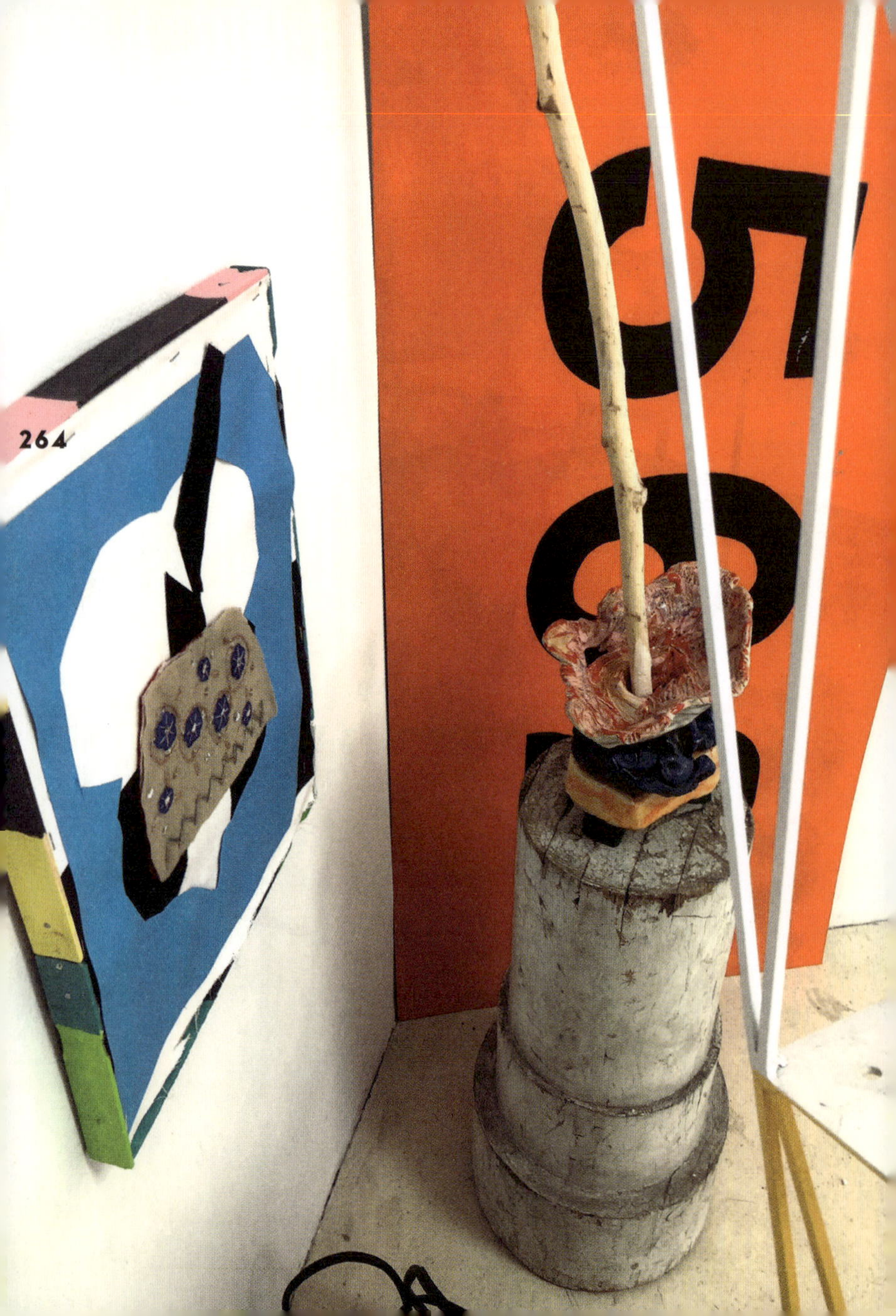
264

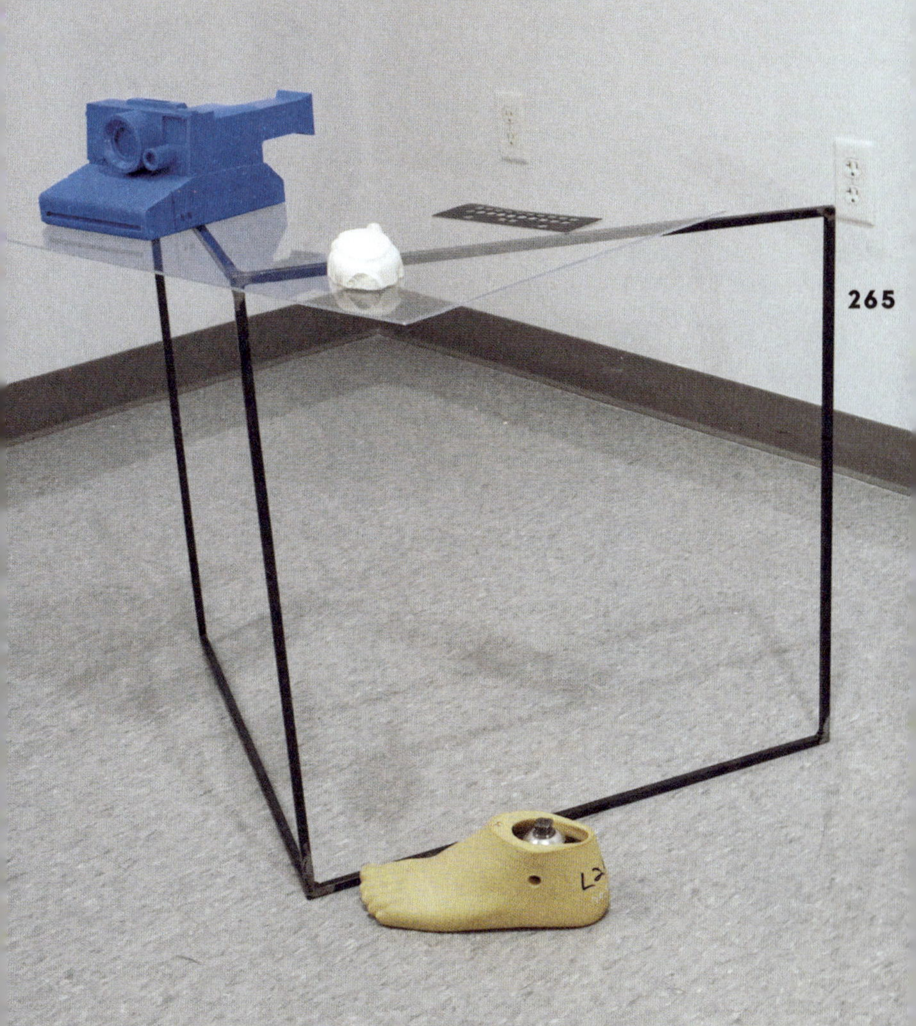
265

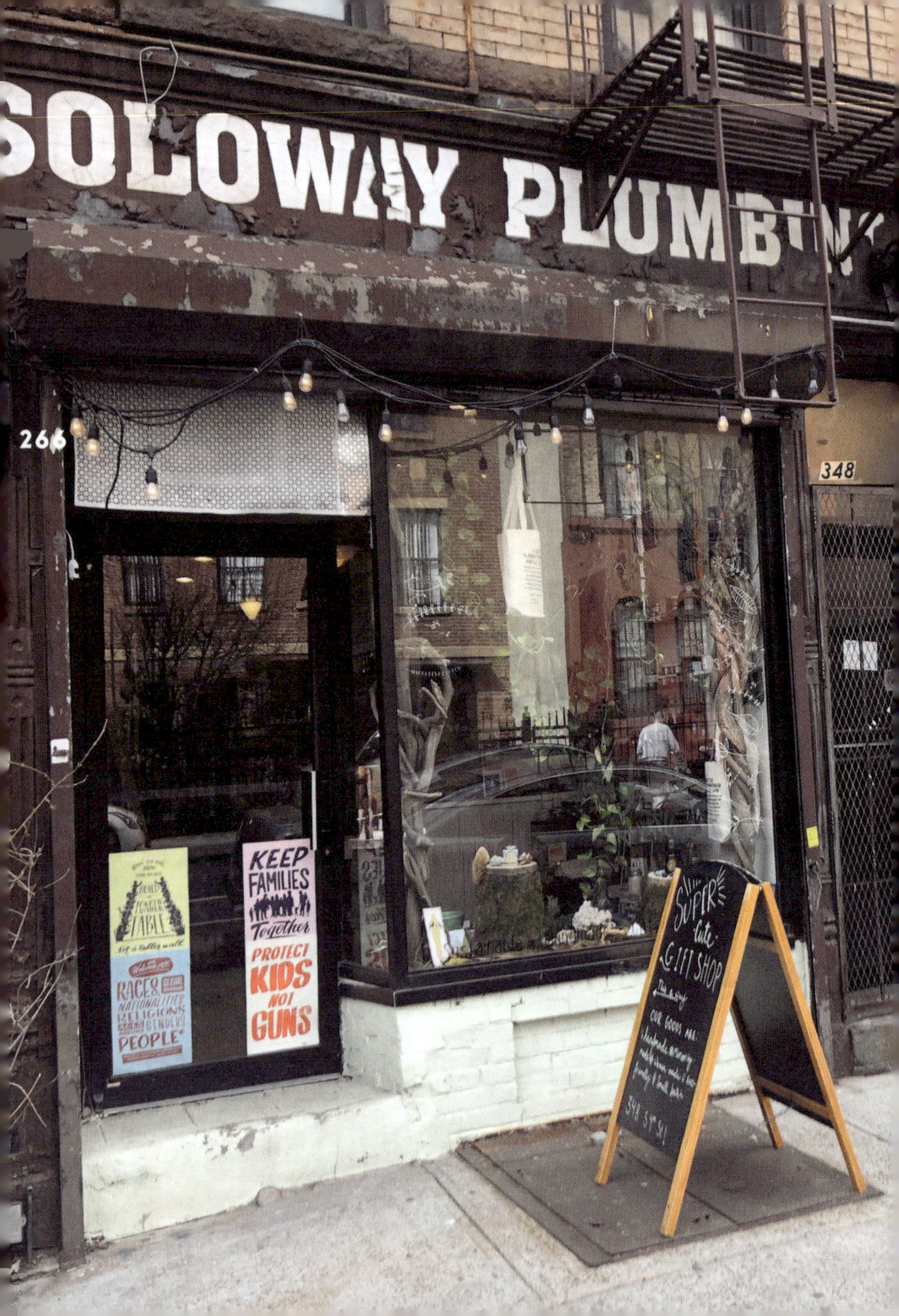
SOLOWAY PLUMBING
266
348
KEEP FAMILIES Together
PROTECT KIDS NOT GUNS
SUPER cute GIFT SHOP
348 ST St

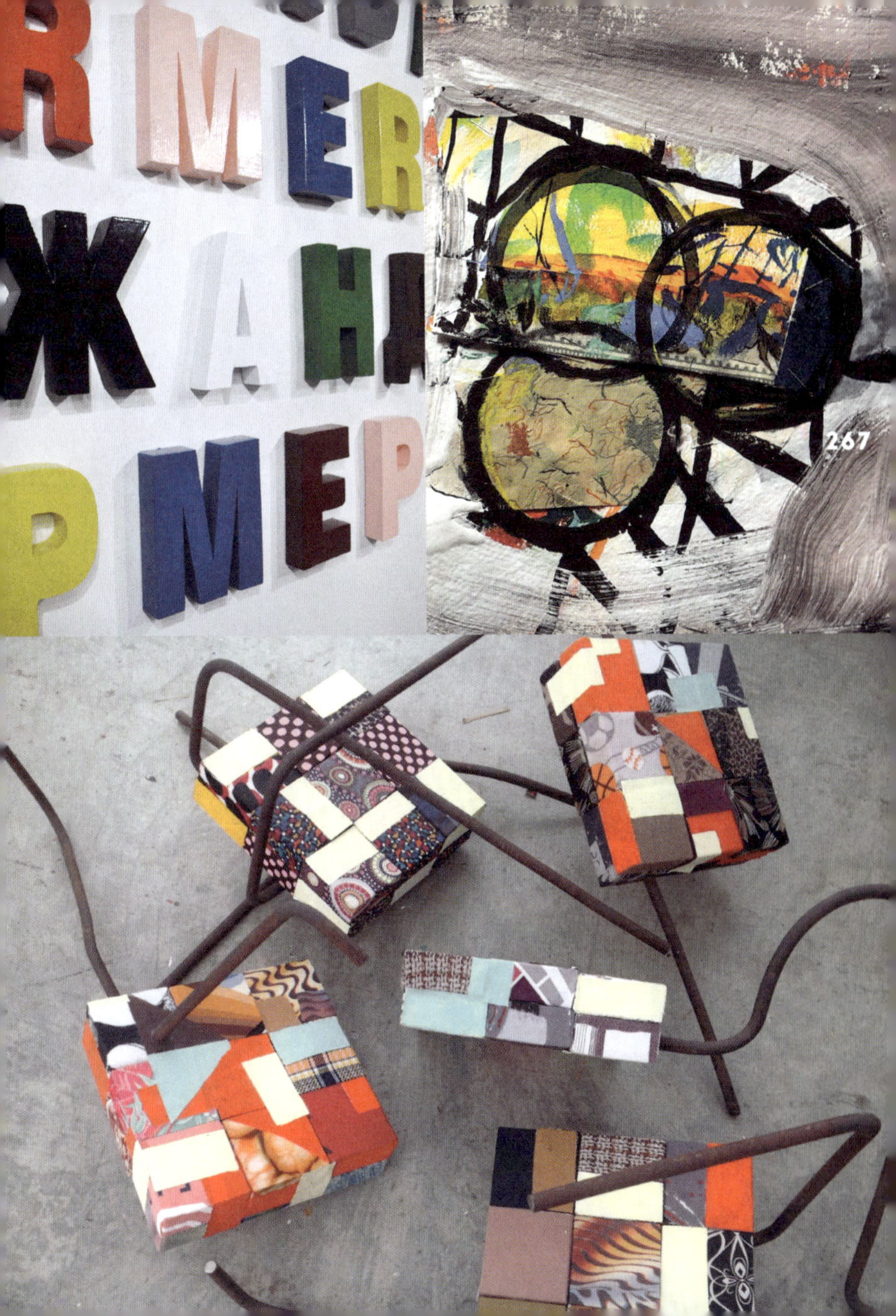
267

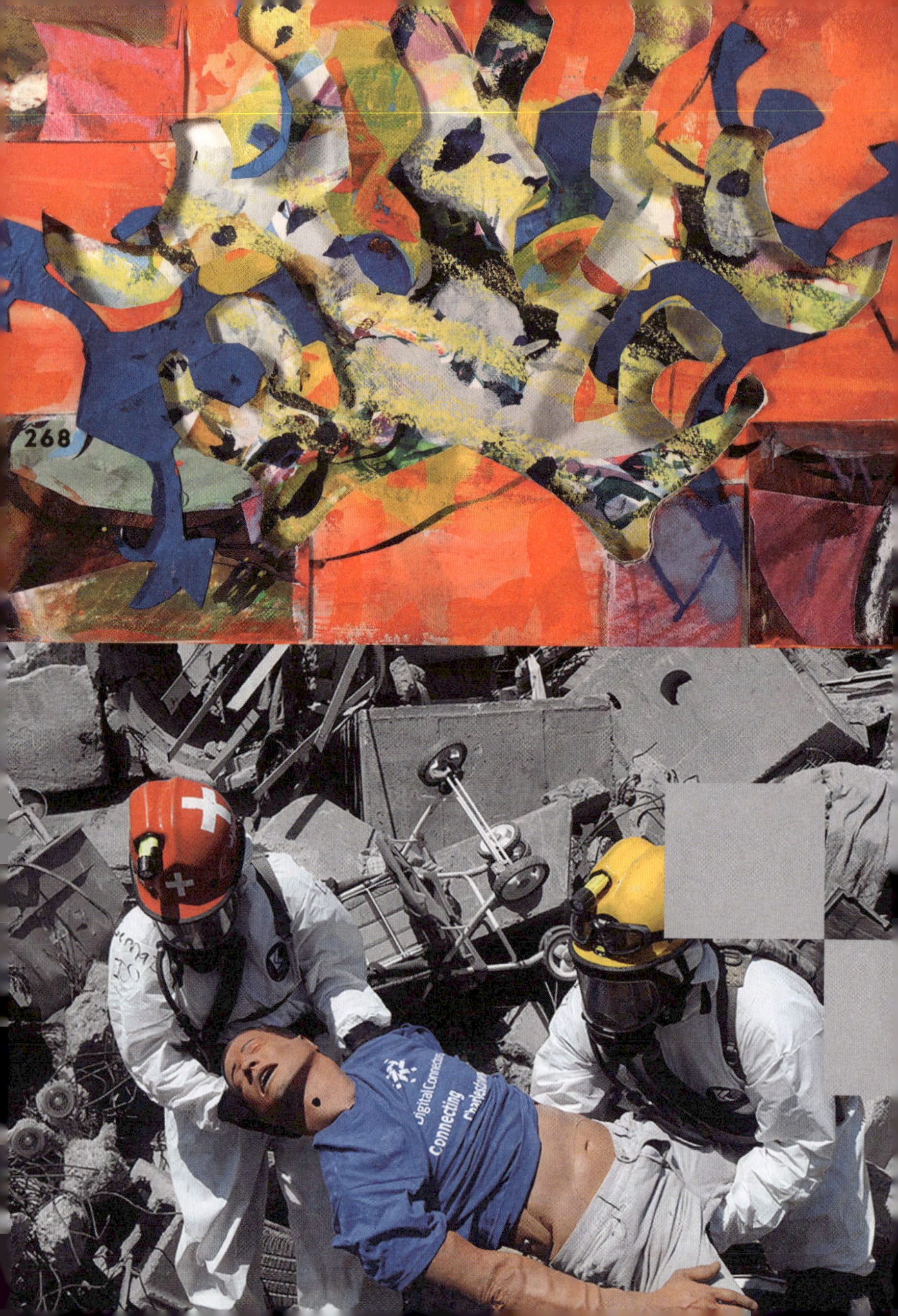
268

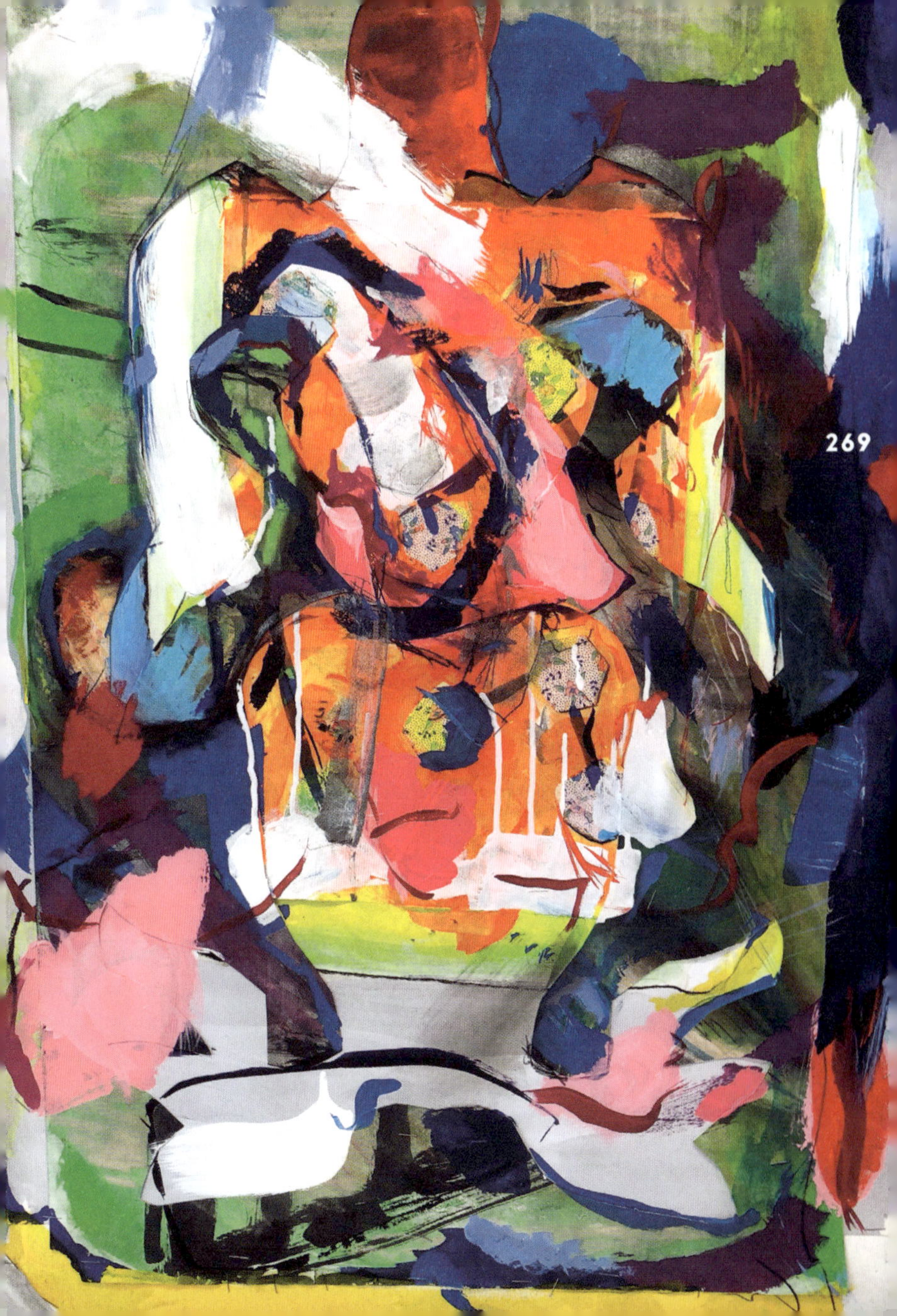

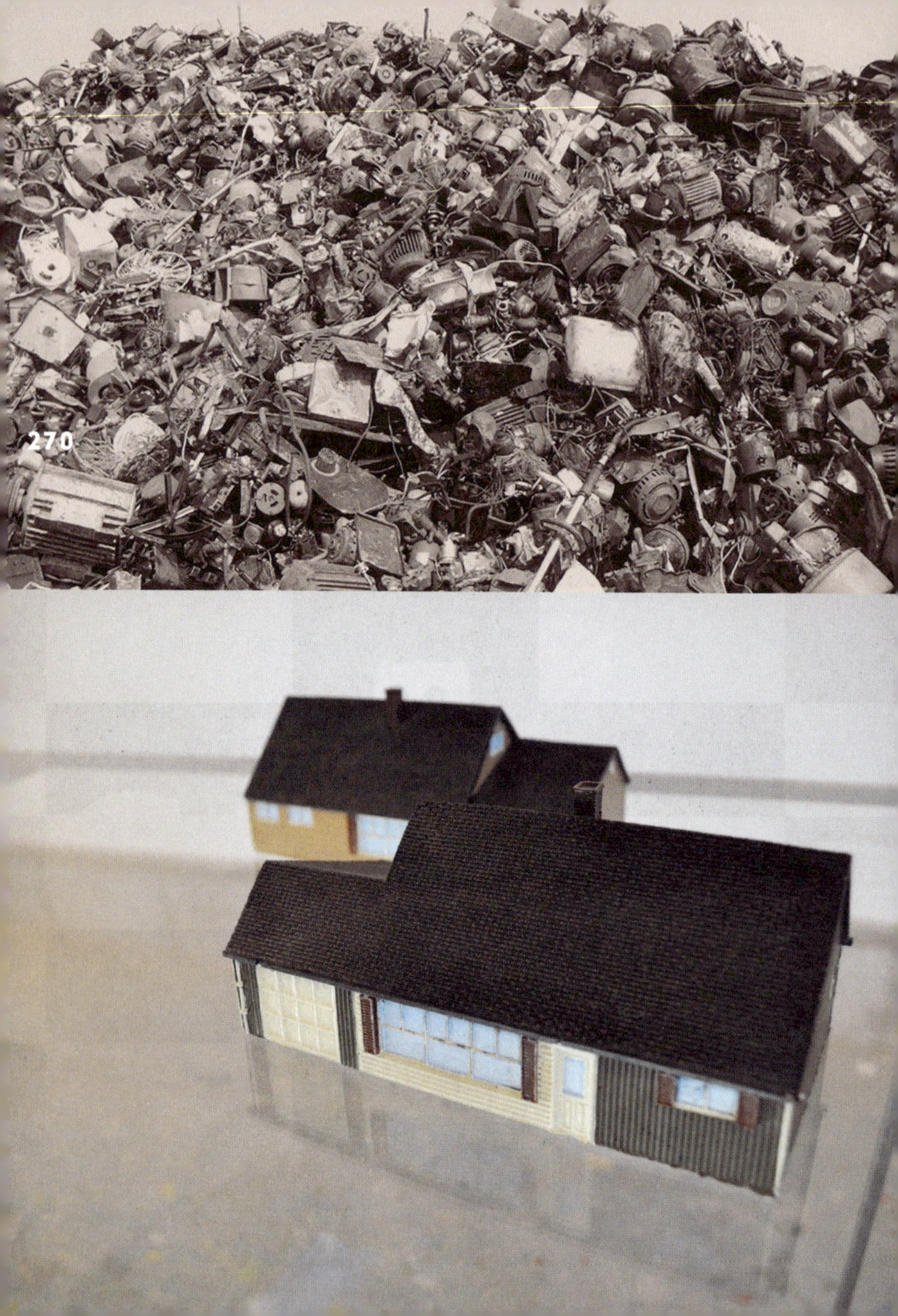
270

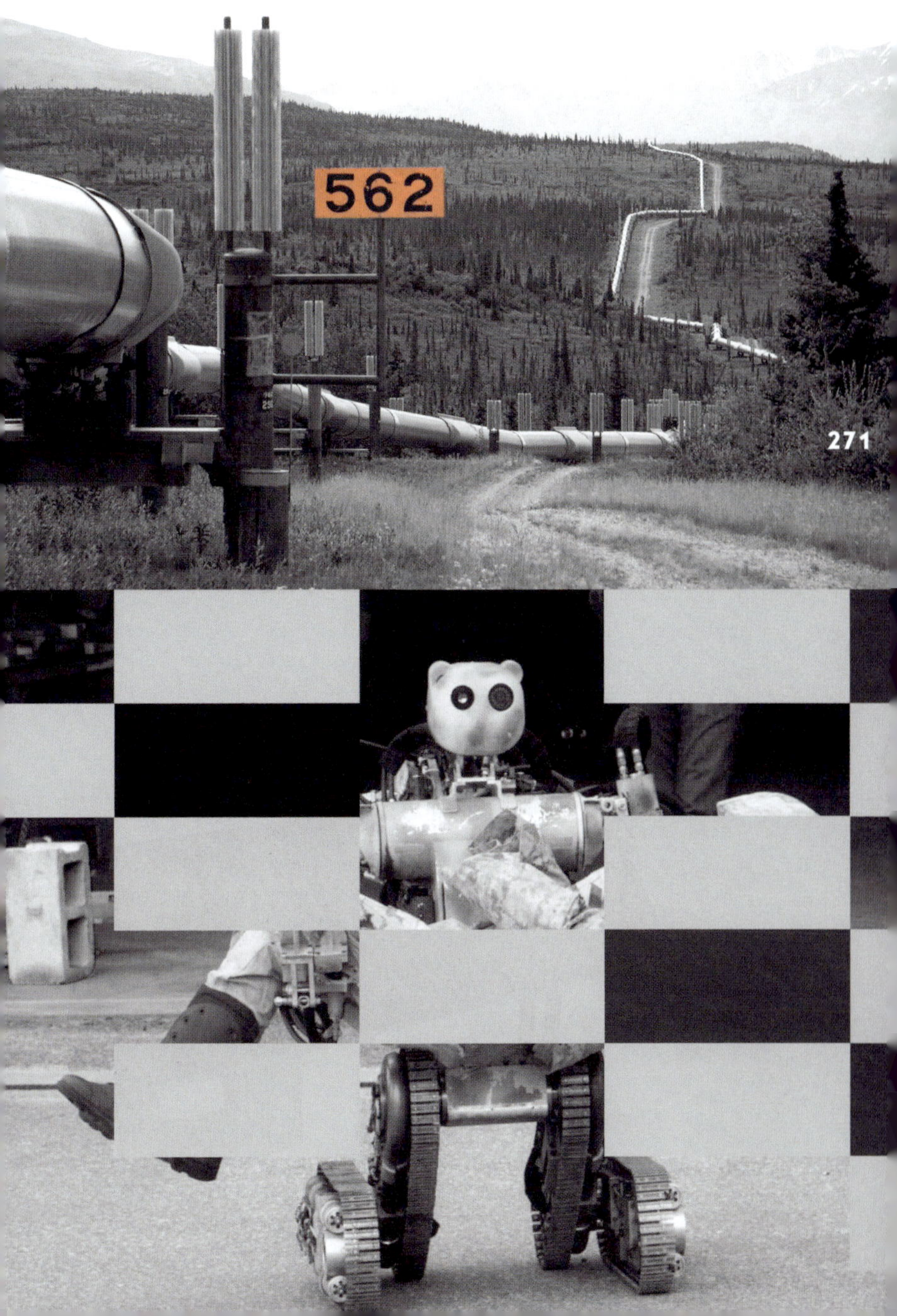
562

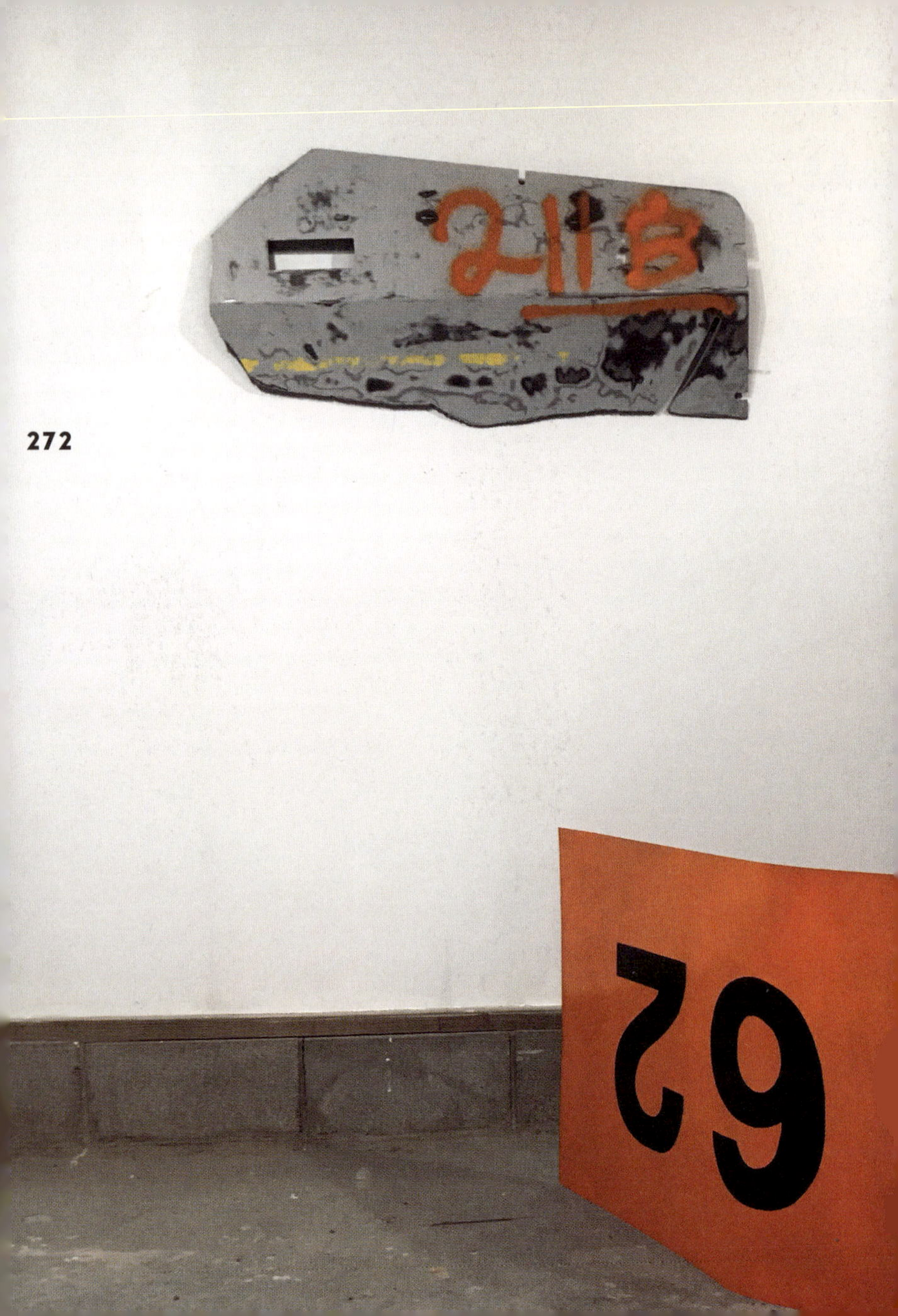

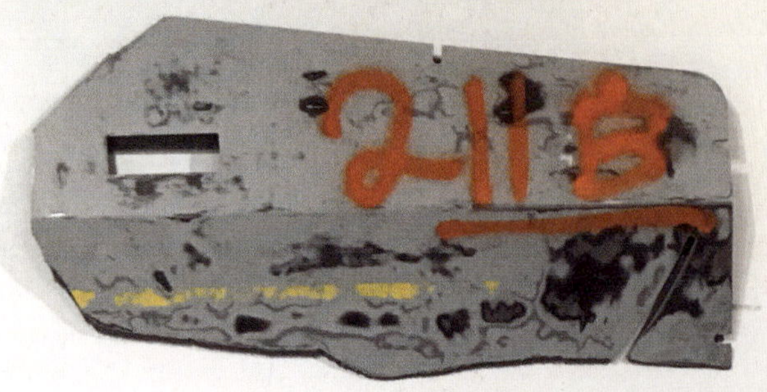

272

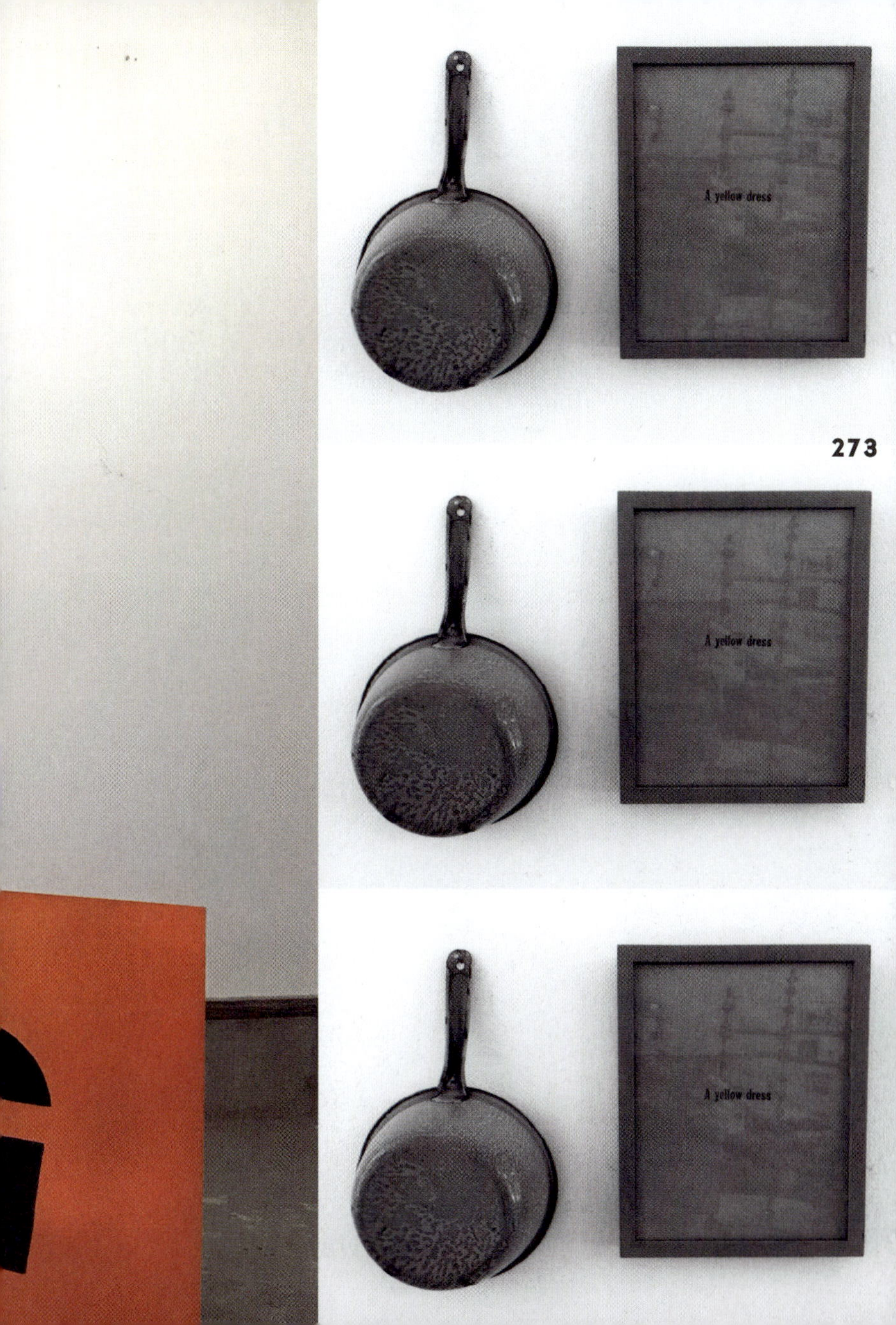

273

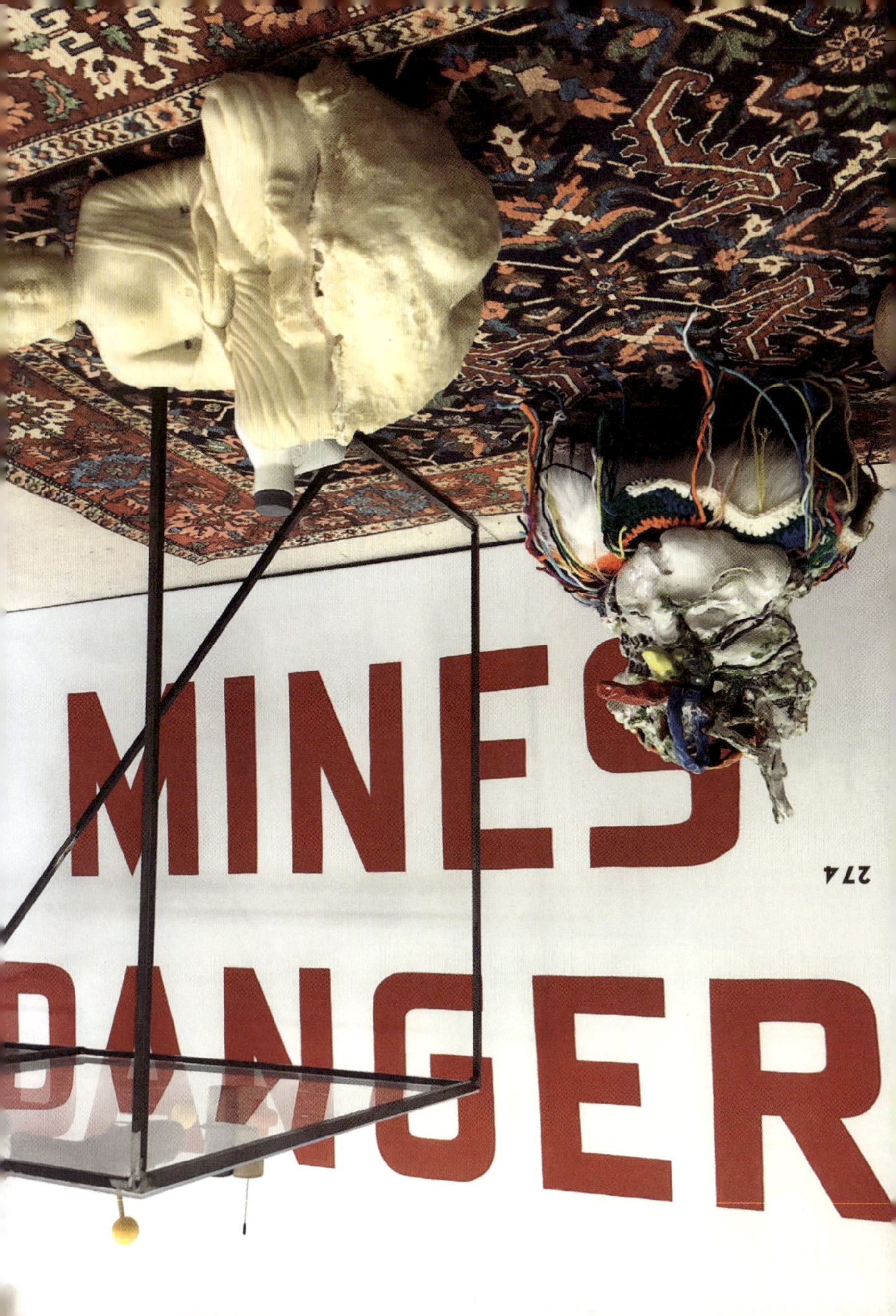
MINES
DANGER

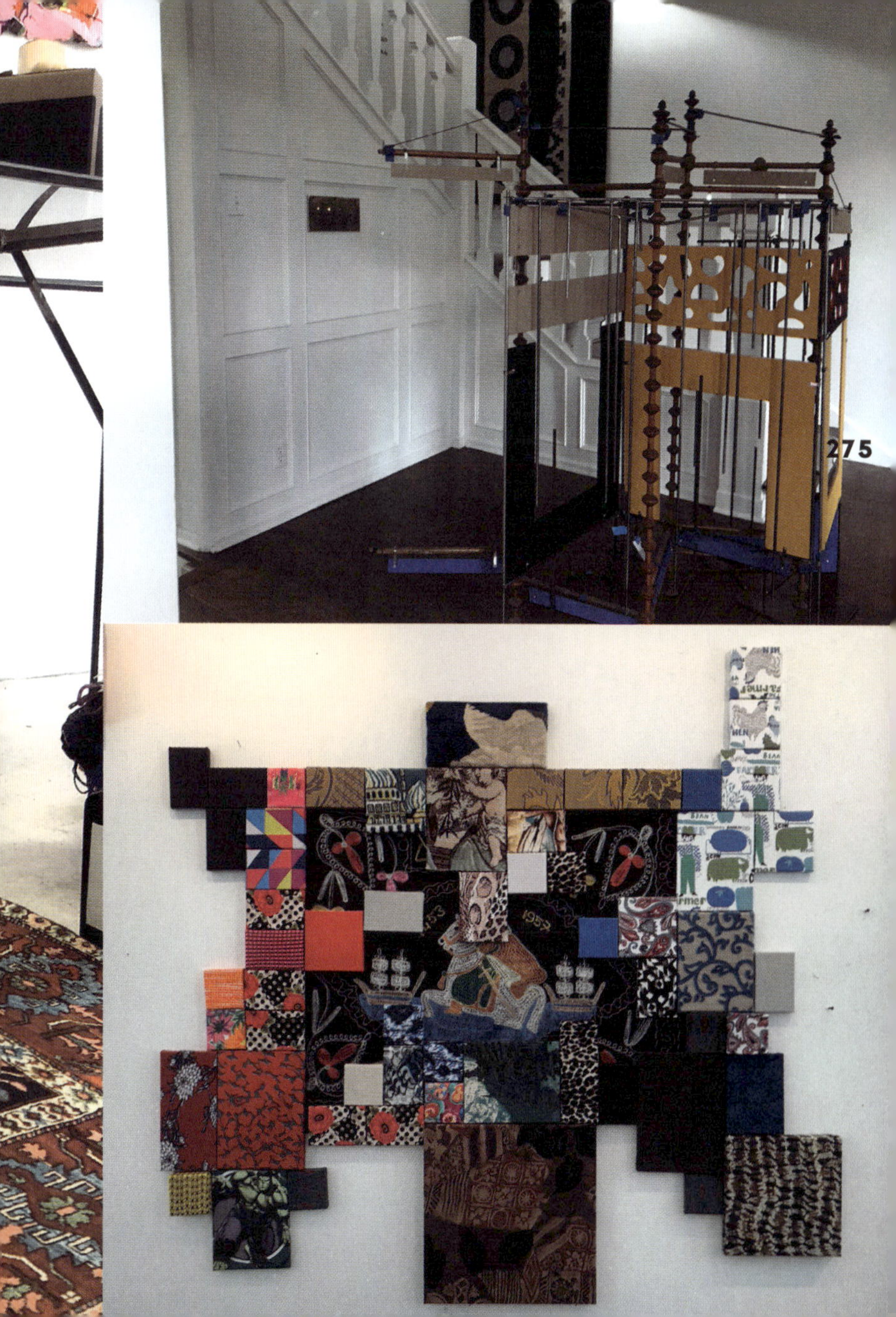

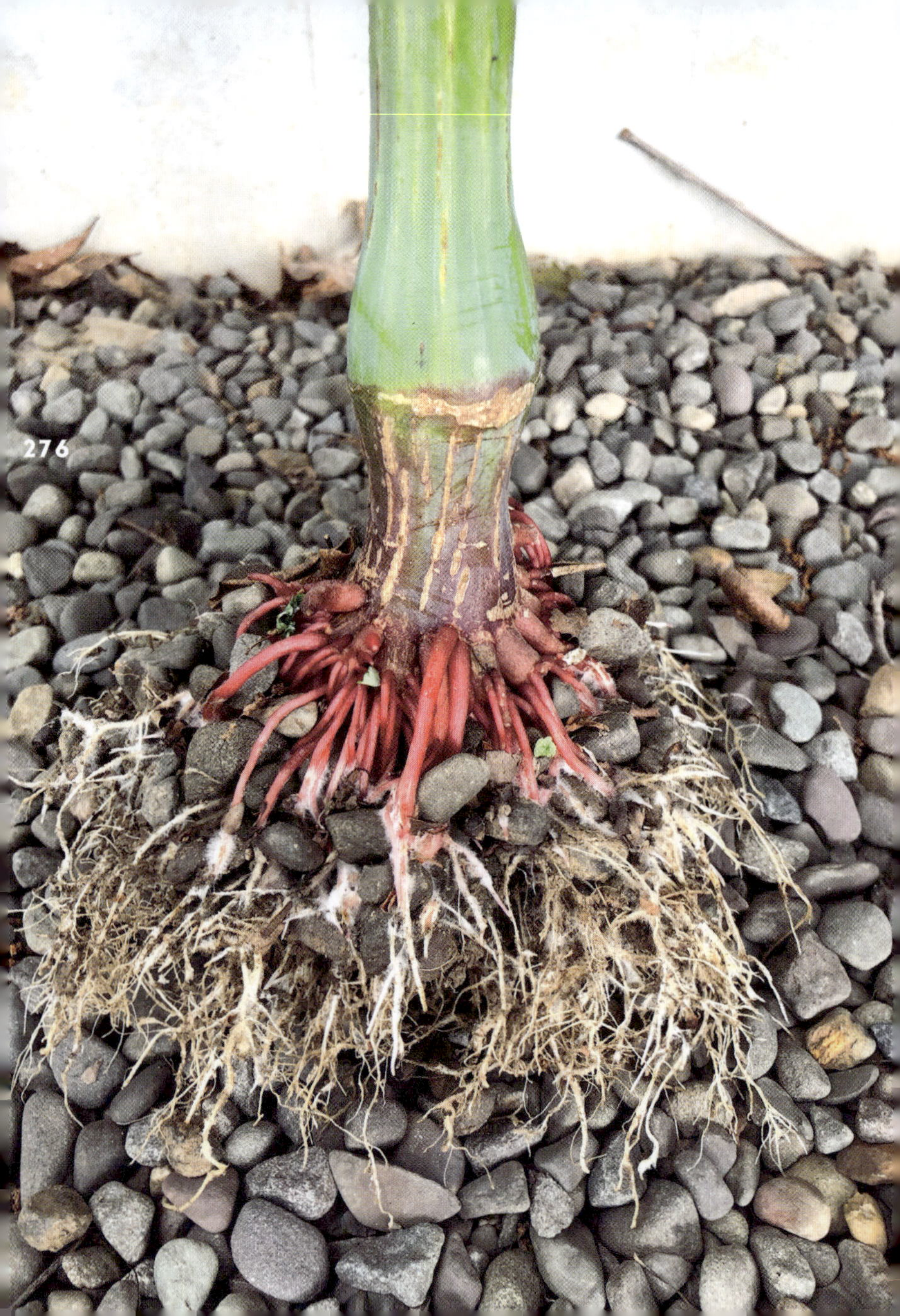
276

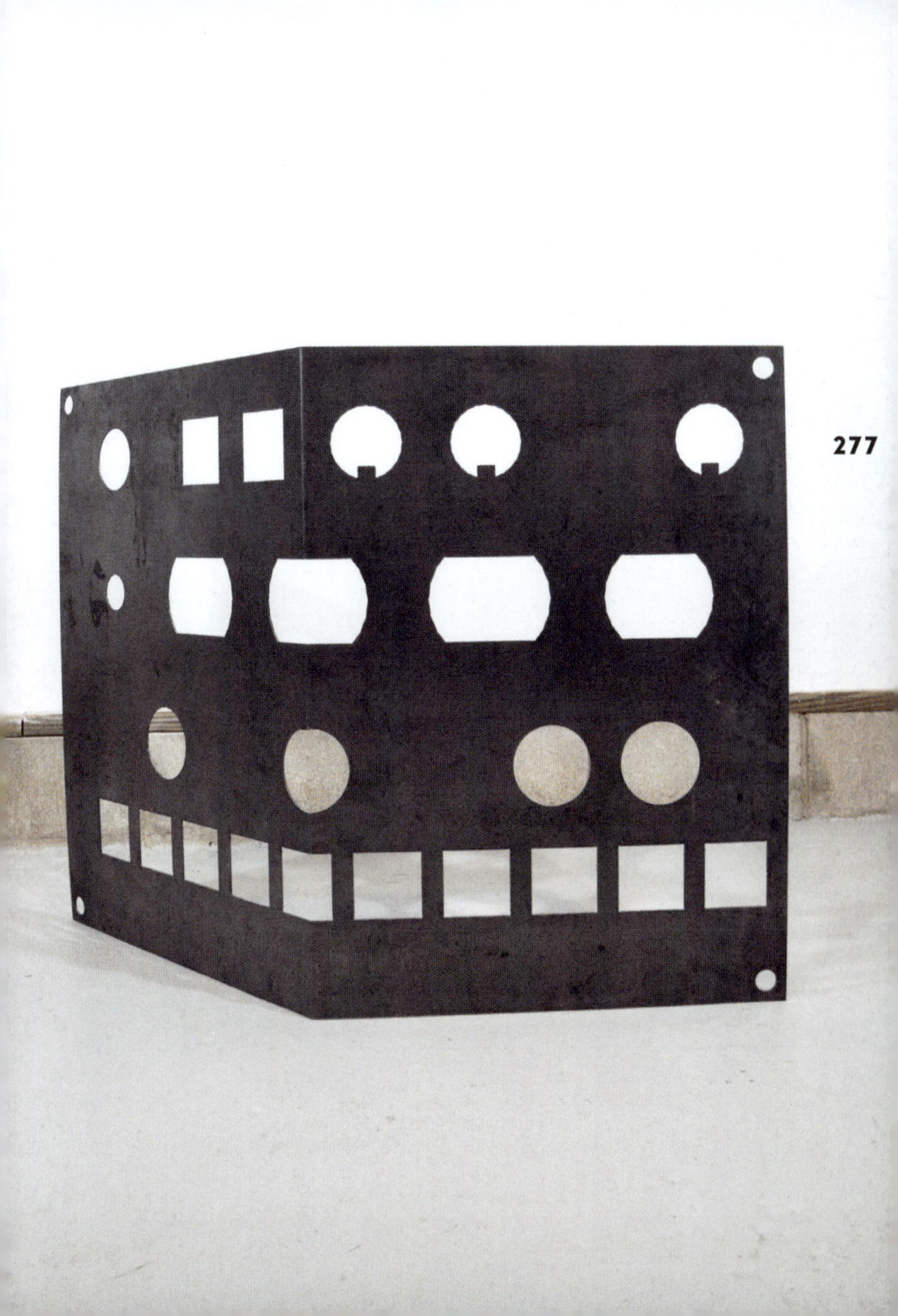

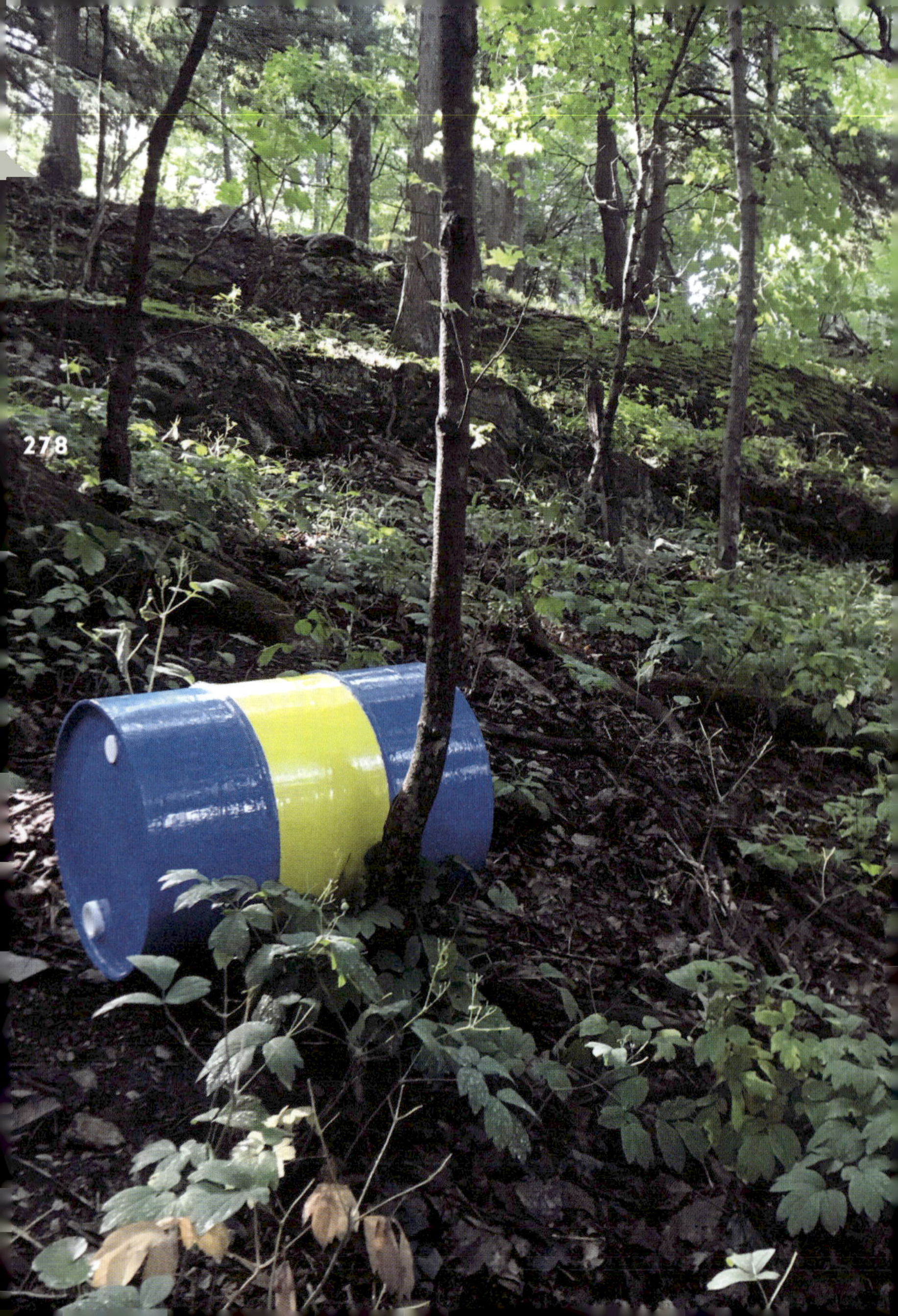
278

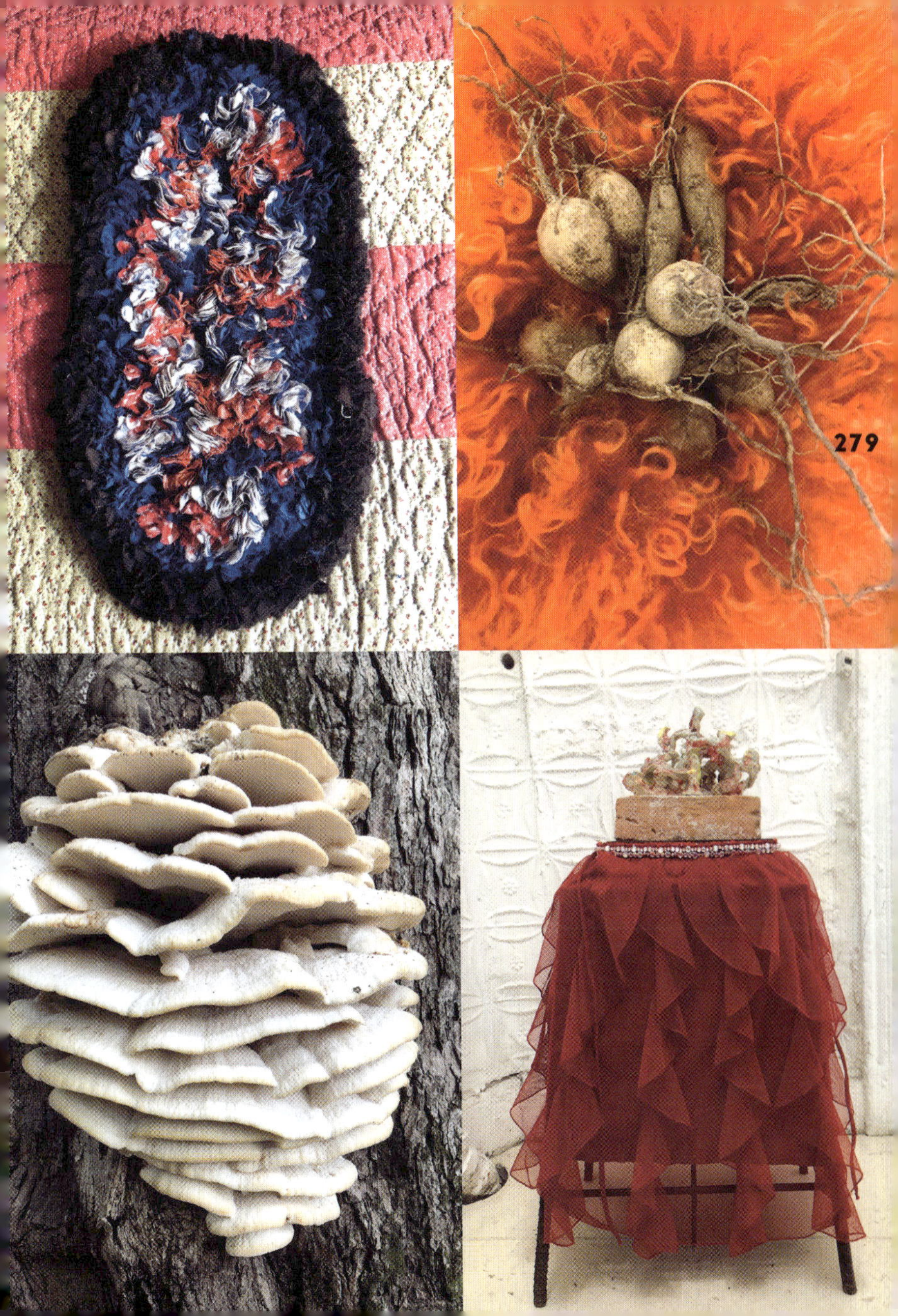

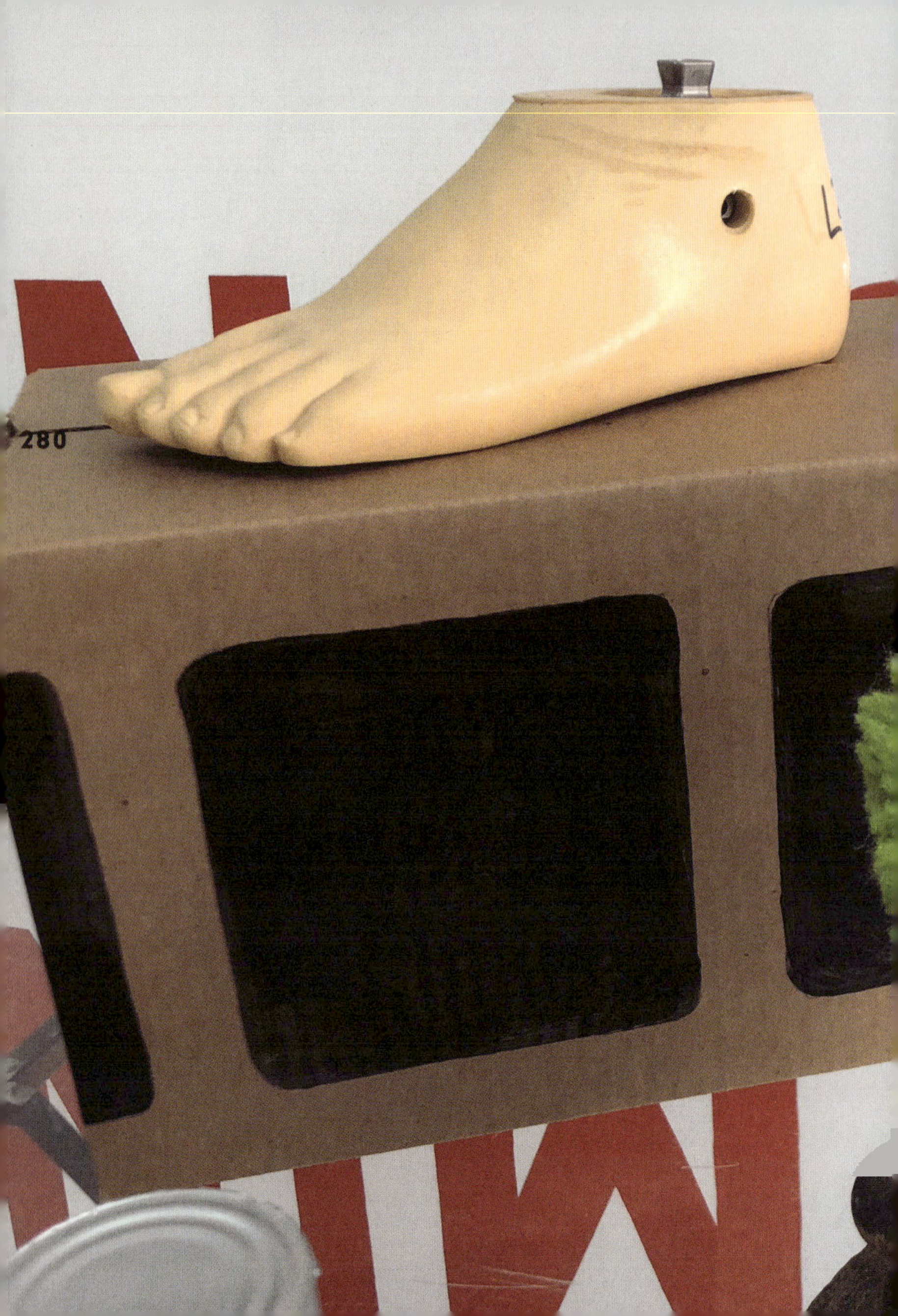
280

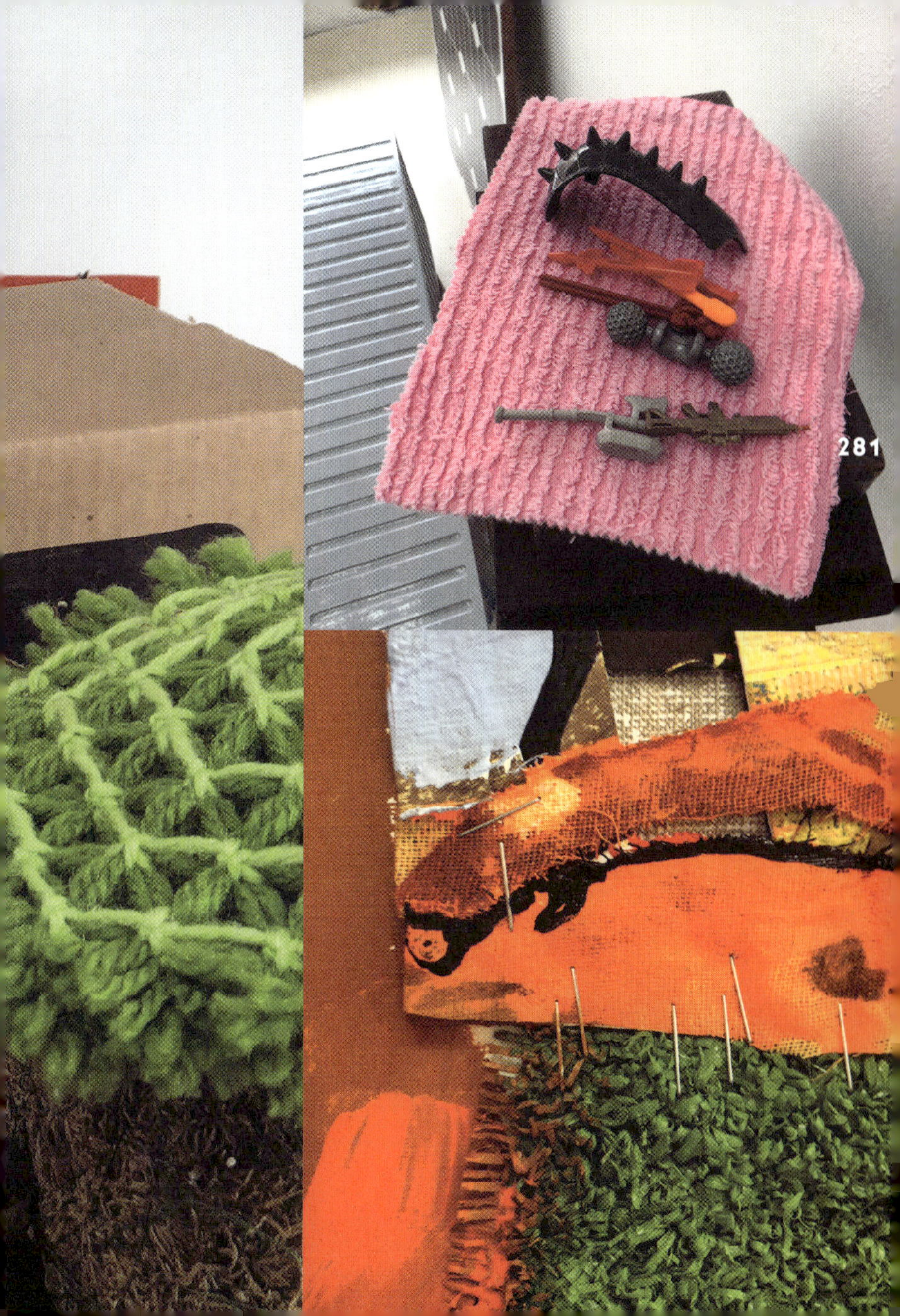
281

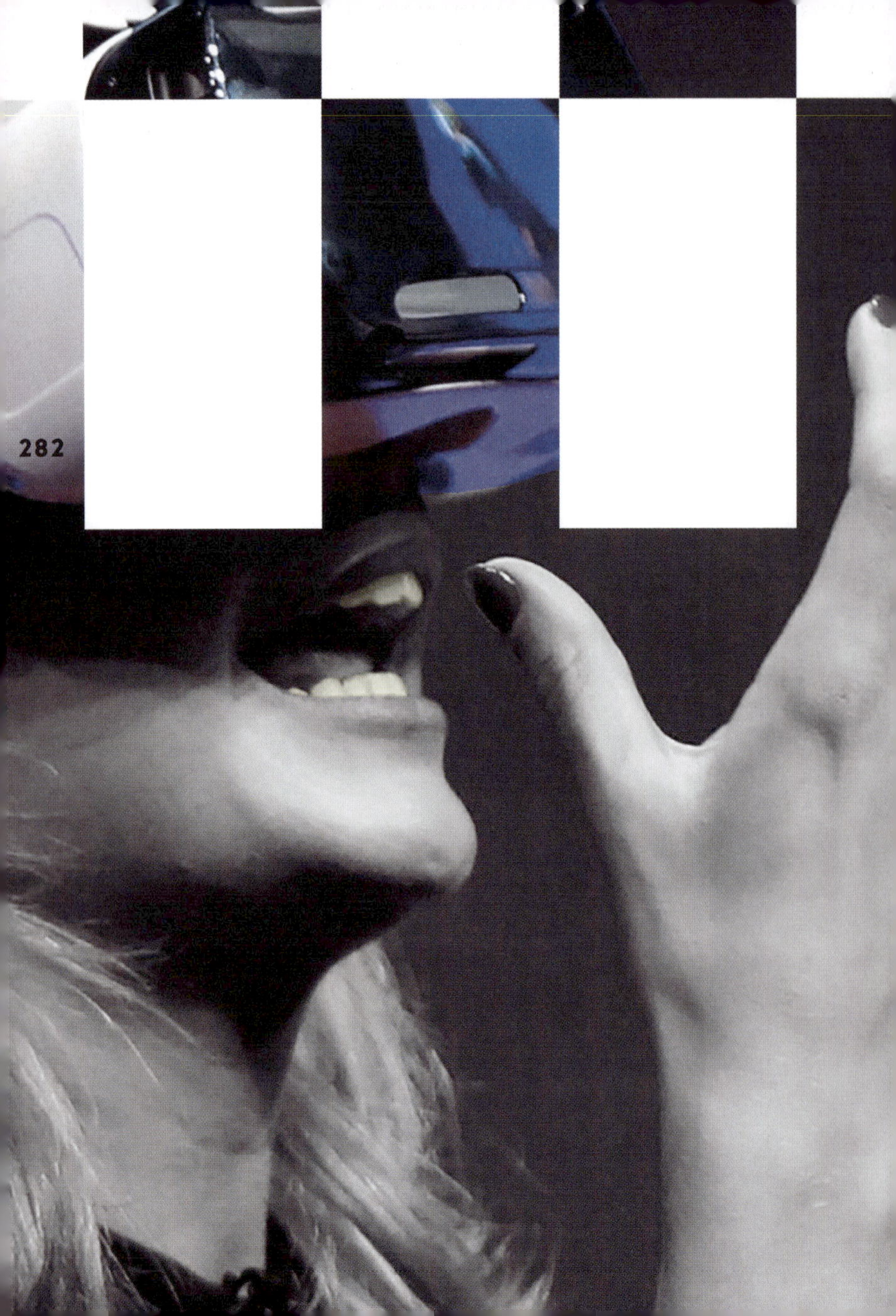

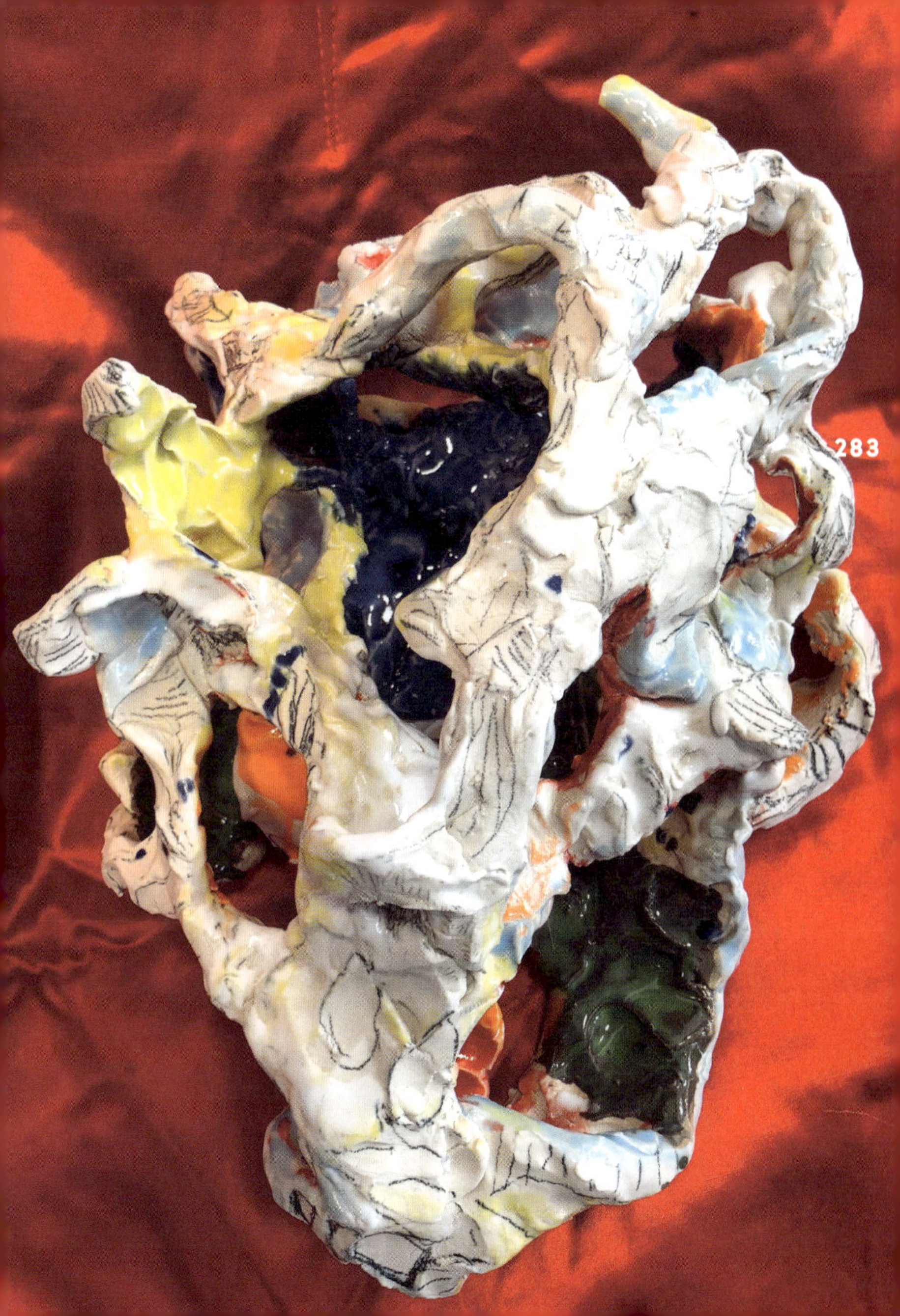
283

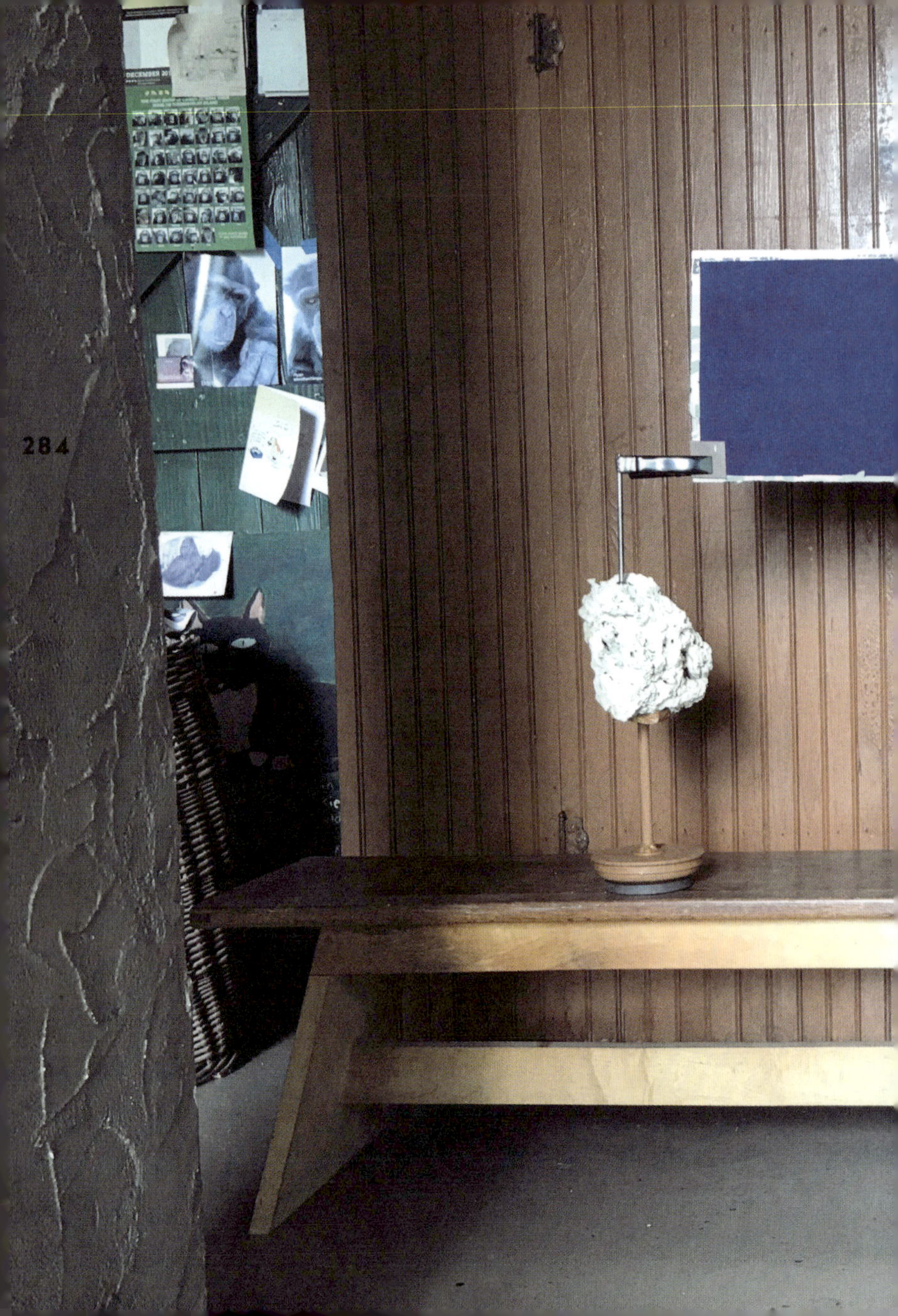

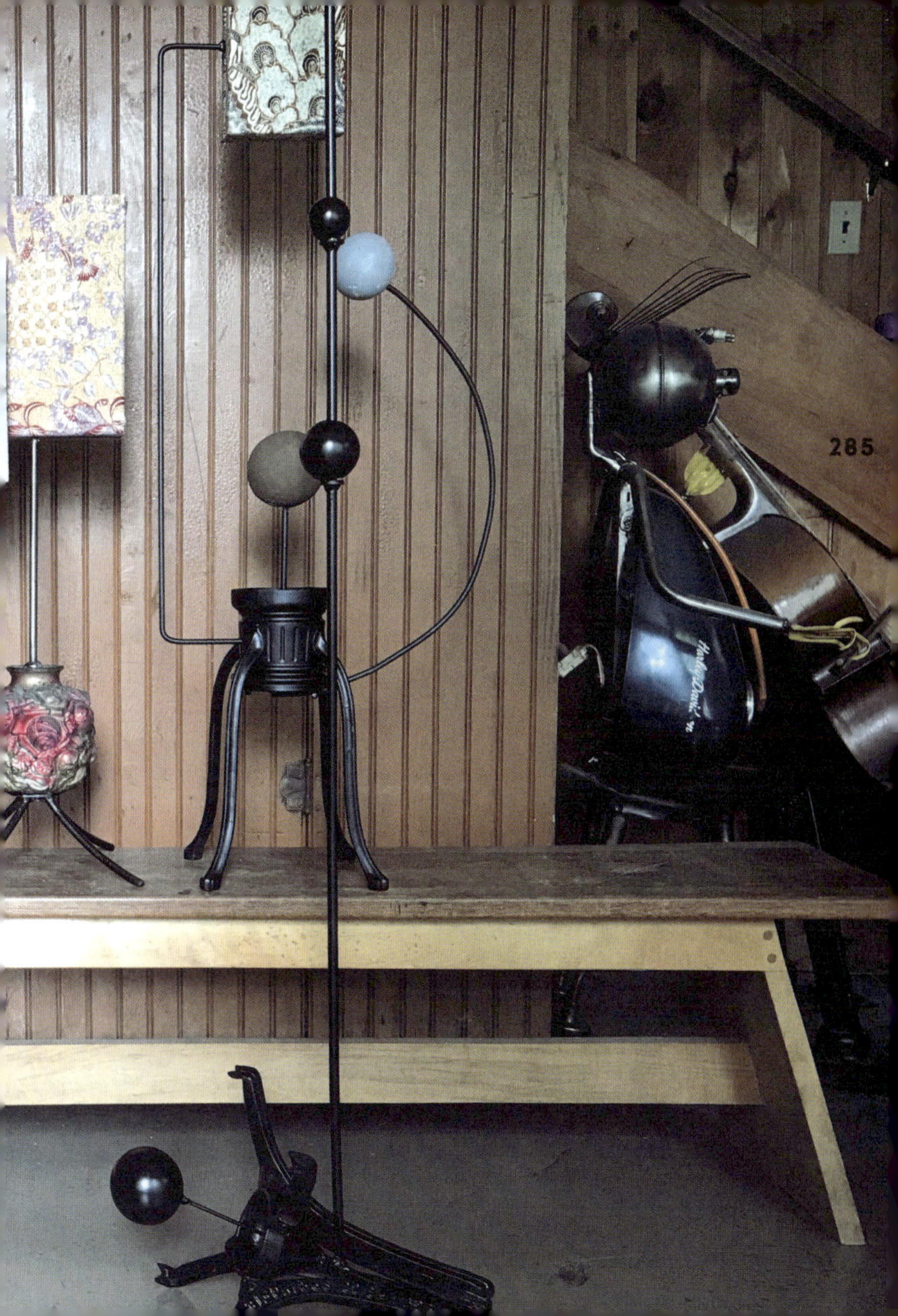

285

contributors

STAN ALLEN is an architect and George Dutton '27 Professor of Architecture at Princeton University. From 2002 to 2012, he was dean of the School of Architecture at Princeton. His architectural firm, SAA/Stan Allen Architect, has realized buildings and urban projects in the United States, South America, and Asia. He was one of 12 architects chosen to represent the U.S. in the American Pavilion at the 2016 Venice Architecture Biennale, and his work was featured in the 2017 Chicago Architecture Biennial. In addition to numerous articles and project reviews, his architectural work is published in *Points + Lines: Diagrams and Projects for the City* (Princeton Architectural Press, 1999), and his essays in *Practice: Architecture, Technique and Representation* (Routledge, reissue 2008). *Four Projects: A Stan Allen Sourcebook* was published by ORO Publishers in 2017, and in 2020, Park Books published his most recent book, *Situated Objects*.

CHARLES CURTIS is a cellist. His long creative relationships with experimentalists such as La Monte Young and Marian Zazeela, Alvin Lucier, Éliane Radigue, and Tashi Wada have brought into being a body of distinctive works modeled on his cello-playing and performing persona. *Naldjorlak* (2003–2005) by Éliane Radigue is a concert-length, solo cello work made collaboratively with Curtis, in which the wolf of the cello functions as the reference for the tuning of the entire instrument. Curtis is Distinguished Professor of Music at the University of California, San Diego.

PRADEEP DALAL is a Mumbai-born artist and writer based in New York. His work has been shown at EFA Project Space, New York (2019); Callicoon Fine Arts, New York (2017); Sala Diaz, San Antonio, Texas (2017); and Murray Guy, New York (2011); among other venues. His photographs have been included in publications such as *Blind Spot*, *BOMB*, *Cabinet*, *Grey Room*, *Nueva Luz*, and *Rethinking Marxism*. His artist book, *Bhopal, MP* (2017), was excerpted in *Chandigarh Is in India* (The Shoestring Publisher, 2016); and his essay, "A Bifocal Frame of Reference," was published in *Western Artists and India: Creative Inspirations in Art and Design* (Thames & Hudson, 2013). He recently published *Photography in the Sensorium* with Fia Backström for the Pratt Photography Imprint (2021). He co-chaired the Photography Department in the MFA program at Bard College, Annandale-on-Hudson, New York, from 2015 to 2020. He has also taught at Pratt Institute, Cooper Union, and the International Center of Photography. He directs the Andy Warhol Foundation Arts Writers Grant in New York.

STACY WAKEFIELD FORTE is a New York–based book designer and artist who works for both trade and art publishers as a professional desgner of commercial books, and also creates collaborative and personal artists' books that have been collected by and shown at institutions all over the world, including the Whitney Museum; the Museum of Modern Art, New York; and the Brooklyn Museum. She studied design at the Rietveld Academie in Amsterdam with an emphasis on book arts.

ANNA FRIZ is a sound and media artist born on the unceded territories of the Coast Salish peoples in the city presently known as Vancouver. She specializes in multichannel radio transmission systems for installation, performance, and broadcast, as well as works in which radio is often the source, subject, and medium of the work. She also creates multichannel audiovisual installations, and composes works for theater, dance, film, and solo performance that reflect upon public media culture, political landscapes and systems, time perception, the intimacies of signal space, and speculative fictions. Friz is Assistant Professor in the Film and Digital Media Department of the University of California, Santa Cruz.

MAXIMILIAN GOLDFARB is an artist who produces projects in many forms. Goldfarb has completed past works with support from the Harpo Foundation, the Elizabeth Graham Foundation, the Pollock-Krasner Foundation, The Kaplan Institute, the Foundation for Contemporary Arts and the Experimental Television Center. He has participated in numerous exhibitions in venues including Sculpture Center, NY; Stadsgalerij, NL; Western Front, BC; White Columns, NY; The Drawing Center, NY; and Nina Freudenheim Gallery, Buffalo, NY. Goldfarb is interested in the generative potential of publication and radio transmission platforms. He is co-author of *Architectural Inventions* (Laurence King Publishing, UK, 2012), *Deep Cycle* (M49, 2010), *Handbook for Human Machines* (Pilot Editions, 2015), and *Remote Viewing: 500 Tableaux* (Publication Studio, 2017). Goldfarb is a co-founder of Incident Report in Hudson, NY. He serves on the Board of Directors of Wave Farm and is an Assistant Professor of Sculpture in the Department of Art at the University at Buffalo.

JULIA KLEIN is an artist and the publisher of Soberscove Press, which she founded in 2009. The press is guided by

Klein's interests in collaboration, documentation, process, and the relationships between various forms of work within singular artistic practices. *Wolf Tones* is the third book project Klein has worked on with Nancy Shaver.

ANN LAUTERBACH is a poet and essayist. She has published ten volumes of poetry, including *Or to Begin Again* (2009, nominated for a National Book Award); *If in Time: Selected Poems 1975–2000* (2001); and, most recently, *Spell* (2018), all from Penguin Books, which also published a collection of essays, *The Night Sky: Writings on the Poetics of Experience* (2005). Lauterbach's poems have been published widely in journals, magazines, and anthologies, and her work has been translated into French, German, and Spanish. She has written many essays on contemporary artists including Felix Gonzales-Torres, Taylor Davis, and Cheyney Thompson. Lauterbach has received numerous awards, including fellowships from the Guggenheim Foundation and the MacArthur Foundation. She is Schwab Professor of Languages and Literature at Bard College, where she was co-chair of Writing in the multidisciplinary MFA Program for twenty-eight years.

CATHERINE LORD is a writer, artist, and curator whose work addresses issues of feminism, cultural politics, and colonialism. She is the author of the text/image experimental narrative, *The Summer of Her Baldness: A Cancer Improvisation* (University of Texas Press, 2004); the conceptual translation *Sa Calvitie, Son Colibri: Miss Translation* (L'une Bevue, 2007); and, in collaboration with Richard Meyer, *Art and Queer Culture, 1885–2005* (Phaidon Press, 2011). Her critical essays and fiction have been published widely, and she has contributed to catalogs for exhibitions including *WACK! Art and the Feminist Revolution*. Lord's curated exhibitions include *Pervert*; *Trash*; *Gender, fucked*; and *Memories of Overdevelopment: Philippine Diaspora in Contemporary Visual Art*. Her work as a visual artist was included in the inaugural Site Santa Fe Biennial (1995) and has been shown at numerous venues, including the New York Gay and Lesbian Film Festival, Post Gallery (Los Angeles), and La MaMa (NYC). She is Professor Emerita in Studio Art at University of California, Irvine.

MATANA ROBERTS is an alto saxophonist, internationally recognized composer, and mixed-media visual artist whose work has forged new conceptual approaches to considering narrativity, history, community, and political expression within improvisatory musical and visual structures. www.matanaroberts.com

NANCY SHAVER is an artist who has been exhibiting work for more than 40 years. In 2018, she was included in *Outliers and American Vanguard Art* (National Gallery, Washington, D.C.), and *One Day at a Time: Manny Farber and Termite Art* (MOCA, Los Angeles). Other recent exhibitions include *VIVA ARTE VIVA* (La Biennale di Venezia, 2017); *Nancy Shaver: Reconciliation* (The Aldrich Contemporary Art Museum, 2015); and *Robert Gober: The Heart is Not a Metaphor* (Museum of Modern Art, 2014–15). Recent gallery exhibitions include Derek Eller Gallery (NYC), 12.26 (Dallas, TX), Atlanta Contemporary (GA), and Parker Gallery (Los Angeles). Shaver has received fellowships and awards from the Guggenheim Foundation, Anonymous Was a Woman, the Pollock Krasner Foundation, and the Louis Comfort Tiffany Foundation. A co-founder of Incident Report in Hudson, NY, Shaver also runs the store, Henry. She has been teaching in the Bard College MFA Program for more than 20 years.

STERRETT SMITH studied painting with Jim Gahagan, an American colorist who directed the Hans Hoffman School at Goddard College. She graduated from the San Francisco Art Institute with a BFA in painting in 1980, where she studied with Hassel Smith, Franklin Williams, Robert Hudson, and Angela Davis. She also studied in San Francisco with Helen Palmer, Diane Di Prima, Ian Grand, and Charles Ponce in the training of the intuition, the Kabbalah, and Somatic Knowledge. She was part of the group of artists and poets in Jess and Robert Duncan's household and Diane Di Prima's circle. She has been painting and making sculptures ever since.

DAVID LEVI STRAUSS is the author of numerous books, including *Co-illusion: Dispatches from the End of Communication* (MIT Press, 2020), *Photography and Belief* (David Zwirner Books, ekphrasis series, 2020), *From Head to Hand: Art and the Manual* (Oxford University Press, 2010), and *Between the Eyes: Essays on Photography and Politics*, with an introduction by John Berger (Aperture 2003; new edition, 2012). *In Case Something Different Happens in the Future: Joseph Beuys and 9/11* was published by Documenta 13 (2012); and he co-edited, with Michael Taussig, Peter Lamborn Wilson, and Dilar Dirik, *To Dare Imagining: Rojava Revolution* (Autonomedia, 2016; Italian edition by Elèuthera, Milan, 2017). Recently, Strauss, Taussig, and Wilson also co-edited *The Critique of the Image Is the Defense of the Imagination* (Autonomedia, 2020). Strauss was a Guggenheim fellow in 2003 and received the Infinity Award for Writing from the International Center of Photography in 2007. He is chair of the graduate program in Art Writing at the School of Visual Arts in New York.

image index

MG	Maximilian Goldfarb
NS	Nancy Shaver
SS	Sterrett Smith

Notes on source images:

MG— The objects I produce are in direct contact with their sources, connecting image and articulated form. My intention is to extend the material phenomena and contextual imprints often lost in transmission, closing distance from guarded, inaccessible, or overlooked places and spaces. Simple geometric forms applied to the picture plane serve to reprioritize elements by either excluding or emphasizing what I find most salient about the image. All artworks pictured are from a single, ongoing series, *500 Tableaux*, based on my collection and recalibration of found source imagery (2015–21)..

NS— My source images tend to present singular things that others have made, fashioned as care would have it, to meet a specific desire or longing. They are all aspects of a collective need to see through making. Craft has no standard here. To "see" something outshines every production. Everything shines in my eye as a viewer.

Unless noted otherwise, the subjects of all source images are in the collection of Nancy Shaver. "Merchandise at Henry" references Henry, a retail store run by Shaver at 348 Warren Street in Hudson, NY.

SS— My work begins in the gap between things. I cut, patch, bandage, bind, wrap, reassign, and reassemble; there is tending to do. A source image might key a possible manual reparation of a rupture and can direct and encourage fluency.

*Unless noted otherwise, all images are courtesy of the artists. Source images are indicated by **bold text**. Images on multi-image pages are listed from top to bottom, and clockwise from top-right where applicable.*

292

138—MG. *No._Mines Danger*, 2018. Enamel on aluminum; 48 × 72 × .75 inches / **NS. Garden at home.**

139—MG. *No._Medals of Commendation*, 2017. Enamel on wood; 58 × 63.5 × 1.5 inches. / **SS. Transfer station.**

140—NS. *Mostly blue, for E.G.* (detail), 2020. Wooden boxes, cardboard boxes, paper, Flashe acrylic; 76 × 18.5 × 10 inches. Photo: Jeanne Liotta.

141—**SS. T-bone on tile.**

142—**SS. Roadside spring / MG. Pipe breach / NS. Naga necklace from Nagaland, India, maker anonymous.**

143—**SS. Leverage / NS. Costumed dolls from Equator, a business (Merchandise at Henry), maker anonymous.**

144-45—NS. *China*, 2018 (mirrored). Found red boot, Chinese baby hat, plumbing connectors, yarn; 24 × 8.5 × 7 inches. Photo: Adam Reich.

146—**NS. "Cowboy Boots for the Whole Family," Sears Catalog, c. 1960. / SS. Donkey youth.**

147—**MG. Model food / MG. Capsule recovery rehearsal.**

148—MG. *No._Boulder*, 2020. Cast pigmented ultracal; 17 × 14 × 13 inches; and MG. *No._Barrel*, 2020. Enamel, newspaper, sonotube; 17 × 17 × 24 inches / MG. *No._Taser*, 2021. Sandblasted enamel, plastic, modeling paste on cardboard; 12 × 6 × 2 inches / SS. *Beverly*, 2020. Wood, plaster, fabric, paper, plastic, foam, acrylic; 31 × 20 × 16 inches.

149—NS. *T-shirt, Mary*, 2018. T-shirt mounted on canvas panel; 8 × 10 inches.

150—SS. *Still*, 2019. Fabric, paper, wax, copper wire, wood; 22 × 13 × 10 inches.

151—SS. *Upside Down Banana Saddle, for Maya*, 2021. Paper, ceramic, fabric, hair extension, acrylic; 19 × 15 × 12 inches.

152-53—**MG. Anti-ballistic (mirrored).**

154—**NS. Black-and-white baby's crocheted dress and knitted sweater with sleeve extended, maker anonymous.**

155—NS. *Physical and Visual Texture*, 2019. Canvas stretchers, dress and jacket fabric; 18.5 × 15 × 2.5 inches. Photo: Adam Reich / NS. *Corner to Center Grids*, 2018. Wooden blocks, men's shirt fabric, dress fabric, paper, Flashe acrylic, oil pastel; 10.5 × 10.75 × 3.5 inches.

156—**MG. Skull / NS. Merchandise at Henry.**

157—SS. *Buster*, 2019. Ceramic, fabric; 12 × 5 × 5 inches.

158—NS. *Jackson's Aunt Theresa's Vest*, 2018. Ladies' auxiliary vest; 18 × 25 inches. Collection of Jarrett Buckheister. Installation view: *Love and Trouble* (2018–2019) in *One Day at a Time: Manny Farber and Termite Art*, Museum of Contemporary Art, Los Angeles.

159—**SS. News-clipping about stone sizers / NS. Plastic toy box from the collection of Lisa Scull, maker anonymous.**

160—MG. *No._Shiu Fu (single)*, 2018. Enamel, wood, cast plastic, straw; 10 × 18 × 42 inches / MG. *No._Maersks*, 2019. Enamel, wood; 8 × 18 × 41 inches.

161—MG. *Shiuh Fu No. 1* / MG. *No._Spoons Bundle*, 2021. Whittled driftwood; dimensions variable (approx. 11 × 6 × 4 inches).

162—SS. *First Occasion*, 2019. Wooden stool, ceramic; 13 × 15 × 11 inches / NS. *Abstraction and Figuration #1*, 2017–2018. Mass produced products, wooden platform, 14.5 × 49.5 × 21.5 inches. Photo: Adam Reich.

163—**NS. Woman's hat, cir. early twentieth century, maker anonymous / SS. "Please Take," transfer station / MG, radar antenna enclosures.**

164—NS. Installation-in-progress, 2015. Installation view: *Greater New York*, MOMA PS1, 2015, Long Island City, New York.

165—SS. *Richie*, 2019. Ceramic, rope, string, yarn, paper; 13 × 10 × 5 inches.

166-67—**NS. Pitcher, cir. twentieth century, maker anonymous (merchandise at Henry).**

168—**MG. Solar module/drum** / NS. 2 *Teapots: Form and Image*, 2019. Two Victorian teapots, forms for ironing, metal; 16 × 12 × 6 inches / **MG. Street view mast.**

169—NS. *Early Work*, 1986. Frame, cardboard, green paint; dimensions unknown.

170—**MG. Cooling chimneys / MG. Container stack.**

171—NS. Studio photograph with *Floating Sentinel*, 2019 / **NS. Merchandise at Henry.**

172—NS. *Dominate and Defeat T-shirt*, T-shirt mounted on canvas panel, 8 × 10 inches. Installation detail: *Love and Trouble* (2018–2019) in *One Day at a Time: Manny Farber and Termite Art*, Museum of Contemporary Art, Los Angeles.

173—SS. *Gaelic Punk,* 2020. Ceramic, fabric, wax, linen, concrete; dimensions variable.

174—NS. *Computer Blue Plaid with Red and Yellow*, 2019. Canvas panels, blue plaid fabric, paper, Flashe acrylic; 26 × 13 × 3.5 inches / NS. *A Luxury of Red*, 2018. Wooden blocks, dress fabric, Japanese fabric, red scarf, paper, Flashe acrylic; 10.25 × 10.75 × 3.25 inches. Installation detail: *Alex Olson & Nancy Shaver: Waters*, 2019, 12.26 Gallery, Dallas, TX. Photo: Kevin Todora.

175—NS. *Lares and Penates*, 1991. Found objects (coffee pot and planter, armatures); 8 × 18.5 × 9 inches / NS. *To Richie Rich #2*, 2014. Found metal, wooden blocks, dress fabric, Japanese fabric, Flashe acrylic, house paint; 11.25 × 26 × 16 inches / **MG. Prosthetic eyes.**

176-77—**MG. Medical-imaging arm.**

178—**NS. Textiles in black and white, makers anonymous (merchandise at Henry) / SS. Freon.**

179 — NS. *Drawing Post #2*, 2021. Wooden farm-tool, metal, cardboard, paper, colored pencil, China marker; 62 × 15 × 5.5 inches.

180 — NS. *Small Sentinel*, 2017. Wooden blocks, fabric, plumbing parts; approx. 11 × 20 × 1.5 inches. Installation detail: *Wolftones*, 2019, Soloway Gallery, Brooklyn, NY.

181 — SS. *At-with-in, for Ann*, 2020. Fabric, paper, acrylic; 46 × 33 inches.

182 — NS. Garden at home, 2018 / NS. Hooked rug, early twentieth century, maker anonymous.

183 — NS. Box made by Katie and Lizzie Glover-Jones for their grandmother, Elaine Glover / SS. *Yokohama*, 2020. Ceramic, string, wood, wire, fabric; 12 × 11 × 19 inches.

184 — SS. "Defining painting through apples."

185 — NS. *T-shirts mounted on panels*, 2018. T-shirt on mounted on canvas panels; 8 × 10 inches. Installation detail: *Love and Trouble* (2018–19) in *One Day at a Time: Manny Farber and Termite Art*, Museum of Contemporary Art, Los Angeles.

186 — SS. *Catkin, for Carolee*, 2020. Paper, netting, fabric, pencil, acrylic; 58 × 48 inches / NS. *Seven/Ten Split*, 2018. Bowling bag, croquet balls, wooden blocks, dress fabric, T-shirt fabric, wire, metal, paper, Flashe acrylic; 14 × 25 × 18 inches / **SS. Nancy at Henry, 2020.**

187 — MG. *No._Stock 1 and Double*, 2021. Carved walnut, Potomac River driftwood; approx. 16 × 10 × 3.5 inches / NS. Works by John Jackson, NS, and B. Wurtz. Installation view: *Nancy Shaver: Reconciliation*, 2015. Aldrich Museum of Contemporary Art, Ridgefield, Connecticut / **SS. Early spring.**

188 — SS. *Trenched*, 2020. Shell casing, fabric, cardboard, paper, acrylic; 25 × 12 × 12 inches / SS. *Traveler,* 2019. Metal, wood, fabric, ceramic, wire, wax; 18 × 15 × 12 inches.

189 — NS. *In The Wings*, collaboration with Emi Winter, 2015. Hand-loomed rug, natural dye, metal armature, wooden blocks, dress fabric, paper, Flashe acrylic, house paint, oil pastel; 16 × 38 × 82 inches.

190 — SS. *La Donna e Mobile*, 2019. Copper wire, fabric, wood, rope, spray paint, foam; 29 × 13 × 5 inches.

191 — SS. *McNamara*, 2020. Ceramic, foam, cord, fabric, rope; 14 × 7 × 7 inches.

192 — NS. *Moving Left* (detail), 2020. Canvas, baby's quilt cir. 1860, panels, paper, Flashe paint; dimensions variable.

193 — NS. Studio photograph of *Fishes, Silver, and Gold*, 2019; and *Fishing—A construction*, 2018.

194-95 — MG. Dollys.

196-97 — (from 197, top right): **SS. "Eat what you like, fight, turtle wax"** / **MG. End-effector / SS. "Busting in or busting out?"** / NS. *Paisley Landscape, a large spacer*, 2020. Paisley fabric, cotton tapestry fabric, dress fabric; 17.25 × 29 × 2 inches / **SS. Shadow** / SS. *Circe*, 2020. Fabric, pencil, ink, paper, acrylic; 58 × 50 inches.

198—MG. *No._Jackboots*, 2020. Stained lumber; 14 × 6 × 36 inches.

199—MG. *No._End Effector*, 2019. Paper on cardboard; 18 × 36 × 6 inches.

200—SS. *Big Toe*, 2021. Plaster, fabric, wire, paper; 21 × 20 × 6 inches.

201—NS. *Standardization, Variation, and the Idiosyncratic*, 2016. Installation view: *La Biennale di Venezia*, 2017, Venice, Italy.

202—**NS. Patchwork quilt, cir. early twentieth century (detail), maker anonymous (merchandise at Henry)** / NS. *Standardization, Variation, and the Idiosyncratic*, 2016. Installation view: *La Biennale di Venezia*, 2017, Venice, Italy.

203—NS. *Spacer*, 2018. Fabric over canvas panels, approx. 35 × 40 inches. Installation detail: *A part of a part of part*, 2018, Derek Eller Gallery, New York City.

204—NS. *Characters for a Play*, by Katie Glover-Jones and Lizzie Glover-Jones.

205—NS. *Blue Pool*, 2018. Wooden platform, wooden blocks, dress fabric, T-shirt fabric, Japanese fabric, found fabric, paper, Flashe acrylic; 75 × 50 × 10 inches. Installation view: *Gathering Texture, Following Shape*, 2019, Parker Gallery, Los Angeles, California.

206—**SS. Rosehips / MG. Garbage vortex / SS. Paisley (merchandise at Henry).**

207—SS. *Island Lung*, 2021. Ceramic, wood, plaster, wire, canvas, fabric; 24 × 15 × 13 inches.

208-09—(from 209, top right): NS. *Piano Keys*, 2018. Wooden block, dress fabric, paper, Flashe acrylic, house paint; 12.75 × 10.75 × 3.25 inches. / NS. *Blue, and a Leopard Square*, 2017. Wooden blocks, dress fabric, plaid fabric, Flashe acrylic; 10.25 × 10.5 × 3.25 inches / NS. *Blue Kilter*, 2016. Wooden blocks, paper, Flashe acrylic; 12 × 11.5 × 3.25 inches / NS. *Aspects of Denim #2*, 2016. Wooden blocks, denim, dress fabric, Flashe acrylic, house paint; 10.75 × 10.75 × 3.25 inches / NS. *Aspects of Denim #1*, 2016. Wooden blocks, denim, paper, Flashe acrylic, house paint; 14.5 × 14.5 × 3.25 inches / NS. *Central Flower*, 2018. Wooden blocks, dress fabric, plaid fabric, paper, Flashe acrylic; 10.25 × 10.5 × 3.25 inches.

210—SS. *Arc/Tunnel*, 2019. Pencil on paper; 10 × 12 inches / **MG. Cattle system / SS. Junking.**

211—**NS. Jewelry box, maker anonymous / MG. Pack bots.**

212—**MG. Overpass.**

213—SS. *Bark*, 2021. Ceramic, paper, acrylic, fabric, string, cardboard; 30 × 19 × 13 inches.

214-15—(from 215, top right): NS. *Sampler of Crochet Patterns* (merchandise at Henry) / **MG. Pipeline** / MG. *No._99 Knives* (detail), 2020. Ninety-nine knives hand-carved from various driftwood, branches, and scrap-wood on custom steel and plexiglass tables; dimensions variable / NS. *Trees, Signs, Tools*, 2019. Dress fabric, canvas panels, Flashe acrylic, house paint, china marker, thread; 9 × 36 × 1.5 inches. Installation detail: *Alex Olson & Nancy Shaver: Waters*, 2019, 12.26 Gallery, Dallas, TX. Photo by Kevin Todora / **SS. Studio photograph of stuffed frog, utopian parking space** / MG. *No._ 360˚*, 2018. Archival printed mylar; 3 × 8 × 14 inches.

216 — NS. *Yellow Light*, 2020. Driftwood, metal, cardboard boxes, paper, silver paint, China marker; 23 × 9 × 14 inches / **MG. X-band radar**.

217 — NS. *Plastic Telephone*, cir. 1960. Kitchen decoration, 5 × 7.5 × 1.75 inches. Installation detail in numerous exhibitions: *Reconciliation*, 2015, Aldrich Museum, Ridgefield, CT; *Standardization, Variation and the Idiosyncratic*, 2016, *La Biennale di Venezia*, Venice, Italy; *A part of a part of a part*, 2018, Derek Eller Gallery, New York City; *Love and Trouble*, 2018–2019, *One Day at a Time: Manny Farber and Termite Art*, Museum of Contemporary Art, Los Angeles; *Wolftones*, 2019, Soloway Gallery, Brooklyn, NY; *Fastness, slowness and Monstrous Beauty*, 2020, Derek Eller Gallery, New York City.

218-19 — NS. *An Abundance*, 2020. Shiny dress fabric, lace, bedspread, African fabric, Japanese fabric, paper, Flashe acrylic, house paint; 20 × 36 inches.

220 — **SS. White House** / MG. *Small Object Array* (Molecule, SAE, Torch, Truss, Mallets, JPL, etc.), 2018. Installation view: Small Object Array, 2018, University at Buffalo, Project Space, Buffalo, NY / **SS. Cloud.**

221 — NS. *Block and Ball*, 2017. Found metal, wheel, wooden blocks, dress fabric, Flashe acrylic, house paint; 19.5 × 13.75 × 17 inches.

222-23 — **SS. Flower arrangement.**

224 — MG. *No_Tallship*, 2019. Scrap wood, hemp, canvas, thread, clasps; 54 × 22 × 52 inches.

225 — **SS. Mom's pincushion (needle-point by Heidi Thiel, pin placement by Mary Smith)** / MG. Installation view: *Karl & Antikythera*, 2018, University at Buffalo, Project Space, Buffalo, NY.

226 — **MG. Partially buried boat** / MG. Installation view: *Karl & Antikythera*, 2018, University at Buffalo, Project Space, Buffalo, NY / MG. *No._IED*, 2018. Various materials; 9 × 8 × 5 inches.

227 — NS. *Standardization, Variation, and the Idiosyncratic*, 2016. Installation view: *La Biennale di Venezia*, 2017, Venice, Italy / SS. *Sky Top*, 2019. Shells, ceramic, wire, yarn, cord, paper, Astroturf, artificial plants, wood; 19 × 14 × 10 inches.

228-29 — **NS. Sears Catalog, cir. 1960.**

230-31 — (from 231): MG. *No._Antikythera Mechanism*, 2018. Acrylic and modeling paste on cardboard; 14 × 15 × 2 inches / SS. *Strut*, 2019. Fabric, ceramic, yarn; 8 × 14 × 10 inches / MG. *No_ Globe (downside)*,

2021. Enamel on acrylic; 18 × 18 × 18 inches / **NS. Conch shell souvenir art (merchandise at Henry), maker anonymous / NS. Sculpture by Hawkins Bolden / SS. Elephant still life.**

232—MG. *No._Gendarmeri*, 2021. Enamel on polystyrene, dimensions variable (letters: approx. 10 × 9 × 2 inches) and MG, *No._Cruise*, 2020. Cardboard on steel frame, dimensions variable (ship: 97 × 22 × 34 inches).

233—SS. *Fillip*, 2021. Ceramic, fabric, wire, wax, string, paper; 20 × 12 × 6 inches.

234—NS. "Roses," photograph of fabric.

235—SS. *Chickadee*, 2019. Fabric, acrylic, paper; 33 × 26 inches.

236—MG, NS, SS. Installation view: "Wolf Tones II", in *Nancy Shaver: fastness, slowness, Monstrous Beauty*, 2020, Derek Eller Gallery, New York City / **MG. Predator** / MG. *No._42nd Attack Squadron*, 2019. Enamel and vinyl on plasma-cut steel; 54 × 30 × 12 inches.

237—MG. Minefield / NS. Handmade stool, 1967, maker anonymous (merchandise at Henry) / SS. Tool shed trellis.

238—MG. *No._Mines Danger*, 2018. Enamel on aluminum; 48 × 72 × .75 inches / MG. *No._Rug Sim*, 2018. Archival print on synthetic canvas, on foam carpet pad; 60 × 44 × 1 inches.

239—NS. *Collections—Love and Work*,

2017. Evening bags; handmade snow shovel; baby hats from China, Afghanistan and Uzbekistan; panel of drawer knobs; tin-can covers; metal rods; plumbing parts; wooden platforms; 44.5 × 87.5 × 58 inches. Photo: Adam Reich.

240—MG. Cable diver / MG. Workstation block.

241—MG. *No._Landcam 2*, 2019. Rapid-prototyped ABS plastic; 3 × 5.5 × 2.5 inches and *No._Buddha (1/4)*, 2019. Cast concrete; 3 × 3.5 × 4.5 inches / MG. *No._99 Knives* (detail), 2020. Ninety-nine knives hand-carved from various driftwood, branches, and scrap wood on custom steel and plexiglass tables; dimensions variable.

242—MG. *No._Sign (Sweatlodge)*, 2018. Wood and concrete; 6 × 28 × 72 inches.

243—NS. *Red, Scraps of Yellow, and Blue*, 2004. Wooden box, cardboard boxes, charcoal, Flashe acrylic; 13 × 8 × 8 inches / NS. *Camouflage Fruit Box*, 2009. Cardboard boxes, paper, house paint, Flashe acrylic; 16 × 21.5 × 4 inches. Included in exhibitions at Feature, New York City, 2007; Derek Eller Gallery, New York City, 2008.

244—SS. Nancy's sentinels at Henry / SS. Birch bark cuts / MG. *No._Buddha*, 2017. ast foam; 14 × 8 × 10 inches, and MG. *No._SAE (1/10)*, 2017. Enamel on cast ultra-cal; 2 × 4.75 × 10 inches, and MG. *No._Rug Sim*, 2018. Archival print on synthetic canvas, on foam carpet pad; 60 × 44 × 1 inches. Installation view: *Wolftones*, 2019, Soloway Gallery, Brooklyn.

245—SS. *Head for L.G.*, 2021. Ceramic, styrofoam, wire, fabric, paper, cardboard; 25 × 19 × 19 inches.

246-47—MG. *Modules 1–6*, 2018. Enamel on MDF; each module: 24 × 48 × .75 inches. Installation view: *Repeater*, 2019, Nina Freudenheim Gallery, Buffalo, NY (mirrored).

248—**SS. Sweepings.**

249—MG. *No._ Högertrafikomläggningen*, 2021. Stitched Naugahyde; approx. 16 × 7 × 3.5 inches / MG. *No._Keyboard*, 2021. Enamel on wood in vinyl, 8 × 15 × 2 inches / **SS. Seed collection.**

250—SS. *Sudsy Bone*, 2020. Acrylic, pencil, paper; 39 × 37 inches.

251—SS. *Tinct*, 2019. Ink, acrylic, paper; 30 × 22 inches / **SS. Fountain.**

252-53—(from 253, top right): MG. *No._ Hand*, 2019. Whittled lilac branches; 6 × 9 × 1 inches and *No._Soup*, 2019. Enamel on cast ultracal; 3 × 3 × 4.5 inches / MG. *No._Torch 3*, 2019. Enamel on cast ultracal; 2 × 2 × 8 inches and *No._Can*, 2019. Enamel on cast ultracal; 3 × 3 × 4.5 inches. Installation view: *Repeater*, 2019, Nina Freudenheim Gallery, Buffalo, NY / MG. *No._Navigator's Shirt*, 2019. Hand-stitched, archival-printed Mercator map on synthetic fabric; dimensions variable (folded shirt: approx. 14 × 16 × 4 inches) / MG. *No._Siren*, 2018. Cast hydrocal, 9 × 5 × 2.75 inches and *No._Truss*, 2018. Enamel

on wood, 19 × 4 × .5 inches. Installation view: *Repeater*, 2019, Nina Freudenheim Gallery, Buffalo, NY.

254-55—SS. *Boogie Leaf*, 2020. Wax, board, artificial greenery, acrylic; 20 × 30 inches.

256—**NS. Refrigerator at home, 2018 / SS. News clipping about bag containing cheese in late fourth–early third century, B.C., Southern Siberia.**

257—SS. *Beltway*, 2020. Fabric, paper, ink, acrylic; 37 × 34 inches.

258—NS. Studio photograph of *Two Plaid Sentinels*, 2018.

259—**SS. "Boo, Thanks."**

260-61—NS. Studio photograph of early version of *Work and Love*, 2018.

262—NS. *Looking for a Cup of Coffee*, 2015–2018. Found base, metal rod, wooden blocks, fabric, paper, Flashe acrylic; 35.5 × 11.5 × 12 inches. Photo: Adam Reich.

263—**MG. Surgical system.**

264—MG, and SS. *Beaver, 2020*, wooden column, glazed ceramic, beaver honed wooden stick, acrylic; 12 × 72 inches and SS. *Industry Dog*, 2019. Fabric, wood and acrylic on panel; 13.5 × 17.5 inches. Installation view: *Wolftones*, 2019, Soloway Gallery, Brooklyn, NY. Photo: Sterrett Smith.

265—MG. *No._Landcam*, 2018. Rapid prototype, ABS plastic on acrylic and steel frame; 6 × 7 × 5 inches and *No._PTT*,

2017. Cast ultracal. 7 × 3 × 1.5 inches and *No._Prosthetic Left*, 2018. Foam and metal; 10 × 4 × 4 inches. Installation view: *Karl & Antikythera*, 2018, University at Buffalo, Project Space, Buffalo, NY / MG. *No._ Landcam*, 2018. Rapid prototype, ABS plastic on acrylic and steel frame; 6 × 7 × 5 inches.

266 — Photo: Ann Bobco.

267 — SS. *Trinoculars*, 2019. Paper, linen, acrylic on paper; 14 × 16 inches / NS. *A Gaggle of Clutter: Form and Line*, 2016. Metal rods, wooden block, dress fabric, Flashe acrylic, house paint; 32 × 53 × 48 inches, variable / MG. *No._Gendarmerie*, 2021. Enamel on polystyrene; dimensions variable (letters approx. 10 × 9 × 2 inches).

268 — SS. *Deputy* Dog, 2019. Paper, pastel, acrylic, gouache; 11 × 16 inches / **MG. Disaster rehearsal.**

269 — SS. *Peak Peek*, 2019. Fabric, acrylic, paper; 34 × 24 inches.

270 — **MG. Waste pile** / MG. *No._Model Homes*, 2018. Enamel on cast plastic; each house approx. 9 × 4 × 4 inches.

271 — **MG. Mile marker / MG. Infantry rescue rehearsal.**

272 — MG. *No._Mile Marker 562*, 2020. Enamel on sheet metal; 24 × 48 × 6 inches and *No._42nd Attack 211B*, 2020. Enamel on plasma-cut steel; 39 × 19 × 4 inches.

273 — NS. *A Yellow Dress*, 1987–89. Found saucepan, frame, paper, ink; 12 × 18 × 4.5 inches (three times).

274 — MG. *No._Buddha*, 2017. Cast foam; 14 × 8 × 10 inches and MG. *No._Mines Danger*, 2018. Enamel on aluminum; 48 × 72 × .75 inches and MG. *No._Rug Sim*, 2018. Archival print on synthetic canvas, on foam carpet pad; 60 × 44 × 1 inches. Installation view: *Wolftones*, 2019, Soloway Gallery, Brooklyn.

275 — NS. Installation view: *Gathering Texture, Following Shape*, 2019, Parker Gallery, Los Angeles, California / NS. *A Patchwork: The Crusader—1453, 1957, 2019*, 2019. Canvas panels, souvenir scarf from Turkey, various American fabrics; approx. 40 × 46 inches.

276 — **SS. Root.**

277 — MG. *No._Console*, 2021. Plasma-cut steel; 30 × 42 × 9 inches.

278 — MG. *No._Barrel 1/5*, 2020. Enamel, newspaper, and sonotube; 17 × 17 × 24 inches.

279 — **SS. Roots and fur** / SS. *Skirted*, 2019. Clay, fabric, brick, steel; dimensions variable. Installation view: *Wolftones*, 2019, Soloway Gallery, Brooklyn, NY. Photo: Sterrett Smith / **SS. Tree shelf / SS. Shaker rug and quilt, makers anonymous (merchandise at Henry).**

280 — MG. *No._Block*, 2019. Acrylic on cardboard; dimensions vary (each block is 8 × 8 × 16 inches) and MG. *No._Foot*, 2019. Foam, rubber, hardware; 11 × 4 × 4 inches. Installation view: *Wolftones*, 2019, Soloway Gallery, Brooklyn. Photo: Sterrett Smith.

281—SS. *Bedspread*, 2019. Plastic toy guns, paint, wood, metal, fabric; dimensions variable. Installation detail: *Wolftones*, 2019, Soloway Gallery, Brooklyn, NY. Photo: Ann Bobco. / SS. Untitled (detail), 2019. AstroTurf, staples, linen, acrylic; dimensions unknown. Installation detail: *Wolftones*, 2019, Soloway Gallery, Brooklyn, NY. Photo: Ann Bobco.

282—**MG. VR goggles.**

283—SS. *Ennead*, 2019. Ceramic, fabric; 13 × 10 × 8 inches.

284-85—NS. Studio installation of new work, 2020.

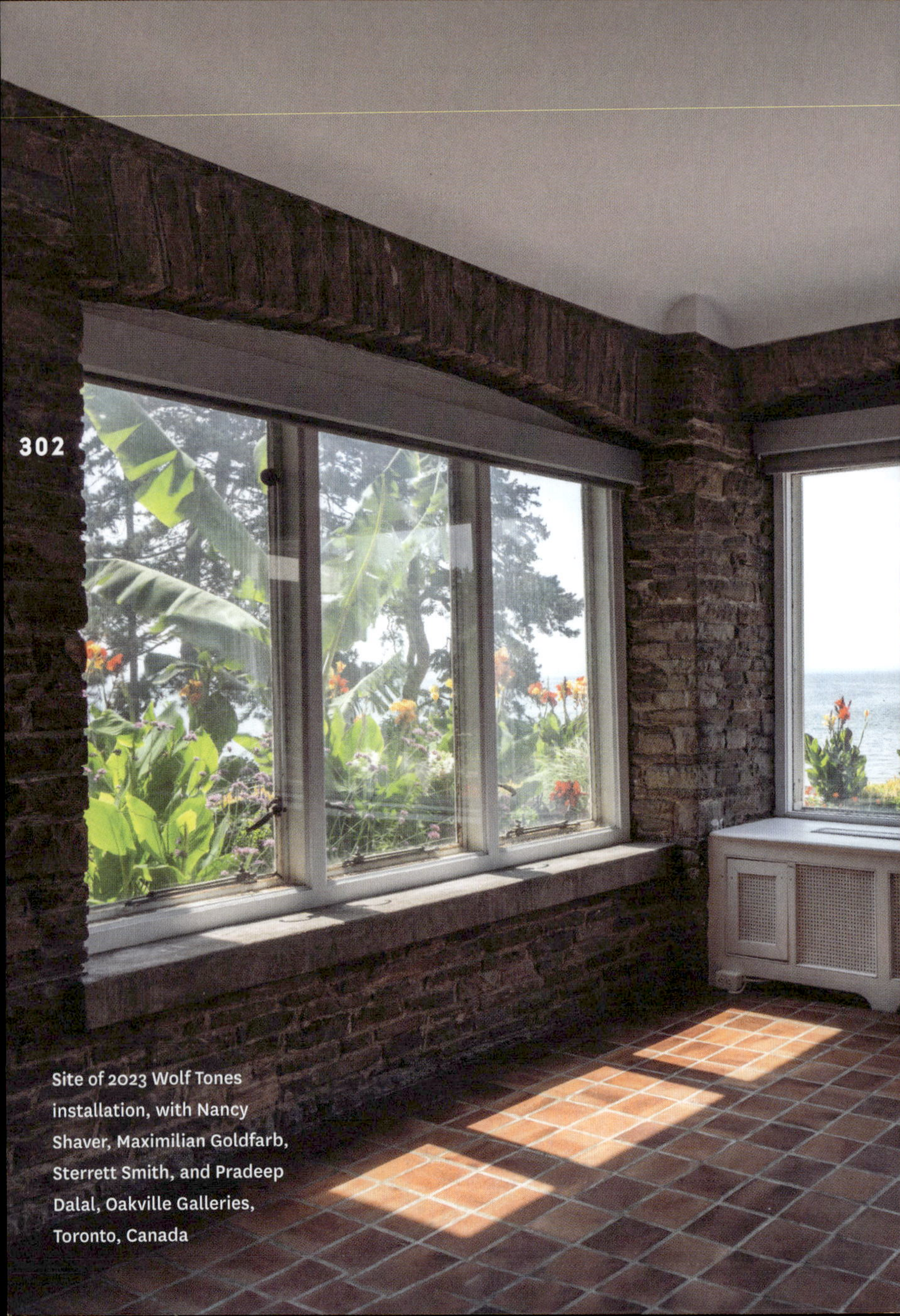

Site of 2023 Wolf Tones
installation, with Nancy
Shaver, Maximilian Goldfarb,
Sterrett Smith, and Pradeep
Dalal, Oakville Galleries,
Toronto, Canada

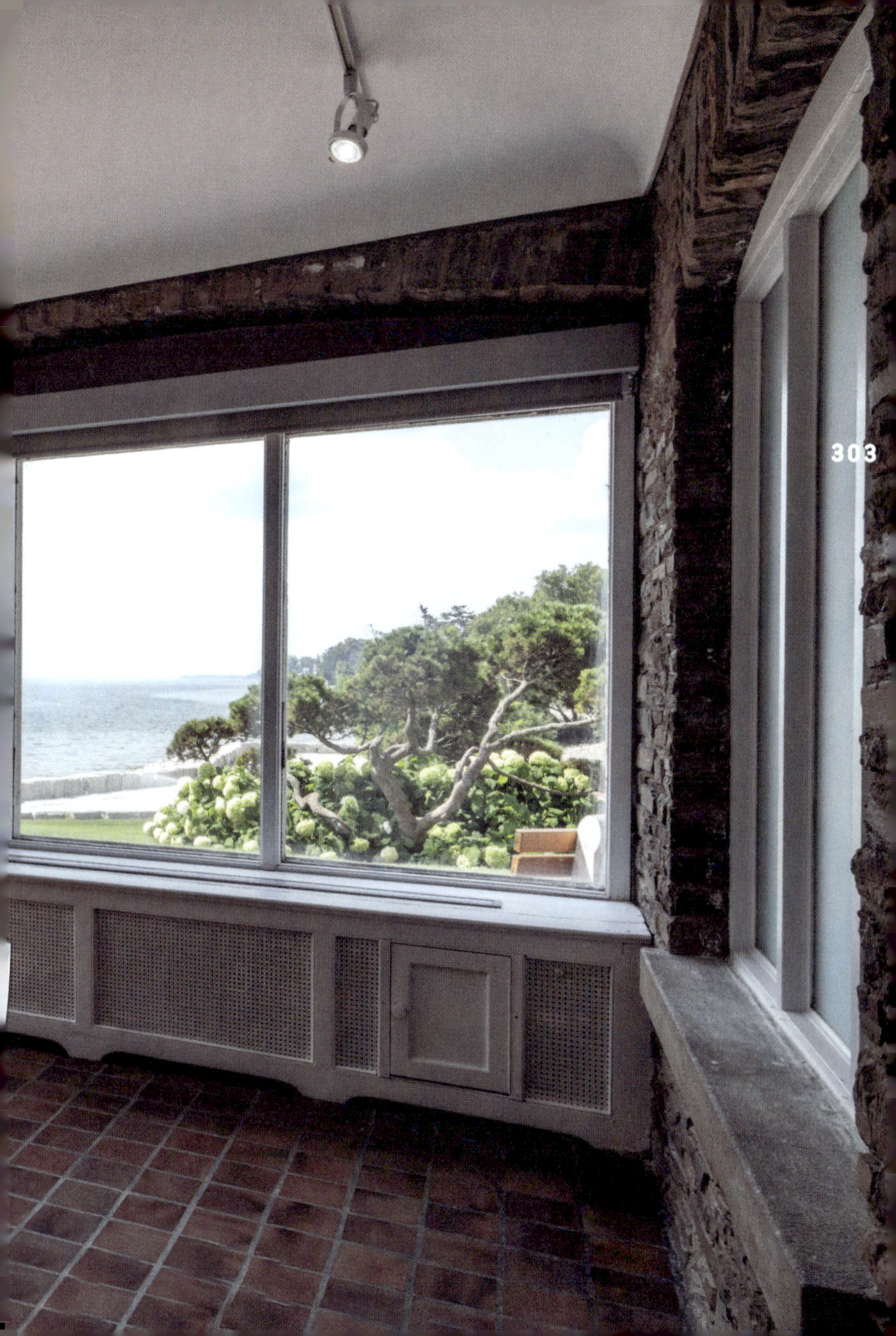

Soberscove Press
Chicago, Illinois
soberscove.com

Wolf Tones © 2022 Soberscove Press
All artworks © the artists
All texts © the authors

All rights reserved. No part of this
publication may be reproduced, stored
in retrieval systems, or transmitted in
any form or by any means, electronic,
mechanical, photocopying, recording or
otherwise, without the prior permission
of the copyright holder.

Cataloging-in-Publication Data is
available from the Library of Congress.

ISBN 978-1-940190-28-0
Editor: Julia Klein
Copyediting: Corina Copp
Design: Stacy Wakefield Forte
Printed in Lithuania

Distributed by
ARTBOOK | D.A.P.
75 Broad Street, Suite 630
New York, NY 10004
artbook.com

Our thanks to
Soloway, Derek Eller,
Frances Loeffler,
and Julia Klein.
—Nancy Shaver,
Maximilian Goldfarb,
Sterrett Smith